Labour and the Wage

OXFORD LABOUR LAW

General Editors

Professor Alan Bogg, University of Bristol; Professor A. C. L. Davies, University of Oxford; Professor Keith Ewing, King's College London; and Professor Mark Freedland, University of Oxford

This series has come to represent a significant contribution to the literature of British, European, and international labour law. The series recognizes the arrival not only of a renewed interest in labour law generally, but also the need for fresh approaches to the study of labour law following a period of momentous change in the UK and Europe. The series is concerned with all aspects of labour law, including traditional subjects of study such as collective labour law and individual employment law. It also includes works that concentrate on the growing role of human rights and the combating of discrimination in employment, and others that examine the law and economics of the labour market and the impact of social security law and of national and supranational employment policies upon patterns of employment and the employment contract.

ALSO AVAILABLE IN THE SERIES

Principled Labor Law
U.S. Labor Law through a Latin American Method
Sergio Gamonal C. and César F. Rosado Marzán

Living Wage
Regulatory Solutions to Informal and Precarious Work in Global Supply Chains
Shelley Marshall

Bullying and Behavioural Conflict at Work
The Duality of Individual Rights
Lizzie Barmes

The Concept of the Employer
Jeremias Prassl

The Labour Constitution
The Enduring Idea of Labour Law
Ruth Dukes

The Legal Construction of Personal Work Relations
Mark Freedland FBA and Nicola Kountouris

A Right to Care?
Unpaid Work in European Employment Law
Nicole Busby

Regulating Flexible Work
Deirdre McCann

Welfare to Work
Conditional Rights in Social Policy
Amir Paz-Fuchs

EU Intervention in Domestic Labour Law
Phil Syrpis

Labour and the Wage

A Critical Perspective

ZOE ADAMS

OXFORD
UNIVERSITY PRESS

OXFORD
UNIVERSITY PRESS

Great Clarendon Street, Oxford, OX2 6DP,
United Kingdom

Oxford University Press is a department of the University of Oxford.
It furthers the University's objective of excellence in research, scholarship,
and education by publishing worldwide. Oxford is a registered trade mark of
Oxford University Press in the UK and in certain other countries

First Edition published in 2020

Impression: 1

Published in the United States of America by Oxford University Press
198 Madison Avenue, New York, NY 10016, United States of America

British Library Cataloguing in Publication Data
Data available

Library of Congress Control Number: 2019953152

ISBN 978–0–19–885889–8

Printed and bound by
CPI Group (UK) Ltd, Croydon, CR0 4YY

To my parents, for always believing in me, and to my friend Adam, for showing me how to believe in myself

General Editors' Preface

Labour law scholarship has always been imbued with a keen sense of its historical development. Sometimes, certain ideas are so pervasive that they become invisible, part of the taken-for-granted background which then provides the point of departure for argument and critique. One such idea is the 'autonomy' of social and economic relations from legal norms, and the relative impotence of legal norms in shaping those relations. It is an idea that has run like a golden thread through the discipline, from the heyday of industrial voluntarism and *collective laissez-faire* through to state of the art theories on reflexive governance and juridification. Valiant attempts to repudiate this axiom of autonomy have often ended up reproducing those very same assumptions. Labour lawyers have explored ways in which legal interventions could be designed more effectively to secure desirable social and economic outcomes in society. It was as if the law was simply a purposive instrument, rather like a knife, that could do its work better on the intractable material of social and economic life. Yet this law-as-instrument approach presupposes the severability of the legal from the social.

In *Labour and the Wage: A Critical Perspective*, Zoe Adams provides a highly original and rigorously argued intervention in these scholarly debates. Using a genealogical method of inquiry, situated in a deep knowledge of legal and social practices, she presents a 'constitutive' view of the relationship between legal norms and social reality. On this approach, it is profoundly mistaken to conceptualize law as an instrument or tool that can be used, more or less successfully, to bring about changes in the social world. Our social world and our ways of being in that world are already framed through legal norms. These legal norms embody a specific form in capitalist relations. These insights are then developed within the context of the contemporary crises and challenges of labour regulation: employment status, the living wage, casualization. In so doing, the book traces the historical evolution of the law's core organizing categories in employment, such as the wage–work bargain. It is only by exposing the contingency of the law's evolutionary path, and what she describes as 'law's ontology', that the emancipatory potential (and limits) of the legal form can be understood. This is scholarship of the highest quality, which synthesizes theoretical, historical, and doctrinal insights to produce a remarkable contribution to enduring debates in labour law. We are confident that it will come to be regarded as a landmark work in the field, and we are delighted to welcome it into the series.

ALB, KDE, MRF, ACLD
November 2019

Acknowledgements

I would like to thank the editors of the *Oxford Monographs on Labour Law* series and everyone at Oxford University Press for their patience and support throughout the preparation of the manuscript.

This book is based on my PhD thesis, 'A Social Ontology of the Wage', although there is little left of the original text because I have refined, re-written, and edited as my ideas have developed. I would not have had the opportunity to do this had I not been offered a Junior Research Fellowship at King's College, Cambridge, and had I not been surrounded by such wonderful and supportive colleagues.

I would like to extend a special thanks to my PhD supervisor, and colleague, Professor Simon Deakin. I have always been inspired by Simon's work, and I am incredibly grateful for the time and effort he has, and continues, to devote to me and my academic career. I would also like to thank my PhD examiners, Professors Judy Fudge and John Bell, whose feedback has proven invaluable in the preparation of the manuscript.

There are also a number of colleagues in the wider labour law community to whom I would like to extend my thanks: Dr Jeremias Adams-Prassl of Magdalen College, Oxford, who has been an invaluable source of support to me since the beginning of my PhD; Professor Nicola Kountouris, with whom I had the privilege of working with in the summer of 2019, and whose ideas have helped me improve and refine many aspects of the text; Dr Liam McHugh Russell, a legal scholar whose work I have long admired; and Andrew Sagar, a colleague, and friend, whose critical insights continue to push and challenge me in ways that help me further refine, and improve, my analysis.

Finally, and above all, I would like to thank my parents, and my dear friend Adam, without whose tolerance, understanding, and support this book would not have been possible. I dedicate this book to the three of you.

Table of Contents

PART II

Table of Cases

Table of Primary Legislation

TABLE OF UK STATUTES

Table of Secondary Legislation

UK STATUTORY INSTRUMENTS

1

Labour Law from an Ontological Perspective

1.1 Labour Law's 'Crisis': Low Pay and Under-Inclusive Employment Status

Low pay and under-inclusive employment status are some of the most pressing problems facing workers today.[1] Nonetheless, as is clear from a recent government review into modern working practices, labour law often seems incapable of providing meaningful responses to these problems.[2] For many, this is a sign that labour law is, once again, in crisis. This crisis, it is said, is due to several factors: a global 'neoliberal' policy agenda; a failure or lack of adequate enforcement of existing rights; unnecessarily rigid and complex legislation and case law; and various 'economic' factors, such as globalization, the growth of non-standard forms of work, and developments in technology.[3]

Faced with such a 'crisis', some labour lawyers have called for a 'more purposive' approach to labour law, a 're-alignment' between its 'goals' and 'means'.[4] The premise of such interventions is that these 'problems' are not new, and that, as such, labour law already has the 'means' with which to address them. After all, they argue 'labour laws' ... '(like all other laws), are a means to an end; we need them, and use them, to advance societal goals' and/or to uphold certain (universal) values.[5] The task in this view is simply 'to understand, and articulate, [these] goals—to explain to ourselves (and to legislatures, courts, employees and employers) the purpose of [labour] laws at the deepest possible level', and 'to reconsider our means—to ask what we need to change or improve in the laws themselves in order better to advance the goals [identified]'.[6]

[1] Matthew Taylor, 'Good Work: The Taylor Review of Modern Working Practices—GOV.UK' (2017) 36. See also the government's response: HM Government, 'Good Work: A Response to the Taylor Review of Modern Working Practices' (2018).

[2] Taylor (n 1).

[3] Simon Deakin, 'Labor Law: The Pragmatist's Guide—Comments on A Purposive Approach to Labour Law' (2017) 16(1) Jerusalem Review of Legal Studies 28.

[4] Guy Davidov, *A Purposive Approach to Labour Law* (OUP 2016).

[5] Julie McClelland, 'A Purposive Approach to Employment Protection or a Missed Opportunity?' (2012) 75 Modern Law Review 427; Davidov (n 4); Gunther Teubner, 'After Legal Instrumentalism', in Gunther Teubner (ed), *Dilemmas of Law in the Welfare State*, vol 3 (De Gruyter 1986); Richard A Posner, *Economic Analysis of Law* (Wolters Kluwer Law & Business 2014). See also: *Autoclenz Ltd v Belcher* [2011] UKSC 41; [2011] 4 All ER 745 (Lord Clarke).

[6] Davidov (n 4) 4. While Guy Davidov's work is a key example of such an approach, the tendency to see labour law in what Alan Bogg calls 'prophylactic' terms is extremely common. See the

Labour and the Wage. Zoe Adams, Oxford University Press (2020). © Zoe Adams.
DOI: 10.1093/oso/9780198858898.001.0001

This so-called purposive approach to labour law makes a number of assumptions about the role of law in a capitalist society, and thus about the relationship between law and social practices. These assumptions are seldom made explicit. The purposive approach takes it as given, for example, that the purposes of a particular rule, or body of legal doctrine, can be derived from some abstract notion of what 'Parliament' intended, certain universal 'values', and/or some unspecified body of 'authoritative' academic opinion.[7] Contributing to an emerging tradition in labour law scholarship that emphasizes the importance of 'deriving' labour law's purpose from a consideration of its 'philosophical foundations',[8] such an approach implicitly posits an extra-legal world in which problems exist, and a legal world in which these problems are 'solved'. In this way, it largely reproduces the view that law 'intervenes' in society (or the market), to realize outcomes that by assumption could not be achieved absent such intervention.

The result of these assumptions is that labour law's putative failures, whether it be to provide for wage security or an appropriate coverage of labour protection legislation, tend to be ascribed to a lack of political will, to a failure to pursue the 'right' goals, to exogenous 'problems' to which labour law has failed to adapt, and/or to a lack, or failure of, enforcement. Potential systemic or structural causes tend to be downplayed, therefore—as do the inherent, or structural, limits to law's capacity to address them.

This book offers an alternative perspective. It argues that it is unhelpful to talk about what labour law *should* be doing, and how, without a deeper understanding both of what law is, its ontology, and the nature of the society to which it is specific. Before thinking about what sort of rules we need, and thus what 'goals' to pursue, what is required is not abstract moral or philosophical theorizing; rather, what is required is an express engagement with questions of ontology: exploring the conditions from which law, and labour law, developed, and the practices and relations in the context of which it came to be. This, it will be argued, means situating our analysis of law within a social ontology of capitalist society—a theory of its unique features, or structures, and engaging, expressly, with questions of legal form.

By adopting such a perspective and exploring the distinguishing or unique properties of law and its relationship with capitalism, this book will show that there are inherent limits to what law can achieve in a capitalist society—regardless of the purposes to which it is put. These limits are not purely political, determined

discussion in: Alan Bogg, 'Labour, Love and Futility: Philosophical Perspectives on Labour Law' (2017) 33 International Journal of Comparative Labour Law and Industrial Relations 7.

[7] Ruth Dukes, 'Identifying the Purposes of Labor Law: Discussion of Guy Davidov's A Purposive Approach to Labour Law' (2017) 16(1) Jerusalem Review of Legal Studies 52 <https://doi.org/10.1093/jrls/jlx017> accessed 5 November 2019.

[8] Hugh Collins, Gillian Lester, and Virginia Mantouvalou (eds), *Philosophical Foundations of Labour Law* (OUP 2018).

by disagreement over the goals that should be pursued; nor are they due to apparently exogenous factors such as globalization or technology. Rather, these limits are inherent in what law is, in the form it assumes, and in the functions it performs in the context of the capitalist system. These limits need to be considered when it comes to thinking about how we engage with law, and, relatedly, labour law, and of whether, and if so, how, it might be 'used' to bring about social change.

The book is divided into two parts. Part I develops a Marxist inspired critical 'social ontology' of law that explores the nature of law, its distinguishing features and its relationship with the practices and relations that are uniquely constitutive of capitalist society. In so doing, it advances a constitutive conception of the law market and law-society relationship[9] that stresses law's contradictory roles in the emergence and reproduction of capitalist social relations—and, relatedly, in the emergence, and reproduction, of the (capitalist) market.

Part II develops a genealogical analysis of the social category of the wage, tracing the evolution of this category through legal discourse and the shifting repertoire of legal concepts (the 'wage', the 'salary', 'remuneration') through which it has been denoted over time. In so doing, it sheds new light on the problems of low pay, under-inclusive employment status, and the role of the legal system in perpetuating, and potentially constituting, these problems. Significantly, it will also help to distinguish those historic, and contingent, factors shaping contemporary approaches to wage regulation from the systemic or structural constraints on law as a historically evolved mode of regulation.

While the focus of this book is labour law, and its critique is directed at trends common in labour law scholarship most specifically, the analysis presented should also be seen as contributing to a wider literature that has been concerned in recent years with revitalizing the Marxist legal tradition by engaging with questions of legal form (as distinct from content), particularly in the context of international law and human rights law. Like this book, this Marxist literature emphasizes the importance of engaging with questions of legal form with a view to better understanding its limits, and its emancipatory potential.[10]

[9] I use relationship loosely here. The ontology presented suggests that law does not exist *in relation to* society, but is *part of society*, even if it assumes an 'independent' or autonomous form *within it*. For a critique of the use of the term 'relationship' when speaking of the law's autonomy, see: Christopher Tomlins, 'How Autonomous Is Law?' (2007) 3 Annual Review of Law and Social Science 45.

[10] China Mieville, *Between Equal Rights: A Marxist Theory of International Law* (AAKAR Books 2016); Susan Marks, 'International Judicial Activism and the Commodity-Form Theory of International Law' (2007) 18 European Journal of International Law 199; Robert Knox, 'Marxism, International Law, and Political Strategy' (2009) 22 Leiden Journal of International Law 413; Paul O'Connell, 'Law, Marxism and Method' [2018] Forthcoming in tripleC: Communication, Capitalism and Critique (2018); Grietje Baars, *The Corporation, Law and Capitalism: A Radical Perspective on the Role of Law in the Global Political Economy* (Brill 2019). While Hugh Collins has also engaged with Marxist approaches to law, I do not include his work in this scholarship because of its relative neglect of (the significance) of questions of form. That being said, his book is an excellent summary of the Marxist legal tradition in the UK (prior to the 1990s): Hugh Collins, *Marxism and Law* (OUP 1982).

The rest of this introductory chapter will explain some of the key ontological premises underpinning the analysis, explain in more depth the trends in the existing literature that have motivated the book, before outlining the argument to follow. It concludes with a more detailed breakdown of the remaining chapters.

1.1.1 Ontology

This book's call to ontology is a response to two concerning tendencies that can be detected in legal and labour law scholarship: first, a perennial framing of law as a regulatory response to social problems that exist in some unspecified extra-legal realm, rather than as a participant in the processes and structures that give rise to them; and second, a consistent privileging of questions of legal content (the rules that are enacted) over questions of form. Engaging with ontological questions directly, questions about the nature of society; its basic building blocks; how it emerges/is reproduced/ transformed; how it relates to 'us' (as members of society, and as theorists/scholars studying and developing theories about it); *and* with questions about what it means to make claims about the nature of reality, this book will provide much-needed clarity, and greater theoretical consistency, to labour law scholarship. At the same time, it will make clear why engaging with questions of form is so important: for shedding light on why labour law seems to struggle to remedy problems such as low pay and under-inclusive employment status, and for shedding light on the broader question of the limits, and potential, of labour law when it comes to bringing about social (structural) change.

The social ontology elaborated in this book is inspired by a combination of critical realism, and the ontology implicit in Marx's critique of classical political economy. It is a praxis-based ontology that sees social reality as inherently dynamic, or processual, emerging (and thus being constantly transformed/reproduced) but existing independently from (ie as being irreducible to), the conscious interactions of human agents (between each other and with nature). While social reality is an emergent product of such interactions, it is independent from the actions of any particular agents, and so, exists independently from them and their conception. In this sense, it is objectively real; it has its own distinct mode of being, and makes an irreducible difference to the course of events. While this ontology is elaborated in detail in chapter one, it is worth outlining certain key premises by way of introduction.

First, the term 'social structure' is used here to describe the web of relations that exist between the social positions (worker/employer; husband/wife) into which individuals are born/which they assume, and from which they act. These positions—and the relations between them—condition the interests individuals have (conceived objectively), and the resources at their disposal (power, money) when it comes to acting (engaging in specific practices). This structure exists regardless of whether individuals are aware of it, but the constraints embedded in that structure (that confront individuals as they assumed different positions) are only causally efficacious to the extent that they are interpreted, and understood, by social agents in some way: my position as a worker only limits my options to the extent that I realize I have no choice but to work in order to live—even if I do not need to have any understanding of the specific structures that explain that lack of choice. In this sense, social structure has an inherent conceptual dimension. This does not mean, however, that the social structure can be reduced to the level of subjective consciousness: what it means to occupy the position of worker, and thus what it means to engage in the social practice of work, is not something that any individual can decide for himself. Rather, it depends on how those positions and practices are (and have historically been) collectively understood within a given population, and thus on the shared framework of meaning that 'unites' them, and makes possible their mutual interaction. This conceptual framework is, moreover, also an emergent product of conscious human praxis—it emerges from repeated interactions between individuals, and between them and their material (and social) environment; hence, it too is rooted in the material.

The structure of society thus presupposes both the objective positions people occupy, and the relations they enter into, and the shared conceptual framework that informs agents as to the significance and implications of those positions, and which guides them when it comes to fulfilling, or engaging in, particular practices. It always, moreover, pre-exists a given round of human agency in the sense of being a precondition for (further) action. The causal powers of social structure exist independently from those of human agents, therefore, in the sense that the structure of society (and various components of that structure) makes an irreducible difference to the course of events. No outcome can be explained in terms of the actions or beliefs of individual agents alone, therefore, nor can they be explained solely in terms of structural (eg market) forces. Rather, every outcome, and the way those outcomes come to be perceived (conceptions of them), must be explained by reference to the *interaction* between various aspects of the social structure (and, by implication, both its conceptual and material dimensions)—including law—and the actions of (socially situated) human agents.

Third, if social reality emerges through conscious human practice, knowledge practices must be seen as part of the process by which the objects of knowledge themselves emerge and change. The way society is thought and understood thus influences its nature, just as much as the nature of social practices influences how it is thought and conceived. The ontological question cannot, then, be neatly or completely separated from the epistemological question. Far from existing in some autonomous realm of thought, invoked to describe or conceptualize a 'mind-independent' reality, concepts must be seen as part of that reality, and so, as something to be explained by reference to the practices and relations in the context of which they come to be, and thus by reference to the nature of the society in which they are formed.

Finally, given the above premises, social reality, and our theories about it, is always historically and contextually specific—specific to the particular form of society in which those theories are produced. It follows that we can never produce a universally valid theory of social reality *in general*; we can only ever produce a theory of the particular form of society in which we exist. And, if social reality emerges from human practices, different forms of society can, this book will argue, be distinguished (for analytical purposes) by reference to the nature of the dominant mode of production—the (regular and pervasive) practices through which human life (biological, cultural, social, etc) is reproduced, and the social relations into which individuals must enter for this purpose. When it comes to understanding the nature of law, therefore, it follows that we can only make claims that are relevant to the particular form that law assumes in capitalism.

These premises have some important methodological implications that will guide the analysis presented in this book:

Given that conceptual phenomena (including norms, theories, beliefs, etc) are socially produced, we cannot assess labour law, capitalism, or socio-economic outcomes such as low pay, by reference to some 'external' normative standard (of justice, efficiency, or fairness).[11] The standards we invoke, and the concepts we use to 'describe' the world, are products of the very system to which they are applied, and so, must also be grasped contextually and historically. This does not mean subscribing to the subjective values motivating social struggles at particular moments, nor does it imply a radical form of moral relativism. Rather, it means invoking as our normative standard, norms and expectations that are immanent in the social totality under investigation, immanent, that is, in the social practices from which it develops. Rather than advancing certain normative arguments from the perspective of the worker, 'unequivocally accept[ing] the worker's perspective as the appropriate analytical and normative focus for employment law's fundamental concerns';[12] and rather than criticizing socio-economic outcomes by reference to some putative 'external' standard of efficiency or fairness, this book explores which rules and institutions capitalism *itself* requires. That is, it explores what is essential to, or necessary for, capitalism's 'self-reproduction'. And this also means exploring the limits, and potential that exists, within capitalism, for those requirements to be met in practice.

By proceeding at the level of capitalism's deep structures, the enquiry allows us to distinguish systemic, irreducible features of capitalism and capitalist law, from

[11] Of course, we could do this, and many labour law scholars do this, but it is not productive for the purposes of critical theory: unless we can justify the particular standard we invoke (why *this* theory of justice rather than another), our critique is unlikely to motivate change.

[12] Jeremias Prassl, *The Concept of the Employer* (OUP 2015) 2.

the historical and contingent forms they assume in particular socio-historical contexts. In this way, we can better expose the contingencies, path-dependencies, and decisions behind what might otherwise appear as natural or inevitable, thereby revealing the scope that exists for change. By exploring law at a structural level, so as to develop a theory of the irreducible features of the legal form, we can better understand the limits, and potential, of law when it comes to realizing the particular purposes attributed to law at various times, and/or bringing about *structural* change.

By shifting away from an analysis of the effects of markets, and capitalist economic practices, towards an analysis of the processes and practices that generate them, such an approach opens the door to a more far-reaching critique. Rather than thinking about what labour law can (or should) do to remedy adverse outcomes that are otherwise taken as inevitable, the approach adopted in this book makes it possible to problematize the very processes by which those outcomes are produced—potentially opening the door to much more far-reaching programmes for reform.

1.2 Background and Outline of Argument

1.2.1 Naturalistic Approaches

Mainstream legal (and economics) scholarship is, for the most part, rooted in an approach to legal and economic analysis that is *naturalistic*. That is, it accepts as given the processes that generate socio-economic outcomes, focusing its analysis and critique on its observable effects. Rather than exploring the conditions of possibility of markets and law (and the social relations that underpin them), it simply assumes their existence. By implication, it tends to take it as given that markets, and capitalist economic processes more generally, are self-constituting and self-sustaining—capable of guaranteeing the conditions for their own functioning. Of course, this strand of scholarship does not (necessarily) deny the importance of law for the market's *efficient* operation, or that law contributes to socio-economic outcomes; but it does, implicitly, take law as something that 'responds' when something goes 'wrong', operating on a pre-existing reality, rather than being something that is integral, and implicit, in that reality itself.

In these naturalistic accounts, law and markets are implicitly treated as if they are externally or contingently related, rather than dialectically, and intrinsically related. The market is spoken about as if it is 'an independent entity, something with its own logic, its own laws and requirements',[13] that law can either support

[13] Kerry Rittich, 'Making Natural Markets: Flexibility as Labour Market Truth Special Issue: Continuing towards an Economic Sociology of Law' (2014) 65 Northern Ireland Legal Quarterly 323, 323.

and facilitate, or restrict. As a result, the legal framework through which market practices take place (and the social relations underpinning them) becomes self-justifying—taken for granted in the way that the market is conceived. Private property rights and freedom of contract tend to be seen not as legal constructs, but as natural rights, which the legal system and the state more generally are bound to respect. These rights then come to circumscribe the limits in which 'public' law can operate, limiting what Parliament can legitimately require of employers and workers through protective labour legislation, while, at the same time, preventing the courts from imposing rights and obligations on contracting parties to which they have not freely agreed. While it assumed, where private law is concerned, that 'the courts are merely respecting and enforcing the parties' choice, not imposing on them particular types of economic relations',[14] regulation that imposes rights and obligations on the parties to which they have not agreed is seen as an illegitimate usurpation of judicial power. Thus, while the courts tend to defer to Parliament as the only body capable of 'legitimately' restricting a 'natural' freedom of contract, they simultaneously adopt a restrictive approach to statutory interpretation. Private law rules (as expressions of those 'innate' rights) are, then, implicitly deemed to be more desirable than coercive public regulation. This is not only because the latter restrict individual freedom but also, because in doing so, they impose outcomes on society that diverge from the competitive outcomes 'required' by the market.

These accounts largely take as given that labour law 'qualifies' private law rules, and so has to be explicitly justified by reference to its effects on the market's functioning; whether in terms if enhancing efficiency or promoting fairness. And, at the end of the day, if a choice has to be made between an approach that 'allows the market to decide' on controversial political questions about distribution, and one that involves particular individuals or groups (such as trade unions, or the state) deciding such questions—the former will, inevitably, prevail

The 'naturalistic ontology'—or, rather, the tacit naturalism that prevails when ontological questions are neglected—circumscribes beliefs about what labour law can achieve, and shapes conceptions of the 'problems' it is said to address. As a result, it has had a profound influence on labour law scholarship and practice. In policy-making circles, for example, labour law is often presented as a mechanism for *enhancing* worker 'choice', *preventing* employer abuse of power, and minimizing transaction costs—facilitating, in other words, 'free' competition.[15] While the problem of under-inclusive employment status is recognized to be problematic, it is implicitly conceptualized in terms of positive transaction costs—information asymmetries—and so, is to be addressed by providing clearer guidance to workers

[14] Hugh Collins, 'Independent Contractors and the Challenge of Vertical Disintegration to Employment Protection Laws' (1990) 10 Oxford Journal of Legal Studies 353, 376.

[15] London, Department of Trade and Industry, *Fairness at Work* (Cmnd 3968, 1998); Taylor (n 1).

and employers (through the use of statutory definitions) about the options available to them: facilitating 'informed' choice by firms and workers about their rights and obligations.

In the courts, a similar attitude prevails: employment status, the question of who is, or is not, an employee *in law*, is seen as a simple question of fact that depends on what the parties *actually* agreed. There is no room, therefore, for imputing contracts of employment with a view to *shaping* working practices in light of broader considerations of public policy. It is not, then, within the capacity of the courts to provide, for example, casual workers with greater stability, and security, of employment where this does not reflect how the working relationship is conducted in practice. Not only would this require the courts to make a political decision that it is for Parliament to make, but any form of regulation that deprives individuals of the right to 'choose' the working arrangement that best suits their immediate preferences is excluded:

> There is no doubt that zero-hours contracts are a matter of very great concern. This is because they are often, although not always, *cynically constructed agreements*, framed by the employer in order to avoid their legal duties. *I do not believe that the common law can successfully deal with them alone.* ... The courts cannot simply ignore express terms or apply some general doctrine of unconscionability to invalidate a contract because of unequal bargaining power. The remedy must lie in legislation. *Even then, there are real practical difficulties because there is a not insignificant number of people for whom the flexibility of a zero hours contract, when they can pick and choose their work, is a real benefit.*[16]

In labour law scholarship, therefore, labour law is frequently presented either as a necessary corrective to market failure,[17] attributed, variously, to transaction costs, limited information, and/or inequality of bargaining power, or as a mechanism for improving the negative side-effects of 'markets forces'—as a tool for redistribution.[18] In the latter case, labour law is deemed to be necessary to promote certain universal values (of fairness, dignity, or justice, etc) which are deemed to be more important than economic efficiency; in relation to the former, by contrast—an approach that epitomizes the 'neoliberal' approach to labour law—efficiency, and fairness, are assumed to be promoted, in equal measure, through the competitive process.

[16] Patrick Elias, 'Changes and Challenges to the Contract of Employment' (2018) 38 Oxford Journal of Legal Studies 869, 884 (emphasis added).

[17] This is particularly clear in the *Taylor Review*, but see also: Alan Hyde, 'What Is Labour Law?' in Guy Davidov and Brian Langille (eds), *Boundaries and Frontiers in Labour Law* (Hart Publishing 2006) 37 at 53. Hyde also suggests that labour law can be seen as a mechanism for overcoming collective action problems in market settings.

[18] For example: Guy Davidov, 'A Purposive Interpretation of the National Minimum Wage Act' (2009) 72 Modern Law Review 581.

1.2.2 Constitutive Approaches

In the above naturalistic accounts, structural features of capitalism rarely enter into the scope of the analysis. Rather, the focus, for the most part, is the market and the relationships that are established through it. Inequality of bargaining power is thus seen as something that arises at the inter-personal level—between individual workers and their employers—rather than something that characterizes a structural relation between groups.[19] Exploitation appears not as an inherent feature of the capitalist labour relation, therefore, but as an exception—a product of immoral conduct by individual employers that would not, by definition, exist in a zero transaction cost world of perfect competition.

The failure by labour law scholars to engage with the structural features of capitalism has had a particularly profound influence on how the personal scope of labour law is construed, particularly by the courts. Rather than something rooted to a historically specific social relation, dependent wage labour, labour law is seen as a tool for promoting certain 'universal' values, or solving common transaction cost problems—the analytical boundaries of labour law have thus been blurred. That is not to say that the boundary between dependent workers and other working relations has ever been easy to draw *in practice*. Rather, it is to say that today, the analytical or conceptual boundary has been obscured. Even at the theoretical level, there appears to be no convincing basis for confining labour law to a particular type of working relationship at all. This has led many labour law scholars to attempt to 're-conceptualize' labour law (and its scope) in various ways: as '[encompassing all those] regulatory techniques and values that are properly applied to *any market* that, if left unregulated, will reach socially suboptimal outcomes because economic actors are individuated and cannot overcome collective action problems'; as encompassing all those aspects of law 'which bear upon human capital deployment';[20] or even in the form of a 'law of economic subordination and resistance'.[21]

Once the structural features of capitalism, and the alienated form of labour that is intrinsic to it, are excluded from the scope of the analysis, labour law loses its sense of identity—its boundaries—entirely.[22] At the same time, the premise that law 'intervenes' in a pre-existing reality, that labour law 'alters' outcomes generated by non-legal processes, and/or that it 'qualifies' the private law rules that *facilitate* the (natural) market's operation—seem self-evident. The legal system's

[19] Guy Palermo, 'Power, Competition and the Free Trader Vulgaris' (2016) 40 Cambridge Journal of Economics 259.

[20] Brian Langille, 'Labour Law's Theory of Justice' in Guy Davidov and Brian Langille (eds), *The Idea of Labour Law* (OUP 2011) 144 (emphasis added).

[21] Harry Arthurs, 'Labor Law as the Law of Economic Subordination and Resistance: A Thought Experiment' (2012) 34 Comparative Labor Law and Policy Journal 585.

[22] Mark Freedland, 'From the Contract of Employment to the Personal Work Nexus' (2006) 35(1) Industrial Law Journal 28.

role in *producing* the outcomes that labour law is invoked to change is, implicitly, ignored, as is its role in the emergence, and reproduction, of the unequal and exploitative social relations that underpin them.

Some labour law scholars, variously inspired by institutional economics, strands of Marxism and legal realism, have, however, engaged more explicitly with the origins, and evolution, of labour markets, making possible a more nuanced, constitutive conception of law, and labour law, than that which prevails in the naturalistic accounts presented above. This constitutive approach emphasizes that real-world markets are always legally saturated; structured, and constituted by a pre-existing set of rights and entitlements, established, to a great extent, by law.[23] Individuals' preferences, their interests and opportunities, and even their beliefs about what is fair and legitimate, are profoundly shaped by the broader legal framework in which economic exchange takes place, in other words, and this prevents a conceptualization of the market as independent from law and legal discourse.[24]

Of central importance to these accounts is the observation that labour is not a natural commodity, but is 'fictive' in the Polyanian sense of being instituted or socially constructed.[25] Private law rules are no more 'natural' and inevitable than labour law rules are, and they are each profoundly implicated in market outcomes. Such constitutive approaches stress the importance of understanding labour law as a historically evolved mode of regulation, and thus the role of labour law in the emergence, and reproduction, of capitalist social relations.

These scholars have also shown that, contrary to the assumption implicit in the naturalistic approach, labour law does not post-date an earlier era of freedom of contract, responding after the fact to defects in the market's operation. Rather, functional analogues to modern labour law and social security law, co-evolved with markets, and the vertically integrated firm, and are in this sense constitutive of, and integrally inter-related with them.[26] Labour law determines the subject matter of the contract, the rights in the labour (power) acquired by the wage, while at the same time putting in place certain mechanisms of protection and co-insurance as a basis for the reproduction of labour power.[27] Labour law works in tandem with the property law framework, with company law, tax law, as well as

[23] See, for example: Robert L Hale, 'Coercion and Distribution in a Supposedly Non-Coercive State' (1923) 38 Political Science Quarterly 470; Simon Deakin and others, 'Legal Institutionalism: Capitalism and the Constitutive Role of Law' [2015] University of Cambridge Faculty of Law Research Paper; Evgeny Pashukanis, *Law and Marxism: A General Theory* (revised edn, Pluto Press 1987).

[24] Lauren Edelman, 'Rivers of Law and Contested Terrain: A Law and Society Approach to Economic Rationality' (2004) 38 Law Society Review 181; Lauren Edelman and Robin Stryker, 'A Sociological Approach to Law and the Economy' in Neil J Smelser and Richard Swedberg (eds), *The Handbook of Economic Sociology, Second Edition* (Princeton University Press 2010); Rittich (n 13).

[25] Judy Fudge, 'Labour as a "Fictive Commodity": Radically Reconceptualizing Labour Law' in Guy Davidov and Brian Langille (eds), *The Idea of Labour Law* (OUP 2011.

[26] Simon Deakin and Frank Wilkinson, *Labour Law and Economic Theory: A Reappraisal* (ESRC Centre for Business Research 1998).

[27] Simon Deakin, 'The Contribution of Labour Law to Economic and Human Development' in Guy Davidov and Brian Langille (eds), *The Idea of Labour Law* (OUP 2011).

non-legal institutions such as the family, to co-determine the nature and extent of the worker's wage dependency, and as such, to shape the nature, and extent, of the employer's superior economic power both in the market and in production.[28]

In this way, 'constitutive' scholars show, labour law operates alongside (and through) private law, to produce, directly and indirectly, differential distributions of income; to promote or hinder the organisation of the parties; and to structure the freedoms and liabilities of workers and employers in ways that can be exploited when it comes to making decisions over how working relationships should be arranged. At the same time, legal discourse profoundly shapes the particular form of subjectivity through which market activity is sustained, and thus plays an integral part in the emergence and reproduction of 'rational' behaviour.

One of the implications of this analysis is that the structural power imbalance that characterizes the trading conditions between capital and labour is not a 'natural' feature of some abstract market place, nor the product of the parties' 'naturally' 'free' agreement; it is a situation in which law and legal institutions play a central part. Private law rules are not neutral as between market actors, therefore generating occasional externalities that social legislation is required to 'correct'. Rather, the legal system operates as an integrated whole to secure the formal subordination of labour to capital intrinsic to the capitalist mode of production, while, at the same time, reconciling this with the requirements of social reproduction. Far from interfering in a natural process, therefore, social legislation and statutory employment rights are an integral part of the process by which labour markets are rendered politically and economically sustainable.[29]

Labour law has an integral role to play in deciding who has access to labour (power) and on what terms, ensuring that subordination and dependence, on the one hand, and social protection, on the other, can be mutually interrelated features of employment relations in capitalist market economies. Employment relationships cannot be seen to be solely constituted by the terms of the parties' agreement, therefore, for while individual agreement is a prerequisite for the formation of any work relationship in a capitalist society which refuses to recognize the legal validity of forced labour (itself an institutional decision and not a state of nature), the contract the parties make is deeply embedded in a prior framework of laws and norms, which together define the circumstances under which labour is commodified.[30] This includes private law rules, as much as 'publicly' constituted regulations. In this sense, labour law is an integral element in the reproduction of the relationships which together characterize capitalist society, and so, cannot be seen as a mere instrument used to ameliorate the 'side-effects' of a natural, market-led process.

[28] Mark Harvey and Norman Geras, *Inequality and Democratic Egalitarianism: Marx's Economy and Beyond and Other Essays* (OUP 2018).

[29] Antonella Picchio, *Social Reproduction: The Political Economy of the Labour Market* (CUP 1992); Deakin and Wilkinson (n 26).

[30] Deakin (n 3).

While this constitutive approach does go much further when it comes to embedding its theory of law, and labour law, in the context of capitalism, the structural or systemic features of capitalism and their relationship with the *form* of law remain relatively under-explored. It is thus not clear from this account which aspects of labour law are historical and contingent; and which structural or systemic. It does not really engage, therefore, with why labour law might struggle to remedy social problems such as low pay and under-inclusive employment status, nor with whether labour law may have *inherent* limits on its capacity to do so. These are all questions that the ontological approach developed in this book can, however, help us address.

1.2.3 A Novel Conception of Law's Constitutive Role

1.2.3.1 Law and Contradiction

By engaging expressly with ontological questions, with the nature of law as a historically specific form of social regulation, and thus its relationship with practices and relations that are distinctive to capitalist society, this book advances a novel theory of law's constitutive role that grasps its, and labour law's, essential, and distinguishing features. In so doing, it sheds new light on law's necessary, but contradictory, role in reproducing the practices and relations unique to capitalist society.

To speak of law as playing a constitutive role in capitalism, it will be argued, is to recognize that capitalism is grounded in two contradictory logics: the logic of capital accumulation, and the logic of social reproduction. These two logics presuppose each other, but they exist in perpetual conflict. While social reproduction is a precondition for capital accumulation, the process of capital accumulation tends, in practice, to undermine the conditions required to sustain it. This includes not only the social needs that must be met for labour power to be sustainably reproduced, but also the particular form of subjectivity that must be sustained for a decentralized market to function. These requirements cannot, moreover, be met *through* the market, because, in the market, decisions are (and must, necessarily be) taken by reference to quantitative (or 'abstract-general') considerations—(costs, price, profit)—rather than the qualitative (or 'concrete-particular') considerations that are relevant to whether social needs can actually be met in practice.

These contradictory requirements, between that which is presupposed by markets, and thus surplus value production, and the material and cognitive conditions that underpin them, must be mediated through law and institutions—that is, 'outside' the market. And this, it will be argued, is a central element in law and labour law's constitutive role—its necessary role in reproducing the practices and relations that are unique, and intrinsic, to capitalism. This, it will be shown, has important implications when it comes to understanding the limits and potential of labour law as a historically evolved mode of regulation: its capacity, that is, to bring about social change.

1.2.3.2 The Constitutive Role of Legal Concepts

It follows from the above analysis that law's constitutive role has both a material and a cognitive dimension. That is, the contradiction inherent in capitalist society manifest not only as a contradiction between the material processes of capital accumulation, and the material processes of social reproduction, but also, as a contradiction between the way the world appears from the perspective of market practices (where workers, and employers, appear as equal and free) and the way the world appears in the context of the (inherently unequal) conditions in which individuals live and work. This means that a theory of law's constitutive role must grasp not only law's influence over the distribution of wealth and income, that is, its role in structuring rights and entitlements, but also the cognitive dimension of this role: the constitutive role of legal concepts.

In mainstream accounts, legal concepts tend to be seen as empty shells, as abstract and unnecessarily complex linguistic formulae that legal scholars ascribe to social phenomena, leaving policy-makers to fill with legal content. Thus, in the words of Guy Davidov,

> [w]e are free to *devise* the categories of 'employee' and 'worker'. We should, therefore, start from asking what group of people should enjoy the legislation, based on the purpose of the legislation, and devise these legal concepts accordingly.[31]

In this book, however, legal concepts are seen as emergent social forms that arise in the context of historically specific sets of practices. They presuppose the wider conceptual framework in which those practices are embedded, and which provides the shared framework of meaning that unites a given society, but they nonetheless possess distinct properties of their own as a result of the particular, inter-related practices from which they developed and in which they participate—the formulation, interpretation, and application, of legal rules and doctrine.

Individual legal concepts have meaning for the legal system only within the wider network or framework of linked ideas and categories through which new concepts are formulated and existing concepts reproduced and refined. They are only meaningful because of their relationship with the legal system's past practices and communications, which are, at any given time, embodied in this wider framework of categories. To take the practical example that the book explores in some depth, the legal concept of the wage, while to some degree reflecting existing

[31] Guy Davidov, 'The (Incomplete) Purposive Revolution: A Comment on The Legal Construction of Personal Work Relations' (2013) 7(1) Jerusalem Review of Legal Studies 90 (emphasis added). See also Taylor (n 1) 35–36.

practices, it is also influenced by meanings attributed by the legal system to these social existents in the past, and which are bound up in the concepts which are at the law's disposal at that point in time. Hence, legal concepts constrain the evolution of the law as much as they facilitate it[32]—independently from the intentions of judges or policy-makers.

The process of conceptualization is shaped by the legal system's existing conceptual structure, leading to path-dependencies that 'lock-in' assumptions and beliefs that correspond with conditions that may no longer hold, but which continue to influence the path of the law.[33] And, crucially, because conceptualization takes place by reference to a historically specific set of social relations and practices, legal concepts embed assumptions about the world that are themselves profoundly shaped by, and to some extent specific to, the practices and relations of capitalist society—and the contradictions intrinsic to it. This embeds contradictions in legal discourse, it will be shown, which reflect those that exist in society more generally.

Not only do legal concepts influence how law and social practices develop—quite independently from the content of the rules they are used to express—but the process by which legal concepts are formulated and applied to social reality is not passive; it is not a task of simply 'fitting' facts within pre-existing conceptual boxes. Rather, conceptualization is inherently normative: to describe an activity as work, for example, is to imply that it ought to be regulated in a similar manner to other forms of work, and so, (potentially) subject to (inter alia) labour law. At the same time, however, such subsumption is an act of constitution: by referring to an activity as work we change expectations and attitudes towards it, as well as perceptions of worth, and value, and thus potentially, the nature of the activity itself. How the legal system describes, or conceptualizes, social phenomena influences the nature of that phenomena, as well as what it is believed it is possible/impossible/necessary to 'do' with it—including what is appropriate, and acceptable, when it comes to regulation. A failure by legal officials to engage with the meanings embedded in legal concepts, cannot only lead to unforeseen and often unintended effects, therefore; it can also deprive us of an important opportunity to influence how society, or certain practices/relations, develop.

This brief discussion highlights something of importance for the analysis to follow. The concept of society presupposes the 'shared conceptual framework' that unites a given population and lends a particular meaning and significance to their practices and relations. And while this framework emerges from their practices, it is also, necessarily, an emergent product of the way that the various competing discourses (and conceptual frameworks) that emerge from different spheres

[32] Simon Deakin, 'Juridical Ontology: The Evolution of Legal Form' [2015] Historical Social Research/Historische Sozialforschung 170, 181.

[33] Simon Deakin, 'Evolution for Our Time: A Theory of Legal Memetics' (2002) 55 Current Legal Problems 1, 40.

of activity, interact. Everyday concepts of, for example, property, contract, employee, cannot be reduced to the particular meanings these concepts have in legal discourse, therefore, but how they are understood *in law*, necessarily influences (and is influenced by) everyday understandings, as well as the various meanings attributed to those concepts in different spheres of interaction (the economy etc). However 'removed' from reality legal discourse may seem, therefore, however 'abstract' its concepts, those concepts are still inherent in that reality, and participate in the process by which it emerges, develops, and is reproduced.

This conception of the constitutive role of legal concepts informs the methodology adopted in Part II of this book: a legal genealogy of the wage. The wage, it will be argued, is a social category, inherent in capitalism, and refers to the social form that workers' subsistence assumed in the context of the capitalist mode of production. It takes a particular form, however (is conceptualized in a particular way), in legal discourse as a result of the particular functions law performs vis-à-vis regulating the ways in which workers' subsistence is guaranteed in practice. A legal genealogy, then, is an analysis that traces how the wage has been conceptualized, and thus the various legal terms with which it has been denoted, in legal discourse, over time. This method allows us to shed light on how the specifically *legal* conceptualizations of core capitalistic categories contributes to the reproduction of the system in which those legal conceptualizations participate—and thus on the constitutive role of law, and legal concepts, in particular.[34]

In the same way that an ontological approach allows us to interrogate the deep structures that lie behind the immediate, surface-level appearance of things, genealogical analysis allows us to look behind a particular discourse, or concept, to explore its conditions of possibility. Tracing the evolution of a particular concept over time, genealogy allows us to read contingency into the past,[35] to expose all that which is implied by the existence of something that otherwise appears as natural or self-evident. In this way, it allows us to problematize conventional assumptions about the meaning, and function, of the wage, exposing the various meanings, and significances, attributed to that category in legal doctrine and discourse over time.

As the social form assumed by workers' subsistence in the context of capitalism, the wage is a particularly useful form to explore for the purposes of this book because it is central to our understanding of the historical specificity of capitalism, as well as its contradictions. This is because the contradictions inherent in capitalist social relations (most particularly, between the processes of capital accumulation and the process of social reproduction) find expression in a contradiction at the heart of the wage itself. On the one hand, the wage is the market price of the commodity, labour power, which is exchanged in the labour market. As with any other

[34] A similar task was undertaken by Baars in relation to the concept of the corporation: see Baars (n 10).

[35] Emilios Christodoulidis, 'Labour Constitutionalism in a Genealogical Key' [2018] Jurisprudence 1.

price, the wage functions to coordinate decision making in the market. On the other hand, the wage is the cost of reproducing that commodity, a process which is not confined to the market but takes place in society more generally: this is the function of social reproduction. These two functions are not only conceptually and materially distinct, they are frequently in conflict: the price the market assigns to the labour commodity is not always, and not necessarily, that which is required to cover its costs of (re)production.

The genealogical analysis will shed light on the role of law, and legal concepts, in reconciling the contradictory functions of the wage, therefore, tracing the evolution of this category through legal discourse, over time. By locating itself in the context of a particular society, Britain, and a particular legal system, moreover, the analysis will help us better identify the truly systemic, or structural, properties of law, by revealing the contingencies, path dependences, and decisions influencing how this contradiction has unfolded in a particular, historical context.

1.3 Outline

1.3.1 Part I

Part I of this book explores, at an analytical, or structural-systemic level, the nature of law as a social category, or form, which is unique, and integral, to capitalism. This part of the book isolates the distinguishing and intrinsic features of law as a historically specific mode of regulation, with a view to understanding these features by reference to the practices and relations in the context of which they came to be.

Chapter 2 develops a Marxian inspired ontology through which to explore law's relationship with capitalist social relations and the nature of its constitutive role. While the ontology draws primarily on Marx's critique of political economy, it also engages with insights from the philosophy of critical realism. Critical realism, it is argued, provides a social ontology that helps us better understand how structure and agency interact to produce particular outcomes, and thus the different ways in which law might contribute to the problems it is often called upon to address.

Chapter 3 develops these ideas to explore law's ontology more directly: developing a theory of the legal form. This analysis will help tease out some of the inherent or structural limits on law as a mode of regulation. Few mainstream or critical legal or labour law texts[36] have engaged with the origins of the capitalist

[36] While some scholars, including members of the school of critical legal studies, have engaged with law and labour law from a Marxist perspective, they have not paid much attention to the *origins* and *form* of law to the extent advocated here. For a UK example, see: Hugh Collins, *Marxism and Law* (OUP 1982).

legal form (as distinguished from other forms of social regulation and/or law's substantive content); as such, they have tended to neglect the historical specificities of this form and its significance for law's capacity to bring about social change.[37] Chapter 3 explores these questions by engaging with the Marxist theory of law as refined by Evgeny Pashukanis, and, in so doing, teases out some implications for our understanding of labour law.

Chapter 4 develops the analytical framework that will underpin the historical, genealogical analysis in Part II where some of the insights of Part I can be explored in more depth. The purpose of Part II is to move from a *conceptualization* of capitalism, and law under capitalism, to a *historicization* that explores how the processes, or logics identified in Part I have unfolded in real historical time: how the defining features of capitalism, and law, have manifested, or expressed themselves, in a particular country, and legal system, in practice, and how the law's conception of a core capitalistic category, the wage, has influenced capitalism's development..

1.3.2 Part II

Part II comprises a legal genealogy of the wage, tracing, through legal texts and discourse (cases, legislation, Hansard, Select Committee reports), the various concepts through which that category has been legally denoted. Each chapter of Part II focuses upon a different period in the development of capitalism, and/or a different aspect of the wage and its regulation. The intention is not, however, to present a chronology of the wage's development; the chapters are, for the most part, structured thematically. Chapters 5 to 7 explore the development of minimum wage legislation, beginning with the decline of the feudal system of land tenure, before exploring developments in wage regulation throughout the nineteenth and twentieth centuries. It discusses, in particular, the Truck Acts of 1831, the Trade Board Acts, and the wages council system. Chapter 8 then analyses, in depth, the modern minimum wage framework, focusing on the conceptual structure of the National Minimum Wage Act and Regulations (1998–2019), and the prevailing conception of the wage implicit in it. Chapter 9 draws on this analysis to show how viewing modern debates over employment status through the lens of the wage can shed new light on some of the tensions in the case law and, relatedly, some of the challenges facing society when it comes to securing to workers the sort of 'social wage' that capitalism itself requires.

[37] Notable exceptions include: Knox (n 10); O'Connell (n 10); Baars (n 10); and Christopher Tomlins, 'How Autonomous Is Law?' (2007) 3 Annual Review of Law and Social Science 45.

1.3.3 Scope and Clarification

The term 'labour law' is most frequently used to describe the various rules, institutions, and doctrines developed to regulate employment relationships in the early twentieth century. In this book, however, the term labour law is used in a much broader, analytical sense. In this context, the term refers to the particular body of rules, institutions, and doctrines that emerged with the generalization of wage labour, and which are concerned, most directly, with regulating the terms on which employers gain access to labour power, and workers to the wages they need to live. That being said, for reasons of space, the analysis in Part II does not cover all aspects of labour law so conceived. Rather, it concerns only those aspects most relevant to the question of wage regulation. Thus, while the relationship between contractual 'wage' payments and the various other mechanisms that contribute to workers' take-home pay, such as the tax and social security system, is explored indirectly, through the way it influences how the wage is conceptualized in legal discourse at various points in time, no attempt is made to explore the tax or social security systems in detail. Similarly, while the book discusses aspects of collective labour law where relevant, a chronology of this aspect of labour law is outside the scope of this work.

PART I

2
An Ontology of Capitalism

2.1 Introduction

The ontology developed in this chapter draws inspiration from two traditions: critical realism and the immanent social critique associated with Marx's mature critical theory. It is intended, first, to help us distance ourselves from the instrumental conceptions of law criticized in Chapter 1 (where law is seen as a neutral instrument for promoting certain 'values' or pursuing particular purposes), without, however, retreating into a form of 'idealism', privileging abstract concepts over the specific historical contexts in which legal ideas take hold; and second, to explore the relationship between structure and agency in detail, and the historically specific relationship between law and capitalist social relations in particular, so as to help us better understand how the structure of capitalism might limit, but also potentially empower us, when it comes to using law, and labour law, to bring about social change—a question that will be addressed in more detail in Chapter 3.

2.2 Critical Realism

Critical realism is a philosophy of science based around several ontological and epistemological premises.[1] It emerged as a 'third way' between positivism, and the 'idealist' or post-modern critique that developed in response to it.[2] Rejecting the premise that reality can be reduced to subjective experiences, whether it be empirically observed events (positivism), or discourse, theories, and concepts, critical realism sought to show how maintaining a clear distinction between ontology and epistemology might help ground socio-scientific research.

[1] Some of the principal texts in this field include: Roy Bhaskar, *The Possibility of Naturalism: A Philosophical Critique of the Contemporary Human Sciences* (Routledge 2014); Roy Bhaskar, *A Realist Theory of Science* (Routledge 2013); Margaret Scotford Archer, *Realist Social Theory: The Morphogenetic Approach* (CUP 1995); Dave Elder-Vass, *The Causal Powers of Social Structures* (CUP 2010); Berth Danermark, Mats Ekstrom, and Liselotte Jakobsen, *Explaining Society: An Introduction to Critical Realism in the Social Sciences* (Routledge 2001). For more user-friendly introductory texts, see: Andrew Collier, *Critical Realism: An Introduction to Roy Bhaskar's Philosophy* (Verso 1994); Roy Bhaskar, *The Order of Natural Necessity: A Kind of Introduction to Critical Realism* (CreateSpace Independent Publishing Platform 2016).

[2] Including the 'idealism' of the critical legal studies tradition (critiqued at length in: China Miéville, 'The Commodity-Form Theory of International Law: An Introduction' (2004) 17 Leiden Journal of International Law 271.)

Labour and the Wage. Zoe Adams, Oxford University Press (2020). © Zoe Adams.
DOI: 10.1093/oso/9780198858898.001.0001

Central to this agenda is the premise that while human knowledge is inherently mediated and fallible, and thus 'constructed', it is still knowledge of some actually existing (intransitive) reality, the nature of which necessarily influences the *form* of our (fallible) knowledge claims.[3] The features of that reality that we identify can, for this reason, help us to understand how different interpretations, or discourses, come to be. This opens the door to explaining why certain things appear to us as they do, and thus to better understanding even our 'mistaken' theories and assumptions.

Critical realists emphasize that our experiences of reality (that which we observe or perceive through our senses) do not exhaust that reality. Rather, the task for science is to explain those experiences by reference to the underlying structures that give rise to them (without which they would not exist). Reality is structured, therefore, in the sense that, in addition to the events and outcomes that we (may or may not) directly observe and perceive, there exist deep, underlying 'structures' that account for them, but which are rarely observable on the surface. Because we only have access to the 'surface' of society, therefore, (its forms of appearance), to gain knowledge of reality (its underlying essence) requires thinking, conceptually (through thought-experiments etc), about the structures that must exist for those experiences to be possible.

Critical realists do not, therefore, assert that their conception of social reality is inherently 'true', or assume that certain 'facts' are beyond question. Instead, they stress that competing accounts must be judged by reference to their explanatory power, their capacity to make sense of a wider range of empirical phenomena.[4] The transcendental method they employ, along with their willingness to engage with existing theories, is such, they claim, that their theory is, at least, the 'best' available at the present time.

This method involves a process of retroduction—a form of transcendental argument that seeks to explain what the world must be like for a particular phenomenon (or a particular practice) to exist as it does; to reveal its conditions of possibility.[5] It starts with some (apparently) uncontroversial claim about the world (such as the existence or materiality of human beings) and explores what (perhaps more controversial) claim/s must also be true for this to be the case: for X experience to have taken place (an apple falling on one's head), Y must exist (gravity). By applying immanent critique to this process,[6] scrutinizing *why* and under what

[3] K Robert Isaksen, 'Reclaiming Rational Theory Choice as Central: A Critique of Methodological Applications of Critical Realism' (2016) 15 Journal of Critical Realism 245.

[4] Tony Lawson, *Economics and Reality* (Psychology Press 1997); Paul A Lewis, 'Tempered Steele? On the Merits of Critical Realism and the "Ontological Turn" in Economics' (2011) 23 Critical Review 207; Tony Lawson, 'A Realist Theory for Economics' [1994] New Directions in Economic Methodology 257, 271.

[5] Danermark, Ekstrom, and Jakobsen (n 1).

[6] Isaksen (n 3); Danermark, Ekstrom, and Jakobsen (n 1). The conception of 'immanent critique' employed by critical realism is perhaps best seen as a form of *internal critique*. This criticism of this concept is elaborated more fully below.

conditions X is (deemed to be) uncontroversial, and thus taken for granted in the context of particular theories, critical realists commit to an iterative process that involves the continuous refinement, and development, of existing theories and conceptions of the way the (social) world 'is'.[7] Its social ontology is not 'produced' out of thin air, therefore, but is constructed from what already exists; refined, and developed, however, in light of new experiences.

The starting point for the critical realist social ontology is that certain social predicates must exist for particular actions/interactions to be possible.[8] That is, certain widely observed features of reality, such as the fact of someone going to work, presuppose certain positions (worker) and relations (labour–capital (class); worker–employer (individual) etc), certain institutions (money, the state), and a shared framework of meaning that allows us to identify what counts as work in a particular context. This implies that there is a real social structure that causally influences the actions of individual agents (is a precondition for certain types of action), and so is ontologically irreducible to individuals and/or their mental conceptions.[9] That is, certain structures pre-exist, and are conditions for, certain types of action/interaction, and so must be independent from the 'human agents' that undertake them.[10]

For critical realists, this social 'structure' essentially consists of a web of relationships between (internally related) social positions—husband/wife, employer/employee, father/son, etc—which individuals assume (or are born into) and which provides the context from which they engage in 'socially positioned' practices.[11] This structure, and thus the positions people assume and the practices they perform, exist independently from the particular individuals occupying them at a given moment—what it means to be a worker does not depend on the properties of a particular individual assuming the role of worker at a particular time. These positions—and the relations between them—condition the interests individuals have (conceived objectively), and the resources at their disposal (power, money) when it comes to acting (or engaging in specific practices). Social structure thus exists independently from individuals' subjective awareness of it; a 'worker' has an interest in obtaining high wages and stable employment, and is constrained in the options available to him when it comes to developing his life plans, as a result of the position (into which he was born, or which he subsequently assumed) in the web of relationships that constitutes society—even if, for that structure to affect his

[7] Roy Bhaskar, *Dialectic: The Pulse of Freedom* (Routledge 2008).

[8] Bhaskar, *Possibility of Naturalism* (n 1) 34. It should be noted here that Bhaskar's ontology has been refined by other critical realists since, and it is the most convincing version of this theory that is presented here.

[9] ibid 35–39.

[10] For a critique of the logic of this argument, see: Tuukka Kaidesoja, 'The Concept of Social Structure in Roy Bhaskar's Critical Realism' [2009] Jyväskylä Studies in Education, Psychology and Social Research 376.

[11] See Roy Bhaskar, *Scientific Realism and Human Emancipation* (Routledge 2009) 52.

behaviour, he has to have some awareness of the constraints under which he acts (not necessarily an awareness of the structure itself, but some conception of what it means to be a worker dependent on wages to live).[12]

Social structure consists of more, therefore, than the web of relations into which individuals are born and/or which they assume in different contexts, and from which they act. Social reality always has a conceptual dimension: it is conceptualized reality.[13] Social practices are only social practices insofar as they are performed, and interpreted, in light of a shared framework of meaning (shared 'cognitive framework'), a framework that makes it possible to identify a particular action (or sequence of actions) as something (as work, as football, or as shopping), and which informs agents about what is expected of them in terms of fulfilling that practice.[14] As Jaeggi puts it 'practices are social in the fundamental sense that what is performed can be understood only in a context of socially shaped meanings and socially constituted institutions (broadly conceived)'.[15] While the positions people assume exist independently of their (and the theorist's) knowledge of them, their causal power (capacity to make a difference to the course of events) depends on how those positions are conceptualized, the rights, duties, etc commonly associated with the position denoted by the term 'worker', for only then will they influence social interaction.

As Bhaskar argues:

> all activity, including purely economic activity, necessarily has an ideational component or aspect ... it is un-thinkable except insofar as the agent has a conception of what s/he is doing and why s/he is doing it. The crude base-superstructure distinction must be rejected and replaced by a conception of the different ideologies[16] associated with the different practices, in any particular formation.[17]

If individuals are to participate in society, and engage in social practices, therefore, they cannot but draw on the shared norms, beliefs, and assumptions that are shared within a given population at a particular time—a shared 'cognitive framework' that emerges from, and is reproduced/transformed through, the web of (inter-related) practices that constitute a particular 'form' or 'structure' of society.[18]

[12] On the relationship between the 'conceptual' (or ideological) and the material, see: Douglas V Porpora, 'Cultural Rules and Material Relations' [1993] Sociological theory 212.

[13] Roy Bhaskar, *The Order of Natural Necessity: A Kind of Introduction to Critical Realism* (CreateSpace Independent Publishing Platform 2016) 38.

[14] For a similar view, see: Rahel Jaeggi, 'Towards an Immanent Critique of Forms of Life' (2015) 57 Raisons politiques 13.

[15] Rahel Jaeggi, *On the Critique of Forms of Life* (Ciaran Cronin tr, Belknap Press 2018) 57.

[16] Cognitive framework is perhaps a better term than ideology here; Bhaskar employs the term somewhat loosely.

[17] Bhaskar, *Possibility of Naturalism* (n 1) 86.

[18] I use the term 'cognitive' to emphasize that it is the particular system of meaning, rather than the precise linguistic terms (concepts) that is significant here, although the term 'conceptual' is arguably

Social reality is, then, concept-dependent. But that does not mean that the conceptual is *exhaustive* of social reality: many structures emerge from the actions of previous agents, but continue to be causally efficacious even though they may not currently be being reproduced through conscious practice (eg a prior distribution of capital). Moreover, while social reality is as it is because of how it is conceptualized, social structure, including the conceptual, has its origins in (socially conditioned) intentional or conscious human praxis, and thus interactions with and between material beings and/or objects. It is, then, always rooted in the material. While the 'cognitive' and 'material' may be analytically distinct, in the sense that the positions people assume, and the interests they have, exist independently from the concepts people hold, in the 'dialectic of history' they necessarily interweave.[19]

Social reality is not, however, simply the web of (conceptualized) relations and practices that form the context for individual actions: social reality also has lower level 'material' parts—social forms or entities with which individuals interact and which are themselves inherent in, and emerge from, social practices (eg the social practice of exchange presupposes the social form of money, and relatedly the institutions of the state and legal system, each of which have a material, as well as a conceptual basis). Critical realists explain the existence of such forms by reference to the concept of emergence: material objects assume new forms as a result of the way they are relationally positioned in the context of different practices, and, as a result, those objects come to perform new functions.[20] While the capacity of, say, gold, to function as a means of exchange is constrained by its physical properties (durability etc), there is nothing inherent in those properties that lends it the form, or function of money. Rather, it is the way that gold came to be relationally positioned in the context of various inter-linked practices that gives rise to money, and its emergent capacity (or 'power') to function as a means of exchange (and, relatedly, a measure of value).

Social reality is, moreover, structured, or internally differentiated. Repeated interactions between particular positions, and in the context of particular sets of inter-linked practices, can give rise to 'emergent systems', or spheres of interaction, which, while embedded in the broader social structure, interacting with other emergent spheres, nonetheless possess distinct, emergent, properties of their own.[21] Thus, we can speak of the economic, legal, political, etc 'systems', as certain

more appropriate as it emphasizes that this system of meaning is not reducible to the level of individual consciousness.

[19] Douglas V Porpora, 'Tony Lawson from a Sociological Point of View' (2017) 41 Cambridge Journal of Economics 1525.

[20] Tony Lawson, 'Social Positioning and the Nature of Money' (2016) 40 Cambridge Journal of Economics 961.

[21] Tony Lawson refers to these 'spheres' as 'communities'. See the discussion in: Simon Deakin, 'Tony Lawson's Theory of the Corporation: Towards a Social Ontology of Law' (2017) 41 Cambridge Journal of Economics 1505.

internally related practices that generate their own, internal structure (web of relations), and, in turn, their own discourses and belief systems. The legal system, for example, is part of society, but is, nonetheless, an emergent 'totality' that is constituted by various internally related positions (judge, lawyer, legislator, etc) and entities/forms (courts, Parliament, statutes, etc), emerging from, and being reproduced through, a particular set of regular, and internally related, practices. At the same time, these practices presuppose and interact with other practices taking place elsewhere/outside the system (exchange etc). These internally related practices and positions also generate a unique legal discourse—a discourse, a particular belief system and particular way of seeing the world, with which individuals must engage if they are to 'successfully' participate in legal practices, and thus in the legal system.

It is in this sense that the legal system is emergent: while the legal system would not exist without the individual positions and social forms of which it is comprised, it is nonetheless 'more than the sum of its parts': it has the capacity to influence behaviour by reason of the way that these lower-level components relate to each other, and, in this sense, possesses emergent properties that are not possessed by those components in isolation. The legal system's capacity to influence behaviour, for example, is not a property possessed by a statute, a judge, or a legislator, taken collectively, or in isolation; it is an emergent property of the relations and interactions between these various components of the system. And while legal discourse has meaning only by reason of the broader linguistic framework, and social discourses, in which it is embedded, legal concepts nonetheless come to possess distinct meanings of their own, meanings which are specific to the practices and contexts in which legal actors are engaged, and which, in turn, shape, and are shaped by, those practices.

It is the emergent properties of social forms (and thus structure) that explain how the causal properties of social structure, and its various lower-level components (positions, entities, discourses, etc) can be distinct from those of human agents, even if they emerge through their (previous) interactions.[22] It thus explains how social structures can exist independently from the individuals whose behaviour they condition, forming the context into which they are born, and from which they act, while nonetheless being (often unconsciously) reproduced/transformed through their interactions.

In the same way that social structures cannot be reduced to the actions of individual agents, because they pre-exist them and possess properties that agents do not possess whether collectively or in isolation,[23] the discourses, theories, and belief systems that frame and lend significance to social practices are more than

[22] Bhaskar, *Possibility of Naturalism* (n 1) 50.
[23] Bhaskar, *Possibility of Naturalism* (n 1) 46; Archer (n 1) 139.

the words we actually say, or the beliefs that are actually held at a particular time. This is because they consist of implicit rules about what can be said and in what context,[24] rules that are both a product of collective understandings shared between particular groups, and of a discourse's internal structure, of what has been said in the past.

Discourse, or systems of meaning (the 'conceptual' or 'cognitive') both frame, and are reproduced/transformed through, the actions of human beings. They are emergent forms, therefore, in the sense that they emerge through human interactions, and, inhering in particular practices, make a difference to what is done and how, influencing how individuals conceive themselves, and the world, and the reasons they form for acting. The form of those discourses is influenced in part by the structure of the world in which those actions take place and in part by the pre-existing concepts, ideas, and beliefs of the persons engaging in them. They are not pure constructions, therefore, for while they influence behaviour at a conceptual, or psychological, level, they nonetheless emerge from concrete practices.[25] They depend, in turn, on collective understandings, and so cannot be altered nor disposed of through individual actions. While the form that discourses and discursive/meaning systems take can, moreover, be influenced by human agents, not only are the actions of those agents always already socially conditioned, or framed, but the form they take is also influenced by the objective features of the world from which they abstract, and with which agents engage when they undertake any form of social activity.

These observations have important implications for our understanding of law. They suggest, for example, that while law might influence behaviour through its distribution of rights and resources and its application of material sanctions, it also operates at a cognitive, or conceptual, level. That is, somewhat invisibly, legal discourse structures social practices, influencing agents' conceptions of themselves and the world, and in this way, influencing their behaviour. Certain practices might themselves possess a juridical dimension, be structured by legal norms and concepts, moreover, regardless of whether legal rights and obligations are expressly invoked or engaged. Furthermore, because social reality has its origins in praxis, the form that legal discourse takes cannot be separated from the broader context, the framework of inter-related practices and relations, from which it developed.

The above is not an exhaustive account of the critical realist ontology, but it highlights particularly well three points of interest for law and legal analysis:

[24] Tony Lawson 'Comparing Conceptions of Social Ontology: Emergent Social Entities and/or Institutional Facts?' (2016) 46 Journal for the Theory of Social Behaviour 359.

[25] Dave Elder-Vass, *The Reality of Social Construction* (CUP 2012); Philip Gorski, 'As Critical Realism Meets Social Constructionism - Dave Elder-Vass, The Reality of Social Construction (Cambridge, Cambridge University Press, 2012)' (2013) 54 European Journal of Sociology/Archives Européennes de Sociologie 461.

First, the causal independence of structure and agents, and thus their mutual implication in socio-economic outcomes. The positions people hold, and the discourses, ideas, and beliefs that frame social practices, do not determine, but only condition which opportunities agents seize and the capacities they exercise in a given situation;[26] nor do discourses about the world determine the beliefs individuals *actually* hold and the reasons they form when acting: agents are always capable of (socially positioned) reflexive choice. How individuals think, how they act, and thus the choices they make, are always already conditioned by the structural positions they find themselves in (the web of relations into which they are born), and the shared discourses, languages, and belief systems, with which they must engage (whether consciously or not) if they are to interact with others, and participate in society/particular spheres of interaction. This suggests that when explaining social problems, or outcomes, (such as low pay), we must pay attention to the complex ways in which the positions from which individuals act, and the assumptions embedded in the practices they participate in, influence how they understand their interests, and preferences, and thus what it is right/beneficial/legitimate to do. In so doing, we cannot exclude the possibility that law is already part of the 'problem' that it is being called upon to address.

Second, the mutually constitutive nature of the conceptual and the material. This suggests that it is important to engage not only with the way that power and resources are distributed throughout society (the objective positions from which individuals act and into which they are 'born'), but also, the conceptual frameworks, discourses, and belief systems, that influence how individuals conceive the world, and how practices develop—and, the relations and interactions that exist between them. Once again, law may be implicated in both these aspects—influencing how rights and resources are distributed, but also, individuals' world views, and how they conceive their interests and preferences—that is, how they choose to act.

Finally, the path-dependent nature of social structures, the continuing influence on the present, of structures (both past distributions of resources and historical ideas and assumptions) that emerged from (structurally conditioned) practices, and interactions that took place in the past. This refers not only to the way that past interactions might produce particular webs of relations (a particular distribution of rights and resources) that continue to constrain the interests and options available to different individuals and/or groups, but also to how historical assumptions about the world come to be embedded in different discourses and so continue to influence how society is conceived, and thus potentially how social practices develop.

[26] Lawson, Economics and Reality (n 4); Archer (n 1).

2.3 From Critical Realism to Marx

The critical realist social ontology allows us to move away from the limitations of the naturalistic approach, and, in particular, the idea that law is a mere instrument that social actors can design, and use, for particular purposes. So too does it distance us from the methodological individualism implicit in such approaches—that is, the premise that we can explain socio-economic outcomes solely by reference to the actions and decisions of human beings (whether economic agents or legal actors such as judges and policy-makers). In turn, it allows us to engage with the role that emergent structures and agency play in influencing socio-economic outcomes, including the emergent discourses and belief systems that frame particular actions, whether or not individuals are aware of such structures, or their effects, in practice.

Before we can draw on the insights from the analysis of critical realism so as to study, more specifically, the nature of law and markets, some inconsistencies and tensions in the critical realist approach must be addressed. Critical realists assert that the conceptual (the shared framework of meaning that unites a given society), emerges through material practices, thereby locating discourses, theories, beliefs, etc *within* the social reality of which knowledge is sought. At the same time, however, they suggest that knowledge exists *outside* reality, that it is causally influenced by it, but nonetheless existing in some sense autonomously from it—in some 'external' realm of thought. This allows them to claim to have developed a theory of social reality *in general* notwithstanding that they can, by definition, only have developed that theory in light of experiences in, and through practices undertaken within, the particular form of society in which that theory was elaborated.[27]

If social reality emerges through human praxis, however, there can be no 'pre-social' realm in which knowledge about the world can be produced; no place outside society from which to develop a theory of what society is like. Ontologies can only ever be (socially produced) theories of actually existing societies, therefore, of the particular form of society in which that ontology is developed. As we shall see, this observation has important implications for our understanding of the ontological status of concepts (such as law, markets, or society.)

If social reality is always necessarily a conceptualized reality (even if it has its origins in material practices), the nature of social reality, and of particular features of that reality (such as law) can only be assessed relative to the particular form of social reality in which a given concept (or form) of law (or market etc) exists. We simply cannot separate, in other words, the question of how social forms appear, and come to be conceptualized in particular conditions, from the question

[27] For a similar critique, see: Richard Gunn, 'Marxism and Philosophy: A Critique of Critical Realism' (1989) 13 Capital & Class 87; Andrew Brown, 'Reorienting Critical Realism: A System-wide Perspective on the Capitalist Economy' (2007) 14 Journal of Economic Methodology 499.

of their underlying essence, or structure (the reality or nature of law). How social forms such as law appear to us influences how we engage with them, and so, how they appear and are commonly conceptualized must be seen as part of the process by which a given society, and certain features of that society, emerge and are reproduced. Rather than dismissing appearances as illusory therefore, as obscuring the real structures that underpin them, we must explain those appearances by reference to the role they play in the practices that are constitutive of the system in which they come to be.

To understand the nature of law, therefore, and its role in society, we must begin by identifying the distinctive or unique features of the particular form of society in which it (a particular conception of law) and we, exist, before exploring how certain categories, or concepts, integral to that society (law, markets, value, labour) contribute to the emergence, and reproduction, of its constitutive practices and relations.

Following Marx, and consistently with the premise that social reality emerges through human praxis, therefore, this book argues that different forms of society can be distinguished by reference to the nature of the dominant mode of production—those practices which must be regularly carried out (given the state of technological development), if society is to persist. The concept of 'mode of production' does not imply the existence of some determining economic sphere that is in some sense separate from society more generally. Rather, the term itself denotes the entire structure of a given society; its basic form and underlying logic. The mode by which, or activities and relations through which, human societies reproduce themselves have profound implications for the basic structure of society, in other words, including the form of its power relations, and the beliefs and ideals of its members. This is not to suggest that all activities, and all spheres of life, are mere reflexes of 'real' economic relations. Rather, it is to recognize that social life, and the basic structure of society (including its politico-legal dimensions) is profoundly influenced by the nature of the activities through which human life is (re)produced, the activities without which all other practices and relations would not be possible.[28]

In *Capital* Marx presented his theory of capitalism in, and through, an immanent critique of classical political economy. Here, and consistently with the above observations, he set out to understand *why* capitalist social relations appeared as they did, in particular socio-historical conditions, including why the classical political economists had 'universalized' that which was historically specific. While he did not argue that markets are by definition perfectly competitive, or that, in practice, prices will be equivalent to value (socially necessary labour time),[29] he nonetheless

[28] Karl Marx and Friedrich Engels, *The German Ideology*, vol 1 (International Publishers Co 1970) 31.

[29] Marx equates value and price only in *Capital*, volume 1. In volume 3, however, he makes clear that, in the long run, competition between firms and between industries leads to an equalization of the rate of profit, such that commodities sell not at their values but their prices of production. While prices are

took seriously that the theories of his predecessors were the product of experiences *in capitalism*, and that their ideas, and mistakes (or 'ideological distortions'), could be explained by reference to real, objective tendencies and contradictions inherent in capitalism itself. The task was not to dismiss their ideas, therefore, but to explore why the market came to be conceptualized in a particular form in particular socio-economic conditions—to explore what it is about the essence or structure of capitalism that explains its 'distorted' or 'inverted' forms of appearance.[30]

Crucially, by adopting such an approach, Marx showed that the contradictions inherent in capitalist society, (between the processes of capital accumulation and the process of social reproduction; a reflection of the contradiction between exchange and use value at the heart of the commodity) extend to (and are reflected in) a contradiction between the way that capitalist social relations manifest in experience (and thus the concepts through which it is denoted), and its material 'essence'. The material 'essence' of capitalism, he argued, is the unequal and exploitative relationship between capital and labour (the relations of production), a relation that is presupposed by the existence of the market, and which is brought about through direct legal, or political, force. The ideal form in which the market is experienced, however, conceals this essence by (among other things) presenting capital and labour as equal and free, and law, and the state, as independent from the market, neutral vis-à-vis individual legal subjects. This self-presentation of the market, and law, is intrinsic to the nature of market practices, in the sense that, without these beliefs, those practices would cease to be. And, by concealing the reality of labour's inequality and exploitation, the market's self-presentation makes these practices both possible and sustainable, and, in the process, ensures the reproduction and expansion of capital. Hence, the distorted form in which the relations of capitalism present themselves, he concluded, is part of the essence of those relations, essential for sustaining those practices over time.

Recognizing this contradictory unity between essential relations and the misleading forms in which they are experienced is, as we shall see, of particular importance when it comes to understanding the nature of law. In Marxist scholarship, law is often described as 'ideal' or 'ideological', or as part of the 'superstructure'.[31] In Marx's work (and in contrast with the naturalistic view outlined in Chapter 1),

rooted in, and fluctuate around, labour values, they necessarily and systematically deviate from them. See: Patrick Murray, *The Mismeasure of Wealth: Essays on Marx and Social Form* (Brill 2016), 288–89. See also: Karl Marx, *Capital, Volume III* (David Fernbach tr, Penguin Books 1981) 279.

[30] On this point, see: Geoffrey Pilling, *Marx's 'Capital': Philosophy and Political Economy* (Routledge 1980) Chapter 2. The relationship between form and appearance is also important for grasping the relationship between volumes 1 and 3 of *Capital*.

[31] Karl Marx, *Capital, Volume I* (Penguin/New Left Review 1867) Preface. See the discussion in Hugh Collins, *Marxism and Law* (OUP 1982) Chapter 4. This misreading of Marx can also be seen in: Simon Deakin and others, 'Legal Institutionalism: Capitalism and the Constitutive Role of Law' (2017) 45 Journal of Comparative Economics 188.

however, references to base and superstructure do not imply that law is causally secondary to some real economic relations that exist in the 'base'. Rather, the appearance of a distinction between base and superstructure, between law (and politics) and the economy, is an ideological consequence inherent in the nature of capitalist social relations—how capitalism presents itself in experience.[32] In capitalism, the social relations of production manifest themselves in the form of ostensibly independent economic and non-economic spheres, and their doing so is integral to the nature of that system and its reproduction.[33] This is not a purely ideological separation, moreover, but has objective, institutional, foundations. We must not explain away, or dismiss as an error of thought, the differentiation of the politico-legal and the economic, therefore, but must explore what it is about the capitalist mode of production that necessitates, or explains, this apparent differentiation of spheres—the particular forms that the legal, political, and economic aspects assume (and are commonly conceptualized) in the context of capitalism.[34] This observation must now be born in mind as we turn to explore the nature of capitalism in more detail.

2.4 Capitalism

In *Capital*,[35] Marx shows that capitalism is a system in which the unique social goal of production is the production and realization of surplus value[36]—the accumulation of capital. Capital, he argues, refers to a historically specific form of wealth: money advanced into circulation with a view to extracting more money from circulation.[37] It thus presupposes commodity production and generalized

[32] Evgeny Pashukanis, *Law and Marxism: A General Theory* (revised edn, Pluto Press 1987) Chapter 2.

[33] Derek Sayer, *The Violence of Abstraction: The Analytic Foundations of Historical Materialism* (Blackwell 1987).

[34] TR Raghunath, 'Marx's Theory of Ideology' (PhD thesis, McMaster University 1988) 17.

[35] While much of the following analysis presupposes Marx's labour theory of value, it is not necessary to subscribe to this view to appreciate the point being made about the relationship between law and markets, and law and capitalist social relations. Even so, while there have been numerous critiques of this theory over the years, (see in particular: John E Roemer, 'New Directions in the Marxian Theory of Exploitation and Class' (1982) 11 Politics & Society 253; John E Roemer, *A General Theory of Exploitation and Class* (reprint 2014, Harvard University Press 2014); Eugen von Böhm-Bawerk, *Karl Marx and the Close of His System* (Ludwig von Mises Institute 1949); Herbert Gintis and Samuel Bowles, 'Structure and Practice in the Labor Theory of Value' (1981) 12 Review of Radical Political Economics 1) responses to these critiques include: Murray (n 29); Postone Moishe, *Time, Labor, and Social Domination: A Reinterpretation of Marx's Critical Theory* (CUP 1995); Hans Ehrbar and Mark Glick, 'The Labor Theory of Value and Its Critics' [1986] Science & Society 464; Fred Moseley, *Money and Totality: A Macro-Monetary Interpretation of Marx's Logic in Capital and the End of the 'Transformation Problem'* (Brill 2015).

[36] On the method and mode of presentation of Marx's theory of capitalism, see: Moseley (n 35).

[37] Karl Marx, *Capital, Volume I* (Penguin/New Left Review 1867) 331. Marshall discussed various definitions of capital in Appendix E of his *Principles of Economics*, but wrongly attributed to Marx a definition whereby capital consisted of physical capital goods (means of production). However, Marx

exchange—each of which are implied by the existence of money, a social form which is also unique to capitalism. Consistently with the above premises, however, Marx developed this understanding of capitalism through an analysis of the fetishistic forms in which capitalism presents itself in experience (and thus, as experienced in a context of competition), the most basic of which being the commodity, and thus the widely prevalent practice of buying and selling commodities in the market.[38]

Marx observed that the market that appears on the surface of capitalist society is not the same as pre-capitalist markets—simple exchange or barter—where buying and selling takes place simultaneously. Rather, the capitalist market is a decentralized sphere of economic interaction, wherein prices function to coordinate behaviour. Buying and selling does not take place simultaneously; supply and demand is mediated by money, a 'universal equivalent' that measures not how much an individual is willing to pay for a particular commodity, but how much of *any* other commodity a particular commodity can purchase in the market: its (exchange) value.

In pre-capitalist societies, producers would exchange surplus goods for other goods, not with a view to accessing money, but in order to access particular use-values. Because exchange was local and irregular, the ratio at which goods exchanged depended on a mixture of customary understandings of just prices,[39] and/or subjective valuations of a good's utility. No class of goods had a value around which its price gravitated, in other words; 'prices', or the ratio at which goods exchanged, varied between transactions, locations, and over time.

In capitalism, by contrast, the prices of commodities, the ratios at which they exchange, displays a distinct pattern.[40] In this sense, commodities seem to have a 'real' exchange value. That is, it is possible to say, for example, that five litres of milk *tends* to exchange for eight loaves of bread, such that we can speak of their mutual replaceability: of their entering into relations of equivalence (eight loaves of bread= five litres of milk). If five litres of milk is equal to eight loaves of bread, and each is equal to a given measure of money (a particular price), all these things (money, milk, bread) must have something in common that makes it possible to equate them. Given that all commodities have different physical properties, however, and different uses or 'use-values', their physical qualities cannot be the common substance that they share. Rather, the substance common to them, the substance that

clearly emphasizes that the concept presupposes the existence of money, and thus, generalized commodity exchange: hence its historical specificity. See: Moseley (n 35) 8–9.

[38] David Goldway, 'Appearance and Reality in Marx's "Capital"' (1967) 31 Science & Society 428, 433.

[39] See: James Davis, *Medieval Market Morality: Life, Law and Ethics in the English Marketplace, 1200–1500* (CUP 2011).

[40] For a detailed analysis of Marx's understanding of prices, exchange value, and value, see: Murray (n 29) Chapter 9.

Marx described with the concept of *value,* must consist of something else. That something, as we shall see, is 'abstract labour'.

When we abstract away the qualitative differences between (the concrete properties of) different commodities, the only thing left that they have in common is that they are produced by human labour. Nonetheless, the products of labour only have an exchange value (as well as a use-value), and only share the common substance of value in a society in which exchange is generalized, and in which all economic actors are dependent on the market for existence. The human labour that is common to commodities, then, and which is the substance of value, is human labour as it exists in a society of generalized commodity exchange; a society in which the producers are excluded from the means for production. In such societies, and as a result of that exclusion, human labour assumes a particular, *abstract* form. Exercised only if and to the extent that it can be alienated in the market, labour in capitalism is necessarily abstracted (or alienated) from its concrete qualities and immediate use.

In capitalism, by reason of their exclusion from the means of production, workers' capacity to work can only be exercised if, and to the extent that, the right to put that capacity into action is transferred to someone in possession of the means of production: a capitalist employer. It is capital, and not the individual worker, therefore, that decides what concrete form workers' capacity to work will take: *how* they will work, and *what* they will produce. Labour in capitalism is thus labour, the nature and purpose of which is dictated not by the needs of the direct producer but by the 'needs' of capital. In such a context labour ceases to be (primarily) meaningful or purposive activity, an end in itself (concrete labour), valued as a result of its concrete qualities and becomes something that is treated, socially, as a (general) means to an end: 'mere' labour. For workers, it becomes a means to acquire the products of the labour of others (commodities) through money (the wage); for capitalists, it becomes a mere means to the production and realization of surplus value, or, to the appropriation of profits.

While a detailed analysis of the process of surplus value production is outside the scope of this book, it follows from the above observations that abstract labour, as the substance of value, must necessarily be the substance of 'surplus value' and thus of capital. In the capitalist labour process, in the course of producing, of transforming use-values into new use-values, therefore, workers do not merely transfer the exchange value of the means of production to the new product ('productive consumption'), but also *add new value* to that product. In effect, then, workers (taken collectively) must expend more abstract labour (measured in time) than is embedded in the labour power purchased by the wage. Given that the value of anything, including labour power, consists of the amount of abstract labour time required (or which is socially necessary) to produce it, therefore, the price of labour power will tend to gravitate around the socially necessary costs of producing the subsistence goods required to maintain the average worker (and his dependents).

Once workers (taken at a social level) have worked as long as it would take to produce those goods (hypothetically), then they will no longer be replacing old value (ie transferring old value to the end product), but will actually be adding new value that can be realized when the product is sold in the market.

Surplus value production, and thus capital accumulation, is only possible, then, as a result of the particular structure of social relations in the context of which labour assumes an abstract form. It presupposes, in other words, the exclusion of workers from the means of production and subsistence, and their being 'empowered' to access those means through the market.[41] Capitalist markets, wherein economic competition functions to distribute society's productive inputs (including labour power) and society's total surplus value, already presuppose, then, the *historically specific categories* of abstract labour, (surplus) value, and the commodity—none of which would exist but for workers' exclusion from the means of production and subsistence, and their capacity (legal and practical) to access the both through the market.

Significantly for the purposes of this book, and as will be explained in more detail below, neither of the things listed above would be possible but for certain legal institutions, including private property, contract, and the contract of employment. The private property framework is implied by, and necessary for, that exclusion; contract is necessary to facilitate the sale of labour power to capital; and the contract of employment in particular for facilitating the subsumption of labour to capital so as to secure (and support) capital's control over labour in production, and its right to appropriate the product. This is one sense in which law cannot be seen to be causally secondary to markets, in the way that the naturalistic approach would suggest, responding to 'problems' or 'failures' that emerge therein: law plays an integral role in the emergence and reproduction of the capitalist market—and, relatedly, in the emergence, and reproduction of the social relations that underpin it. It is, in fact, as we have seen, one of the fundamental preconditions for the emergence of capital itself.

We might say, then, that one dimension of law's constitutive role consists in establishing the initial, and ongoing, conditions on the basis of which capitalist economic practices take place, ensuring the differential distribution of resources that makes possible a mode of production based on commodity production and free wage labour. In this way, it provides the foundation for the unique social process through which surplus value is produced, and as such, by which capital can be accumulated.[42] But law does not only play a role in establishing the material conditions for the emergence of competitive markets and the capitalistic production process: law is essential to the process by which those markets operate, and

[41] Karl Marx, *Capital, Volume I* (Penguin/New Left Review 1867) Chapter 6.

[42] Robert Hale, 'Coercion and Distribution in a Supposedly Non-Coercive State' (1923) 38 Political Science Quarterly 470.

are reproduced, over time. And, in this context, an important aspect of its role lies in facilitating the widespread coordination without which generalized commodity exchange could not take place. As we shall see, however, its capacity to perform this coordination function is contingent not only on how well it obscures the material inequalities and exploitation that underpin the market framework and which is presupposed by them, but also how well it regulates capitalist social relations, shaping market practices in such a way as to render them, and the social relations in which they are embedded, socially and economically sustainable.

2.4.1 Law's Functions: Coordination and Regulation

Capitalist markets are, as we have seen, characterized by the fact that decision making is coordinated by a decentralized pricing mechanism that tends, in the long run, towards an equilibrium between supply and demand. For this to be possible, prices must embed information about the costs of producing commodities (their value), reflecting past decisions taken in relation to other commodities in a market setting. For prices to embed this information, agents must know that decisions have been, and will continue to be, taken freely (and thus solely by reference to the information embedded in prices). While markets existed in the feudal era, based primarily on custom; as we saw above, they lacked the universal categories of price and value as social forms arising independently from the subjective valuations of individual actors.[43] These categories could only emerge in a system in which the stability of property, and the enforceability of agreements (contract), could be, *and could be believed to be*, guaranteed.

Law, under capitalism, appears (presents itself) as neutral as between individual agents, applying equally to all, reinforcing belief in equality of right—the premise that individuals are equally free and capable of participating in exchange. It thus plays an integral role in instituting individuals as legal subjects, sustaining the particular form of subjectivity and conception of legitimate power that emerges from, and is integral to, commodity exchange. This subjectivity is also essential to the emergence of the pricing mechanism because it helps sustain belief in prices as a reflection of a commodity's *value*, rather than something that arises as the result of the will of a particular individual or group. Combined with a state monopoly on coercion, this helps maintain an alignment between prices and value (in the long run) so as to facilitate coordination in a way that is conducive to accumulation.

The problem, however, is that, in a context of structural inequality, the above described form of subjectivity is vulnerable to disintegration—it appears to contradict the reality in which individuals live and work. It is not, therefore, self-sustaining,

[43] Karl Marx, *Grundrisse: Introduction to the Critique of Political Economy* (Penguin Books 1973) 156.

and so must be upheld, and reinforced, through an authoritative discourse on which individuals cannot but draw when participating in those practices if they are to coordinate their behaviour. The particular form in which law appears in experience, therefore, and thus the way it presents itself through its discourse, is essential to the process by which a particular conception of the competitive process, as independent from law and politics, is sustained, a conception that is presupposed by, and *necessary* for, the practices through which it is reproduced.

Intrinsic to capitalist markets then is a particular cognitive framework in which law appears as independent and autonomous, and markets as self-constituting and self-sustaining. Because this framework contradicts, or denies, the reality of inequality and domination on which capitalistic production is based, it is often described as ideological, or as a mechanism of concealment.[44] But this framework, the particular image of the world that legal discourse presents, does not come about by the active deception of the ruling class: it emerges from, and inheres in, social practices, even if it takes a distinct form once it is embodied in a juridical discourse on which individuals must draw in the course of those practices in order to coordinate behaviour, and enforce their rights.

This cognitive framework makes possible the assumption that commodities exchange at their value, and thus that prices reflect costs of production—making possible decentralized and 'efficient' coordination. In this framework, law's only role appears to be to protect individuals' natural rights to property, and to contract (as those rights are subjectively experienced in everyday exchange), and/or to intervene in the event of (what we now refer to as) market failure—that is, when experiences deviate from the expected norm of competition.[45] The reality of competitive markets is, however, quite different. This is so, not (or not only) in the sense that real-world markets are liable to fail, that 'perfect competition' rarely exists in practice, rather it is so in a much deeper sense: the capitalist market has an inherent tendency to undermine its own conditions of possibility.

First, capital's expansion is, necessarily, limited by the material and human basis of value production—both the social needs that must be met for labour power to be sustainably reproduced and the material, or human, properties of labour power itself. And it is precisely the human, and material, dimensions of value production that remain obscured in the cognitive framework that is intrinsic to the market. While labour must appear in the market as a pure commodity, or a mere value, it can never be treated as such in practice. This is so not only because labour is

[44] This is particularly true in the context of critical legal studies. See, for example: Karl E Klare, 'The Public/Private Distinction in Labor Law' [1982] University of Pennsylvania Law Review 1358.

[45] I am not suggesting here that the majority of the population are ignorant of the 'regulatory' role of even the neoliberal state. As Susan Marks points out, one can be aware of the 'reality' behind ideological forms, but insofar as one acts *as if* those forms of appearance are true, one nonetheless participates in the reproduction of the relations and practices they 'conceal', and thus of the ideologies themselves. See: Susan Marks, 'Big Brother Is Bleeping Us—With the Message that Ideology Doesn't Matter' (2001) 12 European Journal of International Law 109.

inseparable from the human person, and so presupposes the social processes and activities through which workers themselves are reproduced (and, relatedly, socialized, educated, etc), but also because labour in production is inherently concrete. In production, capital is faced not with pure human effort, but with embodied individuals, with needs, and interests, and an inherent capacity for, and tendency towards, resistance.[46] Not only does capitalist production presuppose, then, that the needs of workers be met in practice (a 'socially necessary wage' or 'social wage'), regardless of the outcomes 'dictated' by the market (as conceived from the perspective of price competition),[47] it also presupposes a means to secure their cooperation, and efficiency, in the production process itself. We might say, then, that it presupposes the socio-economic functions that have historically been performed by labour law institutions, even if it does not necessarily presuppose any particular rules or doctrines.

Second, the laws of capitalist production 'assert themselves as coercive laws of competition, and are brought home to the mind and consciousness of the individual capitalist as the directing motives of his operations'.[48] The problem, however, is that these laws are brought home as an imperative for individual capitalists to maximize profits in order to survive. Maximizing the profits of an individual firm is not, however, the same as maximizing surplus value production—where surplus value is a product of capitalist activity taken collectively/socially. Many activities can generate a profit (charging for access to natural resources or intellectual property etc; financial speculation, where firms profit by charging high interests on loans; or commerce (buying cheap and selling dear)) but that does not mean it contributes to surplus value production very much, or at all.

As Foley explains:

> Each capitalist is in effect a free-rider on the whole system of generation of surplus value. Capitalist exploitation is an externality from the point of view of capitalists as a class. One way to appropriate surplus value is to exploit productive wage workers by lowering costs through raising their productivity or depressing their wages, but this is far from the only way. The actual exploitation of productive wage workers is important because it is the mode of appropriation of surplus value that contributes indirectly to the global pool of surplus value. There are many other modes of appropriation of surplus value, such as monopolization of sectors of the market; marketing and advertising; establishment of intellectual property rights through patents, copyrights, and trademarks; ownership of scarce energy

46 Geoffrey Kay and James Mott, 'Concept and Method in Postone's Time, Labor and Social Domination' (2004) 12 Historical Materialism 169; David McNally, 'Beyond the False Infinity of Capital: Dialectics and Self-Mediation in Marx's Theory of Freedom' in Robert Albritton and John Simoulidis (eds), *New Dialectics and Political Economy* (Springer 2003).

47 Chapter 4 will explain why even 'perfectly competitive 'markets cannot guarantee a 'social wage'.

48 Marx, *Capital, Volume 1* (n 32) 347.

> or other natural resources; superior cleverness in arranging financial transactions or structuring financial property rights; and controlling medical treatment.[49]

The exploitation of productive wage labour (abstract labour) may, then, be the only way in which surplus value can be produced, but it is not the only route to profit. Many capitalists make use of other forms of surplus labour extraction—forced labour, voluntary labour, etc—as well as forms of rent extraction (and other forms of purely parasitic activity), in order to make a profit, and, in doing so, divert resources away from more productive (of surplus value) activities, and, crucially, away from social reproduction.[50] They profit at the expense, in other words, of other capitalists, and the long-run interests of the system. The problem here results from the inherent conflict that exists between the interests of capital as a class (and, by definition, workers) in sustainable accumulation, and the interests of individual capitalists, as conceived in a context of competition, in profit-maximization. It is this same conflict that incentivizes individual firms to depress wages below the socially necessary level (below subsistence level), a strategy that simply shifts those costs onto society.

To put this another way, capital accumulation, and thus the reproduction of capitalism as a system, is an emergent by-product of the competitive process: of the pursuit of self-interest by individuals in the market. While the competitive process is necessary for accumulation, producing the unique incentives to invest that lie at the core of capitalism's expansionary dynamic, it is not *sufficient* for it. This is because it is always in the interests of an individual capital to try to 'cheat' the system—whether by engaging in parasitic activities (such as rent-seeking) or by depressing private cost below social cost. This strategy only works, however, insofar as other capitalists do not do the same. It is in this sense that we might say that the goal of capital accumulation, a precondition for social reproduction, requires mechanisms existing outside the market capable of limiting or subordinating the pursuit of individual self-interest to the collective requirements of sustainable accumulation. Historically, such a function has been performed, primarily, by the state.

What are the implications of this analysis for our understanding of law? It suggests that, not only do capitalist markets *presuppose* certain legal-institutional foundations (or conditions of possibility), they also presuppose mechanisms, such as minimum wage legislation, restrictions on working time, health and safety

[49] Duncan K Foley, 'Rethinking Financial Capitalism and the "Information" Economy' (2013) 45 Review of Radical Political Economics 257, 264.

[50] A discussion of the distinction between productive and unproductive labour is outside the scope of this book. However, the distinction is not material for this analysis because unproductive labour can still be productive for an individual capital (that capital can appropriate surplus labour time) and the wages of those workers still constitute a 'charge' on the overall surplus value available to society for investment.

legislation, etc (or functional equivalents), capable of restricting an already legally constituted 'freedom', so as to guarantee the conditions that the market, and relatedly capital accumulation, presupposes.

2.5 Conclusion

What the analysis in this chapter suggests is that law's function in capitalism is, like capitalist social relations more generally, inherently contradictory. On the one hand, law both provides the initial material conditions of possibility for the emergence of capitalist social relations and is implicated in, and partly constitutive of, the market practices through which those social relations are reproduced. On the other hand, however, the reproduction of those practices, and thus the social relations presupposed by them, depend on legal mechanisms (minimum wage laws, labour laws, and other 'restrictions' on competition) that necessarily contradict the assumptions intrinsic to those practices, and, relatedly, which are intrinsic to law. Law's form and function exist, then, in perpetual conflict: law must always present itself, and its relationship with markets (and capitalist social relations more generally) in a way that fundamentally contradicts the relationship that *must* exist in practice, and the functions that must be performed, if capitalism is to be sustainable.

If this is so, it would seem too that beyond the political/class struggles that influence the law's substantive content, and which influence which laws and institutions prevail at different times, the *form of law*, the medium through which power must be exercised in the context of capitalism, would seem to place limits not only on what law can achieve—and thus how far it can challenge the structures of the system—but also, how far it can mediate capitalism's (and its own) contradictions in practice. Law must always operate, in other words, through a conceptual framework that systematically contradicts the reality of law's role, and state power, in the system in which its exists. The nature of this conceptual framework, that is, of the legal form, will now be explored in depth.

3
Legal Form

3.1 Introduction

The previous chapter observed that law assumes a particular form in capitalism, and that its doing so is integral to the process by which (specifically capitalist) markets, and the social relations presupposed by them, emerge, and are reproduced, over time. It also suggested, however, that this form exists in perpetual conflict with the regulatory function law must perform if market practices, and capital accumulation more generally, is to be sustainable. The task for this chapter is to *explain* the emergence of this form of social regulation (and thus the processes by which it assumes this form) so as to better understand its relationship with the practices and relations in the context of which it came to be.

In undertaking such a task, the chapter draws on the work of the Marxist scholar Evgeny Pashukanis whose 'commodity form' theory of law has inspired much Marxist legal scholarship, including the recent work of scholars such as Robert Knox, China Mieville, Paul O'Connell, Susan Marks, and Grietje Baars, to name just a few. Working primarily in the field of international law (Marks, Mieville, Knox); public law and human rights (O'Connell); and/or company law (Baars), these scholars have sought to use an analysis of the legal form, its origins and its relationship with capital, to explore its limits, and potential, to law as a mode of regulation.[1]

Like these scholars, this chapter places emphasis on the importance of exploring the form of law, as distinguished from (but not to the neglect of) its substantive content, isolating those features of law that explain the 'lawness' of legal rules, and explaining those features by reference to the social practices in the context of which they came to be. Like Pashukanis, moreover, the chapter explores the conditions in which law tends to appear and be conceptualized in a particular historically specific form (as independent, neutral, and autonomous from the market (and society)) without assuming that it does so perfectly, or unconditionally, in practice.

[1] Evgeny Pashukanis, *Law and Marxism: A General Theory* (revised edn, Pluto Press 1987); Robert Knox, 'Marxism, International Law, and Political Strategy' (2009) 22 Leiden Journal of International Law 413; Paul O'Connell, 'Law, Marxism and Method' (2018) 16 tripleC: Communication, Capitalism & Critique. Open Access Journal for a Global Sustainable Information Society 647; Grietje Baars, *The Corporation, Law and Capitalism: A Radical Perspective on the Role of Law in the Global Political Economy* (Brill 2019); Susan Marks, 'International Judicial Activism and the Commodity-Form Theory of International Law' (2007) 18 European Journal of International Law 199; China Mieville *Between Equal Rights a Marxist Theory of International Law* (Aakar Books 2016).

Labour and the Wage. Zoe Adams, Oxford University Press (2020). © Zoe Adams.
DOI: 10.1093/oso/9780198858898.001.0001

The third and fourth sections of this chapter build on the analysis of the legal form, drawing on systems-theoretical approaches to law with a view to better understanding how legal form and content interact.[2] In particular, it explores how the legal form, and thus abstract concepts such as the legal subject, and the values of freedom and equality with which it is associated, lend different meaning to legal rules depending on the lower-level concepts with which they are combined (concepts such as employee, the corporation, the wage). It explores the processes by which meaning comes to be embedded in those concepts, and how these processes constrain, but potentially also facilitate, labour law when it comes to addressing social problems, such as low pay and underinclusive employment status, and/or when it comes to bringing about more far reaching social change.

3.2 Legal Form

The starting point for the commodity form theory of law is the premise that the process by which the products of labour (and labour power itself) assume the form of commodities parallels the process by which individuals assume the form of legal subjects. Generalized exchange requires mutual recognition of property rights, and in this sense the legal relation between subjects is not a response to, but is actually intrinsic in, the value relation: it is one of its necessary modes of appearance.[3] As exchange becomes more widespread, therefore, relations between individuals increasingly assume the form of relations between legal subjects—equals before the law.[4]

For commodities to enter into relations of equivalence they must be taken to market. The persons taking those goods to market must, therefore, have the capacity to dispose of and acquire goods in a market setting. They must be secure that their property is protected, and the agreements they enter into can be enforced. The individuals taking these goods to market assume the form of equal, but independent, persons; equal, that is, in their capacity for ownership, their freedom to dispose of and acquire property, and their disability from exercising coercion—in the rights they enjoy before the law.

As we have seen, (capitalist) markets are not arenas in which isolated exchange transactions take place. They are spheres of recursive economic activity—of universal and regular exchange—where not only society's surplus but also its productive inputs are allocated through the market. It is the regularity of these exchange practices that gives rise to prices, a quantitative expression of (or the form

[2] See: Niklas Luhmann, *Law as a Social System* (Klaus A Ziegert and Fatima Kastner trs, OUP 2004);Simon Deakin, 'Juridical Ontology: The Evolution of Legal Form' [2015] Historical Social Research/Historische Sozialforschung 170, 171–72.

[3] Mieville (n 1) 87.

[4] Pashukanis (n 1).

of appearance of) the value of a commodity.[5] In the long run, prices appear to gravitate around the value of commodities because high-frequency exchange between economically motivated actors embeds information about the decisions taken in relation to those commodities in prices, facilitating coordination. For the right sort of information to be embedded in prices, however, decisions to buy and sell must be, and must be assumed to be, taken freely, solely by reference to the information embedded in prices—they must be based on considerations about a commodity's value or costs of production.[6] For this to be possible these decisions must be taken (and be believed to have been taken and likely to be taken in the future) free from constraint and coercion. So too must they be taken with confidence that the rights acquired will be protected, and agreements enforced. It is in this sense that the free and equal legal subject as a bearer of legal (property) rights is inherent in capitalist market practices, just as the independent state and legal system are before which those rights can be enforced.

This does not mean, however, that the legal subject does not have its origins in practice. Rather, individuals assume a particular identity when they participate in exchange and this becomes self-perpetuating and reinforcing as exchange becomes more widespread.[7] It is the embodiment of this identity in a particular juridical discourse, however, that makes this identity sustainable. Its perpetuation through legal discourse is necessary because the way capitalism presents itself in the context of market practices conflicts with the material conditions in which individuals live and work—the social relations that underpin the market framework. It is only by being expressed at a relatively abstract level and being communicated through a discourse on which individuals cannot but draw if they are to assert their rights that this particular conception of the human being comes to be seen as natural, inevitable, and/or inherently true of human beings.

The free and equal legal subject presupposes the publicly constituted legal system and the state—a third party before whom an individual's 'inherent' (equal) rights can be asserted and enforced.[8] The structure of the legal system—its functional independence from the market—and the existence of a public state monopolizing force beyond the market, are also, therefore, essential

[5] Karl Marx, *Capital, Volume III* (David Fernbach tr, Penguin Books 1981) 25. Marx explains the relationship between value and prices in volume 3 of *Capital*. Whereas his analysis of value in volume 1 is the analysis of capitalism's essence, his analysis of price in volume 3 is of how that essence appears on the surface of society—the two necessarily diverge. In a context of competition, commodities exchange not at their values, but at their prices of production (in the long run; in the short-run, market prices fluctuate around prices of production depending on the strength of effective demand).

[6] Karl Marx, *Capital, Volume I* (Harmondsworth: Penguin/New Left Review 1867) part 1.

[7] Pashukanis (n 1) 95–96; 111–12.

[8] ibid chapter 5. To clarify, the state is the historically contingent form that the 'external' source of coercion, presupposed by capitalism, actually assumed as capitalism developed. The *form* of the state is thus intrinsic to capitalism; the actual, historically existing model of the nation state may not be—an observation that may be important for theorizing capitalism in an era of 'globalization'.

aspects of the legal form because they are presupposed by the legal relation and the particular form of subjectivity that emerges from, and is perpetuated through, exchange.

There is, however, an important juridical or conceptual element at play here. There is more to the state and legal system than the existence of the physical state and legal structures themselves. Contract is integral to the market—providing stability to the parties' expectations.[9] In turn, it is an expression of the parties' autonomous will, and so reinforces their beliefs in their own freedom and equality. Nonetheless, the possibility of enforcement is inherent in the bindingness of agreements, and it is this which lends them contractual form. This means that coercion is implicit in market relations, and it is only the particular form in which the state appears in legal discourse that makes it possible to reconcile this coercion with the freedom and equality of the legal subject.[10] Legal discourse actively constructs the foundations for its own legitimacy, therefore reinforcing belief in an independence and autonomy which is systematically negated by the role that the state and legal system actually play in the context of capitalism. That is, its role in bringing about the conditions for a system of social relations that is founded on inequality and domination.

In legal discourse, therefore, the state only ever appears as an independent 'third party,' representing the impersonal interests of the system, sustaining the idea that there is equal protection for the 'natural' rights of all. This dogmatic figure, encapsulated in the concept of the rule of law, is reproduced through legal discourse, helping to sustain the legal system's legitimacy. The state in capitalism is therefore more than just the material embodiment of power, that is, the practical mechanism through which order is secured. It also has a semi-autonomous existence as a legal concept that is reproduced through legal discourse. This concept, moreover, has its origins in the practices and relations of commodity-producing society. In this sense, the concept, and not (only) the state itself, is integral to law's capacity to stabilize property rights and uphold faith in the bindingness of agreements. The legal concept itself is thus essential when it comes to facilitating cooperation in the market.[11]

Exploring the legal form requires, therefore, going beyond a recognition of the particular legal institutions that underpin the market—the private property framework, the institution of contract, and the contract of employment—to identify the elements of the legal form that make these institutions possible. Property and contract themselves emerge from capitalist social relations to which a particular legal discourse, or normative system, is intrinsic.[12] Contract is qualitatively

[9] ibid Chapter 4.
[10] ibid Chapter 5.
[11] ibid 147.
[12] ibid 119–20.

different from exchange, and property from possession, by reason of the juridical form in which they are expressed and the system of (internally related) concepts of which they form a part. Property is more than exchange; it is the form that factual possession takes when it ceases to be precarious. Likewise, contract is the form that agreements take when the freedom to bind oneself is given concrete form by the prospect of third-party enforcement.[13] Each of these institutions presupposes the fundamental features of the legal form: the free and equal legal subject, the independent state and legal system, and the principle of the rule of law—the principle which legal rules must respect to be perceived as legitimate in a society of equal subjects, and which, as a result, constrains how far the state can actually 'intervene' to secure the conditions for sustainable accumulation (and social reproduction).[14]

This analysis reveals that legal discourse reflects the social relations of capitalist society, but it does so in a 'mystified form'. This form is not purely ideological, or 'defective' in some way, misrepresenting the reality of the social relations they represent, but *necessary* for (or integral to) their existence and reproduction. This reiterates the point made in Chapter 2, that the way that features of reality present themselves are part of what makes them what they are. By presenting social relations as their inverse, the legal form helps uphold the assumptions that are intrinsic to the market practices through which those relations are systematically reproduced.

3.3 Law, Contradiction, and Social Change

If the market is to function, legal rules must be expressed in a form that reinforces belief in the freedom and equality of the subject, and the independence of the state. This makes the legal system's capacity to coordinate (and regulate) behaviour dependent on its ability to uphold, and reproduce, the cognitive framework that the market presupposes—a framework that contradicts the material realities of life and work in capitalism; that is, the inequality and exploitation inherent in the social relations of production. It also contradicts the reality of state power, and the role the law plays in (differentially) distributing rights and resources between groups. There is, as a result, a contradiction embedded in legal discourse that reflects that which exists in capitalist society more generally: the legitimacy of the legal system presupposes conditions (inequality and exploitation) and functions ('regulating' an 'autonomous' market) that its existence, form, and mode of operation systematically negates. This makes law's legitimacy, and thus its capacity to

[13] ibid 41.
[14] ibid 105–06.

facilitate coordination, inherently fragile, along with the practices that are intrinsic to the market.[15]

This contradiction makes the legal system's reproduction (and thus its capacity to maintain its form and be recognized as law) contingent upon its capacity to mediate the tensions that exist in capitalist society—between the way the world appears from the perspective of market practices, and the conditions that must exist to sustain them. If the legal system were to merely assert the reality presupposed by its concepts, to assume the truth of the world as it appears from the perspective of exchange, the legal system would be sapped of all credibility and legitimacy. The legal system would be experienced as entirely disconnected from society, and specifically from the conditions in which legal subjects live and work. If it were to depart too far from that assumed reality, by contrast, it would no longer be able to meaningfully communicate with market participants, and thus act as a reliable guide for behaviour. In order to maintain its own legitimacy, therefore, and to be capable of influencing behaviour, the legal system has no choice but to *shape* society, to attempt, through its discourse, to narrow the gap between the world as it appears in its discourse, and the material conditions required to sustain it—the gap, in other words, between fact and norm.

Law's contribution to the reproduction of capitalist social relations is not a purpose' consciously attributed to it by human agents, but is inherent in the form that it assumes in capitalism: the stable juridical concepts through which legal rules and decisions are expressed, and through which law's autonomy from social relations is discursively reproduced. This form lends law the capacity to facilitate coordination, and this is integral to the market practices through which capitalist social relations are systematically produced. Law's capacity to perform this coordinating function, and thus to reproduce its form over time, presupposes that it actively shapes those practices to bring about the conditions that are required to sustain them—reconciling the inherent conflict that exists between capital accumulation and social reproduction, between the interests of individual capitals in profit-maximization and the interests of capital in general in sustainable accumulation. It is in this sense that we can say that law performs both a 'coordination' and a 'social reproduction' function. Each function follows from, and is implicit in, the form law assumes in the context of capitalism.

Law is thus both causally independent from, and integrally related to, market practices and relations. This causal independence is a product of the form that social regulation assumes in capitalism, and thus is essential to law's nature and function. Law is not, although it is often seen to be, a mere instrument for implementing

[15] On Capitalism's 'inherent' crises of legitimation, and the particular form they assume in neoliberal capitalism, see: Nancy Fraser, 'Legitimation Crisis? On the Political Contradictions of Financialized Capitalism' (2015) 2 Critical Historical Studies 157.

political programmes. In a society of commodity-owning subjects, a system of social regulation must be functionally independent from society to be seen as legitimate; only then is the exercise of coercion necessary for capitalist production and exchange compatible with the unique system of coordination that is intrinsic to it. One of the implications of this autonomy, whether in terms of the material separation of legal institutions from the market, or the discursive expression of that separation through the concept of the rule of law, is that the legal system evolves according to its own evolutionary dynamics, rather than generating direct responses to social demands.[16] The legal system's evolutionary path is profoundly shaped by the push and pull of the contradictory forces that are internal to the legal system: the tension between consistency and responsiveness to change, between asserting the 'factual' reality of the cognitive framework on which market activity depends, and which is presupposed by the legal system's central concepts, and its need to operate through that framework so as to bring about the conditions it presupposes.

The image of itself that the law does, and arguably must (in the sense that it must do so from the perspective of capitalism's, and the legal system's reproduction), project—an image that is integral to social and economic stability—thus creates internal problems for the legal system when it comes to sustaining this image over time. The law's ability to uphold its autonomy depends simultaneously on the 'mediated' responses it provides to social change and its capacity to adapt itself in line with those changes so that it can continue to be seen as a reliable and legitimate guide for behaviour. Because law is necessary for, and integral to, the practices through which capitalist social relations are reproduced, it cannot afford to lose sight of the conditions that must be in place for the market to function; but its ability to bring about those conditions is constrained by the particular form that legal discourse must take if it is to be recognized and accepted as law.[17] The legal system cannot entirely ignore social inequalities therefore, but it can recognize and engage with them only through the prism of equality of right. Every time labour law 'recognizes' and attempts to address the inequality between labour and capital, therefore, it can do so only by first conceptualizing that inequality as an inequality between individual legal subjects—and thus, as a deviation from the 'norm' of equality and freedom. By definition, then, structural inequalities tend to be obscured in legal and labour law discourse: social relations can only become an 'object' of regulation if conceptualized in an inherently individualistic form.

[16] This observations establishes a link between Marxist scholarship on law and capitalism and systems theoretical approaches, such as that of Niklas Luhmann. See: Luhmann (n 2). The systems theoretical literature informs the discussion of legal concepts later in this chapter.

[17] Or, in systems theoretical terms, its autopoiesis; the conditions for its self-reproduction.

3.4 Legal Form and Legal Concepts

The above analysis reveals the distinguishing features of legal discourse. It raises the question, however, as to how the legal system maintains, or systematically reproduces, its form over time. In order to explain this, a shift in perspective is required, focusing less on how the legal system and legal discourse emerges, and more on how the legal system, as an emergent totality maintains itself (its form) and the lower-level components through which it, and its distinctive discourse, emerges over time. This means thinking in more detail about the codifying or condensing function of concepts (in the sense of linguistic terms), and the relationship between the form of law and its ever-changing substantive content.

Concepts are the means through which information about the world can be stored, analysed, and structured. In this way, they facilitate the conceptualization of new experiences by providing a framework by reference to which those experiences can be assessed, or interpreted. Legal concepts perform a similar function: they acts as stores of information that have been coded by the legal system as relevant to its operations providing structure to legal decisions. Legal concepts collectively express the system's memory, the way in which it has previously coded information entering the system from other social discourses, and the particular legal responses that have been developed, refined, and adapted to deal with them over time.[18] Concepts help to ensure consistency in the application of legal rules by informing the legal system as to how similar situations have been dealt with in the past, allowing, at the same time, distinctions to be made so that it can remain responsive to change.

Legal discourse is continually shaped by interactions between information drawn from society and the internal processes and concepts that lend this information meaning within the system, helping to reproduce the legal system's legitimacy while providing it with the capacity to adapt and change. By ensuring that law is never seen as a mere instrument for implementing political programmes, or for providing direct responses to social and economic demands, the self-referential nature of legal discourse helps preserve the image of the legal system's neutrality, while nonetheless ensuring that legal change will never be entirely random or uninformed.[19]

The abstract character of legal discourse is not only important for reproducing the image of law's autonomy from social relations therefore, it also helps the system to reduce complexity, contributing to stability and consistency within the system and clarity in its communications with society. Because the legal system is always open to external influence, through the legislative and judicial process, and as a

[18] Ulrich Preuss, 'The Concept of Rights and the Welfare State' in Gunther Teubner (ed), *Dilemmas of Law in the Welfare State* (De Gruyter 1986).

[19] Gunther Teubner, *Autopoietic Law—A New Approach to Law and Society* (De Gruyter 1987) 67.

result of the codifying or condensing function performed by its concepts, it is able to combine, however imperfectly or contingently, consistency in decision making with openness to the environment in which it is embedded.

It follows from this that legal concepts must be expressed at a high level of abstraction so as to increase the circumstances in which they can be usefully deployed, and thus contribute to stability and consistency within the system. These abstract concepts can be made more concrete, however, by being linked with other concepts in the construction of specific rules and decisions. For example, while the legal concepts that are constitutive of the legal form are the core categories through which substantive legal rules and decisions are constructed, they are given distinct meanings in different contexts through the lower-level concepts with which they are linked in different aspects of doctrine. They can thus be more or less sensitive to the factual specificities of the contexts to which they are applied. In turn, through these varying and complex linkages, new meanings can emerge, allowing for the meaning of even these higher-level concepts to change over time, as they are interpreted in new ways in light of changing circumstances.

The more the legal system is called upon to deploy its concepts the greater its capacity to refine and adapt them to changing circumstances. This provides scope for variation, and as such, for concepts to perform new functions and assume new meanings, as they are deployed in new contexts over time. This is why the judicial and legislative processes are so important: they provide an opportunity for the legal system to draw on social information and codify it for future use, and thus for the system to prove its neutrality and its willingness to respond to change. Moreover, it is through these processes that lower-level concepts, specific to particular practices or areas of law, develop, and are harnessed to perform new functions. The problem, however, is that, because only a small fraction of the legal conflicts that arise in society will result in litigation, and because social influence over legislation is unequally distributed, certain discourses will inevitably exercise a disproportionate influence over the law's development.[20] The result is a process of legal evolution informed by a fragmented and distorted picture of the world that often favours the interpretation and interests of particular groups.[21] Which groups the process favours is, in particular, influenced by the pre-existing distribution of rights and resources, and so is already the product, in part, of law; implicating the law in the very social inequalities it helps to reproduce. The self-referential nature of legal discourse is such, moreover, that the interests served by a particular doctrine, or the values embedded in a particular concept, will often exercise influence over the law's development long after the interests they serve, and the beliefs they reflect,

[20] Simon Deakin, 'The Contract of Employment: A Study in Legal Evolution' (2001) 11 Historical Studies in Industrial Relations 5.

[21] For a similar critique, see: Peter Goodrich, *Reading the Law: Critical Introduction to Legal Method and Techniques* (Wiley-Blackwell 1986) 188.

have ceased to be. Thus, law not only reflects a delayed and imperfect response to social demands, it also constructs its solutions by reference to an image of the world that will often skew the solutions it formulates, leading to often unexpected results.[22]

The self-referential nature of legal discourse, which limits how far law can adapt to changes in society, is essential for preserving the consistency integral to the law's capacity to be seen as legitimate and to act as a meaningful guide for behaviour. The meanings embedded in legal concepts cannot, therefore, be disregarded. Legal rules and decisions must be expressed through a language that already makes sense, both in the context of legal discourse and in society more generally. And this language must reinforce ideas shared throughout society concerning the legitimacy of power in the context of capitalism. The scope for using law to bring about substantial changes in the structure of society will be dependent, therefore, on what can be achieved through a conceptual framework that presupposes at a basic (juridical) level that formal freedom and equality are either already vindicated or have been violated as a result of the 'autonomous' acts of human beings.

Capitalist society may, therefore, presuppose the legal form and thus the concepts of the free and equal subject and the related idea of equality of right, but the *form* of those concepts does not determine the meaning that form lends to law's (and by implication, labour law's) substantive content. The meaning that concepts lend to substantive legal rules will always be influenced, in part, by the understandings embedded in the contexts to which they are applied, and thus the social practices and relations which legal concepts 'lend' legal form. While social practices and beliefs will always already be framed or conditioned by legal discourse, and thus by past understandings embedded in the law, they are not determined by them, but, rather, will shift in line with changes in society. This provides scope for feedback, with the interpretation of legal rules by social and legal actors influencing the meaning of the concepts through which legal rules are constructed albeit indirectly, and allowing for evolution in the content of the concepts themselves.

To describe a company as a legal subject, for example, invokes certain connotations about capacity, freedom, rights, etc attached to prior legal subjects. But the application of that concept to new contexts will, in turn, influence the meaning of the concept itself. The same is true of concepts such as the 'employee' and the 'wage'. In practice, how the legal system's constitutive concepts, such as freedom and equality, come to be conceived, and thus the 'colour' they lend to legal rules, is determined by concrete legal and social practices which, while they may exhibit a high level of regularity or stability, are not fixed.

[22] Niklas Luhmann, *Ecological Communication* (University of Chicago Press 1989) 61.

3.5 Legal Form and Labour Law

The legal form must always shape social relations into a recognizable object. This means it must conceptualize social relations in a particular form so as to render it amenable to (legal) regulation. Because this form is the form appropriate to, and inherent in, commodity exchange, labour law will necessarily presuppose and serve to perpetuate the exploitative class relations that commodity exchange implies. Neither law in general, nor labour law in particular, can, then, be seen as neutral instruments that social actors simply deploy to pursue particular political purposes; whatever the *content* of labour law rules, insofar as that content continues to assume the form of labour *law*, it will, necessarily participate in the reproduction of the very exploitative relations that labour lawyers hope to change.

Labour lawyers need to recognize, then, that the legal form embeds certain assumptions about the nature and origins of certain social problems and about the appropriate (and/or legitimate) way for the law to address them. This not only influences what labour law policies can achieve, but also, what it is assumed to be legitimate and worthwhile for such policies to pursue in the first place. For example, in legal discourse inequality comes to be seen as the product of interactions between individuals rather than of the structures in which those interactions take place; rights and obligations, and thus socio-economic outcomes, appear as the outcome of contractual agreements or the actions of individual subjects rather than as the product of the background conditions in which those individuals exist—conditions produced in large part through law. At the same time, the legal system's assumption (ie the assumptions implicit in legal discourse) about its own neutrality places limits on how far it can qualify or restrict individuals' freedom of contract, and thus how it must justify 'legal intervention' in the market. Thus, the inequality of bargaining power that exists between employers and workers may be seen to justify the courts in looking past the formal contractual wording to the 'reality' of the agreement between the parties—but it cannot extend so far as to permit the courts to impose on those parties a form of work arrangement to which they have not 'freely' agreed.[23]

To avoid perpetuating the very social 'problems' that labour law is invoked to address, therefore, labour lawyers must engage reflexively with the assumptions embedded in the legal form, remaining mindful of the contradiction between this form and the broader functions labour law must perform in the context of capitalism.[24] Rather than accepting, for example, that minimum wages set 'too high'

[23] See the judgment of Lord Justice Underhill in *Aslam BV v Uber* [2018] EWCA Civ 2748. See also comments in: Patrick Elias 'Changes and Challenges to the Contract of Employment' (2018) 38 Oxford Journal of Legal Studies 869.

[24] This is why, as Robert Knox notes, any 'progressive' politics must be capable of taking advantage of content *without falling foul of form*: Knox (n 1) 413.

may have negative effects on employment rates, relying on this to justify a cautious approach to minimum wage regulation,[25] labour lawyers must explore why such dis-employment effects may be observed, and the broader social implications of the mechanisms that account for, or explain them. Similarly, rather than simply assuming that precarious work arrangements that suit workers' and employers' preferences ought not be prohibited,[26] labour lawyers need to problematize the conditions in which such preferences come to be, exploring, at the same time, the broader *systemic* implications of such work arrangements for the long-term sustainability of the system.

Labour law faces a particular challenge in this context. Because the legal system has an innate tendency to conceptualize the relationship between labour and capital as an interpersonal relationship between legal subjects, the structural relations that underpin that relationship tend to remain obscured in labour law discourse, and so remain, implicitly, beyond the purview of law—unless, that is, this tendency is recognized by the courts and its implications considered. This not only makes it difficult for the legal system to secure the conditions for social reproduction in practice—to mediate capitalisms' contradictions—it also places limits on how far labour law can ever be 'used' to challenge, or transform, the basic structural features of the system. In other words, any policy proposal that labour lawyers do advance, however well-conceived, will still have to be operationalized through a legal discourse in which certain features of the world are, implicitly, denied, and, by reason of this denial, these policies tend to reinforce the very structures that constitute the ultimate 'source' or 'cause' of many of the social problems labour lawyers are trying to address.

These issues notwithstanding, however, and as we have seen, the values, such as freedom and equality, embedded in legal discourse do not have, and cannot have, a fixed or pure meaning—changes in social practices and in the nature of the policies that the legal form is called upon to express, will necessarily influence the meaning of these concepts in practice. By being linked in different ways to certain lower-level concepts, and the various practices in which they are intrinsic, the juridical conceptions of equality and freedom of contract can, and necessarily must, evolve.[27] Beyond inherent limits, therefore, labour law contains untapped potential to reshape social relations and the way that capitalism's contradictions express themselves over time. Labour law may not be able to challenge the structural inequalities at the heart of the capitalist mode of production therefore, but

[25] Guy Davidov, 'A Purposive Interpretation of the National Minimum Wage Act' (2009) 72 Modern Law Review 581, 591.

[26] Elias (n 23).

[27] To clarify, *concepts* exist in the complex of social and linguistic usages gathered together by a term; conceptions are particular beliefs or meanings tacit in uses of those concepts. Thus, what is at stake here are the interpretations of juridical terms by judges (conceptions).

that is not to say it cannot make a significant difference in the material conditions of life and work—indeed, its willingness to do so is essential for the sustainability of the system. The challenge is, in Robert Knox's words, to 'take advantage of content without falling foul of form'.[28]

The problem, however, is that because labour law regulates both the exchange of labour power for wages and the unequal and exploitative relationship that the exchange establishes, it is in the labour law context that the contradictions inherent in the form of law express themselves most clearly. Labour law is, then, not only one of the principal sites of class conflict, but also, is one aspect of law whose legitimacy is likely to be most contested. Despite its integral role in the reproduction of capitalist social relations therefore, labour law is one of the areas of law that is most likely to be subject to challenge—by workers and by employers. Therefore, while the political limits that labour law confronts are not insignificant, they can only be fully grasped if conceptualized from within a framework that engages with the contradictions and limits inherent in its form.

3.6 Conclusion

The analyses in this chapter and the previous chapter support the view that law plays an integral role in the emergence and reproduction of capitalist social relations, and the nature of this role influences the form it assumes, and thus the assumptions that are embedded in its concepts. This form is integral to the market practices through which the social relations of capitalism are systematically reproduced and the 'logic' of capital accumulation enforced. But, because these practices have an *inherent* tendency to undermine the material conditions required for their reproduction, the legal form is always at risk of undermining its own and the market's conditions of possibility. Rather than merely asserting the reality presupposed by its concepts, therefore endorsing the image of the world as it appears from the internal perspective of the market, the legal system must somehow operate through those concepts, so as to shape reality, and secure the material conditions required to sustain it.

The analysis suggests, however, that the legal system's capacity to bridge the gap between the assumptions intrinsic to the market, and the objective requirement for some mechanisms of social production—to mediate, in other words, capitalism's contradictions—would seem to depend, therefore, on the malleability of the legal system's concepts and the ability and willingness of legal and social actors to exploit that malleability in practice. This is, moreover, likely to be particularly important in the context of labour law—that is, those aspects of the legal

[28] Knox (n 1) 413.

framework concerned most directly with the terms on which capital gains access to, and makes use of, labour power, and the latter, access to wages. Exploring how, and if, the legal system is able to exploit the malleability of its concepts, and the various factors influencing how well it does so over time, will be explored in detail in Part II of the book.

4
The Wage

4.1 Introduction

Thus far, the concept of the wage has been used in an analytical sense to refer to the social form assumed by worker's subsistence in the context of capitalism. Embedded in the wage, it was argued, are two contradictory, but mutually constitutive functions: the coordination function, reflected in the idea of the wage as a price; and the social reproduction function, reflected in the idea of the wage as workers' costs of living. Employed in this sense, the wage is a social category or form that expresses the price of a generic commodity (labour power) and/or the total social costs of reproducing society's labour power over time. In the rest of the book, these two dimensions of the wage will be referred to as the 'market' wage and the 'social' wage, respectively, where the latter might, in different contexts, be monetary wages, and/or a particular bundle of rights and entitlements which, in combination, are necessary to secure the productivity, health, and well-being of workers (actual and potential) over time.

Compared with Part I of this book, which proceeds at a relatively abstract level, Part II will proceed at a more concrete level of analysis. The task will be to explore the precise mechanisms through which the above dimensions of the wage are given effect in practice—their concrete manifestations—and, relatedly, the various social and legal concepts through which they are variously denoted. At this level, then, the term 'wage' has a more concrete meaning. It is used not (or not only) to refer to the social form assumed by workers' subsistence, but also, and alternatively, to give expression to the various forms in which the social category of the wage is historically actualized/expressed.

The purpose of Part II is not, however, simply to identify the various institutional mechanisms through which workers' living costs have been met at particular periods of time (whether through wage payments, tax, social security, etc). Rather, the purpose of the analysis is to explore legal conceptions of the wage, and the role, within legal doctrine, of the various concepts through which the wage has been legally denoted, placing this analysis in its broader socio-historical context. In so doing, the objective is to observe how (and to what extent) law secures, and has historically secured, the performance of the coordination and social reproduction functions of the wage in practice, to understand the role that these various concepts play in this process. It will also explore how legal and social actors make use of such concepts, and the assumptions embedded in them, and how this influences

Labour and the Wage. Zoe Adams, Oxford University Press (2020). © Zoe Adams.
DOI: 10.1093/oso/9780198858898.001.0001

how particular doctrines, or policies, evolve. Hence, the analysis is not merely a historical, or descriptive, account of the evolution of wage regulation: it is a historical *genealogy* that traces the evolution of labour law and the wage relation *through* the lens of the juridical concepts through which the wage is conceptualized and expressed.

4.2 Genealogy

The analysis in previous chapters suggests that law can be conceived as (but not reduced to) an autonomous, discursive system, constituted through the inter-linking of concepts of varying levels of abstraction. At the core of the system are the highly abstract concepts of property, contract, the legal subject, and the rule of law, concepts that are constitutive of law in the sense that they are of general and universal application, and part of what identifies a particular normative discourse as law. Every lower-level concept, or substantive rule, is constructed through, or implies, these higher level concepts, because they form the basic building blocks through which legal discourse is constructed. Lower level concepts, by contrast, more closely tailored to the factual specifics of different problems or doctrines, are more concrete and so are of (more) specific than general application. Lower level, more fact-laden concepts allow the legal system to condense complex information in a form that is manageable, facilitating consistency at the point of a rule's application, while allowing the legal system to adapt to new, and more complex, situations.[1] Legal concepts never correspond directly with the facts on the ground (or rather, the way those facts are conceptualized in everyday language); but they do vary in their level of abstraction depending on how much factual detail they condense.

At its most abstract, then, the legal concept of the wage (which itself implies the concepts of the subject, property, and contract, etc) can be understood as a concept formed by the legal system to facilitate the identification of payments made in exchange for labour power, condensing, within a single category, the diverse forms of payment and work that emerge in the context of labour relations and in different aspects of legal doctrine. At the same time, however, the wage reflects a partial or one-sided understanding of the function of that payment, and the law's regulation of it, conceived from the perspective of the legal system, and in the context of the particular activities and relations in which it exists.

The particular form in which the social category of the wage is abstracted in legal discourse, and thus the way that different types of payment are grouped within a single concept (the 'wage'), and, separated within that concept (wages, salaries, remuneration, bonuses, tips, etc), are themselves a product of a specific

[1] Simon Deakin, 'Evolution for Our Time: A Theory of Legal Memetics' (2002) 55 Current Legal Problems 1.

set of social relations, and a particular stage of (a particular) society's, and the legal system's own, development. Exploring the evolution of the legal conceptualization of the wage over time, and the various lower-level concepts through which it finds expression, is, as a result, extremely useful not only when it comes to revealing the complex and diverse factual situations embedded in that concept, but also for gaining a deeper insight into the development of the capitalist system more generally. Relatedly, it can help shed light on the role within that system of legal discourse, and of the particular social category, and its legal conceptualization, under investigation.

Given that legal discourse emerges from, and so is shaped by, the practices and relations of capitalist society, while, at the same time, framing those practices, and thus influencing how society develops, legal concepts can be said to act as a medium through which an already legally mediated history can exercise a continuing influence over the present. Because concepts have greater longevity than the experiences from which they abstract, the meanings embedded in legal concepts not only provide the framework through which future experiences are conceived, they also condition what sorts of experiences, and events, are (believed to be) possible.

Legal concepts not only shape the path of the law, therefore, constraining what can be said, and how, they also profoundly shape society's own path of development. By disturbing the assumptions embedded in legal concepts, revealing why certain paths were taken, and why others were not, why different legal concepts were used in different contexts at different times, we thereby open the door to a deeper understanding of how different concepts might be used when it comes to 'changing' our approach towards wage regulation. In this way, we can reveal that, very often, what we thought was inevitable, or immutable, is, in fact, historical, and contingent. At the same time, we can better distinguish those factors that have influenced the legal system's response to problems such as low pay that are contingent and those which might be structural or systemic.

One of the benefits of the genealogical approach, then, is that it allows us to disrupt established discourses about the wage, and wage regulation, to show that alternative conceptions of the wage, and the law's relationship with it, are possible.[2] In this way, it can help us to escape from false teleologies, allowing us to see that concepts which seem to express fundamental truths about the world are in fact contingent and evolving. It can help us reveal not only the limits, therefore, but also the potential of labour law, when it comes to mediating capitalism's contradictions, but also, and potentially, for bringing about social change.

In order to lay the groundwork for this analysis, the next section explores two competing discourses about the nature of wages, and wage regulation, one rooted in a naturalistic conception of the law-market relationship (or, a naturalistic

[2] Emilios Christodoulidis, 'Labour Constitutionalism in a Genealogical Key' [2018] Jurisprudence 1.

ontology), and the other associated with a more constitutive approach like that advanced in chapters one and two. The 'naturalistic' approach will be explored through the lens of neoclassical economics, the basic premises of which find its expression in current 'neoliberal' approaches to wage regulation, but which, in turn, is often reflected in labour law discourse. The 'constitutive' approach will, by contrast, be explored through an analysis of the work of the classical political economists, including Smith, Ricardo, and Marx, and institutional scholars, such as the Webbs, all of whom have been influential, in one way or another, in shaping approaches to wage regulation throughout the course of capitalism's development.[3]

4.3 The Concept of the Wage

4.3.1 Naturalistic Approaches: Neoclassical Economics and the Wage

Neoclassical economics sees economics, as a discipline, as the study of resource allocation in conditions of scarcity—a study, in other words, of the sphere of exchange. Questions of efficiency tend, for this reason, to be conceived in terms of how to secure an optimal usage of resources in order to maximize individual (and thereby aggregate) welfare. In this context, maximum welfare is assumed to require that prices reflect the private (marginal) costs of production, so that supply equals demand. In neoclassical economics, this is said to be achieved by means of a decentralized pricing mechanism in the context of a free, perfectly competitive market.[4]

Neoclassical economics studies labour markets in the same way as it studies markets for other commodities: treating labour like any other factor of production. In its model of the labour market, competition between workers and firms ensures that wages will cover the workers' costs of living: if wages are too low, workers will refuse to work, there will be a shortage of labour relative to demand, and workers will be able to bid up wages until supply and demand are in equilibrium, and wages cover the worker's 'production' costs.[5] If wages are too high, by contrast, employers will be able to bid wages back down due to increased worker competition. Left to its own devices, the market dynamic, driven by the rational

[3] This section is based on sections of: Zoe Adams, 'Understanding the Minimum Wage: Political Economy and Legal Form' (2019) 78 Cambridge Law Journal 42.

[4] Antonella Picchio, *Social Reproduction: The Political Economy of the Labour Market* (CUP 1992); Maurice Dobb, *Theories of Value and Distribution since Adam Smith: Ideology and Economic Theory* (CUP 1975).

[5] John Clark, 'Minimum Wages' [1913] Atlantic Monthly 289, 292.

utility-maximizing decisions of economic agents, will keep the wage in the appropriate market-clearing range so that the production costs of firms, and workers, are fully covered: prices for labour of comparable productivity will be more or less equal throughout the market, and so will be equivalent to private marginal costs of production.

In this account, wages are governed entirely by the relationship between supply and demand. The supply of labour is entirely governed by markets (rather than institutions) and the same goes for its allocation: prices (wages) dictate how labour will be allocated, and used, throughout society, by telling workers and firms how much it is 'worth' in terms of utility. Workers decide to produce more or less labour (power) depending on the relative benefit of an additional hour's work, as expressed in the wage (in light of prevailing prices of consumption goods), as compared with the opportunity cost of lost leisure time. Firms will demand more or less labour depending on the relative value of the worker's output (his marginal product), given prevailing wage rates, and the likely returns from alternative methods of production (such as machinery). In the absence of legal intervention, the prevailing wage rate acts as a reliable guide as to what amounts to a 'fair bargain', so that each party can be confident that they have received something of equal value to that which they provide in exchange.[6]

This image of the self-equilibrating market shifts, however, once the existence of positive transaction costs and market 'distortions', such as employer monopsony, are conceded.[7] Low-wage labour markets have been shown to be monopsonistic, and so are better modelled as such.[8] In such a context, a legislative minimum wage can be justified as a means to 'restore' the market to its equilibrium point. On this view, minimum wage legislation has a place in the neoclassical model, provided it is set at a level that does not exceed workers' marginal productivity—its 'inherent' value (however difficult, in practice, determining such a rate may in fact be).[9] The function of minimum wage legislation is thus, at least in theory, to substitute the wage that would have emerged in competitive conditions: to ensure that employers pay the true 'market' price of labour. That is, to secure workers a true 'market wage'. Implicitly, then, the price that is set by a competitive market is assumed to cover workers' living costs—as the costs of reproducing his commodity. As we saw in previous chapters, however, there are good reasons for thinking that this will not be the case.

[6] ibid.

[7] Alan Manning, *Monopsony in Motion: Imperfect Competition in Labor Markets* (Princeton University Press 2003).

[8] Bruce Kaufman, 'How a Minimum Wage Can Improve Efficiency Even in Competitive Labor Markets: The Webbs and the Social Cost of Labor'(2008) Andrew Young School of Policy Studies Research Paper Series No 08-16.

[9] Clark (n 5).

4.3.2 Constitutive Approaches: Classical Political Economy and Institutionalism

Classical political economy illustrates what happens to our conception of the wage, and minimum wage laws (legislation or collective bargaining), when we see markets not as natural spheres of economic activity, but as emergent institutions in which law and social structures play an integral part.[10] In contrast with neoclassical economics, for scholars such as Smith, Ricardo, and Marx, markets were not spontaneous orders, but institutions; profoundly shaped by politics, custom and the law.[11] Economics was not the study of the market process, but of the process of social reproduction; production, consumption, and exchange all had to be taken into account.[12] Considerations about efficiency were not assessed in terms of how to maximize the (aggregate) utility of economically rational agents, therefore, but with the broader question about how to secure the long-term sustainability of the capitalist system. That is, it was directly concerned with the question of social reproduction.[13] This required more than simply aligning prices with private marginal cost; it required the reproduction, and increase, in the existing stock of productive resources so as to fuel future production, and consumption, and to raise the living standards of the general population.

Because they studied markets in their social context, the classical economists did not see wages as the product of supply and demand; bargaining inequalities were key.[14] The relative bargaining strength was what determined the normal range around which competition would act.[15] By reason of workers' wage dependence and the superior economic strength of employers, however, in the absence of comprehensive collective bargaining and limits on employer combinations, it was assumed that market wages would inevitably diverge from the 'natural' or normative rate required for social reproduction.[16] For the classical economists, therefore, workers and employers were not 'naturally' free agents; the inequality between master and servant, between capital and labour, was seen as an integral element of the system, one recognized to be the product of law and institutions.

[10] Picchio (n 4); Dobb (n 4); Deborah Boucoyannis, 'The Equalizing Hand: Why Adam Smith Thought the Market Should Produce Wealth Without Steep Inequality' (2013) 11 Perspectives on Politics 1051; Antonella Stirati, *The Theory of Wages in Classical Economics: A Study of Adam Smith, David Ricardo, and Their Contemporaries* (Edward Elgar Publishing 1994).

[11] Enrico Sergio Levrero, 'Marx on Absolute and Relative Wages and the Modern Theory of Distribution' (2013) 25 Review of Political Economy 91.

[12] Picchio (n 4).

[13] Boucoyannis (n 10).

[14] David Ricardo, *On the Principles of Political Economy, and Taxation* (London John Murray 1821) 93.

[15] Enrico Sergio Levrero, 'Some Notes on Wages and Competition in the Labour Market' (2011) 1 Sraffa and Modern Economics 360; Adam Smith, *An Inquiry into the Nature and Causes of the Wealth of Nations* (W Strahan and T Cadell 1776) Chapter X.

[16] ibid Chapter VIII, 77.

This recognition, of the embedded nature of markets, led the classical economists to distinguish between the actual costs to society of producing commodities, their natural or social price, and the value of those commodities as expressed in market-prices. In the labour market, this was reflected in a distinction between the natural and the 'market' wage:[17]

> The natural price of labour is that price which is necessary to enable the labourers, one with another, to subsist and to perpetuate their race, without either increase or diminution ... The market price for labour is the price, which is really paid for it, from the natural operation of the proportion of supply to the demand.... It is not to be understood that the natural price of labour, even estimated in food and necessaries, is absolutely fixed and constant ... It essentially depends on the habits and customs of the people.[18]

For the classical economists, this natural wage was the normative standard around which market wages gravitated, a reflection of prevailing fairness norms, and the outcome of past conflict.[19] Because it was established outside the market, determined by customs, politics, and institutions, it was independent from the short-run conditions of supply and demand. Thus, while the market wage might tend, in practice, towards this natural, or customary level, deviations were inevitable. This was due not to 'interferences' in the market's spontaneous processes, but to the unique nature of the labour commodity and its process of (re)production.[20]

At the heart of this classical, or 'institutional', approach is the recognition that labour (power) cannot be separated from its owner.[21] For this reason, labour supply is not dictated by market forces, but by social institutions such as the family, as well as the customs and habits of the working classes. For the classical economists, the question to be addressed, therefore, was whether, and if so how, these processes might come to be reflected in the wage rate so as to secure social reproduction in practice—given that, in a capitalist system, employers have little incentive to pay natural or social wages, and workers lack the bargaining power to demand them.[22]

[17] Ricardo (n 14) 93.

[18] Ricardo (n 14) 93, 99. Thomas Robert Malthus and John Pullen, *TR Malthus: Principles of Political Economy*, vol 2 (CUP 1989) 240.

[19] Karl Marx, 'Instructions for the Delegates of the Provisional General Council' (1866) section 6 <https://marxists.catbull.com/history/international/iwma/documents/1866/instructions.htm#06> accessed 25 December 2019; Friedrich Engels, 'Outlines of a Critique of Political Economy' (1844) 1 Deutsch-Französische Jahrbücher.

[20] Picchio (n 4)

[21] Sidney Webb, 'The Economic Theory of a Legal Minimum Wage' (1912) 20 Journal of Political Economy 973.

[22] Ricardo (n 14) 93; Anne Robert Jacques Turgot, *Turgot on Progress, Sociology and Economics: A Philosophical Review of the Successive Advances of the Human Mind, on Universal History Reflections and on the Formation and the Distribution of Wealth* (CUP 1973); James Steuart, *An Inquiry into the Principles of Political Oeconomy: Being an Essay on the Science of Domestic Policy in Free Nations*, vol 2 (Millar & Cadell 1767) 270; Smith (n 15) 66.

While Ricardo and Smith in particular did not provide an answer to this question, that it had to be answered and that some mechanisms had to exist so as to reconcile the so-called coordination and social reproduction functions of the wage, was beyond doubt.

The neoclassical model largely ignores these questions, by contrast, because it starts from the premise that labour (power) already exists as a commodity that can be sold by free economic agents in a competitive market. Once the worker's wage dependence is taken into account, however, the bargaining process appears somewhat different. If workers have no choice but to work for someone, 'rational' utility maximizing behaviour will not, in itself, ensure that information about worker's 'production' costs are embedded in the wage rate. Even on the terms of the neoclassical model, therefore, we cannot assume that workers will refuse a wage that falls short of the costs to them of working—the opportunity cost of lost leisure time. In conditions of wage dependence, additional leisure time is rarely an option: workers face a choice between accepting the wage offered, seeking out alternative employment or, in modern times, relying on the family, or the state, to support them. At best, therefore, the wage rate will reflect the best wage offered by the firm's competitors, or, in modern conditions, the prevailing rate of social security payments (the worker's 'best' available alternative); actual living costs will not necessarily be incorporated into the wage rate.[23] In the labour market, competition is such that worker and firm self-interest will coalesce around a wage that falls short of that which is 'socially necessary' even if the market clears (in the neoclassical sense).

It may be, then, as Smith argues, that if 'masters ... always listene[ed] to the dictates of reason and humanity' they would willingly pay subsistence wages—otherwise they risk a depreciation in the stock of resources available for productive use.[24] But not only does this overlook that their ability to pay such a wage itself requires some institutional mechanism by which to determine this 'social' wage rate, but also, market competition is such that no single employer has an incentive to pay such wages unless other employers are doing the same.[25] Rather, the competitive process produces incentives for firms to profit *by whatever means available*. Very often, then, this means reducing production costs, such as by depressing wage rates, rather than taking a long-term perspective, investing for the purposes of increasing productivity.

The problem, as Smith agued, is that, in a capitalist labour market workers do not sell themselves outright, they hire themselves to an employer for a particular

[23] There is a further issue with the neoclassical model which is not discussed here: the neoclassical model assumes that shifts in the nominal wage will reflect shifts in the real wage rate. This is not the case: the capitalist can adjust prices to off set higher wages.

[24] Smith (n 15) 82. See also Marx's comments to similar effect: Karl Marx, *Capital, Volume I* (Penguin/New Left Review 1867) 649.

[25] This practice was dubbed 'parasitic' by the Webbs. See the discussion in: Bruce E Kaufman, 'Sidney and Beatrice Webb's Institutional Theory of Labor Markets and Wage Determination' (2013) 52 Industrial Relations: A Journal of Economy and Society 765.

period of time. This means that employers can make use of their labour without having to worry about the long-term effects on their physical and psychological health—this is what distinguishes wage labour from slavery.[26] In the case of slave labour, slaves are an owned asset much like machines; employers stand to lose, therefore, if they do not cover the costs involved both in the day-to-day use of the slave, and the long-term costs involved in securing him a long, and healthy, existence.[27] In the case of wage labour, while employers have an incentive to provide workers with enough money to fuel them throughout the working day, they have no incentive to cover the 'fixed costs' of maintenance and repair[28]—to preserve the value of their human capital over time; workers can be readily discharged or replaced, and so, tend to be treated as expendable.

While neoclassical economics is largely blind to this social cost gap, (a consequence of their supply and demand model of markets), the classical economists were not.[29] The idea of the social cost gap is reflected, for example, in Marx's distinction between labour and labour power and in the arguments of Smith and Ricardo that the gap between the natural and market wage would have to be closed if existing population levels, and the existing rate of profit, were to be maintained.[30] The natural or social wage was thus seen in classical political economy as a de facto wage floor below which the market could not be allowed to fall: the process of capital accumulation had to be subordinated, in other words, to the requirements of social reproduction.[31]

Smith and Marx both expressly defended a system of high wages on not just moral but also efficiency grounds: legislation mandating 'social' wages was in the best interests of society and conducive to economic growth.[32] For each, law, and institutions, did more than 'correct' the market, they were integral to its functioning. As Boucoyannis argues:

> Price limits are misguided only where competition can respond to change and local conditions more effectively'...[33] [T]he key criterion between good and bad intervention is securing the most productive use of capital—and not burdening

[26] Smith (n 15) 80.

[27] This was a central component in the Webbs' campaign for the social wage in the late nineteenth and early twentieth centuries: Beatrice Webb and B Leigh Hutchins, *Socialism and National Minimum* (AC Fifield 1909).

[28] Marx draws this distinction expressly: Marx (n 24) 171–73. See also: Dobb (n 4) 52; James Bonar, 'The Value of Labor in Relation to Economic Theory' (1891) 5 Quarterly Journal of Economics 137, 143.

[29] Bruce Kaufman, 'Adam Smith's Economics and the Modern Minimum Wage Debate: The Large Distance Separating Kirkcaldy from Chicago' (2016) 37 Journal of Labor Research 29.

[30] Smith (n 15) Chapter 5, 71 and 83; Ricardo (n 14) 24, 93. For Marx's in-depth discussion of the content of the 'natural' wage and how it differs from the price of the commodity, labour power, see: Marx, *Capital, Volume I*, 171; Karl Marx, *Wage-Labour and Capital* (Wildside Press LLC 2008) 45.

[31] Smith (n 15) Chapter 5, 71 and 83; Ricardo (n 14) 24–25.

[32] Smith (n 15) Chapter 10, 61.

[33] ibid 62.

> the poor. Regulation of the right kind is thus necessary in [Smith's] 'system of liberty.' The institution of the market has to be 'made' —only the practice of barter, as well as collusion and deceit, emerges spontaneously.[34]'

In classical political economy, labour markets were not spontaneous orders in which legal regulation 'intervened'. Rather, as a constitutive approach would suggest, they were social institutions, with law playing an integral part in the constitution, and reproduction, of the labour commodity and in the conditioning of wages. Contrary to the assumptions of the neoclassical school, therefore, labour power was not, and could not be, treated, institutionally, like any other commodity. Risk shifting mechanisms, such as sick pay and pensions, legislative support for collective bargaining, and/or a minimum wages tied to living costs, could, from this perspective, be seen as part of the broader institutional framework that makes the commodification of labour both possible and sustainable.

4.4 Rethinking the Wage

Because the classical political economists saw labour markets as social institutions, they were able to embrace the complex factors influencing the supply, allocation, and use of labour power in a capitalist economy—and thus the role of the law and legal system in the emergence and reproduction of markets. Labour supply was not governed by rational decision making, but by social norms, customs, and institutions, including labour law, social-security systems, and the family. Decisions about who to hire, and at what price, moreover, were institutionally conditioned, influenced by social norms and expectations and the balance of power between labour and capital. Labour power was not a 'natural' commodity, but something that was treated as such only in certain historically specific conditions.

By adopting the market-based supply and demand model, by contrast the neoclassical economists concealed labour's costs of reproduction, and the institutions that are required to support it. By taking the existence of markets as given, neoclassical economics can admit only a limited conception of labour law as a mechanism for correcting market failures. Only a very tightly circumscribed minimum wage, tied to the market clearing rate, can be permitted in the name of efficiency, which, in the neoclassical frame, is conducive to 'fairness'. By confining employers to paying the private costs of labour, however, this leaves the social cost problem unaddressed, shifting these costs onto the family and the state. In modern times, this problem has tended to be addressed through wage supplements and tax credits—funded by the tax payer. By leaving employers free to exploit social

[34] Karl Polanyi, *The Great Transformation: The Political and Economic Origins of Our Time* (2nd edn, Beacon Press 2002).

resources at a fraction of the cost, however, this simply provides a subsidy to inefficient firms which would otherwise be forced to improve their production methods to compete. By interfering with the information embedded in wages, it risks overproduction (due to artificially low production costs): wasting resources that could be better used elsewhere.

If the labour market is understood as an instituted process rather than a spontaneous order, however, regulation is necessary to constitute, and not simply to adjust, or 'correct' it.[35] As implied in previous chapters, from this perspective, labour law is best seen as something that helps constitute the labour commodity, and regulates the resulting social and economic relations.[36] The specific form that regulation takes depends on the social, political, legal, and cultural context as well as the balance of power between labour and capital, and between different segments of the labour market.[37] But how the law constructs the employment relationship inevitably influences the balance of power between capital and labour, and in this way, the wage rate. Even the market wage cannot be separated from the institutional processes through which labour power is produced (and reproduced), therefore, and which, in turn, constitutes, and regulates, the labour market.

The classical political economists recognized the importance of engaging with the role that custom, politics, and institutions—structures—play in conditioning the supply of labour (and thus the costs of production), and its price. Because the production of labour power takes place in part outside the market, the supply of labour cannot be governed entirely by a mechanical relationship between prices and quantities in exchange: customary standards of living; hours; inclination to work; family structures and power relationships; and the broader legal and institutional environment, all have to be taken into account.[38] These external considerations cannot be expected to be reflected in the wage rate 'automatically': in the real world, as a result not only of imperfect information and transaction costs, but also of broader structures—wage dependence and an inequality of bargaining power—how much workers will accept as wages will not be the same as how much they need to be provided with to cover their costs of reproduction. Rather, what is needed, as a logical, and practical (social), necessity, is a mechanism, or set of mechanisms, capable or imposing on employers an obligation to pay a wage that reflects workers' costs of living, where such reflects workers' (changing) expectations as to their

[35] Picchio (n 4); Mark Harvey and Norman Geras, *Inequality and Democratic Egalitarianism: Marx's Economy and Beyond and Other Essays* (OUP 2018).

[36] Simon Deakin, 'What Exactly Is Happening to the Contract of Employment? Reflections on Mark Freedland and Nicola Kountouris's Legal Construction of Personal Work Relations' (2013) 7 Jerusalem Review of Legal Studies 135, 143.

[37] Judy Fudge, 'The Future of the Standard Employment Relationship: Labour Law, New Institutional Economics and Old Power Resource Theory' [2017] Journal of Industrial Relations <https://doi.org/10.1177/0022185617693877>.

[38] Picchio (n 4); Judy Fudge, 'Feminist Reflections on the Scope of Labour Law: Domestic Work, Social Reproduction, and Jurisdiction' (2014) 22 Feminist Legal Studies 1.

standards of living. A mechanism, in other words, which is capable of transcending distributional conflicts, reflecting fairness norms prevailing in society—as has historically been achieved (in the United Kingdom, but also in most developed capitalist societies), however imperfectly and contingently, through labour law and the contract of employment.[39]

These ideas about the wage, and the role of (both statutory and collective) labour law, were central to the institutional critique of the neoclassical theory of wages that developed in the nineteenth century where the distinction between the 'social wage' and the 'market wage' came to be placed at the centre of the analysis of the labour market.[40] Particularly well-known proponents of this view include Sidney and Beatrice Webb, ardent supporters of the statutory minimum wage and collective bargaining as mechanisms capable of aligning wage rates with the changing needs of different groups of workers.

In line with the critique advanced above, the Webbs criticized (what we now associate with) neoclassical economics on the basis that it ignored the institutional forces that lent structure to the labour market.[41] The existence of such forces is such, they argued, that the agreed wage will rarely reflect the full social cost of labour, notwithstanding that its capacity to do so is a precondition for the efficient and effective functioning of the price system. The market presupposes some mechanism providing the conditions for the payment by employers of a social wage.

> The continued efficiency of a nation's industry obviously depends on the continuance of its citizens in health and strength. For an industry to be economically self-supporting, it must, therefore, maintain its full establishment of workers, unimpaired in numbers and vigour, with a sufficient number of children to fill all vacancies caused by death or superannuation. If the employers ... hire them [workers] for wages actually insufficient to provide enough food, clothing and shelter ... or if they can subject them to conditions so dangerous or insanitary as positively shorten their lives, that trade is clearly obtaining a supply of labour-force which it does not pay for ... [This is] a vicious form of parasitism.[42]

Like the classical economists, the Webbs emphasized that the wage performs not just an allocative or coordination function, but a vital social, or reproduction, function as well.[43] The argument was not simply that to be fair the wage should be

[39] Alan Bogg and Ruth Dukes, 'The Contract of Employment and Collective Labour Law' in Mark Freedland (ed), *The Contract of Employment* (OUP 2016).

[40] For recent contributions see: Geoffrey M Hodgson, *Economics and Institutions: A Manifesto for a Modern Institutional Economics* (Polity Press 1988); Warren Samuels, *The Legal-Economic Nexus: Fundamental Processes* (Routledge 2007).

[41] Sidney Webb and Beatrice Webb, *Industrial Democracy*, vol 2 (Longmans, Green, and Company 1897) 2:671.

[42] ibid 2:751.

[43] ibid 2:750–51.

one that is capable of providing workers with a fair standard of living. Instead, the 'social reproduction' or 'social' wage (referred to by them as a 'living wage') was an analytical concept, expressing the idea that the economy cannot flourish without an adequate supply of workers, which can only be guaranteed if wages allow for the reproduction of the working class.[44] To exclude from empirical models of the labour market the spheres of reproduction and production, was thus to obscure, and fail to engage with, the tensions at the heart of the capitalist system and, in turn, to underplay the constitutive role of labour law.

The Webbs' campaign for a social wage throughout the nineteenth century formed part of their much broader critique of (what we would now refer to as) the neoclassical model of the market. The Webbs sought to emphasize the historical, social, and legal influences structuring the labour market. The essence of the argument was that, while it may be that on the surface the impersonal forces of demand and supply appear to determine the wage structure, in practice, Adam Smith's so-called 'invisible hand' is actually the hand of government.[45] By specifying actors' endowments, and determining the rules of the game, legal and social institutions directly influence labour market outcomes by structuring the bargaining conditions of the parties *ex ante*.[46] It is the man-made institutions of private property, rules of competition, and the contract of employment that make it possible for the logic of self-interest to appear as if it mechanistically determines the 'true' or 'equilibrium' value embodied in the wage. The choice between a system in which firms pay workers poverty wages for inhuman hours, or living wages for an eight-hour working day and universal health insurance, is, they suggested, a political, or institutional one, rather than one that would have to be played out according to any so-called law of nature. Labour law is not a restriction on a freely competitive market, in other words, but is integral to the effective and efficient functioning of the capitalist socio-economic system.

The Webbs went further than more recent purposive approaches in their conceptualization of the wage and minimum wage legislation. In the latter, minimum wages are heavily circumscribed by what the empirical evidence suggests about the possibility of negative effects on employment levels, and where redistribution is seen to operate in opposition to, and thus to be circumscribed by, broader goals of efficiency and growth.[47] The Webbs, by contrast, recognized that efficiency had to be conceived in broader terms than is the case in neoclassical economics, and that

[44] Picchio (n 4). The notion of the social wage always had a gendered dimension, of course, but a discussion of this issue is outside the scope of this book.

[45] ibid 135.

[46] Kaufman (n 26); Sidney Webb and Beatrice Webb, *Problems of Modern Industry* (Longmans, Green and Company 1902).

[47] Guy Davidov, 'A Purposive Interpretation of the National Minimum Wage Act' (2009) 72 Modern Law Review 581; Bob Simpson, 'A Milestone in the Legal Regulation of Pay: The National Minimum Wage Act 1998' (1999) 28 Industrial Law Journal 1; Bob Simpson, 'Implementing the National Minimum Wage - the 1999 Regulations' (1999) 28 Industrial Law Journal 171.

fairness, dignity and efficiency can, and arguably must, go hand in hand. Rather than arguing that minimum wages serve the purpose of upholding human dignity and that this should override efficiency concerns, they refused to accept the narrow supply–demand conception of efficiency, recognizing that even if minimum wages *did* cause unemployment, this could be justified to the extent that they served the end of dynamic, long-run sustainability.[48]

There is, however, an important limitation in the Webbs' argument: they failed to engage critically with the form, and function, of legal concepts. Despite their critique of the neoclassical model, therefore, they too saw law in instrumental terms, treating it as a mere instrument for implementing political programmes. The main constraints on labour law's development were, in this view, political; stemming from government and employer resistance to legal intervention in the market. The role of law in reproducing, and sustaining, the cognitive framework of the market was thus largely ignored—and so too was its *necessary* contribution to the reproduction of the capitalist system. While they moved beyond a naturalistic conception of the market, therefore, their understanding of the ontology of law, of the distinct properties of law as a mode of regulation, was relatively limited. They did not, therefore, engage with the possibility that there might be constraints embedded in the form of legal discourse that influences labour law's path of development in a way that is not, or is not completely, at the 'control' of human agents, or 'political forces'. It follows that there is room to further refine, and develop, this 'constitutive' approach to wages, by linking it with our analysis, in the previous chapter, of the legal form.

4.4.1 Law, Labour Law, and the Wage: An Ontological Perspective

The above analysis shows that neoclassical economics presents the wage as the outcome of rational bargaining. This makes the law appear as exogenous to a natural, market-led process. But, as we have seen, there are limits to the neoclassical approach, not least its failure to acknowledge law's constitutive role. If viewed through the lens of social ontology, neoclassical economics, as an example of a naturalistic ontology, is problematic because it fails to move beyond the surface appearance of the market to explore the deeper mechanisms and processes that give rise to sustain and reproduce labour market practices over time. This would include, for example, various legal and non-legal institutions, class relations, occupational structures, health, education, and other public services, as well as labour law,

[48] The relationship between minimum wages and economic growth was criticized by Keynes who suggested that employment levels are driven more by aggregate demand: John Maynard Keynes, *General Theory of Employment, Interest and Money* (Atlantic Publishers & Dist 2016) Chapter 19.

tax, social security law, and the private property framework in general. As we saw in previous chapters, law's role is particularly important here, not only for bringing about and sustaining the wage dependence and inequality that indirectly compels workers to work, providing the basis for the free contract; but also, through labour law and the contract of employment, for providing support to the employer's control over labour in production, while at the same time limiting through protective labour legislation how far the employer's exploitation of this commodity can extend. In this sense, law is integral to the emergence of the labour commodity and, as a result, the wage.[49]

Law plays a crucial role when it comes to securing the economic idea of the wage as something capable of coordinating decision making in the market. That is, the idea of the 'market wage' as a price of a commodity. This it does, inter alia, by upholding faith that economic decisions are taken rationally and freely, and that property is protected and contracts will be enforced. But, and as argued above, labour markets can only operate, and be sustainable, if the wage that coordinates decision-making behaviour in fact takes effect as an obligation to pay the social, and not just the private costs of production: a social wage. The costs of social reproduction must, therefore, be an exogenous factor conditioning the wage rate. This is important for sustaining consumer demand, and for securing a stock of productive labour for present and future use, as the Webbs argued, but these functions could be conceivably performed outside the market. The reason that this is not sustainable, that is, the reason this function has to be performed through the wage payment paid by a capitalist to his worker, is that, to externalize this social reproduction function in this way, to shift the social costs of labour onto the community or the state, would interfere with the wage's coordinating function, undermining stability in the market.

It is only because prices coordinate decision making that markets can be seen as efficient mechanisms for allocating resources throughout society.[50] This is itself integral to the competitive process as the mechanism by which the 'laws' of capital accumulation are systematically enforced. This presupposes, however, that prices cover the full costs of production. The problem is that, as the classical economists recognized, in relation to labour power, which presupposes the reproduction of the worker himself, this cannot be assumed. Indeed, the coordinating function of the wage may operate in direct contradiction to its reproduction function. The pure market cannot resolve this problem, any more than models of the market which

[49] For an excellent analysis of the co-constituting role of different aspects of the legal framework, see: Harvey and Geras (n 35).

[50] Efficiency is used here in the sense it is used in neoclassical economics, recognizing that it is, however, a historically specific category that cannot be conceived independently from the capitalist system to which it is specific. On the historic relativity of this, and other, economic categories, see: Dennis Badeen, 'A Marxist Critique of the Ontological Foundations of Neo-Classical Economics' (PhD dissertation, York University (Canada) 2011).

presuppose perfect competition are capable of adequately representing it. As the ontology developed in Chapter 2 implies, the task of integrating the coordination and reproduction functions of the wage is one which ultimately rests with the law, and which can only ever be performed contingently, or imperfectly, as a result of the intractable contradictions at the heart of capitalism itself.

The market wage actually presupposes a legally constituted social wage, therefore, which helps embed information about the process of social reproduction within the market process. The meaning and functions of these contradictory dimensions of the wage can now be specified in more detail.

As explained above, the market wage refers to the way in which the wage must appear to the parties when participating in the market. It expresses the exchange value of a commodity, the price that is agreed, or which it is assumed would be agreed (but for market failure), between free and equal legal subjects in a market setting. In neoclassical economics, it is the market-clearing, or equilibrium wage, an 'objective' representation of a commodity's inherent value, something with which it would be 'inefficient' and 'illegitimate' for law to intervene.

The second concept, the social wage, by contrast, embodies the idea of the wage as something that incorporates the social costs of reproducing labour and society over time. It reflects what the legal system must actually require an employer to pay if this cognitive framework is to be sustained: the material conditions that make possible the reproduction of labour over time. This is the legally constituted wage that the legal system must require that an employer pay as a condition for his access to labour. The social wage is not to be equated with the bare necessities for existence, however, for what is required is a wage that is sufficient both to produce an efficient and productive labour force, and to maintain a customary standard of living—thereby helping to sustain the idea that workers are capable of meeting their employers as equals and of acting freely when participating in the market.

How far a true social wage (sometimes referred to as a 'living wage' in popular discourse) can be achieved in practice is an open question. The argument here is an abstract, analytical one that suggests that, at an abstract level, capitalism presupposes the payment by employers of a wage that covers the 'costs of social reproduction'—that bundle of rights and entitlements which are required, at a given time, to secure the health, productivity, and well-being, of labour (as a class) over time. How well such a wage might be achieved in the context of a living, breathing, socio-economic system which, as we have seen, is beset by internal contradictions, is an open question. It is, moreover, something that will depend, to some extent, on the balance of power in society; for what it means to reproduce society in practice is a political question that depends on what a 'normal' standard of living is deemed, or expected, to be. Not only are the mechanisms of wage regulation up for contestation, therefore, but so too is its content.

The challenge for law, of course, is that the concept of the social wage is a social category that reflects the costs, to society, of reproducing labour as a class—and yet, it must be realized in practice through a legal framework which is, of its nature, individualistic. The social wage thus must be conceptualized, and realized, through the lens of a contractual payment made by an individual capitalist to his worker, notwithstanding that a condition of possibility for that payment is various relations and practices all of which exist, to a great extent, 'beyond' the market framework.

Moreover, it must not be forgotten, as argued above, that legal concepts such as the wage do not simply describe social phenomena. In the same way that human knowledge of the world is mediated by the linguistic and conceptual frames through which it is accessed, the legal system's own view of the world is shaped by its existing conceptual framework, how it interprets new facts and information in light of previously conceptualized experiences. Legal concepts are both descriptive and normative, therefore, but even their descriptive element cannot be assumed to directly reflect features of underlying phenomena. Legal concepts combine an expression of social relations as conceived through the legal system's own cognitive processes, and its attempt, in light of this, to project certain values or ideals with a view to shaping them. For this reason, while the legal concept of the wage bears some correspondence to the payment that an employer agrees to make in exchange for labour, it cannot be reduced to it.

Chapters 5 to 8 of this book will show, however, that while the relationship between legal concepts and economic concepts is not direct, the distinction drawn above, between the wage as price and the wage as the cost of subsistence, is not unknown to legal discourse. Legal discourse frequently engages with the idea that the wage performs two vital, albeit contradictory, functions, and has developed different terms through which to give effect to them. During the early to mid-twentieth century, for example, there developed in legal discourse a distinction between the concept of the 'wage', conceived as the price of labour, and 'remuneration', referring to the total sum due to the worker in connection with his employment. While the former tends to be conceived as a payment that depends on time spent working (a payment for commodified labour), the latter concept connoted the idea that an individual who provided his personal services to his employer had a legal right to a guaranteed minimum income from employment.

The alignment between the legal concepts of the 'wage' and 'remuneration', on the one hand, and the economic ideas of the 'market' and 'social' wage on the other, is not perfect, of course, and the legal concepts themselves say little about the amount that has to be paid. Much will turn, therefore, on how any legally mandated minimum rate is set and how it is calculated at a given time. Nonetheless, the broader significance of these concepts and the distinction between them, it will be shown, lie not so much in their capacity to provide workers with a specified amount of income, but in the function that they perform within legal discourse, and society, more generally. The concept of remuneration connotes ideas of stability, regularity, and fairness, while the wage connotes ideas about price, value, and productivity. The legal concept of the wage thus performs a function analogous to the concept of the market wage, reflecting the contractually agreed sum that an employer pays for abstract labour time, while 'remuneration' performs a function akin to the idea of the social wage, imposing an obligation on employers to pay workers that is decoupled from time working. As a result, the concept of remuneration provides a conceptual mechanism through which to shift on to the employer some of the social costs that fall outside the scope of the concept of the wage, as something that expresses the value of commodified labour.

The rest of the book will argue that the concept of remuneration operates, however imperfectly, to ensure that the socio-economic functions of both the market and the social wage are performed: that is, the wage as a price that cooordinates decision making in the market, and the wage as the cost of social reproduction. The concept says nothing of how much an employer must pay for labour, which itself helps to uphold the image of the wage as something that is set by the 'impersonal' forces of supply and demand. Nonetheless, it imposes on the employer an absolute obligation to pay that sum, and requires that, in addition, the employer bear the social costs implicit in the institution of employment. This it does, first, by decoupling the obligation to pay from the provision of labour, such that it becomes a payment for personal service over time, and second, by implying into that concept the obligation to pay not only the contractually agreed rate, but also the costs of certain protective labour rights which help to bridge the gap between that rate and the costs of subsistence.

If the concept of remuneration ensures that the functions of the social and the market wage are reconciled, the question to be asked is why, the existence of this concept notwithstanding, labour law continues to struggle to provide for wage security today. The answer, it will be shown, lies, in part, in the fundamentally contradictory nature of capitalist society, and the impossibility of reconciling, completely, the contradiction between these two functions of the wage, in practice. At the same time, however, the scale of the 'problem' is not inevitable, and can be explained, in part, by reference to the confusion that exists today over the nature and function of these different concepts, and, in turn, with the way legal officials have come to understand their own role. That is, how they understand the form and function of legal concepts, and whether they should be taken to reflect, or shape, social relations—this might be referred to as law's 'internal' ontology, or self-description.

4.4.2 Law's 'Internal' Ontology

Part II of the book will demonstrate that how the courts and Parliament conceive the relationship between legal concepts and social reality has important consequences when it comes to labour law's capacity to perform the different functions of the wage identified above. If the legal system equates the cognitive framework its concepts presuppose with the reality beyond those concepts, it confines itself to passively enforcing rights and obligations that arise from a naturally free agreement concluded in a 'pre-constituted' market setting. It cannot, in other words, go beyond the surface appearance of the market, so as to engage with, and help secure, the conditions that give rise to, and are required to reproduce, it. If the legal system sees its concepts as part of the process through which the 'reality' of the market emerges, however, this opens the door to a much more active role, with the courts interpreting facts in light of the values embedded in legal concepts, operating through those concepts so as to allocate rights and obligations in a way that is better capable of ensuring that both the coordination ('market wage') and social reproduction ('social wage') functions of the wage can be performed.

These different approaches to what is referred to here as 'law's internal ontology' map on to the 'naturalistic' and 'constitutive' approaches advanced in Chapter 1 of this book. The naturalistic approach is reflected in the work of a number of labour law scholars, the Taylor Review of Modern Working Practices (2017), and recent case law concerning the test of mutuality of obligation, discussed in detail in Chapter 9 of this book. It is based on a particular conception of the nature of legal concepts and their relationship with social reality, one that is well captured by the following quote:

> laws-and with them, legal concepts-do not have a 'life' of their own. They do not have an 'internal' or inherent meaning. They have a purpose behind them, when used in a particular context—to advance some societal goals.[51] ... we should therefore *start* from asking what group of people should enjoy the legislation, based on the purpose of the legislation, and devise these legal concepts accordingly.[52]

On this view, 'employment' as well as 'dependent contracting' are social facts or extra-legal relationships that have an existence that is in some sense prior to, or independent from law. The law responds to the existence of these relationships by attaching certain normative consequences to them, depending on which 'status' the parties have chosen. Law shapes the relationship between the parties by imposing rights and obligations to which they have not expressly agreed, but which are part of the 'regulatory package' to which they have consented by expressing their relationship in a form which the legal system has indicated will be recognized as employment. The function of legal concepts such as employee and worker, on this view, is simply to tell the legal system which set of normative

[51] Guy Davidov, 'The (Incomplete) Purposive Revolution: A Comment on the Legal Construction of Personal Work Relations' (2013) 7 Jerusalem Review of Legal Studies 87, 87. See also: Brian Langille, 'Labour Law's Theory of Justice' in Guy Davidov and Brian Langille (eds), *The Idea of Labour Law* (OUP 2011); Hugh Collins, Gillian Lester, and Virginia Mantouvalou (eds), *Philosophical Foundations of Labour Law* (OUP 2018).

[52] Davidov (n 52) 90.

consequences should be applied, given the nature of the relationship that exists 'on the ground'.

From this perspective, law's relationship with social practices is regulatory, constraining behaviour by altering parties' incentives; and facilitative, providing information about the different 'bundles' of rights and obligations that are available to economic agents, and which are assumed to promote mutually beneficial working relationships by (inter alia) minimizing transaction costs, or 'remedying' or 'compensating' for market failures.[53] Labour law appears as something that operates as if from outside, therefore, modifying a pre-constituted economic structure, wherein agents act in light of pre-formed interests and preferences. Employers and workers are treated as having an equal capacity to engage in certain types of action, most particularly, to contract, and to acquire and alienate property. The broader structure in which these agents exist is, then, implicitly ignored. As a result, law's autonomy is seen not in terms of the legal system's causal independence from capitalist social relations, recognizing its status as an emergent system; but in terms of the state's independence from the market—something which, as we have seen, is part of law's self-presentation. This makes 'respect' for an innate freedom of contract seem as a natural 'law' which labour law must respect to be legitimate. Because law plays no role in the process by which economic agents come to be, that is, in constituting them as rational subjects, any attempt to impose constraints on their behaviour is seen as illegitimate. The cognitive framework through which market practices take place is, in other words, taken by the legal system as an expression of a natural reality, rather than something that is itself constituted, and reproduced, through law.

From this perspective, rather than imposing an obligation to pay that is informed by labour law's socio-economic function, constituting the parties' agreement in a form that guarantees the payment in practice of a social wage, the courts see the wage and the parties' rights as pre-constituted realities which it is the legal system's role to simply enforce. The legal system and the market appear, therefore, as alternative forms of social order, with a presumption in favour of the latter due to considerations of economic efficiency; or, what amounts to the same thing, the courts' deference to Parliament as the only 'legitimate' body capable of legitimately placing limits on freedom of contract. And even this statutory 'intervention' is to be narrowly construed; confined to clear instances of market failure.

[53] For an excellent analysis of the distinction between 'regulatory', 'facilitative', and 'constitutive' functions of law, see: Noah D Zatz, 'Working at the Boundaries of Markets: Prison Labor and the Economic Dimension of Employment Relationships' (2008) 61 Vanderbilt Law Review 857; Andrew Lang, 'Market Anti-Naturalisms' in Justin Desautels-Stein and Christopher Tomlins (eds), *Searching for Contemporary Legal Thought* (1st edn, CUP 2017); Lauren B Edelman and Robin Stryker, 'A Sociological Approach to Law and the Economy' in Neil J Smelser and Richard Swedberg (eds), *The Handbook of Economic Sociology, Second Edition* (Princeton University Press 2010) Chapter 23.

The second, constitutive, model is based on the ontology advanced in Chapters 2 and 3 of this book, although similar ideas have been presented in the work of scholars such as Mark Freedland, Nicola Kountouris, and Noah Zatz. From this perspective:

> acts of legal construction of personal work relations, which forge links between the legal character and the legal consequences of a particular personal work relation or set of personal work relations, . . . not only classify personal work relations *but also form or transform them at the same time*.[54]

Rather than law merely ascribing normative consequences to social relationships, in other words, law partly constitutes those relationships. The act of classification itself can, therefore, transform the underlying relations themselves. For example, law generates understandings of what is and is not a corporation, who is or is not an employee, what constitutes a binding agreement, etc, and in this way provides certain 'interpretative scripts' that actors draw upon when negotiating exchange. Employers and employees presuppose certain features of the employment transaction before they even bargain over substantive terms. But law also helps define certain fundamental constructs such as economic fairness, efficiency, rationality, and value.[55] The premise that efficiency is to be defined in terms of utility maximization, for example, and that efficiency is to be assessed in the narrow framework of exchange, is both reflected in, and shaped by, legal discourse as it interacts with organizations and economic actors through the course of disputes.

Legal concepts such as employee and property help to define which interactions and activities are legitimate and which are not, shaping social conceptions about what it means to be employed, and what is expected from a relationship described in these terms. In this way, legal categorizations define opportunities and limits for economic actors, shaping economic thinking about the nature of markets, capitalism, and the relationship between the market and the state. In this way, they shape (and are shaped by) conceptions of legitimacy and fairness that are drawn upon when individuals participate in the market.

Rather than classification, or conceptualization, being purely passive, therefore, it is seen as constitutive: it changes the nature of that being classified as well as the meanings embedded in the concept through which it is denoted. To classify a particular relationship as employment, therefore, not only generates certain normative expectations about the nature of that relationship and how it ought to be regulated,

[54] Mark Robert Freedland and Nicola Kountouris, *The Legal Construction of Personal Work Relations* (OUP 2011) 9. See also: Noah D Zatz, 'Working at the Boundaries of Markets: Prison Labor and the Economic Dimension of Employment Relationships' (2008) 61 Vanderbilt Law Review 857.

[55] Lauren B Edelman, 'Rivers of Law and Contested Terrain: A Law and Society Approach to Economic Rationality' (2004) 38 Law & Society Review 181.

it also potentially influences how employment itself comes to be conceived, and, by implication, how other relationships are conceptualized in the future.

In this approach, moreover, labour law is not simply responding to, or regulating, inter-personal relations between autonomous subjects. Rather, it is applied to inter-personal relationships, but in light of its broader role in a capitalist economy. In this approach, therefore, there is an important difference between the wage that the employer agrees to pay, and the sum he is legally required to pay as a matter of law. The latter cannot be determined independently from broader considerations about labour law's function, and this turns on what is objectively required, and perceived to be required, to secure social reproduction—or, a wage sufficient to ensure a decent standard of living. Thus, the law does not simply enforce the terms of the parties' agreement. The labour market is seen to be embedded in a much broader socio-historical process that secures, however imperfectly, the existence and reproduction of society.

From a policy perspective, this model might recognize a role for law in imposing an obligation to pay wages that is informed by considerations external to the market—the costs of living. The role of statutory labour regulation is not, in other words, limited to that which is required to 'recreate' conditions for perfect competition. Rather, there is an assumption that it is important that employers rather than the state bear the social and not just the private costs of labour, and that it is the role of the state to ensure that this is the case. Whereas in the former, 'passive' model the limit to what the legal system can require the employer to pay is that which is expressed in the 'objective' market wage—that which the employer agrees to pay, or would have agreed but for market failure—in this model, the precise content of the wage is seen as a political question that cannot, by definition, be left to 'market forces'.

The difference between the two approaches can thus be summarized as a contrast between a legal system that actively strives towards securing a living or social wage and a legal system that sees the wage as something the content of which is determined by extra-legal processes. In practical terms, placing a heavy burden on the tax and social-security system to make up the difference between the market wage and subsistence, the latter naturalistic model affects not only how well resources are used and allocated in the market and production, but also the fiscal and regulatory burden assumed by the state. In the long run, it serves to threaten the long-term sustainability, and viability, of the system.

4.5 Conclusion

This chapter has drawn on the ontological framework presented in Chapter 2, and the analysis of the legal form advanced in Chapter 3, to explore the nature, and significance, of the social category of the wage. In so doing, it has identified two, contradictory, functions performed by the wage in capitalism, and identified some of the legal concepts through which that category tends to be conceptualized in legal discourse. In turn, the chapter has shown how different conceptions of the nature of law, and its relationship with the market, influence how the wage is conceived, and, in turn, the law's role in relation to it.

Having shown the importance of a constitutive understanding of law's role for reconciling the contradictory functions of the wage, its function as a price and its function as a source of workers' subsistence, the analysis in this chapter can now be relied on as a frame through which to view the more concrete, historical analysis, of Part II. This analysis begins in Chapter 5 with an examination of the emergence of the 'wage' in the context of the decline of the feudal system of land tenure, and the emergence, over subsequent centuries, of a labour market.

PART II

5
The Emergence of the Wage

5.1 Introduction

In feudal England, property, or more accurately, land, was the foundation of a person's social and legal identity. Individuals were deemed to have been born into a particular social position that determined their rights and obligations; a socio-economic status that implied duties of loyalty and obedience to superiors. In this context, the concept of property had a qualitatively different meaning to modern notions of ownership: it did not imply rights of exclusivity or alienation, but implied status, and personality. Property did not connote a direct or exclusive relationship between an individual and a thing, therefore; property 'rights' went hand in hand with personal obligations, and claims to land were, in effect, claims to the benefit of a personal relation.[1]

In the years following the Norman conquest, only the King had absolute title to land. His subjects held land 'of' the King, enjoying rights conditional on obligations of fealty and obedience.[2] Lords would then grant peasants rights in plots of land in exchange for labour services. This ensured that land would be cultivated, and that peasants would have access to the means of subsistence.[3] Paying rent in personal services was thus both a condition of land-holding, and, by implication, a condition of subsistence for those in occupation. These grants might be in the form of either 'free' or 'villein' tenure, the distinction turning on the nature of the service obligations owed in exchange for the right to occupy. If the services were uncertain and ill-defined, the tenant was classed as a villein; if the services were certain and explicit, the tenant was classed as free. Other villeins were serfs by inheritance; they were born into serfdom. The boundary, between unfree and free, was extremely important: free peasants fell within the purview of the common law. Villeins, by contrast, at least in their relationship with their Lord, were subject only to manorial custom, and so did not enjoy the protection of the King's law.

Legally speaking, a Lord's right to the services of his tenant was derivative of his title to the land.[4] It was thus by way of 'real' action that the Lord could recover

[1] Keith Tribe, *Land, Labour and Economic Discourse* (Routledge 1978); Mary Murray, *The Law of the Father?: Patriarchy in the Transition from Feudalism to Capitalism* (Routledge 2005).
[2] Theodore Plucknett, *A Concise History of the Common Law* (The Lawbook Exchange, Ltd 2001) 13.
[3] Frederick Pollock and Frederic William Maitland, *The History of English Law before the Time of Edward I. Volume 2* (2nd edn, CUP 1898) 146.
[4] Joshua Williams, *Principles of the Law of Real Property: Intended as a First Book for the Use of Students in Conveyancing* (T & JW Johnson 1879) 12–13.

Labour and the Wage. Zoe Adams, Oxford University Press (2020). © Zoe Adams.
DOI: 10.1093/oso/9780198858898.001.0001

services in the event of non-payment—the same form of action available to recover land.[5] A Lord was said to have 'seisin' of his villeins—or, in more modern language, possession of them: the villein was seen as part of the land to which the Lord had title, hence why they were not seen as legal persons in the common law courts. The Lord's power over his villeins was not unlimited, however; not only was it regulated by custom, but also, by his loyalty to the King. Because Lords held land on behalf of the King, they could no more destroy the villein than they could the land. Thus, while the villein could not bring a claim against his Lord in a common law court, he did have a legally enforceable right not to be deprived of his means of subsistence (his 'waynage'), and was protected by the criminal law from being harmed or killed.[6] In combination, law and custom operated to ensure that both land, and labour, could be utilized in a way that was relatively sustainable.

These early ideas of 'tenure' had a long-term impact on the development of the common law, particularly as it related to the (emerging) relationship between master and servant. Implicit in the feudal conception of property was the premise that rights in land gave rise to rights to service, but that in exchange for that service, the service provider ought to enjoy a guaranteed right to subsistence, and certain protections against social and economic risk. The relationship between Lord and villein, or Lord and tenant, was an inherently unequal one, therefore, but it was characterized by mutual obligations of loyalty and obedience on the one hand, and maintenance and protection on the other, governed by customary understandings that were, increasingly, backed up by law.

5.2 The Decline of Feudal Land Holding

In the feudal economy, peasants reproduced themselves by their own labour, while Lords lived off accumulated wealth, and any rent extracted from the peasants living off their land (ie by appropriating their surplus labour). This was not, then, an economy oriented around economic growth; the purpose of production was consumption, not profit/accumulation, and, as such, incentives towards specialization, investment, or technical innovation, while present, were limited.

The fourteenth century was, however, a period of profound socio-economic change. Economic pressures placed a strain on the pre-existing structure of class relations, and relatedly, the form of land-holding. Servile labour was becoming increasingly difficult to secure, and this was only exacerbated by the labour scarcity and rise in wages that was precipitated by the Black Death.[7] Many Lords had little

[5] Pollock and Maitland (n. 3) 2:125–28. For a discussion of this and its link with the action under the Statute of Labourers, see: (1366) YB Mich 40 Edw 3, fo 39a–b, pl 16.

[6] *Magna Carta*, articles 5 and 20: 'waynage' or 'gainage' is defined as: 'The chattels on which the villein depended for his livelihood: such as his farm implements, seed-corn and stock.'

[7] Rodney Hilton, *Bond Men Made Free: Medieval Peasant Movements and the English Rising of 1381* (Routledge 2003) 154.

choice but to let-out their demesne (the land retained by the Lord of a Manor), as they lacked access to the labour that was required for its cultivation.[8] This meant that the use of hired, rather than servile, labour became more common; as did the payment of money rents, rather than the payment of rent in services. As a result of these changes, the position of the villein was considerably improved, and, given the transition to money rents, it became difficult for the courts to deny him/her a legal right to occupy land.[9] Copyhold, a form of free tenure that many villeins negotiated, or bought from their Lords, was gradually replacing villein tenure, therefore, and this was later to give way to the lease as more Lords struggled to exact profits from customary rents.

By the beginning of the fifteenth century, few feudal Lords were cultivating the demesne directly. Depopulation and the low productivity of (servile) labour had forced many Lords to reduce the size of the demesne, leasing portions to these peasant holders, and others to employ hired labour to cultivate the land directly. It was during this period that the common law recognized the lease as a proprietary, rather than a personal, interest in land—making leasehold attractive to tenants and thereby more profitable for 'land-holders'.[10] In this context, persons leasing land were becoming increasingly significant both in the emerging land-market, and as rural employers of labour.[11] There was thus a rising class of peasant farmers, leasing land from (former) Lords at competitive rents, playing a central role as employers. The result of these changes was that, as the tenurial system was falling into decline, the lease and the service relation were becoming key institutions in the social order that was emerging to replace it.[12]

Before the fifteenth century, labour scarcity and the persistence of customary rights over land were such that enclosure and investments in technology, rather than the exploitation of wage labour, offered the greatest opportunities for maximizing the yield of the land. This, rather than the institution of service (ie the exploitation of labour power), was the major source of profit in the emerging agricultural economy, driven by an emerging market in leases more than a market in labour.[13] That is not to say that the institution of service was not significant; it helped to lay the foundations for the market in leases to expand. By absorbing the newly propertyless and supplying them to those in need of labour, moreover, the institution of service helped render sustainable the large-scale enclosures that were

[8] Richard Henry Tawney, *The Agrarian Problem in the Sixteenth Century*, vol 1 (Longmans, Green 1912) 202–03.

[9] Sir Paul Vinogradoff, *Villainage in England: Essays in English Mediaeval History* (Clarendon Press 1892) 71.

[10] Plucknett (n 2) 373. The legal estate in leaseholds was created by the Statute of Gloucester 1278 (6 Edw 1) and 21 Hen VIII c 15 (1529).

[11] Maurice Dobb, *Studies in the Development of Capitalism* (Routledge 1946) 65–66.

[12] We see evidence of this in the commentary in: (1366) YB Mich 40 Edw 3, fo 39a–b, pl 16 (Fyncheden JCP).

[13] Robert Brenner, 'The Agrarian Roots of European Capitalism' [1982] Past & Present 16.

to come during the eighteenth century, and in doing so, helped to pave the way, in subsequent centuries, for the emergence of the labour market.

In the fourteenth century, however, when the first major labour statute was enacted, the majority of those in service were only intermittently propertyless. Wage dependence was not a life-long condition, but a transitionary phase; service provided young adults with the chance to save towards purchasing or renting land of their own.[14] The wage, paid at statutory wage rates, was less significant than the features of the relationship to which it provided access, for it was this that secured workers their subsistence: 'masters' were legally obliged to provide food and lodging.[15]

During the fourteenth and fifteenth centuries land was still abundant relative to labour so peasants could largely resist competitive pressures, supporting themselves from a combination of subsistence farming and selling surplus produce.[16] The service relation was not, therefore, a major component of the emerging agricultural economy. It was, however, a functional parallel to the lease as the legal form by which access to scarce social resources was beginning to be secured, in each case modelled as a particular form of property relation characterized by ideas of 'tenure': the right to benefit from a particularly vital social resource; conditional, however, on certain obligations of fair-use and protection.[17]

In this sense, the lease and the service relation performed complementary roles in the medieval economy as feudal social relations were coming under pressure. They each made it possible for the community to benefit from a scarce social resource that was under someone else's control by making access to that resource conditional upon maintaining and preserving it for the long-term benefit of the owner and the community. Tenants were obliged to cultivate and maintain the land as a condition for their right to peaceful enjoyment, while employers were obliged to maintain their servant/s as a condition for his/her/their obedience.[18]

[14] Ann Kussmaul, *Servants in Husbandry in Early Modern England* (CUP 1981) 61–62.

[15] The composition of the wage-dependent class was only to change from the sixteenth century, as customary land began to be converted to leasehold through large-scale enclosure: Michael Andrew Žmolek, *Rethinking the Industrial Revolution: Five Centuries of Transition from Agrarian to Industrial Capitalism in England* (Haymarket Books 2013).

[16] Richard Biernacki, *The Fabrication of Labor: Germany and Britain, 1640-1914* (University of California Press 1995) 22; Ellen Meiksins Wood, *The Origin of Capitalism: A Longer View* (new edn, Verso 2002) Chapter 5; Martin J Daunton and others, 'Progress and Poverty: An Economic and Social History of Britain 1700-1850' (OUP 1995).

[17] The court emphasized that only those without property of their own could be compelled to serve: (1431) YB Mich 10 Hen 6, fo 8b, pl 30 (Cottesmore J): 'the statute is intended only for labourers, who are vagrants and have nothing on which they live, so they will be forced into service, but a chaplain has something on which to live, to common understanding, like a gentleman'. It also emphasized the link between leasing land to villeins and the obligation on the propertyless to serve under the Statute of Labourers: (1366) YB Mich 40 Edw 3, fo 39a–b, pl 16.

[18] For the tenant's obligation, see:Mark Wonnacott, *The History of the Law of Landlord and Tenant in England and Wales* (The Lawbook Exchange, Ltd 2012) 184. Thus, in 1353 the court confirmed that a failure to provide livery constituted a good defence in an action for departure: (1354) Mich 28 Edw 3, fo 21b, Pl 18. In turn, a person without sufficient land of their own were not permitted to retain a servant under the Statute: (1364) YB Trin 38 Edw 3, fo 12b, pl 1; (1366) YB Mich 40 Edw 3, fo 39a–b, pl 16.

By these means, both the immediate 'owner' and the person most in need of it could benefit from the resource, whether it be land or labour, notwithstanding that demand far outstripped supply. Concurrent property rights, which might be referred to as a form of tenure, made it possible to balance the competing interests of members of the community. In relation to service, the employer was made responsible for covering the costs involved in his use of labour, for maintaining it during the hiring, because the exclusive nature of his rights to it prevented both the worker and the community from interfering to 'preserve' that labour themselves. In this way, ideas associated with tenure (albeit never articulated in these terms) made it possible for the demand for both land and labour to be met, notwithstanding that no competitive market in either land or labour had fully emerged to secure the distribution of each.

The institutions of service and lease-holding thus expressed the differentiation that was taking place in relation to the landlord and employer functions that had previously been combined in the Feudal Lord. Because those in possession of land had to use that land to produce enough to pay competitive rents, this produced new incentives towards innovation and investment. By making possible the differentiation of rent from labour service, moreover, this transaction paved the way for capitalist social relations to develop, marking the gradual emergence, and differentiation, of land and labour as 'fictive' commodities.

5.2.1 The Statute of Labourers and the Common Law

It was the Black Death's effects on the supply of labour, and thus on wages and prices, which provided the impetus for the Statute of Labourers and the Ordinance that preceded it.[19] Prior to the fourteenth century, the regulation of agricultural labour, including wage rates, had been a matter of status and custom.[20] In a context in which the feudal manorial system was breaking down, however, provision of a workforce at acceptable wages was becoming a matter of central governmental concern.[21] The Ordinance, and the Statute that followed it, was thus the 'first attempt of the central authorities to apply to the country as a whole, uniform legislation on wages and prices'[22] Prior to the Ordinance and Statute of Labourers, wages had long been regulated locally, as had prices, administered by the assizes of bread and ale. What was new, however, was the attempt to bring wage and price control

[19] Ordinance of 1349 (23 Edw III c 1–8); (1351) 25 Edw 111, Star 1 c 1.

[20] Bertha Haven Putnam, *The Enforcement of the Statutes of Labourers during the First Decade after the Black Death, 1349-1359*, vol 85 (AMS Press 1970) 3 and 156.

[21] Robert C Palmer, *English Law in the Age of the Black Death, 1348-1381: A Transformation of Governance and Law* (Univ of North Carolina Press 2000) 15–16.

[22] Putnam (n 20) 223.

within the purview of the King, and the common law courts, and to compel service, not by seigneurial custom, but by law.

In its attempt to maintain control over rising wages and prices, the Statute set wages at the rate that had been payable prior to the Black Death, and the payment or receipt of wages in excess of that rate was punishable in the courts.[23] These provisions worked alongside the contract clause, making labour compulsory for the able-bodied poor; for all those under 60 without visible means of subsistence.[24]

The Statute allowed for workers who refused to serve to be summarily punished: the accused had no chance to answer charges against him or her, and would only be released when he/she had agreed to serve as originally ordered. The Statute also reserved Lords a first claim to the labour of their villeins, however, helping them resist tenants' attempts to substitute money rents for rent services, while reinforcing Lords' power over their villeins by making available certain legal remedies to compel the return of a fugitive villein.[25]

These provisions notwithstanding, the Statute should not be seen as an attempt by elites to shore-up a declining feudal order, to re-assert their power over servile labour.[26] Rather, it was a genuine response to the social and economic challenges of the period. When the councillors and commons of Edward II pondered the problem of labour in 1349 and 1351, they framed their response in terms of mortality; a 'scarcity of servants' and the problem of labourers who would not work unless paid 'excessive' wages'.[27] It was not just the Lords, moreover, but also the rising class of peasant tenants that stood to gain from the Statute's provisions.[28] Providing access to labour at reasonable wages, the Statute helped such tenants exploit local markets, accumulate capital, and further expand their land-holding. In this way, it helped pave the way for both the lease and service relation to play a central role in the emerging capitalist system.[29]

The Statute represented a continuation of the policy, implicit in the assizes of bread and ale, that the reproduction of the population was something which it was for the state (or 'Crown') to secure. At the same time, it continued the belief, implicit in the feudal system of tenure, that labour is a resource that belongs to the community, the heart of which having once been the feudal manor.[30] The statute

[23] ibid; James Rogers, *Six Centuries of Work and Wages: The History of English Labour*, vol 2 (GP Putnam's Sons 1884) 228.

[24] Most peasants were neither entirely wage dependent, nor entirely self-sufficient, dependent on some form of wage labour to supplement the household income. See: Christopher Dyer, 'Work Ethics in the Fourteenth Century' in James Bothwell, Jeremy Goldberg, and William Ormrod (eds), *The Problem of Labour in Fourteenth-Century England* (Boydell & Brewer Ltd 2000) 21.

[25] Dobb (n 11) 55; Putnam (n 20), 200–06.

[26] Larry R Poos, 'The Social Context of Statute of Labourers Enforcement' (1983) 1 Law and History Review 27.

[27] Statutes of the Realm, I, 307–08 (23 Edw III), quotations at 307.

[28] Poos (n 26) 36.

[29] Dobb (n 11) 65–66.

[30] Robert Steinfeld, *The Invention of Free Labor: The Employment Relation in English and American Law and Culture, 1350-1870* (UNC Press Books 1991) 60–63.

not only protected Lords' claims to their villeins, therefore, but imposed restrictions on freedom of movement to prevent both villeins and workers from leaving the locality to look for work. The community's right to control how labour was used was parallelled by similar controls over the use of land, with the common law gradually strengthening the legal protection available to both the villein and the lessee. For those with no land of their own, moreover, the Statute guaranteed that the obligation to serve would continue to be conditional upon the worker's access to subsistence. That is, if 'freedom' from the land meant that access to the means of subsistence was no longer assumed, the Statute ensured that, even so, the interests of those working on the land of others would be provided for: now, however, by being given access to a household in which they would be maintained. Rather than producing for himself, and providing a Lord with the surplus, therefore, an employer-landowner now claimed the entire 'product' of a workers' labour, providing, in exchange, reasonable food and board.[31] Servants who could prove that their masters abused them or failed to provide them with adequate food and board, could thus petition the justices to be released from service.[32]

5.2.2 The Common Law Debt Claim

The Statute had been enacted at a time when neither the common law nor the manorial courts proved capable of securing Lords or employers control over, or access, to labour. It was thus shaped both by customary understandings about the relationship between Lord and tenant, and the form of the writ actions through which the institution of service was beginning to take effect.

In order to understand the common law of this period, it is necessary to highlight the distinctive character of the early modern conception of contract. Contract did not connote equality of right. Contract has its origins in the feudal oath of fealty made by a tenant to his Lord. The difference is, however, that the former, gradually formalized as a written contract, was in no way a promise made and accepted by legal equals in the sense in which the contract has later come to be conceived. Contract was not itself intrinsically associated with notions of legal equality as it is today.[33] As we shall see, the 'equalization' of contractual relations had to be fought

[31] Douglas Hay and Paul Craven, *Masters, Servants, and Magistrates in Britain and the Empire, 1562-1955* (UNC Press 2005) 66, 78; George Tait, *A Summary of the Powers and Duties of a Justice of the Peace in Scotland, with Forms of Proceedings, &c., Comprising a Short View of the Criminal Duty and of the Greater Part of the Civil Duty of Sheriffs and Magistrates of Burghs* (J Anderson 1828) 465. Of course, in practice, the labour services provided were of such a nature that there was not always a tangible product to be claimed. Many servants performed services for their employers that assisted in the maintenance of the household.

[32] Richard Burn, *Justice of the Peace and County, Borough, Poor Law Union and Parish Law Recorder* (Shaw & Sons 1838) 789.

[33] Anthony Woodwiss, 'The Discourses Of Production (Part II)' (1987) 16 Economy and Society 441, 474.

for politically and ideologically throughout the course of the eighteenth and nineteenth centuries. The law relating to the labour relationship was, moreover, one of the last spheres in which even a semblance of freedom of contract was achieved. In the fifteenth and sixteenth centuries, therefore, any notion of a general freedom to contract was largely absent.

In the common law, the writ of covenant lay to enforce a written agreement evidenced by deed. Because labour agreements were informal, therefore, prior to the fifteenth century, the common law provided no remedy to a master seeking to enforce an agreement to serve. The only remedy available to a party seeking to enforce an informal covenant at this time was the writ of debt (and/or the writ of detinue). If the claim could not be framed in this form (and thus reduced to a sum certain), the only remaining option was to rely on tort, and, more specifically, the writ of assumpsit.

The writ of debt was available to a party seeking to enforce a simple contract that operated as a grant, such as a title in property or an assignment of a lease.[34] It thus applied to transactions that gave rise to a proprietary interest in the debt being claimed: the price of the interest obtained. The essence of debt was entitlement, often evidenced by an agreement but based on the fact that something of benefit had been provided in expectation of payment.[35]

In the thirteenth and fourteenth centuries, the courts had allowed both workers and lessors to bring a claim in debt to recover unpaid rent or wages, provided that the parties could prove that the property for which the debt was owed had actually been enjoyed: whether it be exclusive possession of property, or exclusive 'use' of labour services.[36] Because debt shifted the focus away from the agreement between the parties, towards its proprietary effects,[37] its application to claims for wages illustrates the pervasiveness of property ideas in the emerging law of master and servant. The premise underpinning these developments was that, the employer having enjoyed the benefit of the service that constituted the subject matter of the 'grant', the worker had become absolutely entitled to the wage that was due for its enjoyment.[38] Given that the obligation to pay both rent and wages presupposed that the obligation on the other side of the contract had been fully performed, neither could be claimed until the end of the 'hiring period.[39]

[34] Alfred Simpson, *A History of the Common Law of Contract: The Rise of the Action of Assumpsit* (OUP 1987) 79–80.

[35] George Hall, *The Treatise on the Laws and Customs of the Realm of England Commonly Called Glanvill* (Clarendon Press 1993); *Alice's Case* (1458) YB 37 Mich Hen 6, fo 8, pl 18.

[36] On what had to be proven in debt, see: (1472) YB Pash 12 Edw 4, f 8, pl 22. See also: David J Ibbetson, *A Historical Introduction to the Law of Obligations* (OUP on Demand 2001) 39. On the point made in the text, see Simpson (n 34) 48.

[37] Ibbetson (n 36) 34.

[38] Simpson (n 34) 48. See also: *Alice's Case* (n 35).

[39] Simpson (n 34) 66. See also: Newton CJ in (1442) YB Mich 21 Hen 6, fo 6, pl 16; (1470) YB Mich 49 Hen 6, fo 47, pl 23; Michael Dalton, *The Country Justice; Containing the Practice of the Justices of the Peace out of Their Sessions. Gathered for the Better Help of Such Justices of Peace as Have Not Been Much Conversant in the Study of the Laws of This Realm.* (W Rawlins and S Roycroft 1690).

Prior to the enactment of the Statute, the options available to an employer were more limited. Service was not, in contrast to wages, reducible to a sum certain that could be claimed as a debt. Employers thus required a means to compel future performance, as well as a right to damages for a failure to perform. The problem was that, under the common law, employers' only remedy lay in trespass,[40] and before the fifteenth century, trespass was only available as a remedy for mis-performance, leaving the employer with no remedy in the event that the worker failed to serve.[41] That trespass was available at all to an employer might be taken as an indication of how the 'harm' was conceived: not as a breach of promise, but as a wrongful interference with some property to which the employer was entitled.[42] A similar action was thus available against a third party for retaining or harbouring another person's servant.[43]

Despite the relative paucity of remedies available to an employer, however, local courts had often provided employers with a right to compel a servant to serve, extending the remedy that had been available to the Lord to recover rent services from a tenant in arrears.[44] It was a combination of these ideas that came to be embedded in the Statute. The Statute made it a criminal offence for a worker to depart from service. The courts equated this with any act of wilful disobedience and elaborated from it both a civil action for damages, and a right to compel the servant to serve.[45] The statutory action for departure had thus been conceived as a tortious action, an extension of the common law action that was available against third parties.[46] The underlying premise seems to have been that the worker, as opposed to a third party, had wrongfully interfered with the employer's rights in his worker's service, giving the employer a right to recover the property of which he had been deprived.

The Statute of Labourers, influenced by the structure of the common law writ actions, and building on local bylaws and customs, set the framework through which the service relation was to develop.[47] Many of its provisions were consolidated and

[40] Recognized in: 23 Edw III (1349); 25 Edw III (1351). See: David Ibbetson, 'Assumpsit and Debt in the Early Sixteenth Century: The Origins of the Indebitatus Count' (1982) 41 The Cambridge Law Journal 142, 153.

[41] Ibbetson (n 36) 81. However, the courts recognized an action for departure from the Statute for a purely executory contract as early as 1367: (1367) YB Mich 41 Edw 3, fo 20a, pl 4. See also: (1373) YB Mich 47 Edw 3, fo 14a, pl 14.

[42] Madonna J Hettinger, 'Defining the Servant: Legal and Extra-Legal Terms of Employment in Fifteenth-Century England' in Allen J Frantzen and Douglas Moffat (eds), *The Work of Work: Servitude, Slavery, and Labor in Medieval England* (Cruithne Press 1994) 206, 218.

[43] On this interpretation, see Simpson (n 34) 48.

[44] Putnam (n 20) 74. The Lord could bring the writ of customs and services to recover rent services from a tenant in arrears. This mirrored the writ of right which lay to recover the land. On this, see: Ibbetson (n 36) 37.

[45] Putnam (n 20) 195. On wilful disobedience and departure see: Dalton (n 39) 94.

[46] Simpson (n 34) 48.

[47] Strengthened through additional statutes throughout the fourteenth century: (1388) 12 Richard II c 4; (1390) 13 Richard II Stat 1 c 8.

extended in the Statute of Artificers 1563, and it was this that provided the legal framework for the regulation of the labour until the nineteenth century.[48] The Statute of Labourers' origins in the declining system of feudal tenure, and its link with the developing institution of the lease, had a profound influence on the way in which this system was to develop. Enacted in part to supplement the customary mechanisms that were beginning to break down, and in part to fill a gap in the common law writ actions, the Statute had firmly embedded in labour law discourse a model of service as a property relation in which certain mutual obligations were implied. Providing employers with a remedy in the event of departure, a good defence to which was the employer's failure to adequately maintain him, the statute made it possible to read-in to the employer's property in service, a servant's right to wages and to be maintained. In combination, this provided a form of 'social wage', a functional substitute for the tenant's right to occupy land in exchange for his Lord's right to his services.[49]

The gradual differentiation of the landlord and employer functions that was taking place throughout the fourteenth and fifteenth centuries did little to change the significance of 'tenure' as a mechanism for guaranteeing the distribution of land and labour in the emerging agricultural economy: the premise that, in respect of land and labour, concurrent interests in the property 'hired' gives rise to mutual rights and obligations that makes it possible to balance the competing interests of owner, hirer, and the community at large. Privity of estate between the parties to the lease, for example, expressed the idea that the existence of concurrent interests in land gave rise to a set of mutual obligations designed to balance the interests of the parties.[50] The lessor's obligation to provide peaceful enjoyment thus presupposed the lessee's obligation to pay rent and to maintain the land and keep it in good repair. In the master and servant context, it is possible to identify a similar idea of privity, even if not explicitly recognized by the courts, a sort of 'privity of service': an *exclusive* relationship into which the courts would rarely intervene. The mutual obligations that this exclusivity implied helped to protect the worker from exploitation (physical and economic harm), while at the same time facilitating the use of his labour by his employer. The common law thus recognized an employer's rights in labour *conditionally*, ensuring that employers would provide servants with adequate food and board, while ensuring that the latter could not take advantage of their employers by making their right to wages conditional on their loyalty and obedience.[51] The common law was thus gradually

48 (1563) 5 Eliz 1 c 4 'Statute of Artificers'.

49 Failure to provide adequate food and board was a good defence to an action for departure: Richard Burn, *The Justice of the Peace, and Parish Officer / by Richard Burn*, vol IV (12th edn, Butterworths 1805) 246–47.

50 William Searle Holdsworth, *A History of English Law*, vol 1 (Methuen 1922) 1:vii, 268 onwards; Simpson (n 34) 19, 46.

51 See, for example: *Hawkesworth and Hillary's Case* 85 ER 435; (1668) 1 Saund 314 discussing the obligations of a master and his apprentice.

paving the way for the emergence of the labour commodity, something that could be used by an employer free from interference; securing the worker's cooperation, but doing so in a way that would be socially, and economically, sustainable. In order to do this, however, it drew more on customary considerations, and concerns of public policy rooted in historic property law ideas, than it did the emerging principles of contract law in which the evolving service relation was gradually being embedded.

5.3 The Evolution and Decline of the Subsistence Wage

By the sixteenth century, most of the land held in England was being held on economic leases, with rents set by law and/or custom increasingly rare; most rents were now being set by the market.[52] In this context, landlords would offer leases to the highest bidder at whatever rent the market would bear, and this provided an incentive to convert the remaining customary holdings to leasehold.[53] In this context, enclosing the land became extremely important. Enclosure increased the revenue that could be gained from the land, and, in this, landowners' interests were aligned with those of the emerging class of tenants who wanted to be able to use the land to make a profit. Large landholdings and technological advancement were essential if tenants were to be sufficiently competitive to meet their rental obligations.[54] In time, the less competitive farmers lost their land, as the more competitive tenants squeezed them out of the market.

This process was a gradual one, and the emergence of a market in leases in no way led, immediately, to generalized wage dependence. In fact, complete wage dependence remained a rarity throughout much of the sixteenth and seventeenth centuries, even though households were becoming increasingly dependent on the market to meet their daily subsistence needs. Prior to the parliamentary enclosures of the eighteenth century, most households could still engage in some form of subsistence farming on the remaining common land, and/or could produce goods that could be traded in the market.[55] Engaging in wage labour was, for most, still only a supplementary source of income, the necessity of which fluctuated considerably season to season.[56]

[52] Wood (n 16), 102–03. Even remaining customary leases that gave rise to greater security of tenure exposed tenants to competitive pressures.

[53] ibid 101.

[54] ibid 103. See also: Robert Brenner, 'The Origins of Capitalist Development: A Critique of Neo-Smithian Marxism' [1977] New Left Review 25.

[55] Wood (n 16), 131.

[56] ibid. See also: Daunton (n 16) 422.

5.3.1 The Statute of Artificers and the Law of Settlement

The Statute of Artificers 1563 was the central piece of labour legislation from the sixteenth to the early nineteenth century. Having re-enacted and extended many of the provisions of the Statute of Labourers, it also made possible the adjustment of wage rates in line with inflation, empowering magistrates to set wages by reference to prices.[57] Legal control over wages, combined with new provisions on apprenticeships, requiring a seven-year apprenticeship as a pre-requisite for employment in a trade, slowed down the development of the labour market in both agriculture and the trades.[58] Despite the emerging market in leases, therefore, wage competition was still largely precluded; a legal compulsion to work and state controls over labour mobility were still the principal mechanisms guaranteeing the distribution and utilization of labour—rather than, for example, a competitive market in labour power. Moreover, in the regulated trades, capitalist forms of employment remained effectively unlawful, and medieval guilds continued to exercise considerable influence over production, wages, and prices.

The Statute of Artificers formed part of a much broader regulatory framework of which the poor law system was an important part. Various types of poor law had been provided since medieval times, and these were developed throughout the sixteenth century through a series of enactments that culminated in the legislation of 1597 and 1601.[59] In this arrangement, the parish was pivotal. Each parish was responsible for appointing 'overseers' to provide relief to the impotent and able-bodied poor, whether in the form of work, or direct relief. Relief was provided on an individual basis, there being no national standard or framework.[60] The overseers were accountable to the local ratepayers, but their appointment and parish accounts were ratified annually by local Justices of the Peace at the Sessions, providing a check on abuse of power.[61]

This tax-funded poor law was possible in England because of the strong centralized state; this provided a framework within which over 15,000 separate parishes could operate. Even so, disputes between parishes were common, with parishes eager to avoid responsibility for paupers moving into the parish in search of work. It was in this context that the Settlement Act of 1662 was enacted, imposing a

[57] Earlier Acts had set national maximum wage rates: (1514) 6 Henry VIII c 3 and (1515) 7 Henry VIII c 5. See also (1445) 23 Henry VI c 13. The new provisions were enacted in the Statute of Artificers, sections 15–19.

[58] Simon Deakin and Frank Wilkinson, *The Law of the Labour Market Industrialization, Employment, and Legal Evolution* (OUP 2005) 206–07

[59] Poor Relief Act, 39 Eliz I c 3 (1597); Poor Relief Act 1601 (43 Eliz I c 2).

[60] Raymond Cocks, *The Poor Law* (OUP 2010)

[61] There is an extensive literature on the poor law. See particularly: Francis Charles Montague, 'The Law of Settlement and Removal' (1888) 4 Law Quarterly Review 40–45; Lorie Charlesworth, 'The Poor Law: A Modern Legal Analysis' (1999) 2 Journal of Social Security Law 79–92; Ross Cranston, *Legal Foundations of the Welfare State* (Weidenfeld and Nicolson 1985).

legal obligation on a parish to provide for its 'settled' poor, laying down the conditions under which a settlement would be gained, triggering the obligations of the parish.[62] One head of settlement was 'service', thereby allowing a pauper to claim a settlement in a parish in which he had served for a full year.

The concept of the settlement was based on feudal ideas about people's ties to particular locations; the idea that land, service, and social protection went hand in hand. Every person, whether villein or free, was seen as a member of some local community to which he/she owed obligations and from which he/she was entitled to some measure of protection; and, when in need, some undefined support. It was these premises that the Elizabethan system of poor law relief expressed.[63]

During this period, the relationship between master and servant, a condition for both statutory wages and the right to settlement (and thus poor relief) was conceptualized as an exclusive property relationship between an employer and the servant's service. It was characterized by the former's exclusive and continuous control over the servant throughout the duration of the hiring, distinguished from the relationship between an employer and a day-labourer, hired by the job or task, by the exclusivity of the relationship and the extent of control. This emerging distinction parallelled similar developments in the law of leases where exclusive possession and control determined the boundaries between a lease and a licence, a boundary that was crucial to an occupier's claim to a settlement under the (alternative) head of renting premises at £10 a year.[64]

Feudal ideas of tenure thus profoundly shaped how both the lease, and service relation, came to be conceived. The capitalist labour relationship did not emerge out of thin air, but was crafted from the existing structures, ideas, and beliefs, of previous periods. Each of these fundamental relations thus took the form, in law, of a property relationship which implied certain mutual rights and obligations, characterized by one party's exclusive possession of an important social resource that was ultimately held 'of' or 'for' its owner, and ultimately, the broader community. In order to give substance to these rights, however, it was necessary for the 'owner' to have excluded himself from interfering with the other party's possession for the duration of the hiring. This was given legal expression in the servant's open-ended obligation of obedience, and the lessor's obligation to provide peaceful enjoyment of land.[65] But the reciprocal or mutual nature of these transactions was implicit; employers and lessors could only enforce these obligations if they undertook to maintain and protect the 'property' in their control. For this reason, the courts

[62] Settlement Act 1662 (13 & 14 Charles II c 12).

[63] Sidney Webb and Beatrice Webb, *English Local Government: English Poor Law History* (Longmans, Green & Company 1929) 314.

[64] *Anon* (1703) 6 Mod 33. See: Wonnacott (n 18) 39–41.

[65] From 1598, it appears that such would be implied from the relationship of landlord and tenant: Wonnacott (n 18) 178.

would read-in, as a matter of policy, these 'maintenance' obligations so as to render the transactions enforceable.[66]

The centrality of property ideas during this period was such that the relationship between the employer and his servant's service was conceptualized as if it were independent from, and took primacy over, the contract between the parties. It was not 'public law' or notions of 'public policy' per se that took precedence, therefore, but the property law principles through which social life in England had long been governed. As a result of this, however, it was actual enjoyment of the property rather than the promise to deliver it, which provided the basis of the parties' ongoing relationship. In relation to land, the obligation to pay rent issued from the land, and could be claimed from anyone enjoying exclusive possession as of right—even if that person had not been party to the original contract. Similar principles were applicable to the service relation; the right to wages 'issued' from the enjoyment of service rather than from the contract. The courts would thus imply a promise to pay from the fact of the service, and thus derive the 'hiring' from the service rather than vice versa. The statutory requirement for a hiring for a year (to claim poor relief) could thus be satisfied either by proof of the agreement, or by evidence of service:[67] 'a contract of hiring may be inferred from the pauper having served a year as a husbandman',[68] 'having served three years as a menial servant, though at first hired for only part of a year',[69] or having 'lived three years as an ostler'[70] the position being that 'a hiring will be presumed from a general service'.[71]

Contracts of service were not extra-legal realities that arose as a result of a free agreement. Rather, they were legally constructed, imputed to dependent labour relationships where there was evidence that a service relationship had come into being, a mechanism through which to give expression to the rights and obligations that were implied as a matter of law, based, however, on long-standing customary understandings of the rights and obligations enjoyed by different groups within a community. This 'active' role assumed by the courts, that is, their reluctance to 'defer' to some abstract notion of 'free contracting' was perfectly consistent with

[66] In the medieval period, it was usual for a tenant to covenant to return the property at the end of the term in the same condition as when the lease had been granted, except in London, Norfolk, and Ely. By the nineteenth century those customs were obsolete, and the usual tenant's covenant had become what it is today: a full covenant to keep and deliver up the demised premises in repair. *Hampshire v Wickens* (1878) 7 Ch D 555. See: Wonnacott (n 18) 184.

[67] *The Parish of Brightwell v the Parish of Henley* (1714) 10 Mod 287, 88 ER 731; *The Inhabitants of Overton v Steventon* (1703) Fortescue 316, 92 ER 869.

[68] *R v The Inhabitants of Lyth* (1793) 5 Term Rep 327, 101 ER 183.

[69] *R v The Inhabitants of Long Whatton* (1793) 5 Term Rep 447, 101 ER 252.

[70] *R v Holy Trinity in Wareham* Cald 141, 2 Bott 539, cited in *R v The Inhabitants of Weyhill* (1760) 1 Wm Bl 206, 207, 96 ER 113.

[71] *Crediton and Wincanton* (1749) Burr Sett Ca 299, cited in *R v The Inhabitants of Weyhill* at 206. But this presumption may be rebutted by facts showing that the relation of master and servant did not exist: *R v Walton* (1790) 3 Term Rep 515, 100 ER 708.

the common law's historic role as guardian of the 'King's' land. Of course, the line between the express and implied contract was blurred by the fact that most labour agreements were oral and informal anyway, and so could only be inferred from evidence of how the parties conducted themselves in practice. Even so, the emphasis was always on the nature of the relationship, this being different from the question of the legal form that would be imputed to that relationship with a view to regulating it.

From the sixteenth century, assumpsit (an action for breach of an (often oral) promise) came to be preferred over debt as a basis for enforcing the labour agreement. Even so, the courts continued to treat the indebtedness, rather than any promise between the parties, as the basis of the obligation. Provided there was proof of service, therefore, they would imply a promise to pay so that the agreement was 'mutual' and so could be enforced.[72] This made the central question for the courts, both in the settlement cases and in claims for wages, whether the master had enjoyed exclusive control over his 'servant' for the full duration of the hiring. The existence of an antecedent promise to serve, or to pay, thus continued to be relevant only if service had not commenced.[73] The right to wages would thus be readily implied, for 'if a man retaineth a labourer or servant to serve him according to [the] statute (of Artificers) though no wages be spoken of upon the retainer, yet the retainer is good, and they shall have such wages as is affected and appointed by Proclamation'.[74] This position was summarized in the nineteenth century where it was emphasized that:

> ... the fact of the service is always capable of distinct proof; *for it is collateral and subsequent to the contract itself*. The pauper served ... he served without any thing being said as to wages. The stress of the argument seems rather to show that there were no certain wages reserved than that there was no hiring ... if the rate of wages were not specified, he would be entitled to reasonable wages.[75]

The 'fact of service' was also pivotal when it came to the master's action for departure. In order to enforce his right to his servant's service in the event that the servant departed from work, the master had to show that he had such a right. This could be implied from the existence of a contract, or, more commonly, evidence of a relationship from which such a contract could be implied. What this meant in practice was that the action was available even if there was no legally

[72] David J Ibbetson, 'Consideration and the Theory of Contract in Sixteenth Century Common Law' in John Barton (ed), *Towards a General Law of Contract* (Duncker & Humblot 1990) 67, 84.

[73] See: *R v Buckingham* (1834) 5 B & Ad 953, 110 ER 1043. See also Lord Kenyon's judgment in *R v Hilton*, 5 TR 672, discussed in: William Theobald, *A Practical Treatise on the Poor Laws, as Altered by the Poor Law Amendment Act ... and an Appendix of the Statutes, Etc* (Sweet, Stevens & Sons 1836) 352.

[74] See: Dalton (n 39) 92.

[75] *R v The Inhabitants of Pendleton* (1812) 15 East 449, 450–51, 104 ER 913, 914–15 (emphasis added).

binding covenant to serve; a hiring (a contract) would be presumed if service had commenced.[76]

5.3.2 The Exceptive Hiring

By the end of the eighteenth century the individuals appearing before the courts in settlement claims were no longer confined to adolescent agricultural or domestic workers, but also included many adults engaged in industry, hired in bulk under standardized, often written, work agreements that set regular hours and clearly defined their duties and rates of pay.[77] The Elizabethan legislative framework was ill-suited to this new context, premised on a society of semi self-sufficient peasant farmers and independent craftsman that was fundamentally at odds with the society that was emerging: one based predominantly on the exploitation of labourers dependent on money wages for subsistence.[78]

It is in this context that the courts developed the concept of the 'exceptive hiring' as a control device, circumscribing the limits of the right to settlement. This concept referred to any contract of service that envisaged periods where 'the master could not have demanded the service at any time throughout the twenty-four hours for the full year'.[79] By invoking this concept, the courts were able to distinguish between those in service, those who alienated their labour absolutely for a fixed period of time, and those that merely sold their labour for wages, excluding the latter from the scope of the wage-fixing and settlement provisions of the Elizabethan framework.

By the turn of the century more and more contracts were being classed as 'exceptive'. This reflected the fact that growing numbers of workers were now being hired in a social and economic context that demanded new forms of work arrangement, ones which were fundamentally at odds with prevailing assumptions about the nature of service. The courts thus began systematically excluding from poor relief all those industrial workers whose contracts reserved to them *any* time during which they were free from their master's proprietary control. Restrictions on hours of work, a right to a day's holiday or time away with friends, or to terminate the contract on short notice, were all classed as exceptions in the contract capable of

[76] (1443) YB Mich 21 Hen 6, fo 8b–9b, pl 19 (concerning an action against a third party for beating a servant where there was no express covenant, but there was evidence of actual service).

[77] *R v Birmingham; R v Kingswinford* (1791) 4 Term Rep 219, 100 ER 983; *R v Norton Bavant* (1835) 3 Ad & El 161, 111 ER 374; *R v The Inhabitants of Mitcham* (1810) 12 East 351, 104 ER 137. But contrast with: *R v The Inhabitants of Hampreston* (1793) 5 Term Rep 205, 101 ER 116; *R v The Inhabitants of Great Yarmouth* (1816) 5 M & S 114, 105 ER 993.

[78] Žmolek (n 15) 555.

[79] *R v The Inhabitants of St Helen's Aukland* (1833) 4 B & Ad 718, 110 ER 626, cited in *The Law Journal for the Year 1832-1949: Comprising Reports of Cases in the Courts of Chancery, King's Bench, Common Pleas, Exchequer of Pleas, and Exchequer of Chamber, 58* (EB Ince 1832).

depriving the worker of a settlement.[80] The essence of the exceptive hiring was thus that the relationship was discontinuous, it did not confer upon the master property in service for a pre-determined period of time but made provision for certain excepted periods during which 'there is not the relation of master and servant'. This was because 'in each short period that is excepted . . . the master would not have dominion over the servant'.[81] Even the possibility of returning home after the factory closed at the end of the day, or remaining at home on Sundays, negated the existence of service: 'a right of control and authority, at least so far as it relates to the general discipline and government of the servant, must reside in the master at all times during the continuance of the service'.[82] A distinction was thus emerging between what was gradually being seen as the epitome of 'free wage labour', a relationship based on exchange, and 'service', a relationship founded in property law principles and to which traditional/customary labour law norms continued to apply.

5.4 An Emerging Market in Labour Power

By the end of the eighteenth century, centuries of enclosures had been concentrating land in the hands of a privileged few. Domestic manufacture and factory industry expanded as growing numbers of people looked to wage labour as their primary, or sole, source of subsistence. This, and the population growth that a rapidly increasing food supply facilitated, contributed to the growing number of workers who were now being employed in manufacturing enterprises in the towns. The developments taking place in agriculture from the fourteenth century onwards had thus gradually paved the way for the emergence of industry. The gradual dispossession of customary tenants and the market dependency that followed had helped to foster the development of cottage industries and the growth of the national market. The result was a large home market for cheaply produced, cost-effective goods, and a 'free' labour force that could be hired to produce it.[83]

During the course of the eighteenth century, the practice of paying money wages had become increasingly common. Money wages and living out was gradually replacing living in and benefits in kind as even agricultural employers sought to respond to higher wage costs by shifting the costs of subsistence onto their workers.[84] Even in agriculture, the practice of paying money wages had slowly freed the labour relation from 'customary' forms of regulation and associated ideas of tenure, much as the commutation of labour rents had in respect of land-holding centuries

[80] *R v Green, Overseers of the Poor of Gateshead* (1852) 17 QB 793, 117 ER 1485. See: Theobald (n 73) 345–57.
[81] ibid 345.
[82] *R v St Helen's Aukland* (n 79).
[83] Wood (n 16), 140–41.
[84] Eric Hobsbawm and George Rude, *Captain Swing* (new edn, Phoenix 2001) 44–47.

before. The growing number of persons receiving cash payments in poor relief also facilitated this process, for this too contributed to the market dependence that would fuel the development of the industrial economy.[85]

Even so, at the start of the century, money income was still only part of a wider package of entitlements: from employers, the Church, charity, and also certain remaining common rights, such as foraging (for agricultural workers). Towards the end of the century, however, when wartime inflation, combined with grain shortages, drove the price of wheat to previously unseen heights, the drive towards substituting living in and benefits in kind with money wages increased, along with rural unemployment.[86] Remuneration was becoming much more a matter of money wages paid by an employer, thereby eroding the importance of perquisites—something which employers were keen to avoid, as they were open to manipulation by workers. The only fringe benefits that survived were under the control of employers; a reward for loyalty and a means for securing deference.[87]

From the end of the eighteenth century, the number of wage assessments had rapidly declined and the higher courts had become increasingly hostile to workers' attempts to compel magistrates to set wage rates.[88] At the same time, the apprenticeship provisions of the Statute of Artificers had fallen into disuse and the right to settlement was being interpreted so narrowly that poor relief was being denied not just to the emerging class of industrial workers but also to many domestic servants and servants in husbandry.[89] This reflected a shift in the prevailing orthodoxy, the emergence of a new political economy committed to 'freedom of trade'.

5.4.1 The Master and Servant Legislation

In a context in which more and more workers were falling outside the scope of the wage-fixing and apprenticeship provisions of the Statute of Artificers, Parliament introduced a new body of legislation concerned with regulating the relationship between 'master and servant'. The Master and Servant Acts, first introduced in 1747, re-enacted and considerably extended the provisions of the Statute of Artificers. The Acts thus extended the sanctions imposed for departure or breaches of work discipline, and over time included within their scope a much broader class

[85] Žmolek (n 15) 357–58.
[86] ibid 553.
[87] Martin Daunton, *Wealth and Welfare: An Economic and Social History of Britain 1851-1951* (OUP 2007) 424.
[88] Deakin and Wilkinson (n 58) 23. See: Lord Ellenborough in *R v Kent Justices* (1811) 14 East 395, 399–400, 104 ER 653.
[89] See for example: Richard Burn, *The Justice of the Peace and Parish Officer* (W Strahan & W Woodfall 1785) 3: 439–40. Here, the fact that the hours of work for a Shearman were limited also had the effect of denying the right to settlement, the limits being construed as evidence of an exceptive hiring.

of person, while further relaxing the assumption as to an annual hiring. Despite bearing a close resemblance to the Statute of Artificers in a number of respects, the underlying rationale was quite different. As Deakin and Wilkinson have argued, the new Acts 'aimed to impose a more rigorous system of work discipline upon the growing numbers of labourers, artisans and outworkers employed in manufacturing, as well as maintai[n] control of the agricultural labour market at a time of considerable upheaval'.[90] Particularly from 1823, there was thus a decisive shift in emphasis away from state control of the economy, towards more direct support for employer control over workers in production, largely through criminal penalties for breach of contract.[91]

The Master and Servant Acts were enacted at a time when the living habits and consumption patterns of the working classes was of particular concern to employers, and the problem of labour discipline subject to much scholarly, and public, debate. Investment in new machinery and production processes in the context of factory production would not be possible without new forms of work discipline and diligence. There was particular concern in this context that high wages would only exacerbate the problem of labour discipline, with Arthur Young saying in 1771 that 'everyone but an idiot knows that the lower classes must be kept poor or they will never be industrious'.[92] There was thus considerable hostility towards any form of legislation designed to regulate wages, and the idea that a master had an absolute obligation to provide for his worker's subsistence needs was falling decisively out of favour.

Prior to the nineteenth century, as we have seen, where a worker without visible means of subsistence contracted to serve, the courts presumed this to be a hiring for a year that would be subject to the labour and poor relief statutes, with the master bound to maintain him for the full year.[93] In the early nineteenth century, this was parallelled by a similar attitude towards industrial workers, with the courts refusing to enforce contracts where the employer sought to retain servants for long periods without promising to maintain them or employ them so as to provide a regular wage. The basic premise was that 'if the [contract of service] withdraws the workman from labouring for the community generally, without any obligation on the masters to employ him, it is invalid, and would be void for want of mutuality'.[94]

Prior to the mid-nineteenth century, the service relation, as something to which statutory wage rates and common law mutual obligations applied thereby occupied

[90] Deakin and Wilkinson (n 58) 52.

[91] 10 Geo IV c 52.

[92] Daunton (n 16) 175.

[93] Douglas Hay and Paul Craven, 'Master and Servant in England and the Empire: A Comparative Study' (1993) 31 Labour/Le Travail 175, 66.

[94] *Pilkington v Scott* (1846) 15 M & W 657, 659, 153 ER 1014 (argument for the labourer). This was upheld by the courts in a number of cases prior to Pilkington: *Sykes v Dixon* (1839) 9 Ad & El 693, 112 ER 1374.

the field as regards (dependent) wage labour.[95] Even for the purposes of the early Master and Servant Acts the courts were emphatic that a contract of service differed from an ordinary contract between legal equals. It envisaged a particular type of relation between master and servant and, to be enforceable, there had to be something provided in consideration for the service itself and not just wages for work:

> The answer to the objection [that there was no consideration] was, that a consideration for the promise would necessarily result, because the plaintiff had paid Bradley for his labour. But so he must have done under any contract; the work must have been balanced by wages; but there is no consideration for the workman's hiring himself to the plaintiff exclusively.[96]

Despite a much broader interpretation in *Lowther v Earl Radnor* in 1806, piece-rate workers, and those not hired to serve a single master exclusively, were thus implicitly excluded from the scope of the Master and Servant Acts, as were 'domestic servants' or those engaged in 'menial' service.[97] The concept of 'service' continued to be confined to those who did not stand 'in the position of two contracting parties' but in the 'relation of master and servant', selling their entire capacity to work, rather than commodified labour.[98] It was with these workers only that the courts associated the concept of service, and its corollary, the implied right to subsistence. This was so whether this took effect through an implied obligation to retain and employ, or through the implied right to be protected and maintained.

Following the Poor Law Amendment Act (1834) and the repeal of settlement by hiring, however, the courts began to take a much more restrictive approach when it came to the personal scope of the master and servant legislation. This reflected their growing hostility towards any form of labour legislation designed to 'protect' the interests of workers.[99] By the middle of the century, they had thus fallen into line with parliament's intention to extend the Act beyond 'servants' in the traditional sense to wage workers generally, anyone who 'contracts ... to serve ...for any time or times whatsoever, *or in any other manner*'[100] including skilled artisans and piece-rate workers not bound to serve one master exclusively for a minimum term.[101] Extending the legislation in this way made available to employers on a

[95] Casual or day labourers were distinguished in legal discourse from servants hired to complete a specific job or task, usually as a supplement to other forms of subsistence. See: Steinfeld (n 95).

[96] *Sykes v Dixon* (1839) 9 Ad & E 393, 112 ER 1374, 8 LJ QB 102, 103–04, cited in Robert J Steinfeld, *Coercion, Contract, and Free Labor in the Nineteenth Century* (CUP 2001) 106.

[97] *Lowther v The Earl of Radnor* (1806) 8 East 113, 103 ER 287. On domestic servants, see: *Kitchen v Shaw* (1837) 6 Ad & El 729, 112 ER 280.

[98] *Lancaster v Greaves* (1829) 9 B & C 628, 109 ER 233; *Hardy v Ryle* (1829) 9 B & C 603, 109 ER 224.

[99] The old poor law was repealed in 1834 and the Statute of Artificers in 1813 by: 53 Geo 3 c 40.

[100] 10 Geo IV c 34 (emphasis added).

[101] *Hartley v Cummings* (1846) 2 Car & K 433, 175 ER 180; *Pilkington v Scott* (n 94); *Lawrence v Todd* (1863) 14 CB NS 554, 143 ER 562; *Re Bailey* (1854) 3 El & Bl 607, 118 ER 1269.

more or less general, or universal basis, criminal remedies as a means for controlling labour.

In this way, for the purposes of the Master and Servant Acts at least, the concept of service had gradually shed ideas associated with the distinctive property relationship between master and servant prevalent in the fifteenth to seventeenth centuries, with the term servant increasingly being used to refer simply to all those who, in one capacity or another, sold their labour power for wages. Only higher-status managerial employees and domestic servants were consistently excluded from the scope of the Master and Servant legislation.[102] In order that contracts at piece wages that sought to bind workers to the employer for long periods of time not be void for 'want of mutuality' moreover, the courts proved increasingly willing to imply an obligation to retain and employ so as not to deprive an employer of the criminal penalties under the Acts.[103] This did not mean that workers had an enforceable right to be paid during lay-off, however, nor any right to a guaranteed minimum amount of work or pay. Rather than implying an obligation to pay where work was not actually provided, therefore, the quid pro quo for service became not a subsistence or social wage (whether a right to be maintained, or, its equivalent, a guaranteed minimum income), but an obligation to provide work in accordance with the state of the trade.[104] Abstract ideas about market 'forces' were thus beginning to set limits on the rights that workers might enjoy in the context of employment.

5.4.2 Free Trade and the Combination Laws

The idea that an employer ought to bear the costs of his worker's subsistence had fallen out of favour throughout the eighteenth century, alongside the Poor Law and the Speenhamland system with which the latter (wrongly) came to be associated.[105] To followers of Adam Smith, the laws of settlement were a restraint on free trade, and the institution of service an affront to freedom and independence.[106] To followers of Ricardo and Malthus, they reflected alternatives to the market as a mechanism for securing an efficient allocation of resources, one that was liable to distort the distinctive incentive structure that lies at the heart of capitalist wage labour.[107] These institutions moved resources out of the real economy, 'interfering' with the laws of supply

[102] *Branwell v Penneck* (1827) 7 B & C 536, 108 ER 823.

[103] *R v Welch* (1853) 2 El & Bl 362, 118 ER 800, 802 (Lord Denman); *Pilkington v Scott* (n 94).

[104] See: *R v Welch* (n 103); *Pilkington v Scott* (n 94).

[105] Adam Smith, *An Inquiry into the Nature and Causes of the Wealth of Nations* (W Strahan and T Cadell 1776) Book 1, 98–99. See also his criticism of slavery on similar grounds, 387.

[106] ibid Chapter 10; Chapter 2.

[107] David Ricardo, *On the Principles of Political Economy, and Taxation* (John Murray 1821) 61.

and demand, thereby reducing the stock of resources available to be paid as wages.[108]

These ideas underpinned the rejection of Samuel Whitbread's Minimum Wage Bill in 1793 and 1800[109] and the Poor Law Commissioners' Report of 1834.[110] By the early nineteenth century, state control of wages and poor relief had been firmly rejected in favour of the more efficient and less coercive mechanism of free competition in the market. Promoting the free circulation of labour had thus become a central tenet of social and economic policy, with the political environment extremely hostile to the very idea of legally regulated wages. As William Pitt argued:

> Trade industry and barter would always find their own level, and be impeded by regulations which impeded their natural operation . . . to promote free circulation of labour . . . would go far to remedy the evils [of low pay].[111]

In line with these ideas, employers were increasingly relying on wages as a substitute for direct control over the labour process. Payment by output was also more common, seen as a way to incentivize workers to maintain a reasonable pace of work. This coincided with a move away from long to short-term hirings, and thus greater precocity and insecurity for the workforce as a whole.[112] As a result, the problem of labour unrest came to be placed at the heart of policy debates over the regulation of labour.

Restrictions on combinations had initially emerged as an integral part of a system of wage-fixing and centralized trade regulation, implied by the wage-fixing and apprenticeship provisions of the Statute of Artificers. In response to labour unrest throughout the eighteenth century, further statutes were passed with a view to targeting combinations in specific industries. The first was enacted in 1720 in the tailor trade, and rendered void and illegal agreements to increase wages.[113] Further targeted legislation followed in a number of trades, followed by a more general combination law in 1749, all of which were linked to some form of wage-fixing machinery.[114] By the end of the century, however, these Acts had been replaced by the Act of 1799 which, for the first time, enacted a general prohibition on worker combinations not coupled by any attempt to regulate wages.[115]

In prior legislation, therefore, prohibitions on combination had been implicit in, and largely incidental to, the regulation of industry; the quid pro quo for which

[108] Žmolek (n 15) 729–30.
[109] Samantha Williams, *Poverty, Gender and Life-Cycle Under the English Poor Law, 1760-1834* (Boydell & Brewer Ltd 2013) 94.
[110] ibid.
[111] William Cobbett, *Cobbett's Parliamentary History of England*, vol 2 (R Bagshaw 1807) 2:703–11.
[112] Daunton (n 16) 182.
[113] 9 Geo I c 27, 12 Geo I c 34, and 13 Geo II c 8.
[114] 22 Geo II c 27.
[115] 39 Geo III c 81. A further Act supplementing this was passed in 1800: 39 & 40 Geo III c 106.

being provisions for setting wages and hours and/or prohibitions on payment in truck. By the turn of the century, however, wage regulation had been abandoned, and with it (decentralized) state control over the economy. In its place, there existed general legislative and common law prohibitions on combinations and a system of wage regulation based entirely on individual freedom of contract (albeit one in relation to which unequal remedies for breach applied).[116]

Closely linked with these attitudes was a growing opposition to the guilds and apprenticeship system. Before the end of the eighteenth century, compulsory apprenticeship and customary wage rates had effectively barred the emergence of capitalist forms of employment in manufacture.[117] Growing divergence of interests between masters and journeymen throughout the century, however, had given new colour to the growing swathes of regulation designed more specifically to suppress worker combinations and facilitate free trade. The hostile attitude towards combination was thus a symptom of a much more widespread feeling of discontent with state control over the economy.

By the 1820s, however, economic orthodoxy was shifting. McCulloch and Hume, supporters of the MP and social reformer Francis Place's Repeal Bill, had made their case for repeal of the combination laws by arguing that unions were incapable of forcing wages above their natural level.[118] The market was itself best placed to keep wages in check, and so would prevent any 'distortions' taking place. If the wage is an objective sum that is fixed by supply and demand, in other words, 'combinations' are not interferences in the market, but part of the process through which free competition ensures the emergence of a 'competitive' wage. The combination laws were unnecessary therefore, and by increasing hostility actually posed a threat to continuous and stable production. It was thus now the *laws against* combination, rather than unions, which were liable to 'distort' the market.[119]

In 1825, the combination laws were repealed, and common action in pursuit of raising wages was legalized.[120] In fact, however, due to developments in the common law of conspiracy and restraint of trade, there was still little scope for collective bargaining.[121] The principle of collective wage-setting mechanisms was thus accepted, but only grudgingly, and parliament made little attempt to directly facilitate it; leaving this, like all other things, to the market.

[116] John V Orth, *Combination and Conspiracy: A Legal History of Trade Unionism, 1721-1906* (OUP 1991) 67.

[117] Deakin and Wilkinson (n 58) Chapter 2. See also: James Andrew Schmiechen, 'Sweated Industries and Sweated Labor: A Study of Industrial Disorganization and Worker Attitudes in the London Clothing Trades, 1867–1909' (1976) 36 The Journal of Economic History 283.

[118] Orth (n 116) 69; John Rule, *The Labouring Classes in Early Industrial England, 1750-1850* (Routledge 2014) 285; Žmolek (n 15) 665.

[119] Žmolek (n 15) 663.

[120] 6 Geo 4 c 129.

[121] *R v Rowlands and Duffield* (1851) 17 QB 671, 117 ER 1439; *O'Neill v Longman* (1863) 4 B & S 376, 122 ER 500; *Walsby v Anley* (1861) 3 El & El 516, 121 E.R. 536.

By the mid-nineteenth century, therefore, space for collective wage-setting mechanisms had formally increased, but for the growing army of 'sweated' workers, the scope for improving terms and conditions through collective mechanisms was marginal. This was compounded by the dispersed and isolated conditions in which many of these workers worked, the effects of which was exacerbated by the fact that the once comprehensive system of outdoor relief had, by virtue of the new poor law, been replaced by a constant threat of the workhouse.[122]

The new poor law reflected a fundamental shift in the way that the law–economy relationship was conceived. The poor law commissioners had argued that the withdrawal of relief was essential for combatting idleness among the working classes, ensuring workers would become 'more steady and diligent' so giving farmers a higher return on capital. This would then enable them to pay higher wages.[123] The commissioners thus 'rejected the notion that society was reciprocal and organic, with social order based upon custom, utility, patronage and deference and substituted a view of society based on an interdependent market economy resting of self-interest, competition, and contract'.[124] The new poor law confirmed the dominant ideology that saw the economy as a natural order in which the state had no role to play, a view which was justified by the 'invisible hand of political economy and by evangelical theology'.[125] The report was entirely consistent with broader policy changes during the period: the repeal of the corn laws, the emergence of a full-time police force and a renewed emphasis on systematic, regular punishment, and the complete removal of all forms of regulation of wages and prices.

5.5 Early Labour Market Regulation

By the end of the nineteenth century it had become relatively easy for capitalist entrepreneurs to set up business, capitalizing on the growing market for cheap manufactured goods, and taking advantage of the courts' more lenient approach to the apprenticeship provisions of the Statute of Artificers.[126] Supporting this move was the growing legislative and judicial hostility towards any form of worker combination designed to raise wage rates or interfere with 'free trade'. There was thus little effective opposition to employers not apprenticed to a trade establishing themselves with a view to putting-out artisanal work to cheaper labour so as to circumvent customary wage rates.[127]

122 Deakin and Wilkinson (n 58) 219.
123 Daunton (n 16) 493.
124 ibid.
125 ibid.
126 *Raynard v Chase* (1756) 1 Burr 2, 97 ER 155; *Smith v Company of Armourers* (1792) Peake 199, 170 ER 128; *Coward v Maberley* (1809) 2 Camp 127, 170 ER 1103.
127 See: Kenneth Douglas Brown, *English Labour Movement, 1700-1951* (Gill and Macmillan 1982) 29–30.

Putting-out, or 'outwork' was attractive to employers because most of the burden of adjustment to fluctuations in demand would be borne by workers who could be laid off, whereas a factory incurred capital charges in slack periods.[128] The fixed costs of factories only made economic sense when demand passed a threshold which offered some guarantee of continuous working and the opportunity for savings to be made from having a centralized source of power. For many employers (who, in practice, were very often middlemen hired by master manufacturers to procure a given quantity of goods), therefore, outwork made considerable economic sense, and enabled many small entrepreneurs to compete in a market that was increasingly being dominated by larger firms.

The putting-out system was based upon an intense subdivision of tasks that would once have been performed by a single artisan or craftsman apprenticed to the trade. By parcelling out individual tasks each of which required minimal skill, employers were able to employ relatively unskilled workers at low wages, increasing the supply of labour, and further depressing artisanal wage rates. The greater the subdivision of tasks, the lower the grade of the worker, and the lower the pay; but at the same time, the more easily standardized, monitored, and controlled was a worker now employed by a master with little or no experience in the trade.[129]

This task-based system was not unique to outwork. It was also characteristic of the internal contracting system that prevailed in many of the factories.[130] In both cases, an implication of the subdivision of tasks was that a number of intermediaries were required to coordinate the production process.[131] In the internal contracting system, for example, contractors or supervisors would contract with the master employer to perform a particular job in return for piece rates, and they would then be responsible for hiring workers and paying them to produce the good (or part of it). In this context, many artisans had been able to retain a relatively privileged position because this role often required familiarity with the trade. Nonetheless, the introduction of a middleman into the equation increased the numbers of those interested in appropriating the surplus generated in production, and this further increased the scope for depressing wages.

In industries in which outwork was common, middlemen or intermediaries were primarily responsible for distributing work between outworkers and collecting it and arranging for its sale. For this reason, they did not need to be skilled in the trade. Given that a single product might be passed to a large number of

128 Daunton (n 16) 185.

129 Barbara Drake, 'The Waiter' in Sidney Webb and Arnold James Freeman (eds), *Seasonal Trades* (Constable & Company, Limited 1912) 81.

130 Craig R Littler, *The Development of the Labour Process in Capitalist Societies: A Comparative Study of the Transformation of Work Organization in Britain, Japan, and the USA* (Heinemann Educational Publishers 1982) Chapter 6; Sidney Pollard, 'Factory Discipline in the Industrial Revolution' (1963) 16 The Economic History Review 254.

131 Duncan Bythell, *The Sweated Trades: Outwork in Nineteenth-Century Britain* (St Martin's Press 1978) 18–19.

workers, moreover, these middlemen often had little choice but to produce on speculation.[132] This gave rise to an even greater incentive to manipulate wage rates in order to shift the risk of unforeseen market fluctuation onto the workers. Charging prohibitive rents for tools or machinery, and imposing fines for poor workmanship were just some of the common strategies employed by middlemen, further depressing the wages of the already chronically underpaid.[133]

5.5.1 The Truck Acts

The outwork system was ultimately a technique invoked by employers and contractors to shift onto workers some of the risks and costs associated with production increasingly tailored to a mass-consumer market. This form of work organization was such, however, that depression of wage rates was the only realistic cost-cutting mechanism at the employer's disposal; most of the capital costs involved in the production process were already born by the workers.[134] If there was an increase in demand, it would only be worth switching to more centralized capital intensive production if the upswing could be expected to continue. Otherwise, any pressure on wage rates would soon be offset by the advantages of having excess workers to hand when conditions returned to normal. The outwork system was not only a problem for workers, therefore, but proved detrimental to the progression towards mechanization, vertical integration, and in-house production. So long as outwork labour remained plentiful, with its price falling ever lower, there was little incentive to invest in labour-saving machinery, nor to take on the prohibitive capital cost associated with factory production.[135] The incentives towards vertical integration and factory production were minimal.

Even for employers, however, neither subcontracting nor outwork was without its drawbacks. The decentralized nature of the production process was such that monitoring and supervising work was particularly difficult. This made it hard both to predict how much could be produced and in what timeframe, and to maintain control over work quality. Lacking any alternative means to control the labour

132 ibid 189–90.

133 'The wages actually received by the workmen ... differ from the price of their work ... [s]uch difference being occasioned by deductions ... [and] other charges made by the "middleman"': Great Britain. Parliament, *Report from the Select Committee on Stoppage of Wages (Hosiery): Together with the Proceedings of the Committee, Minutes of Evidence, Appendix and Index* (Ordered by the House of Commons, to be printed 1855); Richard Muggeridge, *Report of the Commissioner Appointed to Inquire into the Condition of the Frame-Work Knitters.*, vol 15 (Nineteenth Century House of Commons Sessional Papers 1845) 83; Henry Mayhew, *The Morning Chronicle Survey of Labour and the Poor: The Metropolitan Districts*, vol 2 (Routledge 2016) 102–03 117.

134 James A Schmiechen, *Sweated Industries and Sweated Labor: The London Clothing Trades, 1860-1914* (University of Illinois Press 1984) 53.

135 Duncan Bythell, 'The Hand-Loom Weavers in the English Cotton Industry during the Industrial Revolution: Some Problems' (1964) 17 Economic History Review 339, 177.

process, many employers resorted to manipulating the pay system with a view to inducing more efficient work.[136] Low wages were made evermore precarious, therefore, as payment in truck, the imposition of fines, and the making of various stoppages from wages became increasingly common.

In its narrowest sense, the truck system referred to a practice of substituting benefits in kind for money wages in order to artificially depress wage rates.[137] In its broader sense, however, truck involved any attempt by employers to reduce contractually agreed wages, whether by paying in goods, imposing fines and charges, or requiring workers to spend their wages at a shop run by the employer (or associated firm). These practices were most common in industries where subcontracting and the involvement of middlemen were common. This was so particularly in industries with standardized wage rates, for it provided smaller employers with a competitive advantage in an environment in which they might otherwise be squeezed out of the market.[138]

The truck system was, however, inseparable from broader challenges associated with the monetization of the economy. Shortages of small coins meant that many principal manufacturers were obliged to make coins or tokens to enable them to pay their workmen—and for the convenience of the poor employed by them. These tokens were not legal tender, and were only accepted by a few shops which would charge high prices. While, from 1818, the issue of tokens was made illegal, and from 1821, the Mint had begun to produce a larger amount of small coins, employers were still faced with further constraints on the payment of cash wages: liquidity. In industries that required production on speculation (and thus the many export trades), payment in kind was therefore very often the only option available to an employer dependent on being able to increase production at short notice and with no cash readily available with which to pay wages.[139]

In light of this, it is perhaps no surprise that some of the most active opponents of the truck system were the larger manufacturers concerned to put an end to what they saw as unfair competition.[140] Larger employers with adequate capital and liquidity complained that truck was being exploited by small masters with inadequate liquidity as a means to reduce their wage costs. In this context, it was the practice of paying in truck, rather than any proposed legislation designed to suppress it, which appeared as the illegitimate incursion into the parties' freedom.

From a policy perspective, truck was objectionable because it challenged emerging ideas about juridical equality and freedom of contract, central to which

[136] Bythell (n 131) 155.

[137] George Hilton, *The Truck System: Including a History of the British Truck Acts, 1465-1960.* (W Heffer 1960) 14.

[138] ibid 14–15. Truck was not confined to out-work, but it was in this context that the practice was particularly prevalent: Tom Brass, 'Unfree Labour as Primitive Accumulation?' (2011) 35 Capital & Class 23, fn 54.

[139] Daunton (n 16) 426.

[140] Hilton (n 137), 16–17; HC Deb 17 March 1830, vol 23, cols 461–74, 470 (Mr Littleton).

was the emerging idea that the market ensured that workers would be paid the 'true value' of their labour, and that the labour relation was founded on an equal exchange. Policy-makers referred to the truck system as a form of slavery between a worker and his employer,[141] for 'in the truck system'... 'one party is not a free agent, ... [he is] under the complete control of the other ...'[142] Payment in truck was also problematic because it interfered with ordinary principles of contract enforcement, and thus weakened the contract as a mechanism for providing stability in exchange. By preventing a worker from assessing whether his employer had actually paid the wage which he had agreed to pay, this made it difficult for the courts to intervene to enforce the contract.[143] The truck legislation was thus a legitimate exception to the principle of non-intervention because it did not encroach on the parties' agreement, nor did it 'interfere' with the market: '[it] only interpose[d] to ensure the just fulfilment of contracts already made':[144]

> Members who had opposed this Bill had argued upon a false foundation. They had assumed that the labourers were always competent to make contracts, whereas they were in every case in debt to their masters, and therefore it was impossible for them to resist the control of their masters, and they were obliged to take goods from them at any rate. All that this Bill did was, to enable the labourers to know what were the bargains they did make.[145]

Legal control of truck was not conceived as a form of wage regulation, and so was entirely consistent with an economic policy geared towards free markets. The Truck Acts were simply a mechanism for enforcing contracts already (or deemed to be) agreed. Implicit in the Act was a view of the wage as something that emerges spontaneously from the market process, something that is, and ought to be, dictated by the market—not to be distorted, therefore, by either the state or employer abuse of power.[146]

In this sense, the Truck Acts did reflect a subtle shift in attitude; policy-makers were gradually recognizing that law had to play a more active role in the labour market. It was not sufficient to passively enforce contracts and provide protection to private property rights. Labour law had an important role to play in providing the conditions for free competition to emerge because wage-dependent workers, it was now recognized, were inherently vulnerable to exploitation.

141 HC Deb 12 April 1831, vol 3, cols 1256–59 (Mr Whitmore and Lord Sandon).

142 HC Deb 17 March 1830, vol 23, cols 461–74, 461, 463 (Mr Littleton).

143 HC Deb 12 April 1831, vol 3, cols 1256–59, particularly 2159 (Mr Althorpe). See also: *Sharman v Sanders* (1853) 13 CB 166, 138 ER 1161 (Maule J) at 176.

144 David Bailey, *The Truck System: A Book for Masters and Workmen* (1859) 1–3.

145 HC Deb 12 April 1831, vol 3, cols 1256–59, 1259 (Lord Althorp).

146 The Truck Act was supported by the press too, on the grounds that the truck system amounted to a form of 'slavery'. See: *The Economist*, Saturday 18 June 1870, vol 028, Issue 1399, 757.

> But although, looked at in the abstract, he would be free to agree or decline, yet it is evident that viewed in another aspect, he would be compelled to fall in with the terms offered; for it is contrary to common sense to suppose that if there had been nothing to urge him, he would have voluntarily submitted to that reduction of his wages, and exposure to oppression, which would necessarily follow from his agreement [to be paid in goods]. No; there would be the weak power opposed by the strong, and the former consequently obliged to yield; inability on the part of the workman to procure employment under another, — stern want coming upon himself and his family, — and the fact that half a loaf was better than no bread; — one or all of these causes, or some other similar cause, must have been at work to compel him to agree to such a bargain.[147]

The nature of the Truck Act was, however, very different from the nature of wage regulation during the Tudor period. Whereas the latter was concerned primarily with questions of labour supply, and securing workers' subsistence, the former was concerned entirely with the operation of the market. The 'wage' in this context was not a payment for service made in the context of a mutual or reciprocal relationship. Rather, it was the price paid for a commodity: labour power. Thus, the Truck Act defined the wage as 'any money or other thing had or contracted to be paid, delivered or given as a recompense, reward or remuneration for any labour done or to be done'.[148] The link between the wage and labour done, or to be done, rather than service, made explicit this conceptual link between wages and commodified labour. The Act did not, for this reason, presuppose any form of contract or relationship as a condition for its application. Rather, what mattered was the nature of the good produced, and the socio-economic status of the party engaged in producing it. If the worker actually produced the good, therefore, or performed the task envisaged by the contract, he had an absolute right to be paid its market value and this was not something that could be waived by agreement.

The Truck Acts reflect a growing awareness of the possibility, and likelihood, of what we would now refer to as 'market failure'. That is, the courts and parliament were beginning to see a role for the law in substituting the hypothetical market outcome, for whatever resulted in practice. The limits of labour law thus came to be circumscribed by an abstract idea of a perfectly competitive market, even if, in practice, it was recognized that markets frequently departed from this norm. Employers were thus legally required to pay the value of the labour embodied in the product that they claimed from production, the assumption being that this reflected the value of the worker's contribution to the production process. The problem, however, was that this came to express the absolute limit of what

[147] Bailey (n 144) 6. This is echoed in: HC Deb 12 April 1831, vol 3, cols 1256–59, 1257 (Mr Whitmore).
[148] Section 25(3).

workers could expect to receive in connection with their employment: it seems the 'market wage' was expected to perform the functions of both the 'market' and 'social' wages—coordinating decision making, and, at the same time, securing social reproduction.

In a series of cases throughout the nineteenth century, the courts confirmed that the Truck Act was concerned only with ensuring that the value of labour was paid. This meant that deductions by way of charges for machinery were not contrary to the Act, because such sums were not wages, but were deducted as part of the process by which the wage itself was calculated.[149] The courts also held that deductions made in response to poor workmanship (according to the 'customer of the trade') were not deductions from wages, because the value deducted had never been provided. The wage thus corresponded with the value of the benefit received, much as was the case in ordinary sale contracts:

> What is contracted to be paid for his personal labour is wages, and what is more than that is not wages ... the price (of the finished good) is not merely wages so defined, but wages plus an addition for the work done by the stocking frame (capital) ... deductions are admissible if they really come not out of wages properly so-called, but out of previous additions to those wages.[150]

During this period, the courts did not systematically distinguish the claim in debt for unpaid wages, actions for the price in a sale contract, accounts for work and labour, and claims in quantum meruit. In each case, the price could only be claimed if the good was actually received. If the good was defective in some way, the claim was for the value of the benefit received, even though 'formerly it was the practice, where an action was brought for an agreed price of a specific chattel, sold with a warranty, or of work which was to be performed according to contract, to allow the plaintiff to recover the stipulated sum, leaving the defendant to a cross action for breach of the warranty or contract'.[151]

The wage had thus emerged during this period as the price of a commodity. The contract of service had lost its distinctiveness as a contract that envisaged ongoing mutual obligations, for if labour had been rendered, the only remaining obligation lay on the employer to pay for that labour (in time, or output), leaving it to the worker to secure himself his subsistence. The only difference between contracts concluded between independent contractors and their customers, and employers and labourers/or artificers, was thus the degree of protection that Parliament assumed that the latter required in order to be in a position to freely contract—free from the risk of exploitation. This protection was, moreover, only provided in very

[149] *Chawner v Cummings* (1846) 8 QB 311, 115 ER 893; *Archer v James*; (1859) 2 B & S, 61, 121 ER 996.
[150] *Archer v James* (n 149) 84–85 (Byles J).
[151] *Mondel v Steel* (1841) 8 M & W 858, 151 ER 1288 (Pollock B) at 870–71.

exceptional cases, such as in the context of payment in Truck. As summarized by Lord Hanworth in 1931, the position was that:

> The relation between master and servant is established by a contract between them, a contract which is subject to the rules applicable to other contracts except insofar as statute law has superimposed limitations, or rights, inter se.[152]

The distinction between contracts concluded between independent contractors and their customers, and labourers and employers, was said, for the purposes of the Truck Acts, to reflect the distinction between those that sold their labour for wages, and those that agreed a price for a contract, and this turned primarily upon questions of socio-economic status. The purpose of the Act being to secure the payment of wages for labour, the courts tied the Act's scope to the existence of a wage-dependent worker with nothing but 'his personal labour to sell' for 'only then was the payment to him to be classed as wages'.[153] Those in a position to hire others thus fell outside the scope of the legislation, for what they sold to their employers could not, by definition, be equated with their personal labour. In *Riley v Warden*, Rolfe B put this as follows: '[the Act] applies to those who receive wages as the price of their labour . . . and so does not include wages which are the price of a contract'.[154] The purpose of the legislation, he suggested, was to afford protection to a class of persons 'not very able to protect themselves' and as such, those who 'earn their bread by the sweat of their brow'.[155] It was only in 'exceptional circumstances' therefore that the law would 'interfere to prevent persons . . . from contracting in any way they think proper'.[156]

The problem, however, was that it proved difficult to distinguish in practice between those that sold labour from those that sold a finished article—particularly in a context in which piece-rate payments and subcontracting were common. In an attempt to clarify the matter, Erle J suggested that labourers or workmen were those 'engaged in the performance of the work . . . personally labouring . . . [such] that the wages are thereby legally his against . . . his employer'.[157] The requirement that the individual have contracted to provide personal labour, rather than a particular result or task, thus gradually came to be seen as the key test when it came to determining the scope of the Acts.[158] Originally, this was seen as an enquiry that turned primarily on the worker's socio-economic status. Over time, however,

[152] *Sagar v H Ridehagh & Son* [1931] 1 Ch 310 (CA), 326 (Lord Hanworth).
[153] See the test proposed by Pollock CB in *Sleeman v Barrett* (1864) 2 Hurl & C 934, 942, 159 ER 386.
[154] *Riley v Warden* (1848) 2 Ex 59, 69 (Rolfe B).
[155] ibid.
[156] *Sharman v Sanders* (n 143) 176 (Maule J).
[157] *Ingram v Barnes* (1857) 7 El & Bl 115, 119 ER 1190.
[158] See: *Sleeman v Barrett* (n 163); *Sharman v Sanders* (n 143); *Riley v Warden* (n 154); *Ingram v Barnes* (n 157); *Squire v Midland Lace Co* [1905] 2 KB 448.

this hardened into a more much formalistic test that focused almost exclusively on the express terms of the contract. Thus, the parties' rights and obligations became indistinguishable from what they had expressly agreed, regardless of what happened in practice. In *Ingram v Barnes*, therefore, it was said to turn on 'whether the workman who did work with his own hands in performance of the contract was absolutely *bound by the terms of the contract so to do*'.[159]

Dissatisfaction with this position was such, however, that in 1905 the court expressed regret at having to dismiss a worker's case

> ... having regard to the facts disclosed ... as to the nature of the employment and the position of the women clippers, who, though they do sometimes employ assistants, are evidently, *as a class*, wage-earning manual labourers, and not 'contractors' in the ordinary and popular sense, or persons who 'speculate on the state of the labour market' and we venture to express the hope that some amendment of the law may be made so as to extend the protection of the Truck Act to a class of workpeople practically indistinguishable from those already within its provisions.[160]

The formalistic approach that the courts adopted to the question of personal labour was, in part, a result of the courts' hostility towards an Act that they saw as an illegitimate interference with a freedom to contract that was increasingly becoming seen as something that was innate and universal—particularly at a time when the combination laws had been repealed on exactly that assumption.[161] Nonetheless, many of the judges expressed much unease with the under-inclusiveness of the test, and it seems that the test was used primarily to facilitate decision-making consistency in relation to a complex factual question where the stakes, for legal legitimacy, were particularly high. This came, however, at the expense of frustrating the broader purpose of the Act.[162]

However (in)effective the Truck Act(s) proved in practice in terms of eradicating payment in truck, they nonetheless reflect an important juncture in the history of the wage;[163] a period during which its distinctiveness as a payment for a particular type of commodity was being established. Ideas of service had been firmly shed by this time, and the principles applicable to wage claims more closely resembled claims in the sale of goods context than they did long-term relational contracts envisaging ongoing mutual obligations. In terms of their basic rationale, the Acts reflected the growing recognition that where the sale of labour was concerned, the

[159] *Ingram v Barnes* (n 157) 124 (Campbell CJ) (emphasis added).
[160] *Squire v Midland Lace Co* (n 158), 454 (emphasis added).
[161] See particularly: *Archer v James* (n 149) 83 (Bramwell B) and *Ingram v Barnes* (n 157) (Campbell CJ).
[162] See: *Squire v Midland Lace* (n 158) and *Ingram v Barnes* (n 157) (Erle J).
[163] For a critique of their apparent failure, see: *The Economist* (n 146) 757.

legal system had to do more than passively enforce 'free agreements'. However reluctant the courts might have been, it seems that an important role for labour law had been conceded, providing the conditions for freedom of contract to emerge, and operate, in practice. Thus, while claims for wages appeared in the common law as simple contractual claims for service rendered, or goods sold, the contract by which labour was sold was, at this time, gradually being afforded specific statutory protections—however piecemeal—modifying how the common law rules would take effect.

5.6 Sweating, Casualism, and Early Experiments in Wage Regulation

5.6.1 Sweating and the Road towards the Minimum Wage

Despite being one of the central manufacturing centres of the world, England was slow to move towards a vertically integrated, factory-based industrial structure. Particularly outside the larger manufacturing districts, workshops remained remarkably small. Entrepreneurs were unable (or unwilling) to invest in capital-intensive equipment, and so relied instead on a multitude of market-based transactions to organize production. In such a context, the only way to compete with more centralized, industrial models of production, both at home and abroad, was to intensify labour. The problem of 'sweating', low-wage labour in poor sanitary conditions, thus became an increasingly pressing social problem throughout the nineteenth century.

A series of industry-specific inquiries throughout the early nineteenth century notwithstanding, the problem of 'sweating' only began to catch the attention of policy-makers towards the end of the century. Prior to this, Parliament's energies had focused primarily on the problem of child labour. Little time was spent discussing the terms and conditions of the growing number of adult workers forced to subsist on chronically low wages.

By the 1880s, however, following a series of reforms to parliament giving working men more political weight nationally, sweating was 'rediscovered'. Two Board of Trade reports in 1887 and 1888 helped raise the profile of sweated workers, although even these were followed by a further period of inaction, the Board concluding that: 'public attention and public judgment can effectively check operations in which little regard is shown for workpeople and to the quality of production'.[164]

[164] Sidney Webb and Beatrice Webb, *Industrial Democracy*, vol 2 (Longmans, Green, and Company 1897) 2: xli; Select Committee on the Sweating System, vols XVII, 301, para 204.

In the early 1890s, however, public interest in the problem increased, particularly in light of the 1893–94 report of the Royal Commission on labour.[165] This report suggested that the problem could not be addressed by merely tightening up existing mechanisms concerning sanitation in factories and workshops. The problem was ultimately one of 'the payment of wages insufficient for the full maintenance, under healthy conditions, of the workers and their families':[166] the lack, in other words, of a social wage.

Despite characterizing the problem in this way, economic orthodoxy was strongly opposed to any form of state regulation of wages: 'there was no sphere of economic life in which it was considered more important to allow economic forces unrestrained freedom than in the settlement of incomes'.[167] However, given changing beliefs about the role of worker organizations in the 'self-regulation' of markets, this did not mean that nothing could be done. Rather, the problem lay not in the state's failure to regulate the labour market, but the market's failure to reproduce the conditions for its own free operation: workers' failure to self-organize. This diagnosis shifted the emphasis away from calls for a statutory minimum wage onto how to use law to foster collective bargaining.

In 1891, partly in response to these concerns, Parliament enacted the first Fair Wages Resolution, committing the government to paying 'current rates' to its contractors. The premise was thus that the most that could be done was to impose the highest wage 'the market could bear', a wage, it was believed, which reflected what would ordinarily be agreed through free bargaining between both sides of industry. The Resolution thus provided no cause of action to victims of low pay; its principal concern was how to secure fair competition between government contractors.[168] The Resolution invoked the term 'current rates' as the benchmark for what was 'fair', and replaced this with 'union rates' in 1909.[169] It implicitly assumed, therefore, that there is a hypothetical market wage that could, and should, be used as a benchmark when setting a minimum wage, and that, with the assistance of representatives from the industries concerned, this could be identified and enforced. The wage was not, therefore, something that could be informed by considerations external to the market, such as workers' living costs, the purpose of the minimum wage was to 'mimic' the wage that would be agreed in competitive conditions. The Resolution was not, therefore, designed to provide workers with a legal right to fair or subsistence pay. Its purpose was to guarantee that the real market

[165] Royal Commission, *The Labour Question: An Epitome of the Evidence and the Report of the Royal Commission on Labour* (C Scribner 1894).

[166] Webb and Webb (n 164) 2: xli; Select Committee (n 164) vols XVII, 301, para 204.

[167] Sheila Blackburn, 'The Problem of Riches: From Trade Boards to a National Minimum Wage' (1988) 19 Industrial Relations Journal 124, 126.

[168] Otto Kahn-Freund, 'Minimum Wage Legislation in Great Britain' (1949) 97 University of Pennsylvania Law Review 778.

[169] For a background to the changes made to the resolution, see: Brian Bercusson, 'Fair Wages Resolution' (1975) 34 Cambridge Law Journal 39.

price would actually be paid, that the government pay 'not more, nor less, than the current market rate'.[170]

> ... it was not proposed in the Resolution ... that the intention of the Resolution was to stereotype in every case as the rate of wages *current in the market* the rates which Trades Unions might desire. All we undertook to do was to ascertain what was actually agreed upon between the employers and the workmen in each trade, and, so far as we could, to see that that rate of payment was adopted.[171]

Public interest in sweating grew in the early years of the twentieth century. In 1906, the *Daily News* agreed to finance a sweated industries exhibition, the outcome of which was to raise the profile of the sweated worker and highlight how widespread and pervasive the problem really was. The exhibition revealed that sweating was not confined to a small number of sweated trades but was to be found to a greater or lesser extent in almost every occupation—affecting skilled and unskilled alike.[172] In light of this, and the public outcry it caused, Parliament felt it had no choice but to take more decisive action.[173]

In 1907 and 1908, the government established an all-party committee which recommended that wage-fixing boards, based loosely on the boards established in Victoria, Australia, be established in each of the sweated trades. Rather than legislate for a statutory minimum wage, the Act envisaged the setting up of trade boards in the sweated trades where collective organization had either failed or broken down. The boards would then be able to set minimum time and piece rates for the trades concerned.[174]

The premise behind the Act was: that while 'normally, [the organization of labour] is quite adequate to ensure, by the dealing of the market, fair play as between employer and employed',[175] in conditions of extreme competition, these normal principles did not apply. The parties were left so weak and defenceless that they could not be assumed to be capable of acting freely in defence of their interests. Trade boards could thus be justified on the same basis as factory legislation

[170] HC Deb 10 February 1892, vol 1, cols 119–57, 12 (Mr Plunkett). See also 130–32, (Mr Buxton).

[171] HC Deb 10 February 1892, vol 1, cols 119–57, 128 (Mr Plunkett). See also 130–31 (Mr Buxton) (emphasis added).

[172] Sheila C Blackburn, '"Princesses and Sweated-Wage Slaves Go Well Together": Images of British Sweated Workers, 1843-1914' [2002] International Labor and Working-Class History 24, 38.

[173] Mr Asquith expressed 'little doubt' that there was nothing to be done but to find some way to make provision for a minimum wage: 'Mr. Asquith On Sweated Labour', *The Times* (London, 15 December 1908) 4. *The Times Digital Archive*. Web. 12 March 2019.

[174] Ramsay McDonald's favoured solution had been a system of licensing for homeworkers, enabling inspectors to locate all instances of homework so that examples of poor treatment would not go unchecked. Legislated minimum wages were not the favoured option even in 1907: 'Mr. Ramsay Macdonald On Sweated Labour' *The Times*, (London, 12 October 1907) 12. *The Times Digital Archive*. Web. 12 March 2019.

[175] HC Deb 28 April 1909, vol 4, cols 342–411, 345 (Mr Lyttleton).

targeting women and children. In the absence of collective organization and in light of extreme competition, in these industries there was no market in the ordinary meaning of the word; the boards were not even exceptions to the principle of non-intervention:

> [The Trade Board Bill] does not deal with the question whether State action can, or ought, to control wages. The general rates of wages throughout the country will be settled by other means than this Bill—that is by economic forces. It is generally accepted that State interference with the remuneration for labour can only be justified in exceptional cases where two fundamental conditions are absent—I mean the mobility of labour in its true sense and effective organisation ... applied exclusively to exceptionally unhealthy patches of the body politic where the development has been arrested in spite of the growth of the rest of the organism.[176]

Despite consensus on the need for the Act, the debates surrounding its enactment reveal conflicting views about the nature of law and its relationship with the market. Opposition to the Act had been based primarily on the fear that minimum rates would necessarily raise prices and/or unemployment. As Arthur Balfour argued:[177]

> [T]hese wages are not fixed by competition, but it is a forced sale of value. It is not competition value. It is a forced sale value. It is grossly unfair of anyone to say that a forced sale represents the true value of the article sold. A forced sale never gives a true market rate of wages ... Whatever your view on Protection may be, you are now interfering not with the fair value of wages but with the cost at which certain articles may be introduced ... If you think that the raising of wages in this country will make the cost of production greater, you are driven, to the inevitable conclusion that you are going to hand over the trades to foreign sweated labour. You are absolutely bound to make provision to deal with that difficulty. Under this Bill the only provision you can make is to exclude the industry in question from the beneficent operations of this measure.

In Mr Tennant's view, however, such a view was too simplistic. The Trade Boards Act might actually *change* the incentives of the parties in such a way that

> they may ... have a chance to make arrangements by which they will be able to avoid some of the very violent competition which they now wage against each other, and they may be able to effect considerable economy... [Furthermore] ... there are certain profits of the middleman—exorbitant profits, as some of us

[176] ibid 344 (Mr Tennant).
[177] Trade Boards Bill, HC Deb, 28 April 1909, vol 4, cc 342–411, col 388.

> think—which will disappear. Trade boards in their establishment will bring together not only the workpeople but the employers ... It is ridiculous to assume that a rise in wages must bring about an increase in price ...

Even if this were so, however ...

> it would be better that the worker should be employed on a lesser demand, with reasonable hours of work at a fair rate of wages, than on a great demand with long hours at sweated rates of wages.[178]

The debates reveal a tension between the idea that naturally free parties ought not be deprived of that freedom by circumstances beyond their control, such as unfair competitive practices and employer abuse of power; and the idea that certain institutional preconditions would have to be in place before that freedom could even emerge. In the latter case, there was far more room for law to shape the content of the wage, rather than simply shore-up the mechanisms by which it was to be enforced. It was not clear, therefore, whether law was to be seen as a constituent element in the formation of markets, or simply as a corrective mechanism that responded to 'defects' in a pre-constituted and (largely) self-reproducing competitive system. Either way, there was now consensus at least on the premise that the market could not operate entirely independently from state support: law's regulatory and facilitative roles were, at the very least, acknowledged.

In the end, the Trade Board Act, perhaps the first 'modern' minimum wage legislation, came to reflect many of the same assumptions that had underpinned the Fair Wages Resolutions. It rejected any active role for the law in shaping the content of the wage in the sense that the wage rate was conceptualized as if it was the wage that would ordinarily be set by the market. Direct state regulation of wages was still off the table and the role of the boards was simply to identify the true wage that would have been agreed had self-organization not failed. Considerable emphasis was placed, then, on ensuring that wages were not set above that which 'industry could afford'.[179] The boards were thus only to be established in trades where collective organization was absent, and wages were 'exceptionally low as compared with that in other employments ... '[180] In turn, the minister was to have regard to the rates of wages prevailing in the trade or any part of the trade when making such an assessment.

[178] HC Deb 28 April 1909, vol 4, cols 342–411, 346–47 (Mr Tennant).

[179] Discussing the Trade Board Act, the Economist noted that the principal difference between the British Trade Board system and the prevailing systems in Australia was that, in relation to the latter, there was no mention of 'what industry could afford': '*What is Sweating*, *The Economist*, Saturday, 13 June 1925, vol 100, Issue 4268, p 1170.

[180] 9 Edw VII c 22, s 1(2).

The boards were confined to setting minimum rates. Their powers did not extend, therefore, to providing a minimum amount of work or minimum income from employment.[181] They were simply tasked with setting minimum rates for time and piece work by reference to the going rate in the industry in question. As the *Economist* noted in 1925, 'Trade Boards … have to deal with gross deviation from the normal standard of wages, whatever that may be; not to fix, or attempt to fix, anything in the nature of a living wage'.[182]The wage was still something that emerged spontaneously from the forces of supply and demand, therefore, but it was now assumed that in the presence of market imperfections the parties might need assistance when it came to identifying the 'true' price of labour.[183]

In this sense, the Acts were simply to 'give statutory sanction to principles and methods adopted in numberless cases by voluntary agreement'.[184] Their principal purpose was to prevent employers from gaining a competitive advantage by paying less than the true market price, while at the same time preventing the 'weak and defenceless' from undercutting each other to the detriment of the trade.[185] The Acts were as much designed to protect 'good employers' from unfair competitive practices, therefore, as they were to protect the victims of chronically low wages.[186]

5.6.2 The Casual Labour Problem and the Docks

It was not only the problem of 'sweating' that concerned social reformers during the late nineteenth and early twentieth centuries. Equally pressing, particularly in London, was the problem of 'casualism'.[187] During the late nineteenth century, London was predominantly a finishing centre, organized primarily on the basis of small units, and oriented towards a highly seasonable consumer market.[188] Given the low proportion of fixed capital employed, this seasonality necessitated rapid adjustment to demand. This meant that where skilled workers were scarce, firms were reluctant to lay off workers during slack periods. Where skill was less scarce, however, or less necessary, 'casual' labour and intermittent employment was the

[181] Only in 1918 was this extended to minimum piece-time rates and rates for time spent at the workplace waiting for work: 8 & 9 Geo V c 32.

[182] *The Economist* (n 179) 1170.

[183] HC Deb 28 April 1909, vol 4, cols 342–411, 391 (Mr Churchill), referring to the setting of minimum rates of wages that 'has got sufficient backing in the trade to render enforcement of it by prosecution a useful and effective process'.

[184] ibid 350 (Mr Tennant).

[185] HL Deb 30 August 1909, vol 2, cols 974–1016, 1007 (The Earl of Crewe): 'The idea, therefore, is not so much to raise the standard of wage as to fix a minimum wage, raising the price paid by the bad employer to the level of that paid by the good employer'.

[186] HC Deb 04 November 1948, vol 457, cols 1031–69, 1031 (Mr Isaacs).

[187] Gareth Stedman Jones, *Outcast London: A Study in the Relationship Between Classes in Victorian Society* (2nd revised edn, Verso Books 2013).

[188] ibid 21.

most favourable solution. Thus, in practice, most trades retained a core of permanent, skilled workers, and a 'reserve' of casuals that could be called upon when needed.[189]

This is the background to England's—and London's in particular—causal labour problem; a problem that gained considerable public attention from the mid-nineteenth century onwards. Casual labour was not the same as sweating, although there was inevitably considerable crossover between the two issues. The problem with sweating was not (necessarily) that insufficient work was provided, but that the conditions under which that work was done was oppressive, demeaning, and insufficient to 'maintain' the efficiency and health of the workforce. The problem with casual labour was one of 'under-employment'—absolute wages may have been (and very often were) relatively high compared with other industries, but an over-supply of labour, and a reluctance by firms to retain workers long term, prevented the majority from earning a regular, or sufficient, wage.

Seasonality of production was, to some extent, off set by the possibility of combining work in different trades, where the seasons affected demand at different times. No two trades followed exactly the same seasonal pattern, so there was no risk that the labour market would suddenly become swamped with workers at a particular period.[190] In the really skilled trades, moreover, seasonality was off set by the willingness of employers to pay proportionately more so that their 'prized' workers could live comfortably in the off-season—and be willing to return when production resumed. In less skilled trades, on the other hand, the syncopation of seasonal troughs allowed workers to dovetail one seasonal occupation with another: many skills were transferable between different sorts of consumer goods, and thus between different trades.[191]

These observations notwithstanding, however, seasonal unemployment was still a considerable problem for many workers. If seasonality was unpredictable, as it was in the docks, for example, 'dovetailing' was rarely a possibility. Nor did it adequately cater to the challenges posed by (unpredictable) trade depression or the effects of a 'bad winter'. Moreover, where the supply of labour is plentiful (where the primary source of labour is unskilled), there is little incentive for employers to maintain a continuous level of employment. Seasonality thus tends to breed casual employment, and casual employment breeds further casualization, reducing incentives for employers to invest in new forms of work organization/fixed capital.

The 'casual' labour problem was not confined to any single trade. Like sweating, casual labour was endemic in many industries, even if each trade was affected slightly differently. Industries particularly badly affected included the riverside

[189] ibid 33–34.
[190] ibid.
[191] ibid 39–40.

industries, and other forms of transportation (omnibus drivers, road haulage, and 'cab-men'); in building, catering, the baking trade, barbers, etc.[192]

Casual labour was not, then, a problem unique to the docks. Even so, it was with the dock workers that the 'problem' of casualism came to be most frequently associated.[193] This was due, in part, to the scale and visibility of the problem, and also to the efficiency concerns it generated given the importance of the trade to Britain's global position.[194]

5.6.2.1 Decasualization in the Docks

Historical accounts recite the appalling conditions faced by dock workers as they gathered at the stands (colloquially known as 'pens') at the ports, hustling and jostling for work. Foremen, employed by the shipowners would often be charged with recruiting men (and supervising their work) for what was known as a 'turn'—a half day's work.[195] If men were not recruited, they had to go home and return in the afternoon to try again. Each dock might host over 100 employers; many men would 'try' their luck only at a few, regular, stands, hoping to gain preferential treatment by proving loyalty—often frustrated, however, due to the influx of 'irregular' casuals, 'stealing' their jobs.[196]

Like many casual industries, dock labour had always combined permanent employment for some, with a reserve of casuals; as a result of the seasonality of the trade, and the uneven flow of ships and cargoes. In the early 1800s, however, dock-labouring was generally seen as 'part of a regular trade' that would tend to be passed down through the family. Regular employment was common, for between ten and twelve months of the year at least, and at a reasonable wage.

Sailing ships were less prone to fluctuations in terms of the number of labourers employed than the steamships of the late nineteenth century were, and when the vessels came in, turnaround time was not so pressing. Steamships were quite different: turnaround time had to be rapid, and those 'hands' which were employed, would often be required to work all night, with little or no notice. Firms using port services became increasingly dependent on rapid turnover and quick movement of cargoes across quays. This placed pressure on dock companies and contractors to deploy men in large numbers and in short, intensive bursts of activity—at whatever cost to the regularity of employment.

The gradual introduction of machinery, and the 'increase in the number of applicants' had, by the end of the century, transformed the industry into a casual

[192] ibid 60–61.

[193] Gordon Ashton Phillips and Noel Whiteside, *Casual Labour: The Unemployment Question in the Port Transport Industry, 1880-1970* (OUP 1985).

[194] Steven Tolliday and Jonathan Zeitlin, *Shop Floor Bargaining and the State: Historical and Comparative Perspectives* (CUP 2010).

[195] Detailed descriptions of the 'jostling' and fighting at the dock gates can be found in Charles Booth, *Labour and Life of the People…*, vol 4 (Williams and Norgate 1891) 202.

[196] See the analysis in: ibid 200.

employment, 'only fit for the failures of society', or men whom 'a revolution in their own trade has forced into taking any precarious work they can find'.[197] The removal of regulatory restrictions in the early nineteenth century, the lowering of cost of entry (due to a reduction in the price of vessels), and a growing import trade, thus created new problems for both workers and employers.[198] The number of employers increased dramatically and, with the new poor law, swathes of the 'destitute' came to gather at the docks every day with a view to obtaining employment—as a last 'option' before the workhouse.[199]

As employers grew in number, so the labour market at the docks became more fragmented. Each firm sought a supply of workmen sufficient to cater for maximum needs; no matter how occasionally it could hire them. The problem, however, was that the more that the labourers were immoblized in one sector of the market, the more casual they became—unable to seek employment from the many other port employers in need of labour at the docks.[200]

This system of causal labour could flourish only so long as there was a plentiful supply of unskilled labour. This was facilitated not only by the broader legal framework—most particularly, the new poor law—but also by the willingness of employers to offer (relatively) high wages. This was, of course, a false promise that rarely translated into subsistence pay. The relative freedom that dock work implied also attracted many workers to the docks when their own trade was slack (a freedom which Ernest Bevin later referred to as a 'freedom to starve'). In combination, these factors gave rise to a chronic over-supply of labour.

While there was a period when London companies tried to offer steady work to most of their hands, the intense competition of the 1830s and 1840s made the system too costly.[201] By the middle of the century, casualism was widespread—albeit with subtle differences between docks. Even attempts to regularize engagements, through, for example, a system of 'preferences', did little to ameliorate under-employment. While the casual system was not universally opposed, the dockers being fond of the relative freedom they perceived,[202] by the end of the century, working and living conditions were such that there was considerable

[197] *The Times* (London, 29 August 1889) Issue 32790, 8.

[198] Vernon H Jensen, *Hiring of Dock Workers and Employment Practices in the Ports of New York, Liverpool, London, Rotterdam, and Marseilles* (Harvard University Press 1964).

[199] Eric Taplin, 'Dock Labour at Liverpool: Occupational Structure and Working Conditions in the Late Nineteenth Century' (1977) 127 Transactions of the Historical Society of Lancashire and Cheshire 133. See the discussion in: Booth (n 195) 201.

[200] Charity Organisation Society, *Special Committee on Unskilled Labour (1908) Qs 751-2.* A witness before the select committee added the following details: 'The first thing … is this, that there is a chain put up right across the entrance to the dock and the contractors are on one side of the chain and the men the other.… You can imagine for a moment from 1,500 to 2,000 men crowded together, the front men forced up against the chain and the men; the bad men are climbing over the heads of those in front, and the contractor behind the chain is picking out the men, generally his own favourites, or somebody recommended by his own favourites.'

[201] Phillips and Whiteside (n 193) 21.

[202] Taplin (n 199); Phillips and Whiteside (n 193); Jensen (n 198) 122.

bitterness among the workers. This situation led to the first major strike in 1889, and a protracted campaign, by unions, for 'decasualization'.[203]

The 1889 dock strike had a long-lasting effect on industrial relations in the ports, leading to the establishment of the Dock, Wharf, Riverside and General Workers' Union, which continued thereafter (alongside other emerging unions) to play a prominent role in the docks in London.[204] Nor, moreover, was the dock labour question, and the challenge of decasualization ever far from the public consciousness.[205]

At the heart of the strike had been a campaign for 'work or maintenance', a guaranteed minimum amount of work and/or payment, as a step towards decasualization. At the heart of these demands were proposals for a system of registration. Dockers resented the (non-unionized) 'casual casuals', and their effect on the regular casuals' ability to obtain employment.[206] They thus demanded a register of dock workers so that only registered dockers would be given work—and this was to go hand in hand with a guaranteed minimum wage for those on the register. In fact, however, the outcome of the strike for the workers was more modest; a minimum wage of a sixpence an hour (paid for time actually working): the position of the dock worker was to remain substantially unchanged for decades.[207]

In 1911, following a further strike by the dock workers, experiments in registration began, as did experiments with the centralized payment of wages. These early registration schemes were, however, relatively ineffective.[208] They were voluntary, the number of registered dockers far exceeded ports' demands, and employers continued to make use of unregistered men in conjunction.

The First World War gave a new impetus to the development of registration systems, however, because, for the first time, the docks were faced with a shortage rather than a surplus of labour. In this context, the Board of Trade established Joint Advisory Committees of employers and workers to grant exemptions for military service to dock labour, and these committees soon found it necessary to establish registers so as to determine which workers were to be retained in the industry. Despite reducing the number of casual workers significantly and improving the conditions of the dockers, by the end of the war, underemployment had returned.

Building on the experiences of these early registration schemes, in 1918 the Federation of Transport Workers adopted a program calling, once again, for the limitation of dock work to registered men and a system of guaranteed wages or 'maintenance' to those in the reserve. No progress was made, however, and when

203 Jensen (198) 121.

204 Taplin (n 199).

205 Noelle Whiteside, 'Welfare Insurance and Casual Labour: A Study of Administrative Intervention in Industrial Employment, 1906-26' (1979) 32 Economic History Review 507.

206 HMSO, *Committee of Inquiry into Certain Matters concerning the Port Transport industry: 'Final Report of the Committee of Inquiry under the Rt Hon. Lord Devlin'* (Cmnd 2734, 1965).

207 Jensen (n 198) 121.

208 Phillips and Whiteside (n 193).

negotiations between the Unions and the National Council for Port Employers broke down in 1919, a Court of Enquiry was appointed (the 'Shaw Inquiry').[209] In its report, the Court stopped short of mandating a guaranteed wage, recommending instead a national daily minimum of 16d. Even so, the Inquiry emphasized the importance of tackling the problems of inefficiency and of casual labour, calling attention to the need for decasualization, because unless it was solved 'the prospect of peace at the docks ... will be hopeless'. Casual labour, it declared 'has reached the dimensions of a serious social disease and 'the system of casualisation must if possible be torn up by the roots. It is wrong'.[210]

The Court thus advocated for a decasualization scheme to be worked out by both sides of industry, based on principles outlined by the Court. A central element of this plan was, of course, a guaranteed weekly wage (or 'maintenance'). But once again, no progress was made, and, beyond a series of experiments with registration, little significant progress towards decasualization would be made until the Second World War. While by 1936, there were joint schemes, on a voluntary basis, in a number of ports, 'in no case was any provision made to ensure that dock workers should receive an assured minimum wage with regularity, when full work was not available for them. There certainly was regulation of employment and wages, therefore, but there was no kind of guarantee; a man would turn up, day after day, without getting a call'.[211]

5.7 Conclusion

Prior to the eighteenth century, there was implied in the exclusive nature of the employer's property in his servant's service, certain mutual obligations that helped to balance the interests of the employer with those of the servant and the community. In effect, this provided a form of social wage that placed the social costs of employment on the employer. Thus, while the wage was a payment due for service; implicit in the obligation to pay was a parallel obligation to bear the costs of the worker's subsistence. By making sustainable the growing market in leases and the land enclosures that were to result, this early model of service had been an essential part of the way in which labour law provided the conditions that would be necessary for the emergence of the labour market.

By the end of the eighteenth century, the wage was emerging as the price of a commodity that was sold in a market setting. Like all prices, it was deemed to be set entirely by the laws of supply and demand, and so came to express the limit of

[209] Transport Workers Court of Inquiry, 'Report and Minutes of Evidence of the Inquiry' 2 vols (Cmnd 936 and 937, 1920) ('The Shaw Report').

[210] ibid 8–9.

[211] HC Deb 12 November 1945, vol 415, cols 1753–822, 1754 (Mr Isaacs, Minister of Labour). On the progress made from 1937, see: Jensen (n 198) 132–33.

what the employer could be required to pay for labour. The result of this was that the contract itself, rather than the relationship to which it gave rise, came to be seen as the primary source of the parties' legal rights and obligations. This left little room to read into the wage an implied obligation to provide for the worker's subsistence. In this way, this new conception of the wage expressed a fundamental shift in the way in which the law's relationship with the market was conceived. Rather than being seen as something that itself played a central role in conditioning the distribution of important social resources, the legal system was being conceived as something that 'intervened' to provide support for a pre-constituted market system, 'safeguarding' natural property rights and passively enforcing the terms of 'free' agreements.

These developments led to a fundamental shift in the way in which the service relation was conceived. Rather than something that purchased rights to ongoing service, the wage was now a payment made in exchange for rights of ownership in a disposable commodity. In this way, the concept of property as it related to labour itself underwent considerable change. In practice, this meant that, in order to secure the worker's cooperation in production, employers relied increasingly on extra-contractual mechanisms, such as fines and truck payments, which the legal system reinforced with criminal sanctions for contract breach and restrictions on combination. Because labour now appeared in law as an alienable commodity, proprietary control over workers was preserved in practice, but had been decoupled from the mutual obligations of maintenance and protection they had once implied.

This conception of the law's role in the market soon proved to be unsustainable. This is evidenced in the emergence of sweating, low productivity, and the problems of low and insecure pay that came to plague policy-makers throughout the nineteenth century. The longer-term effect of this, however, was to provide room for new ideas about the nature of the wage, and its relationship with the market, to emerge. The wage was still something that was 'produced' by the market, but it was now assumed that that would be so only if certain institutional preconditions were met. The potential for the market to destroy the foundations for its own existence had thus been recognized, albeit reluctantly, leaving greater room for 'corrective' mechanisms to be introduced.

In line with this, the wage emerged during the late nineteenth century as the objective sum that the parties would have agreed had they been capable of acting freely. By the early twentieth century, it was widely believed that this could only be presumed if collective labour organizations and basic minimum conditions of employment were legally guaranteed. Less clear, however, was the role that law could and should play when it came to guaranteeing that those conditions were in place. Nonetheless, for the most part, an active constituting role for law had been rejected. The consensus was still that there were certain fundamental economic laws that had to be observed if the market was to function. The abstract idea of a pre-constituted market continued to circumscribe the scope for legal intervention in the setting of wages. While new ideas were emerging, as early attempts to regularize dock work demonstrates, the idea that the legal system has a role to play in guaranteeing workers a regular income from employment, and thus in establishing the boundaries in which free competition can operate, had not yet taken hold.

6

Wages, Salary, and Remuneration—Towards a Social Wage

6.1 Introduction

This chapter shows that what began as a basic mechanism for regulating the price at which a commodity, labour power, was sold in the market, securing fair competition between employers, gradually transformed throughout the course of the twentieth century into a legal mechanism designed to secure workers a form of social wage. This, it shows, took the form, not of a minimum rate for labour provided, but of a guaranteed minimum income paid in exchange for employment, expressed through the legal concept of remuneration. The move to a social model of the wage, rooted in the idea of a guaranteed minimum weekly income, was part of a wider acceptance by courts and legislatures of a relational model of the contract of employment, in which there was an implied right to be remunerated for time spent in employment. Linked to this was the idea, also increasingly expressed in juridical language, that the law actively constituted the employment relation and that the courts could, and should, imply contracts of employment in order to provide both parties with greater stability and protection. This attitude was paralleled by attempts by the legislature to 'decasualize' industries to guarantee even those engaged in industries that were, of their nature, casual, a degree of regularity in their work and/or pay.

6.2 A Conceptual History: Wages, Salaries, and Remuneration

Salaries have long been distinguished from wages by reason of their regular, and unconditional, character. The term 'salary' thus presupposes an exchange of work and remuneration of some regularity, and/or an ongoing relationship where the amount of work is expected to fluctuate over time. In turn, the term traditionally implied a degree of independence or autonomy in the work being performed, and would very often be paid in exchange for 'public service' rather than for any given quantum of 'work'. Historically, therefore, the term 'salary' was rarely used outside the context of the periodical payments made to office-holders for tenure of an office.[1] Office-holders, in contrast to workers or labourers, were treated as enjoying

[1] From around 1390 to 1520 commonly applied to the stipend of a priest, especially a chantry

Labour and the Wage. Zoe Adams, Oxford University Press (2020). © Zoe Adams.
DOI: 10.1093/oso/9780198858898.001.0001

property in their office, conferring on them a degree of stability, with the salary seen as a form of rent payable to them as its holder.[2] Conceptualized as if it issued from the office, rather than being attached to any individual or activity, the payment did not vary in accordance with what services were actually being performed. Rather, the salary was effectively a payment for tenure, set at the level required to uphold the dignity and guarantee the performance of the duties of the office.[3] For this reason too, it was payable irrespective of whether actual service was required, because 'it is fit that a public servant should retain the means of a decent subsistence without being exposed to the temptation of poverty'.[4]

The term 'salary' itself is said to have its origins in 'salt money', a payment made to army officials during their service.[5] The salary consisted of meat and drink, of which salt was deemed to be a necessary part.[6] It was paid from a 'salt fund', the availability of which was unconditionally guaranteed, necessary to keep the army going throughout their service.[7] Given the difficulties of transporting large quantities of salt, however, these salt payments were gradually replaced by fixed unconditional money payments, the intention being that the soldiers could then acquire the salt themselves.

While this tale may well be a conventional myth, it still reflects well how the concept gradually came to be conceived in legal discourse as a regular and unconditional payment for the occupation of some position or office, set at a level that reflected the demands of the office and the office-holder's position and status, the payment of which presupposed an ongoing obligation to provide faithful service.[8]

The extension of the salary to professional employees took place gradually. Originally, professional men were not employed (in the capitalist sense or even the legal sense), but provided their services in exchange for a fee from clients. These fees, along with the standards of the profession, were tightly regulated by guilds and professional organizations that restricted membership to the educated, and thus very often the wealthy, elite. During the nineteenth century, however, and

priest: Tushar Rokade, '(8) Salary: Salt Money—Interesting Etymologies— Quora' <https://etymology.quora.com/Salary-Salt-Money> accessed 16 December 2016.

[2] William Searle Holdsworth, *A History of English Law*, vol 1 (Methuen 1922) vii, 269; Paul Matthews, '"Salaries" in the Apportionment Act 1870' (1982) 2 Legal Studies 302.

[3] *Wells v Foster* (1841) 8 M & W 149, 152, 151 ER 987;. Similar views are expressed in *Liverpool Corporation v Wright* (1859) John 359, 369, 70 ER 461 referring to the fees paid in place of a salary. For a discussion of the types of payments and types of office which are deemed to be unconditional and unassignable, see: *Davis v Duke of Marlborough* (1818) 1 Swans 74, 36 ER 303.

[4] *Wells v Foster* (n 3) 152. See also in relation to Emoluments: *Flarty v Odlum* (1790) 3 Term Rep 681, 100 ER 801.

[5] Daniel Greenberg (ed), *Jowitt's Dictionary of Legal Terms* (4th edn, Sweet & Maxwell 2015): The ancients derive the word from sal, salt, the most necessary thing to support human life being thus mentioned as a representative of all others (Plin H N xxxi, 42).

[6] Tushar Rokade (n 1).

[7] William Warner, *Albions England (1612)*, vol 131 (G Olms 1971) 360.

[8] Alfred Denning, 'Wages During Sickness' (1939) 54 Law Quarterly Review 353.

partly as a result of changes in company (and partnership) law, it became increasingly common for independent professionals to join together to provide their services as a partnership or a small, owner-run firm.[9] The partnership or firm would then pay these professionals and a number of clerks and/or agents a fixed annual sum that was independent from the fees paid by clients. The professions thus began operating with a view to profit in a way that they had not before. By these means, there emerged a class of relatively well-to-do professional men (women were often excluded from professional organizations and guilds, or obtained membership only through their husbands) in receipt of a stable income, occupying a position or post that imposed upon them an obligation to serve not merely a client, but the firm through which the provision of services was now being organized.[10] By analogy, these payments came to be classed as salaries, and the obligation to pay those salaries lay with the partnership or company in whose name, or on whose behalf, these persons carried on their profession.

The extension of the salary to professional employees presupposed the existence of a contractual (and relational) model of employment that had not existed when professionals performed services exclusively on behalf of clients. In such a context, it was the contract's relational nature and the salary's certain and unconditional character that came to distinguish it from other payments made in relation to work or service. For this reason, the term excluded payments to the genuinely self-employed, sums 'which a man earns in exercise of his personal skill' where he himself takes the economic risk.[11] It was confined instead to fixed payments for service, either as a consequence of the occupation of a public office or the occupation of a post pursuant to a contract of employment.[12] The extension of the term to cover the latter was, the courts argued, justified because the contract supplied the certainty that is characteristic of the salary, which for office-holders had been provided by their tenure.[13] The contracts of service by which professionals were being hired were thus seen by the courts as providing stability and protection in a similar way as might a proprietary right or interest in the job.

Towards the end of the nineteenth century, the salary was expressly defined as a payment for services rendered under some contract or appointment, computed by time and payable at fixed intervals.[14] Here, the term 'services rendered' did not mean a person's 'actually being called upon to perform duties' but his being 'under

[9] Thomas Marshall, 'The Recent History of Professionalism in Relation to Social Structure and Social Policy' (1939) 5 The Canadian Journal of Economics and Political Science 325.

[10] Alice Clark, *The Working Life of Women in the Seventeenth Century* (Routledge 2013).

[11] In *Re Hutton* (1884) 14 QBD 301 (Lindley J).

[12] In its earlier sense: 'Salarie ... signifies a recompence or consideration given unto any man for his paines bestowed upon another mans': John Rastell and William Rastell, *Les Termes de La Ley: Or, Certain Difficult and Obscure Words and Terms of the Common and Statute Laws of England, Now in Use, Expounded and Explained* (J Johnson Watson & Bangs 1812, 1641) fn 245.

[13] *Re Shine* [1892] 1 QB 522, 527.

[14] ibid (Lord Fry).

an obligation to perform them'.[15] Recipients of salaries might include 'medical advisers, members of theatrical establishments, and even … some descriptions of household servants' therefore, as persons hired to serve, and paid for the fact that they are under an ongoing legal obligation to perform the services required of them, irrespective of whether or not they actually work.[16] This obligation might be based in contract therefore, or for office-holders and servants, some property relationship (or, as conceived in this book, tenure).

The above ideas about the salary are reflected in the modern dictionary definition which defines the salary as a 'fixed payment paid periodically to a person as compensation for regular work'.[17] This definition has been frequently invoked by the courts, and also underpins the definition of 'salaried work' in the National Minimum Wage Regulations (NMWR 1999 and NMWR 2015).[18] It is to be contrasted with the 'wage' in its specific juridical sense: a payment for actual services rendered, most particularly for manual labour, or a payment that corresponds with the provision of some concrete good or measurable output, title to which the employer enjoys by virtue of a contract of exchange.[19] From this perspective, only the wage can be seen as a price 'dictated by' (or even subject to) the market, for the salary has long been seen as an unconditional, mostly contractual, payment set by reference to the skill and status of the individual, and what is needed to sustain that individual and his/her status. It is an individualized payment therefore, rather than one that is subject to market forces, that is, one that is based on the prevailing or going rate for work of a particular skill/type.

The term 'remuneration' was rarely used in legal discourse prior to the sixteenth century, and even then, only in a generic sense to refer to that which was given as recompense for some benefit provided. The term developed a more technical meaning, however, to refer to the various benefits payable to holders of higher status positions such as crown servants, public inspectors, judges, or members of the military, in recompense for their service.[20] Remuneration is a wider term than salary because remuneration means, effectively, 'quid pro quo'. Whatever consideration a person gets for giving his services seems to be a remuneration for them.[21] This would often include a salary, the definite monetary payment made for ongoing service, but also various non-monetary benefits and/

[15] *Emmens v Elderton* 622 (1853) 4 HL Cas 624, 668, 10 ER 606.

[16] ibid.

[17] John Simpson and Edmund Weiner (eds), *The Oxford English Dictionary* (2nd edn, Clarendon Press 1989).

[18] Regulation 21. The dictionary definition has been invoked in: *Greater London Council v Minister of Social Security* [1971] 2 All ER 285; 1 WLR 641, 646.

[19] *Resolute Management Services Limited v The Commissioners for Her Majesty's Revenue and Customs* [2008] STC (SCD) 1202; [2008] STI 2124.

[20] See: Petty Sessions (Ireland) Act 1827, c 67, s 9; Militia Pay Act 1827, c 50, Schedule 1; Clerk of Crown in Chancery Act 1835, c 47, preamble; Superannuation Act 1834, c 24, s.18.

[21] *R v Postmaster-General* (1876) 1 QBD 663, 664 (Blackburn J).

or supplementary payments that might only be payable on the performance of specific tasks or duties.[22]

From the nineteenth century the term 'remuneration' was used increasingly to refer to the total contractual benefits due to a private sector employee in connection with their employment.[23] Many higher-status employees would receive a number of benefits in addition to their salary, such as commissions on profits or benefits in kind, for instance the right to occupy a farmhouse or some other property linked with the business, and this would form part of the contractual remuneration that they could claim if they were wrongfully dismissed.[24]

There was thus a considerable contrast between the rights of a 'contractual' (or relational) employee and the rights of labourers or workmen when it came to the question of payment. The right to be paid wages for labour was quite different from the unconditional right to be paid a salary for time in contracted employment, a right that (most usually) accrued independently from time spent working. In relation to the latter, an employer could not withhold such sums following a breach of contract, but would have to proceed by way of an action for damages. Nor did wage labourers or workmen enjoy the added benefit of a contractual right to remuneration (of which the salary was just a part) for there was no ongoing contractual relationship to which such rights might attach. The only ongoing relationship between the parties arose from the employer's de facto right to secure himself the labour product purchased by the wage; a right which was, for most of the nineteenth century, backed up by the penal provisions of the master and servant regime.[25]

The significance of this distinction between the types of payment that could be claimed by different categories of worker was such that very often it was the nature of the 'remuneration' that determined the question of employment status and thus the scope of labour legislation. The contractor, it was said, looked to 'his profit' and not to wages for remuneration, whereas the workman or labourer would expect to be paid in wages.[26] If the person in question was not a workman or labourer who was paid in wages, therefore, he was someone who had to rely on his contract to secure his right to be paid—whether it be an executory contract of employment (or service) or a contract for services.

[22] For an example of how this operated in practice, see: *Skailes v Blue Anchor Line* [1911] 1 KB 360, 365.

[23] Such as the right to occupy a house: In *Re English Joint Stock Bank v Yelland's Case* (1867) LR 4 Eq 350.

[24] *Saunders v Jones* (1877) 7 Ch D 435.

[25] Robert J Steinfeld, *The Invention of Free Labor: The Employment Relation in English and American Law and Culture, 1350-1870* (UNC Press Books 1991); Claire Mummé, 'From Control through Command to the Control of Discretion: Labour Time, Labour Property and the Tools of Managerial Control in Early Twentieth Century Ontario' (2016) 45 Industrial Law Journal 176, 186–87. Hence, in the settlement cases, workers with weekends or days off were not deemed to be hired under contracts of service: see Chapter 5.

[26] *Marrow v Flimby and Broughton Moor Coal & Fire Brick Company* [1898] 2 QB 588, 598.

In *Gordon v Jennings*, the court made explicit this distinction between the wage on the one hand and the salaries and contractual remuneration of higher status employees on the other.[27] This case concerned the scope of the Wages Attachment Abolition Act 1870.[28] Grove J suggested that although in a broad sense, the term 'wages' might refer to 'any remuneration for services' properly construed:

> The term 'wages' is not applied to the remuneration of a high or important officer of the state or a company, for instance, but to that of domestic servants, labourers, and persons of a similar description. Taking the collocation of the word 'servant' with 'workman' and 'labourer', it is obvious that the reasonable application of the Act is to persons of small means—to servants, such as labourers and workmen receiving small wages at short periods.[29]

This did not include a secretary of a company paid a salary of £200 a year by quarterly payments because:

> ... his position and remuneration can [not] be said to come within the same description as those of menial servants or labourers. His salary is more than sufficient to keep life up; his salary and employment are such as many persons in the position of gentlemen are sometimes glad to get.[30]

Similarly, Lush J argued that the wage was a payment made to those who, absent such wages, 'would be likely to be deprived of their daily means of subsistence'.[31] This did not include the defendant in *Gordon* who enjoyed a relatively comfortable annual salary being employed in a stable and senior post within the company.

By the end of the nineteenth century, the distinction between salaries, wages, and the concept of remuneration was relatively clear—analytically at least. The wage was a payment that was payable in exchange for property in labour, or 'labour rendered', identified by the fact that it was provided by persons with nothing but their labour from which to live.[32] It was, accordingly 'jealously guarded' by the law, as was 'his right to live free from any restrictions as to the mode in which and the place at which his wages are paid'[33] even if the *amount* was dictated (or said to be) not by the law, but the market. The salary, by contrast, was a fixed, unconditional sum paid not for property in labour, but for service, whether provided pursuant to

[27] (1882) 9 QBD 45.
[28] 33 & 34 Vict c 30.
[29] *Gordon v Jennings* (1882) 9 QBD 45, 46.
[30] ibid 46.
[31] ibid 47.
[32] *Riley v Warden* (1848) 2 Ex 59, 154 ER 405.
[33] *Horwood v Millar's Timber and Trading Company, Limited* [1916] 2 KB 44, 51.

a contractual obligation to serve or the occupation of an office. The term 'remuneration', by contrast, might be used to refer to wages and/or salaries as a form of payment received in *recompense* for some benefit, but it also had a more technical meaning in that it referred to any monetary or non-monetary benefits received in connection with employment, whether flowing from an executory contract or tenure of an office.[34]

The distinction between wages and remuneration came to be particularly important in the context of the Workmen's Compensation Acts (1897 to 1906). The Acts provided for compensation in the event of industrial injury, calculated by reference to 'earnings in the employment of the same employer'.[35] They were quite explicitly protective statutes and envisaged an ongoing relationship between the parties, compensating workers for loss suffered because the relationship had been *prematurely* terminated or disrupted due to an accident at work. Given this, the courts drew a sharp distinction between this legislation and the Truck Acts, which 'was passed for a different purpose, and [thus] uses expressions different from those found in the statute we have now to construe'. Rather than equating the term 'earnings' with 'wages' as used in the Truck context, therefore, the court argued that 'the word "earnings" is used, not in the sense in which economical writers use it, but in a popular sense ... the full sum for which the man is engaged to work'.[36] This was taken to correspond with the total remuneration payable in connection with employment: anything that the workman had a legitimate expectation to receive, whether from his employer or otherwise.[37] This included sums which the courts had consistently excluded from the definition of wages under the Truck Acts. It included certain 'allowances' paid to 'meet the cost of board and lodging', for example, said to be 'earn[ed] each time [the worker], *in the service of his employers*, has to spend the night away from home'.[38] The courts emphasized that the term went beyond the wage because it covered the total cost to the worker of providing his service, which, in certain industries, would be far greater if 'the conditions of the employment were such that the workman had to incur some expenses to enable him to perform the services for which he was to be remunerated'.[39] Remuneration, or earnings, was thus to be conceived as a payment for service rendered under a contract of employment, and so was not to be confused with a wage as a payment for labour.

[34] The Income Tax Act 1842, 5 & 6 Vict c 35 was the first Act to directly invoke the term 'remuneration' to refer to the reward 'accruing by reason of employment' (Schedule E).

[35] Workmen's Compensation Act 1897, Schedule 1.

[36] *Abraham Coal Company* [1903] AC 306, 307–08. See also: *Great Northern Railway Company v Dawson* [1905] 1 KB 331.

[37] *Wild v John Brown Ltd* [1919] 1 KB 134 (not applicable on the facts). For further limits, see: *Logan v Shots Ltd.* [1919] SC 131, separating 'earnings' as a worker, and profit as a 'contractor' obtained as part of the same job.

[38] *Midland Railway Company v Sharpe* [1904] AC 349, 354. Emphasis added.

[39] ibid 351.

The term 'workman' that was employed in the 1906 Act included 'any person who has entered into or works under a contract of service or apprenticeship with an employer which is by way of manual labour, clerical work or otherwise'. This was, however, designed to make it possible for the courts to imply a relational contract in contexts in which the 'traditional' relationship of master and servant had previously deemed to have been absent. Thus, when the courts failed to extend the scope of the Act to cab drivers, the relationship between a driver and proprietor having been traditionally classed as one of bailor and bailee, Parliament intervened so as to bring the cab driver within the scope of the legislation.

> I do not think any Member of this House would seek to declare that a taxi-cab driver was not a workman in the real sense of the term. I think I will have the sympathy of the whole House when I say that the Workmen's Compensation Act was last amended it was believed it covered all workmen. I seek in this Bill, which is a Bill of one Clause, to provide that taxi-cab drivers or ordinary cab drivers plying for hire for wages or a percentage of profits or who hire a vehicle for a fixed sum for a day, *in fact no matter what the method of payment is*, that such drivers shall not be contracted out of the Act.[40]

All those in the socio-economic position associated with the concept of the workman therefore, and not only those hired under a particular form of contract in which there was an express right to 'wages', were intended to come within the scope of the Act's protection. The Act thus envisaged an active constitutive role for the courts, implying a relational contract so as to better protect workers' interests in employment.[41] And where the courts proved reluctant to do this, Parliament was willing to intervene. The right to remuneration that had once been the preserve of the higher status 'contractual' employee was thus gradually being extended to those hired at wages, or those in the socio-economic position of wage workers, so as to better protect their interests. Labour law concerns were thus taking precedence over the 'freedom' of individual parties to structure their relationships as they pleased.

6.3 Doctrinal Tensions

The Trade Board Acts had been premised on a particular model of industrial employment, one that continued to associate the wage earner with someone selling his

[40] HC Deb 19 July 1911, vol 28, col 1051 (emphasis added).

[41] Section 7(1). This was modified in 1923, to provide for an added requirement that the overall remuneration not exceed £250 (s 9(1)). The definition was also slightly modified in 1925 (s 3(1)).

commodity in the market.[42] For this reason, the personal scope of the Act turned on the nature of the good produced rather than the form of the contract by which it was provided. The 1909 Act thus provided that any 'shopkeeper, dealer, or trader, who by way of trade makes any arrangement ... with any worker in pursuance of which the worker performs any work' was to be classed as the worker's employer, and any 'remuneration' paid in respect of the good produced, his wages.[43] In effect, the legislation provided for a mandatory minimum price for a particular commodity, failure to pay which rendered the buyer liable for summary conviction. It did not, therefore, give rise to any implied contractual right to be paid minimum wages for labour provided in the context of a long-term relationship where it was presumed that it would be provided on an ongoing basis.[44]

The first minimum wage legislation to depart from this model was the Coal Mines (Minimum Wage) Act 1912. This was enacted in response to the national miners' strike of 1912; an attempt by miners to secure a legislative minimum wage when colliery owners sought to disregard district settlements and 'break their contracts' in response to foreign competition.[45] Rather than providing a mechanism for setting minimum prices for coal punishable by way of fine or imprisonment however, the legislation provided that it was to be an implied term of every 'contract for the employment of workman underground in a coal mine' that the employer will pay the workman wages no less than the minimum rate (set by the board). For the first time, therefore, a form of minimum wage legislation had been enacted that provided a *contractual* remedy in the event of non-payment.[46]

Prior to the 1872 Mines Act, coal mining had been characterized by extensive subcontracting. The dominant organization was the so-called 'butty system' where colliery owners would contract with 'butty workers' to deliver coal at a certain price per ton who would hire a team of men to help them extract it from the ground.[47] The key characteristic of this system was that there was a direct contractual nexus between the butty worker and the colliery company and between the butty worker and the miners, but rarely between the miners and the owners of the colliery. For this reason, payment would flow between colliery owner and butty worker, but not between colliery owner and miner. Instead, the miner would be paid directly by the butty worker who would reserve for himself the lion's share

[42] The courts stressed that the notion of 'trade' was intended to be read in this way: *Skinner v Jack Breach Ltd* [1927] 2 KB 220, 246 (Lord Hewart CJ).

[43] Section 9(1).

[44] Instead, by s 6(5), any agreement in which a lower rate was agreed would be void in its entirety.

[45] HC Deb 19 March 1912, vol 35, cols 1794–97; HC Deb 19 March 1912, vol 35, cols 1723–93 (Mr Cory).

[46] 2 & 3 Geo V c 2, s 1(1).

[47] On the nature and decline of the butty system, see: Arthur J Taylor, 'The Sub-Contract System in the British Coal Industry' in Leslie Pressnell (ed), *Studies in the Industrial Revolution* (Blackwell Publishing Ltd 1960).

of his takings.[48] For this reason, it was an industry in which the truck system had long been endemic.[49]

By the end of the century, however, direct employment had become more common, with colliery owners preferring to employ both colliers and fillers directly, allocating a collier and a number of fillers to a sett and paying the collier for the sett's produce, leaving him to divvy up the sum between the fillers.[50] The trade board model was quite ill-suited to this context, therefore, premised as it was on a simple exchange transaction where the wage appeared as the price of a finished article (or component part) for which an individual worker, or his 'personal labour', was responsible. Here, employers paid a single worker in respect of the output of a group. If minimum wage legislation was to be effective, therefore, it would have to concentrate on what the individual worker received, identifying a single party to be held responsible for guaranteeing that he actually received that sum in practice. To this, a 'contract for employment', a bilateral relationship between two parties, was particularly appropriate as the legal foundation for the obligation to pay a minimum rate.

In the debates surrounding the passage of the Act, Parliament discussed how a minimum wage that focused on what the worker *received*, rather than what the employer paid, might shape employer practices in a way that would be beneficial to the industry and thus to the country:

> If you have those two things—if you have guaranteed, upon the one hand, a reasonable minimum wage, and, upon the other hand, proper conditions for efficiency and regularity of work, you have a twofold incentive to the productiveness of the industry. Why do I say that? On the one hand, in the minimum wage you have an incentive to the management to give to the individual miner, and, indeed, to all the persons employed underground, the fullest facilities to make the most of their time and of their energy, and, on the other hand, adequate safeguards to the employer and an incentive to the men not to take advantage of their slackness or default.[51]

It was in light of this that the Act provided that 'it is to be a statutory term of every contract for the employment of workmen underground in a coal mine, that the employer shall pay to that working man wages of not less than the minimum rate settled under the Act and applicable to that workman ...'[52] so that the workmen

[48] Mike Richardson and Peter Nicholls, *A Business and Labour History of Britain: Case Studies of Britain in the Nineteenth and Twentieth Centuries* (Springer 2011) 158.

[49] For a discussion of work organization in the mines, see: Martin J Daunton and others, *Progress and Poverty: An Economic and Social History of Britain 1700-1850* (OUP 1995) 227–33.

[50] See, for example, the facts of *Richards v Wrexham* [1914] 2 KB 497 (below).

[51] HC Deb 19 March 1912, vol 35, cols 1723–93, 1728 (Mr Cory).

[52] Section 1.

would be provided with 'a right to recover by civil proceedings from the owner *who employs him* wages not less than that of the minimum rate'.[53]

The first case to discuss the significance of the term 'contract for employment' as it appeared in the Act was *Richards v Wrexham*.[54] Here, the claimant was a filler employed in the defendant's colliery. He had been engaged by the colliery manager with whom he had signed a document headed 'Terms of Employment' binding himself to observe the regulations of the colliery and providing the colliery with a right to dismiss him. The colliery would then supply a collier working in a sett with coal and one or more fillers to work under his direction. Each week, the colliery company paid one collier per sett by reference to the weight of the coal produced and the collier paid the filler a daily wage from this sum. There was no express undertaking by the colliery company to pay the filler any wages, therefore, nor was he in direct receipt of the product of the worker's 'personal labour'. It was thus difficult to identify any (pre-existing) liability to pay.

In the Court of Appeal, the majority argued that the filler stood in a relation of master and servant with the colliery. Nonetheless, it held that there was no 'contract for employment *at wages*' between them and so nothing to which the minimum rate could attach:

> The question is not whether the defendants employed the filler in the sense that they selected him, and could discharge him and control him in his conduct in the mine and so on, but whether the contract between the defendants and the filler was one under which the former became *by promise enforceable in law liable to pay the latter wages*.[55]

Proof that the employer enjoyed the benefit of the worker's service did not imply an obligation to pay monetary wages for labour where the direct recipient of that labour was the collier rather than the colliery. The wage was, in other words, a payment not for service, but for a tangible product. The existence of the master and servant relationship was thus insufficient to ground the right to minimum *wages* envisaged by the Act.[56]

Viscount Haldane disagreed with this conclusion. He argued that 'the effect of the [Act] is to make the company the masters who are bound to pay the minimum to the fillers, and a larger sum if they have agreed to pay such larger sum through their agents the colliers'.[57] The colliery company stood in the position of employer because it was the company that claimed the coal and it was the company that enjoyed the power to engage and dismiss.[58] The colliery was the beneficiary of the

[53] HC Deb 19 March 1912, vol 35, cols 1723–93, 1728 (Mr Cory). Emphasis added.
[54] *Richards v Wrexham* (n 50).
[55] ibid 516–17 (emphasis added).
[56] ibid 520.
[57] *Richards v Wrexham* (n 50) 513.
[58] *Richards v Wexham* (n 50) 510–11.

worker's personal service therefore, and there could be implied from this a right to contractual *wages* at the minimum rate. The custom that the colliers be responsible for paying the fillers was irrelevant therefore, for the obligation to pay wages attached to the recipient of service and a contractual obligation to pay the minimum rate could be implied by the courts once the existence of that service relationship had been proven.

When the issue reached the House of Lords it was Viscount Haldane's view that was preferred.[59] Building upon Viscount Haldane's observations, Earl Loreburn emphasized that:

> The payment of wages may be an element in deciding whether the relation of employer and workman exists or not, but if upon the facts of the case it appears that the relation does exist, then in my opinion it signifies nothing whether the wages are paid direct or whether there is some other indirect method or machinery for paying them. If that were not so the whole Act might be evaded simply by providing such machinery.[60]

Lord Atkinson endorsed this approach in *Churm v Dalton Main Collieries*, criticizing *Richards* on the basis that, had it been correctly decided the effect would have been that

> however completely the contract may establish the relation of master and servant, or employer and employee, between the owner of a colliery and his workman underground, the latter is, as against the colliery owner, excluded from the benefit of the Act unless the obligation to pay the workman wages is imposed by this contract upon the colliery owner . . . in effect, all the statute does is to fix a minimum for the wages contracted by an employer to be paid to his workman.[61]

Lord Shaw emphasized that the contractual obligation to pay the minimum wage was an implied obligation that attached to the relationship of master and servant, and so could not be waived by the contract:

> The statute does not say that the implied term is only to enter a contract if the employer has already under it become bound to pay some wages, or to pay individual wages, to each individual workman. It would be a strange answer to this absolute obligation to pay a minimum wage to his servant that the employer should say 'This statute cannot apply to me because I have done better than give him less than the minimum wage: I have bargained to give him no wages at all'.[62]

[59] *Hooley v Butterly Company* [1916] 2 AC 63.
[60] ibid 72.
[61] *Churm v Dalton Collieries Ltd* [1916] 1 AC 612, 624.
[62] *Churm v Dalton* (n 61) 634. See also Lord Parker, 643.

The courts had thus identified the wage, and the employer's obligation to pay it, as something that existed independently from the terms agreed as part of a 'free' bargain. It was instead a legal obligation to pay that arose as a matter of law if a service relationship could be proven. If such a relationship existed, the courts would imply a contract for employment at wages in order not to frustrate the socio-economic function that the Act pursued. This required, it seemed, shaping the social reality of employment in such a way as to secure workers a 'reasonable' wage and, in the process, promote greater efficiency in the industry.[63]

6.3.1 Wages, Salaries, and Remuneration in the Context of Minimum Wage Regulation

Throughout the early twentieth century, the courts became increasingly aware, and began to emphasize, the distinction between wages on the one hand and earnings or remuneration on the other. Thus, if Parliament used the term 'wage' the effect of this was to severely circumscribe the scope of the Statute's protection. This is particularly clear from the court's interpretation of the Metropolis Management Act 1855. Section 62 empowered local councils to 'employ such servants as may be necessary, and to allow such servants ... such wages as [the Council] may think fit'. In *Roberts v Hopwood*, the court had been asked to decide what considerations a Council could take into account in determining its servants' wages. Poplar Borough Council had decided to pay all its workers a minimum wage. This meant that men and women would receive the same rate of pay. In practice, as the court emphasized, this meant that the workers were paid above the market rate—far above that which was paid for similar work in London under industrial agreements between employers and employees.[64] While the Metropolis Management Act 1855 permitted the council to pay such wages as it 'thought fit', the House of Lords upheld a challenge to the legality of the council's decision on the grounds, inter alia, that the council had taken into account irrelevant considerations and 'allowed themselves to be guided in preference by some eccentric principles of socialistic philanthropy, or by a feminist ambition to secure the equality of the sexes in the matter of wages in the world of labour'.[65]

The Act had empowered the council to set wages, and this was seen to be a payment that varied depending upon the quantity and quality of the work. The wage, the court argued, is 'the reasonable pecuniary equivalent of the services rendered ... '[66] or 'the price which the employer pays to his employee for his or her

[63] HC Deb 19 March 1912, vol 35, cols 1723–93, 1728–30 (Mr Cory).

[64] Harold J Laski, 'Judicial Review of Social Policy in England: A Study of Roberts v. Hopwood et Al.' (1926) 39 Harvard Law Review 832.

[65] *Roberts v Hopwood* [1925] AC 578 (Lord Atkinson).

[66] ibid 612 (Lord Wrenby).

services'.[67] The remuneration that the council had set manifestly exceeded that which could properly be classed as wages, therefore, because they 'were far in excess of those [sums] necessary to obtain the services required and to maintain a high standard of efficiency' and so exceeded the 'market price' of labour.[68] This was, according to the court, something that was, 'for any well-recognized form of labour ... ascertainable and can be ascertained'.[69] For this reason, sums exceeding this amount were to be classed as a gift, or a gratuity, and as such, something that the council was not empowered to pay under the Act.[70]

That Parliament had used the term 'wage' in the Trade Board Act, the first attempt to intervene with the amount that workers were paid, was thus significant in circumscribing the scope of early minimum wage legislation. In *France v James Coombe & Son*, for example, this had the effect of confining the claimant's right to the minimum rate to the time spent producing the 'good' that was characteristic of the trade to which the Wages Order applied. This meant he could not claim the minimum rate for time performing quasi managerial duties, rather than manual work:

> The Trade Board Acts was obviously a scheme to provide minimum wages for a particular class of persons employed in the trade ... as soon as this worker ceases to perform the work [described in the order] he is employed under a general agreement of service ...[71]

The majority interpreted the reference to wages in the Act as referring to the price of labour, rather than to what a worker might be entitled to receive by way of income or remuneration from employment. Lord Blanesburgh adopted a different view, however, and suggested that:

> [The Trade Board Act requires] that the worker shall receive at least the minimum rate of remuneration for the work actually done, *or for the time spent in statutory employment.*[72]

He argued that the minimum rate was payable irrespective of whether the worker actually worked. This was so even if he was engaged in work to which the Order did not apply, provided the work was connected with his employment. This, he suggested, would be necessary to give effect to the Act's purpose in circumstances where the employer's rights in the worker's labour were so extensive and exclusive

[67] ibid 596 (citing Bankes J).
[68] ibid 596.
[69] ibid 594.
[70] ibid 600.
[71] *France v James Coombes & Co* [1929] AC 496, 523 (Lord Warrington of Clyffe).
[72] ibid 505–06 (emphasis added).

as to prevent him from accessing his subsistence elsewhere. It would have been different if the Act required an employer to provide a minimum amount of work. Because it didn't, however:

> ... during the periods when the employer is not bound either to employ or pay him he must be left at liberty either to obtain his minimum wage from another employer, or to exercise his skill for his own benefit. In no other way can the minimum or subsistence wage which for workers of his trade the Acts essay to provide be found for him ... [This required that] for *the whole time of his service* there [be] payable to the worker a wage at the minimum time-rate.[73]

His Lordship thus read the minimum wage as a right to be paid a minimum remuneration for time spent in employment.[74] Much as the medieval courts had, he assumed that those entitled to benefit from a worker's ongoing service ought to bear the costs of maintaining the provider of that service throughout the entire term of employment, if, that is, his employment of that worker prevented the latter from obtaining his subsistence elsewhere.

The courts were becoming increasingly aware that Parliament's choice between the concepts of 'wage' and 'remuneration' had significant consequences for workers when it came to the scope of legislative protection—even if, in practice, the use of conceptual language was never (inevitably) entirely consistent. By the beginning of the twentieth century therefore, it seemed as if the term 'wages' (or 'rates') was being invoked in legislation principally concerned with the regulation of the market, and in this context the court tended to interpret the term 'wage' quite narrowly. The term 'remuneration', or 'salary', by contrast, tended to be invoked only in those contexts concerned more generally with employment or the regulation of the labour relationship and/or the social costs of production, and it is these terms that are found in the National Insurance legislation, the Income Tax Act, and, as we have just seen, the Workmen's Compensation Acts.[75] The Coal Mines (Minimum Wage) and Agricultural Wages Acts were unique, therefore, for introducing a right to minimum *wages* that was conditional upon the existence of a contract *for* employment, or *of service,* rather than being tied to the provision of labour. This left open the question as to whether the rate was payable for service, time spent in contractual employment, or only for labour furnished as the use of the concept of the wage would suggest.

In *Pockney v Atkinson*, decided under the Agricultural Wages Act 1924, the court implied from the reference to 'wages' a right to be paid the minimum rate

73 ibid 506–07 (emphasis added).

74 This view was decisively rejected by the rest of the court, however, for it: 'ignores the clear distinction between employment for which alone the minimum wages are provided and employment in the business generally for which no such provision is made' ibid 523 (Lord Warrington).

75 National Insurance Act 1911, 1 & 2 Geo V c 55; Income Tax Act 1842, 5 & 6 Vict c 35.

only for time actually working.[76] Here, an agricultural worker had been hired for a year pursuant to an agreement that he would be paid a weekly sum that was higher than the minimum rate specified in the Order. The worker wrongfully left his employment before the end of the term, and sought to recover the minimum weekly rate for the period during which he had been employed. The court dismissed the claim. There was a distinction to be drawn, it argued, between an obligation to pay the minimum rate for labour actually provided, and an obligation to secure that a minimum weekly sum was actually received.[77] The purpose of minimum *wage* legislation was not to protect contractual expectations, but to prescribe the minimum price at which certain types of labour could be bought and sold, and it was into this category that the Act in question fell:

> if the worker had served his time he would have been paid his wages, but in the present case the employer refuses to pay wages to the man because the man did not carry out his contract to serve a certain time ... There is all the difference in the world between saying that a man shall be paid at a certain rate per week and saying that he shall be paid weekly at that rate.[78]

By contrast, in *Seabrooke & Sons v Jones*, Hewart CJ, referring to the Act's requirement that 'In fixing minimum rates a committee shall, so far as practicable, secure for able-bodied men such wages as in the opinion of the committee are adequate', argued that the Act had been intended to guarantee a minimum weekly income, irrespective of the amount of work available, so as to secure the 'amount of wages which would have been payable if the [week's hours] had been fifty'.[79] This interpretation took account of the fact that the power to set minimum wages was conceived in the Act as a power to fix minimum rates that are not only *adequate*, but 'enable a man in an ordinary case to maintain himself and his family in accordance with such standard of comfort as may be reasonable in relation to the nature of his occupation'.[80]

In *Smart v Spencer*, discussed in more detail below, Somerville J rejected this interpretation as it was inconsistent with the fact that Parliament had used the term 'wage' to refer to the minimum rate.[81] Clear wording would be required, he suggested, before minimum *wage* legislation could be interpreted as setting minimum rates of payment that extended beyond time spent working. It was this view that, in this context at least, appears to have prevailed.[82]

[76] By the Agricultural Wages (Regulation) Act 1924, 14 & 15 Geo V c 37, s 7(1): '... any person who employs a worker in agriculture shall, in cases to which the minimum rate is applicable, pay wages to the worker at a rate not less than the minimum rate ...'

[77] *Pockney v Atkinson* [1930] 1 KB 197. See particularly Lord Hewart CJ, 209–10.

[78] *Pockney v Atkinson* (n 77) 204.

[79] *Seabrooke & Sons v Jones* [1929] 1 KB 335, 340.

[80] Section 2(4).

[81] *Smart v Spencer* [1948] 2 KB 105.

[82] For a different approach, see: *Devonald v Rosser & Sons* [1906] 2 KB 728.

By the beginning of the twentieth century, while a relatively clear distinction had emerged between the wage, a concept intrinsic to the market, and the concepts of the salary and remuneration, contractual payments due for employment, the precise relationship between them remained unclear when it came to legislation concerned directly with how much a worker was entitled to be paid. It was still the case that only in rare circumstances would the courts imply a contractual right to remuneration where the worker was engaged in manual work at relatively low wages.[83] The contractual right to be remunerated for employment remained largely the preserve of higher status employees, those individuals capable of bargaining for such rights in their contract.[84] Similar premises underpinned Parliament's exclusion from the National Insurance Act of 1911 those higher paid employees whose remuneration exceeded £160, for such persons' contracts were deemed to provide them with adequate protection.[85]

Before the Second World War there was not, it seems, any significant move towards assimilating the positions of the two classes of worker, although ideas were beginning to surface which might suggest a gradual move in that direction. In the common law, the courts continued to be relatively reluctant to imply a contract of employment unless a service relation of kinds could be proven, and in the early years of the twentieth century these were rare. In many major industries, such as mining, shipbuilding, iron and steel, subcontracting and casual work rather than direct and open-ended employment, remained the norm, and so too did the presumption that workers' right to be paid was limited to their right to wages.[86]

6.4 The Relational Model of the Contract of Employment

Experiences during and after the First World War helped to foster the development of new ideas about the state's role in the economy. The state took a much more active role in production during this period and this centralization stimulated a movement towards mass manufacture based on a more reliable and continuous consumer demand. Production became less intermittent as a result and this helped to fuel the expansion of machine-based industry, and with developments taking place in company law this was to lead to a more centralized, vertically integrated form of control.[87]

[83] For a case in which this was deemed not to apply, see: *Hulme v Ferranti* [1918] 2 KB 426 (refusal to imply a notice period or an obligation to provide work to a piece worker).
[84] As in *Devonald* and in *Seabrooke*, each of which concerned relatively high-status employees with supervisory roles.
[85] See the list of exemptions in National Insurance Act 1911, first schedule, part II.
[86] Simon Deakin and Frank Wilkinson, *The Law of the Labour Market Industrialization, Employment, and Legal Evolution* (OUP 2005)
[87] Maurice Dobb, *Studies in the Development of Capitalism* (G Routledge 1946) chapter 8; Leslie Hannah, 'Managerial Innovation and the Rise of the Large-Scale Company in Interwar Britain' (1974) 27 Economic History Review 252.

The output rigidity inherent in this model made it more efficient to hire workers long term and keep production going, irrespective of fluctuations in the market, than it was to hire them on short-term contracts so as to respond to short-term fluctuations in demand. For this reason, wage costs began to be seen as a kind of overhead, more akin to a salary than a wage, and, in time, came to be seen as something that purchased the right to integrate the individual within the enterprise with a view to making use of their ongoing service.[88] This process was to be given a further push in the post-1945 period with nationalization and the rise of the large-scale public enterprise.[89]

The developments taking place in the inter-war period also led to greater firm specialisation, and this helped to lay the foundations for industry and sector level collective bargaining mechanisms to develop.[90] This process was assisted by the fact that compulsory arbitration during the First World War had helped to convince the government of the importance of state support for the 'self-regulation' of industry. This meant, however, that assumptions about the (il)legitimacy of wage regulation did not much change. The focus became not how to develop alternatives to the trade board model, but how to build upon it to promote joint regulation. The question of low pay remained a problem of price regulation, requiring measures to stimulate fair competition, rather than any direct intervention in the setting of wages.[91]

Even so, war-time experience of national wage settlement had proliferated proposals for industrial relations regulation at a national scale. National schemes of wage negotiation and ideas about national minimum wages failed, however, to survive the post-war slump. The main reform to come out of this period built on the Whitley Committee's recommendation for expanding the trade board model as a way to foster collective bargaining. In this respect, the Whitley Committee report advocated shifting the focus away from using trade boards to target 'sweating', towards seeing the boards as precursors for *voluntary* collective bargaining. They were to be an alternative to the ideal, namely, joint industrial councils, and would be established voluntarily by both sides of industry. Trade boards were thus to become 'a temporary expedient facilitating organization within the industry, so that, in the course of time, the workers of the employers will not have need of the statutory regulations'.[92] These proposals resulted in the Trade Board Act 1918.

The Trade Board Act 1918 extended the wage fixing powers of the boards to include powers to set general minimum piece rates, and overtime rates. They could also determine the normal number of hours per week or per day.[93] The

[88] Dobb (n 87) 362.
[89] Deakin and Wilkinson (n 86).
[90] Dobb (n 87) 363.
[91] See particularly: Ministry of Reconstruction. Committee on Relations Between Employers and Employed, *Second Report on Joint Standing Industrial Councils* (HM Stationery Office) 659.
[92] HC Deb 17 June 1918, vol 107, col 61, 70 (Mr George Roberts, Minister of Labour).
[93] Section 3(1)(c).

only rates that were mandatory, however, were minimum time rates. The Act did, however, simplify the procedure for establishing boards, and this led to a proliferation of the industries covered by wage orders. However, this expansion depended on the continuation of the post-war boom. As soon as the boom broke, the trade boards came to be seen as something that delayed employers' ability to reduce wages, 'restricting' the market's capacity to self-adjust.[94] In such a changed economic environment, the mood shifted, and the creation of new boards stopped. The government simply ended all expansion of the system. In April 1920, the minister, Dr Thomas Macnamara, said that it was 'desirable, in the present circumstances, to proceed with caution in the establishment of the new Trade Boards'.[95]

Employers saw the boards as inhibiting their capacity to reduce wages in the way they could in other industries. This led them to campaign to amend the 1918 Act so as to allow them to agree a lower rate with their workers, replacing the rate fixed by the boards. In September 1921, this campaign led to the appointment of a committee, 'to inquire into the working and effects of the Trade Boards Acts and to report what changes, if any, are required'.[96] The committee concluded that the Act had unjustifiably extended the degree of state interference in the settlement of wages. Only a change in government prevented the committee's proposals for a radically scaled back version of the trade board model, more restrictive even than the 1909 Act, from passing into law.

The 1930s saw a shift in the (Labour, and later Coalition) government's attitude towards the trade boards. As the depression wore on, wage regulation came back in favour as part of a policy of economic protection.[97] The establishment of new boards was resumed, but this time only if they were desired by both employers and trade unions: state 'interference' was justified, it seemed, provided prior consent had been obtained. During this period, the government provided subsidies and/or licences to employers with a view to limiting the number of producers. Part of the price for state protection was, however, that the employers so protected had to commit to paying fair wages.

Two industries in particular received considerable attention during this period: road haulage and dock work. As we saw in Chapter 5, the challenge in the dock industry was that, unless greater regularity of employment could be secured, and thus a reduction in the number of employers and 'casuals', a guaranteed weekly minimum was unlikely. The Maclean committee, charged to explore the possibility of implementing a system of 'maintenance' concluded that it would be impossible before an efficient system of registration was implemented, it being 'a natural

[94] Frederic Joseph Bayliss, *British Wages Councils* (B Blackwell 1962) 18.
[95] HC Deb 13 April 1921, vol 140, cc 1090-1, 1090.
[96] Ministry of Labour, *Minutes of Evidence Taken Before the Committee of Inquiry into the Working and Effects of the Trade Board Acts* (Cmd 1645, 1922) ('Cave Report').
[97] Bayliss (n 94) 30.

consequence of the work performed ... that to a large extent port employment should be inherently casual ...'[98]

The unions nonetheless continued to argue for 'maintenance' in place of casual engagement by the day supplemented by unemployment benefits; a maintenance payment being something the workers were deemed to be entitled as a consequence of being a registered member of the port's labour force. Mr Bevin had proposed that the payment be funded by transferring the unemployment insurance contributions of state employers and workers to a fund to be administered by the National Joint Committee for the Port Transport Industry, any deficiency being met by a levy on all goods and passengers moving through the ports. The employers, however, could not be sold on the idea of maintenance on the ground of cost. Any distress that could not be met through insurance was, they argued, to be met by public assistance. Given the lack of progress on the question of 'maintenance', it was ultimately agreed to proceed more vigorously with registration schemes and to leave the issue of 'maintenance' for the future.[99] Even so, it was generally accepted that 'registration schemes alone will not provide a solution to the problem of casual employment at the docks' and that what was required was a minimum weekly wage guarantee, pensions, registration, and centralized distribution of labour.[100] For this, however, the dockers were going to have to wait until the Second World War.

The challenge in road haulage was different. The Road and Rail Traffic Act 1933 had imposed an obligation to pay fair wages in accordance with the Fair Wages Resolution, there being no voluntary wage regulation in the industry. The problem, however, was that the existing 'fair wages' resolutions were inadequate as a result of the uneven manner in which the licensing provisions, and thus the fair wage obligations, applied to different aspects of the industry. This problem was exacerbated by the fact that the implementation of the National Joint Conciliation Board's recommendations was frustrated by the lack of effective organization.

In 1938, in light of this, the government introduced the Road Haulage Act 1938. This Act extended to road haulage a model not dissimilar from the trade boards model, with one significant difference: in road haulage the board had the power to fix workers' *remuneration*; the trade boards could do no more than set minimum *rates* for labour. The 'basis' of the Act, it was said, was to ensure that unfair remuneration was not paid.[101]

The Road Haulage Act[102] was less concerned with regulating competition in the market than it was with guaranteeing that workers actually received from their

[98] Vernon H Jensen, *Hiring of Dock Workers and Employment Practices in the Ports of New York, Liverpool, London, Rotterdam, and Marseilles* (Harvard University Press 1964) 131.
[99] ibid 131–32.
[100] Committee on Port Labour, *Port Labour Inquiry Report* (HMSO 1931) 61–70.
[101] HC Deb 11 May 1938, vol 335, cols 1611–57, 1619 (Mr Ernest Brown, Minister of Labour).
[102] (1938) Geo VI c 70.

employers something approximating a meaningful right to subsistence. Despite building on the trade board framework, therefore, the Act conferred on the boards much broader powers, extending over piece and time wages, overtime rates, and holidays with pay; they were to do more, in other words, than merely determine the 'true' price of labour. Thus, while:

> the Bill follows the precedent of previous legislation for the regulation of wages and does not make provision for the regulation of conditions of service or conditions of employment ... it will be possible under the Bill to fix remuneration for overtime and to specify the number of hours beyond which overtime *remuneration* must be paid (etc.)[103]

Stopping short of providing boards with a power to set minimum terms and conditions of employment, the Act nonetheless made provision for setting minimum rates of remuneration and, as a result, provided that the minimum rate would be implied into any contract between a worker and employer providing for a lower rate of remuneration.[104] It did not, therefore, and in contrast to the Trade Board Act, merely impose upon an employer a statutory obligation to pay. It guaranteed to all workers a right to recover by way of civil proceedings what was to be a reasonable remuneration for being employed under an express or implied contract of employment.

The Road Haulage Act made provision for compulsory arbitration in response to complaints by unions and workers concerning the payment of 'unfair remuneration', a mechanism which was regarded at the time as a 'practical experiment'.[105] The purpose of the Act was to 'help industry to self-government',[106] recognizing that '[our] voluntary collective bargaining system is one of the most potent instruments for the stability of our national life'.[107] Determining what was 'unfair' still required that regard be had to collectively agreed rates, but the purpose of this was not now to establish the 'true' market price that would have been agreed had the parties been capable of acting freely, but to determine what was generally regarded as a fair remuneration or return from employment.

It was particularly relevant in this context that a failure to pay fair wages might affect the quality of the work performed, at potential risk to the broader community:

> If we are to have efficient drivers and to assure safety on the roads, it is essential that these men should be paid adequate wages. I am sometimes worried when I see lorries driven by mere boys, very often of small weight, who are probably

[103] HL Deb 29 June 1938, vol 110, cols 387–410, 388 (Lord Templemore).
[104] Section 6(1).
[105] HC Deb 11 May 1938, vol 335, cols 1611–57, 1619 (Mr Brown).
[106] ibid 1620 (Mr Brown).
[107] ibid 1621 (Mr Brown).

> working longer hours than they ought to be called upon to work. From the point of view of the safety of the public it is right that there should be some assurance that men driving lorries should have a wage that would enable them to be as physically perfect as possible.[108]

This concern was particularly so given the tendency for low-wage employers to drive higher-paying employers out of the market:

> I claim to be a big believer in private enterprise, but I like private enterprise to start off on a fair basis as between one man and another. It is not fair that one man should gain an advantage because he is prepared to pay much lower wages than he ought to pay. I believe that the payment of fair and adequate wages is in the interests of public safety, in the interests of the decent employer, and in the interests of the decent employé [sic].[109]

Despite the clear progress made with the Road Haulage Act, the right to 'fair' remuneration was subject to one caveat. Namely, if the Industrial Council decided that an employer had paid 'unfair' rates, it was required to fix the remuneration to be paid 'and in doing this ... must have regard not only to ... appropriate agreements, but also to the *general level of wages in the industry concerned*'. Common practice, then, rather than an objective standard linked to workers' living costs, remained the *primary* concern in making assessments about 'fairness'.[110]

The next issue to be addressed by the government was the question of holidays with pay. Discussions over this matter had begun in 1929 when Parliament debated a private members' bill that sought to introduce a general right to holidays with pay. Despite consensus on the importance of paid holidays, however, both from a welfare and productivity perspective, concern was expressed that a statutory right to paid holidays would distort the price of labour, forcing employers to lower basic wage rates.[111] In relation to agriculture, for example, it was argued that

> ... the principle of those boards is to regulate wages at the highest level which, in the opinion of the boards, the industry is in a position to pay. If you are going to impose an additional burden on agriculture, it must necessarily be taken into account by the agricultural wages boards when they are next called upon to fix the wages of the agricultural worker, and it would, therefore, almost necessarily have the result that the wages would be fixed at a lower level because of the increased charges which were being placed on agriculture by this Bill.[112]

108 HC Deb 11 May 1938, vol 335, cols 1611–57, 1628 (Mr Holdsworth).
109 ibid 1629 (Mr Holdsworth).
110 ibid 1622 (Mr Ernest Brown).
111 HC Deb 15 November 1929, vol 231, cols 2421–503, eg at 2449 (Mr Somerville).
112 ibid 2471 (Sir Rentouil).

Mr Somerville, who was to reiterate this view of the wage in *Smart v Spencer* in his capacity of Justice of the Court, argued that 'in the long run, the question of the rates of pay given by an employer is not settled by the employer himself. The employer pays the highest rate of wages the industry can afford to give'. He went on to argue that 'federations of employers and trades unions really have, in the long run, very little actual influence on the rates of wages paid. They cannot alter the natural law of supply and demand'.[113] The introduction of annual holidays would merely lower the wage rate, therefore, offering workers no net benefit. It was therefore futile for Parliament to even attempt to 'interfere' with market forces, however laudable the aims pursued.

Throughout the course of the parliamentary debates, it was the term 'wages', rather than remuneration that was invoked when discussing the costs of paid holidays. Paid holidays were not yet seen as part of the contractual remuneration payable for employment therefore, but a charge or cost that affected the value of the labour purchased by the wage. Providing for paid holidays in this way was seen to be intimately related to manipulating the wage rate; a form of direct intervention into the market that was still heavily criticized. It was not only an ultimately futile exercise, given the 'law of supply and demand', it was undesirable because 'it means State interference with the liberty of the subject'.[114]

Extending a right to be paid for employment that was distinct from the basic right to be paid wages for labour still seemed limited, therefore, to those whose employment relationships more closely resembled a form of contractual, or personal, service. Parliament was still hostile to the idea of *requiring* an employer to pay for anything other than actual labour:

> ... while everybody who values service must realise that they must give a good measure of reward for that service, they do not necessarily feel that they can afford to do such things as give a week's pay for no work done to every man in the service of some of these great organisations.[115]

It was seen to be particularly important during the debates that 'Great Britain [was] experiencing one of the most difficult times it has ever known. We are facing enormous competition all over the world, and our only hope of being able to hold our position is to reduce the cost of the production of our goods'. This called for particular caution, because

> the introduction of any ill-considered and ill-thought-out Bill of this description [risks further] imperilling the position of the workers of this country, ...

[113] ibid 2443-4 (Mr Somerville).
[114] ibid 2449 (Mr Somerville).
[115] ibid 2480 (Sir James Reynolds).

> increas[ing] the misery which is to-day afflicting the soul of the Lord Privy Seal when he realises his growing helplessness to increase the volume of production in this country, and thus lead to more employment.[116]

Having not yet fully embraced the potential of the concept of remuneration to be used as a mechanism through which to distinguish payments for employment from wages payable for labour, the latter being 'dictated' by the market, the extension of a contractual right to be paid for time not working was only going to be possible as the nature of industrial employment began to change, as employers recognized that it was legal rights in service, rather than labour, that they sought to obtain in the labour market—as they realized, in other words, the benefits of a relational model of the contract of employment.

When a second private member's bill got to the second reading in 1936, it seemed that the situation was changing. The government set up a committee to investigate the possibility of legislating for holidays with pay,[117] there now being broad agreement that holidays with pay should be legally guaranteed.

In 1938, building upon the premises in the Road Haulage Act, Parliament finally enacted its Holidays with Pay Act, empowering trade boards and other industry-specific wage boards to provide up to a week's annual holiday, to which the minimum rate for the industry would apply. Rather than expressing concern over the negative effects of such measures on global competitiveness, it was now believed that 'an increase in the wellbeing of the individual worker means an increase in the efficiency of the industry, and this in its turn means an increase in our general wellbeing'.[118] Significantly, and in contrast with the debates in 1929, this time the right to holiday pay was being phrased as a right to holiday *remuneration*.[119] The shift in opinion over the importance of such intervention was due, in part, to the fact that many employers were making provision for such rights themselves:

> The effect of such a measure would surely be no more than to bring what at present everyone would regard as the backward employers of labour into line with the practice of enlightened employers, whether private individuals or public authorities, at the present day.[120]

The express object of the Act was thus to address remaining status distinctions between blue and white-collared workers, recognizing that wage workers had as

[116] ibid 2450 (Mr Somerville).

[117] Ministry of Labour, *Report of the Committee on Holidays with Pay (Amulree Committee)* (Cmd 5274, 1938).

[118] HC Deb 14 July 1938, vol 338, cols 1553–648 (Mr Ernest Brown).

[119] HL Deb 25 July 1938, vol 110, cols 1094–103, 1096 (Lord Templemore).

[120] ibid 1102 (Earl of Listowell). See also: HC Deb 14 July 1938, vol 338, cols 1553–648, 1555 (Mr Ernest Brown).

much a need for holidays to 'improve their material comfort' as the better paid did.[121] Falling short of providing a right to paid holidays in industry generally, the Act nonetheless paved the way towards transforming the role of the wage boards, for they were now being empowered to set not just wages, but certain minimum rates of remuneration—securing an absolute right to be paid that was for the first time being decoupled from the provision of labour.

During the 1930s, therefore, it might be said that the traditional distinction between wages and salaries was becoming blurred, for even the former appeared as something that was payable not for labour, but for service or employment. In this context, the term 'remuneration' was gradually being employed in place of wages, to refer to all those payments paid *as if* the worker had been working, when he had not. It thus provided a potential bridge between a conception of the wage as price, and the conception of the wage as a cost of production—a right to which workers were entitled. Thus, statutory minimum wage rates were sums that were payable *as if* they reflected prices agreed in the market, for, now that these sums were beginning to be influenced by non-market considerations of fairness, the path was being laid for a much clearer distinction between the market wage and the minimum rates of remuneration that the legal system guaranteed in order to elevate this into a right to subsistence.

In the first half of the twentieth century, however, the coexistence of these different ideas of the wage continued to create tensions in legal discourse, as the cases decided under the Agricultural Wages (Regulations) Act 1924 and the Coal Mines (Minimum Wage) Act 1912, explored above, have already shown. The problem here was that this legislation established a link between wages and the existence of an executory contract of employment, and this made it unclear for what exactly the wage was to be paid; ongoing service or labour rendered. This issue was revisited in *Smart v Spencer*, discussed above, by which time it seems the distinction between minimum wages and minimum rates of remuneration was becoming clearer.

In his judgment, Somerville J drew a distinction between the legal and economic concepts of the wage, a distinction which broadly corresponds with that between remuneration and wages. He argued that there were 'two types of legislation that might impose terms as between employer and employed'. Legislation might provide 'a minimum wage for work done' or might instead provide that 'a man should receive wages in respect of a period when he does not work and is not required to do so'.[122] Legislation of the former type was concerned with the 'primary provision of any contract of service ... what is to be paid for the work which a man contracts to do during the period in question' (market wages). This was different from legislation concerned with what an employer might promise, or be legally required, to pay during periods of sickness or holiday (remuneration).[123] There was

[121] HC Deb 15 November 1929, vol 231, cols 2421–503, 2431 (Mr Hudson).
[122] *Smart v Spencer* [1948] 2 KB 105.
[123] ibid 112.

a distinction therefore, between minimum wage legislation, and legislation concerned with securing reasonable remuneration for employment. The problem for those bringing a claim under the Coal Mines or Agricultural Wages Acts, therefore, was that the presumption was that if the term 'wage' was used there could be no logical basis for imposing (for example) a minimum rate to be paid during sickness and holidays in a particular industry. Such an approach could not be justified simply because wages were thought to be too low. The Agricultural Wages Act (and the Coal Mines (Minimum Wage) Act), having provided for minimum *wages*, had to be construed as being concerned only with regulating the price of labour. They thus said nothing as to what a worker should receive as income from employment.

In light of this, Somerville J suggested that the term 'employed' as it was used in the Agricultural Wages Act had to be taken as referring to time actually working. It was irrelevant that the Act included within the definition of wages certain benefits, such as an accommodation allowance that would be payable independently from time working, for 'the fact that under the Act such a benefit may be reckoned as payment of wages for the purpose of the minimum rate would not necessarily make it wages in other contexts'.[124] Even though the statute hinged the right to the minimum wage to the existence of a contract of service therefore, the wage *rate* itself was only payable for labour. The term 'wages' might incorporate non-monetary benefits not directly linked with work for some purposes, therefore, but these were not wages to which the obligation to pay minimum rates could attach.

It seems, therefore, that co-existing within legal discourse was a concept of the wage akin to the pre-industrial idea of a sum or maintenance cost that is payable for ongoing service, a form of social wage, and the 'economic' concept of a wage as the price payable for commodified labour. But the wage might also be something that expresses not the content of a right to be paid, but something which might go towards proving that there exist legally enforceable rights in labour, a form of 'quid pro quo' for rights in service. For this reason, and consistently with the decision in *Hooley* and *Churm*, Somerville J argued that the obligation to pay wages presupposes enforceable rights in labour, a particular form of social relation characterized by service, but does not necessarily require an express promise to pay monetary wages.[125]

Thus, while 'the payment of wages may be an element in deciding whether the relation of employer and workman exists ... if upon the facts of the case it appears that the relationship does exist ... it signifies nothing whether the wages are paid direct or whether there is some indirect method or machinery for paying them'. The employer will still, it seems, be bound to pay monetary wages.[126]

[124] ibid 115.
[125] *Hooley v Butterly* [1916] 2 AC 63.
[126] ibid 71 (Earl Loreburn).

While the distinction between wages and remuneration was becoming increasingly clear therefore, the wage itself was no longer being confined to that which was payable for commodified labour. It had a deeper significance within the legal system as a right that was specific and integral to a particular social relation, one in which the courts were beginning to believe that certain mutual rights and obligations should (once again) be implied. It was with a view to guaranteeing such mutual rights and obligations that the concept of contractual remuneration and the technique of implying an executory contract, was slowly being embraced. These ideas were eventually to be given legislative expression in the Wages Councils Act 1945.

6.5 Minimum Remuneration Legislation

The Second World War witnessed a sufficiently large extension of the economic functions of the state as to lead to a qualitative reconsideration of the relationship between the state, the law, and the market.[127] Full employment, a steady demand for the products of factories, the emergence of mass production techniques, and a much more significant move towards vertical integration had had a significant impact on the needs and interests of the parties as well as the nature of industrial organization. This, and the erosion of status and skill differentials that compulsory service during the war years had facilitated, meant that standardized terms and conditions could more easily become the norm. This was something that the parties were finding direct employment, on the basis of a contract envisaging mutual obligations of ongoing service and payment, was well-suited to meet.

In 1940, the government enacted the Essential Work Order (EWO) with a view to guaranteeing continuous production during the war period. This effectively made labour compulsory for all, restricting employers' rights of dismissal, and helping to erode status distinctions between workers and across occupations. The effect of these measures was to provide workers of all types with a guaranteed minimum income and a regular working week, while lending trade unions a much more significant role in governing the economy.[128] In this context, the wages these workers received no longer appeared as the price of a tangible good, for they were payable for war service attaching to employment, rather than the provision of commodified labour. The idea behind the Order was that:

[127] Douglas Brodie, *A History of British Labour Law, 1867-1945* (Hart Publishing 2003) chapter 8; Dobb (n 87); Deakin and Wilkinson (n 86) 241–42; Otto Kahn-Freund, 'Minimum Wage Legislation in Great Britain' (1949) 97 University of Pennsylvania Law Review 778.

[128] Howard Gospel, 'Markets, Institutions, and the Development of National Collective Bargaining in Britain: A Comment on Adams' (1998) 51 Economic History Review 591, 155. The practice under the EWO had been to provide guaranteed weekly wages provided that workers were available for work and willing to perform reasonable alternative work.

> The Minister will be able to prescribe the terms of remuneration, the hours of labour, and conditions of service. Remuneration will be on the basis of remuneration for the job. If an engineer is asked to do engineering work, he will get engineer's pay. If somebody else is asked to do a particular job, he will get the pay of that job. If a professional man is asked to do his professional work, he will get his professional pay. If he is asked to do manual work he will get a manual worker's pay. The general principle will be that of remuneration for the *job*.[129]

During this period, all workers received remuneration for their contribution to the war effort; their ongoing service to the country.[130] They did not receive wages in the traditional sense therefore, because 'wages and profits were under the government's control' and their pay was determined outwith the context of the market.[131]

By the end of the war the state had also began taking steps towards universal (rather than selective) social reform. This made possible the creation of new jobs in an emerging consumer-service sector, while at the same time opening up the professions to new recruits to meet the growing demand for public services. In time, this helped to erode customary wage rates and rigid controls over training, further undermining status distinctions between wage workers and salaried employees.

One of the longer-term impacts of the Second World War was to pave the way for the emergence of a unitary class of persons dependent on what was increasingly becoming stable employment for subsistence. The decline of manufacture and the growth of services, coupled with large-scale nationalization of industry was such, moreover, that it was the model of service rather than that of industrial wage labour which was to dominate as the common law adapted itself to these changes. Professionals no longer enjoyed the privileged protected status they had once enjoyed therefore, but nor were wage workers to be left entirely dependent upon their wages for subsistence. In addition to the right to be paid wages for labour, the growth of the welfare state and early social welfare and labour legislation was to provide a relatively comprehensive contractual right to be remunerated for employment for most people.

Particularly significant in this process was the National Insurance Act 1946, bringing within a single class all those 'gainfully employed'.[132] This provided the foundations for uniting salaried employees and wage earners within a single conceptual category, and it was the contract of service that was to be drawn upon for this purpose.[133] By these means, the road was being cleared for the development of

129 HC Deb 22 May 1940, vol 361, cols 154–85, 155 (Mr Atlee). Emphasis added.

130 The Emergency Powers Act 1940 required all citizens to place 'themselves, their service and their property at the government's disposal'.

131 HC Deb 22 May 1940, vol 361, cols 154–85, 156 (Mr Atlee).

132 National Insurance Act 1946, 9 & 10 Geo VI c 67, s 1(2).

133 ibid s 1(2)(a). The term 'contract of employment' was not used explicitly until the Contracts of Employment Act 1963, c 49.

the previously embryonic technique of constituting a relation of service, grounded in the employer's economic power, as a relational contract of service, something that was, in time, to re-embed in the labour relationship the mutual obligations of service and social protection that the legal idea of 'tenure' had once implied.[134]

The relational contractual form had been integral to the labour and social protections being developed during and after the war. But it was also essential to meeting the changing needs of the parties in production. The relational contract helped with the rationalization and stabilization that the large-scale corporate structures emerging during this period required, much as it had contributed to the new business models through which professional services were being carried out in the late nineteenth century. The business models emerging during this period required more than property rights supported by criminal sanctions to guarantee the smooth running of the production process, and rising wage rates and general improvements in the conditions of the working classes were such that economic power alone would be insufficient to secure the cooperation of the workforce. The contract of employment was only available as an appropriate platform upon which to build labour and social rights because it was already becoming central to the way in which the parties themselves sought to protect their interests and expectations. Nonetheless, in so becoming, the effect was to further stimulate the use of this model by the parties themselves.

The emergence (and extension) of the relational contractual model was significant not only for helping to stabilize industrial relations and for facilitating the coordination of labour and social protections, but also because it provided the courts with the resources from which to reconstitute the labour relationship in a new form. Drawing upon the concept of the contract of service (or employment), they were able to express the property relationship at the heart of wage labour in a form in which mutual obligations, similar to those that had once been inherent in ideas of tenure, could again be implied. Now, however, they could be implied in a form that was compatible with the assumptions of the market. Here, integration into the enterprise, rather than the master's household, acted as a functional substitute for tenure, the legal system making the corporation responsible for preserving the persons, and resources, in its 'care'. Drawing an analogy between the salaried employee's contractual obligation to faithfully serve and the pre-industrial servant's duty of obedience, each of which having presupposed a form of 'subsistence wage', the courts had combined within a single institution subordination and dependence, and stability and protection. The courts' ability to do this, however, was inseparable from the fact that Parliament itself was beginning to draw upon

[134] See the discussion in *Benjamin and Another v Minister of Pensions and National Insurance* [1960] 3 WLR 430 where it is deemed to be irrelevant that a waiter not be paid 'wages', or that an agreement not expressly envision 'remuneration' for service. All that matters, on this view, is the nature of the relationship, and thus whether the individual is providing services on behalf of a business or employer.

the executory contract and the associated concept of remuneration, rather than the wage–work exchange, as the foundation upon which to construct a legal framework concerned with the regulation of pay.

6.5.1 The Wages Councils

Both the Wages Councils Act 1945 and the Catering Wages Act 1943 were premised on 'the idea of a joint body working together' to continue the war time policies of full employment and securing reasonable standards of pay and working conditions for all.[135] The former Act was to provide 'for the regulation of the remuneration and conditions of employment of workers in certain circumstances' and to this end provided for the establishment of wages councils which had the power to set not just wages, but holidays with pay, overtime rates, and to prescribe certain minimum terms and conditions of employment. The scheme imposed on the minister a duty to take steps to improve any existing machinery for setting remuneration if it seemed to be inadequate, was likely to become inadequate, or if a reasonable standard of remuneration was unlikely to be maintained.[136]

In contrast to the trade board legislation, the Wages Councils Act was expressly concerned with what the worker received from employment, rather than (solely) what the employer paid for labour in the market. The Act expressly defined remuneration as 'the amount *obtained* or to be obtained in cash by the worker from his employer … *in connection with* his employment'.[137] Moreover, by making *employment* rather than *labour* the reference point for the payment of the rate, the Act firmly embedded the link, emerging in the common law, between the right to a reasonable remuneration and the existence of a particular type of relationship characterized by faithful service and stable employment.

The Act mirrored the Road Haulage Act in that it stated that the effect of a wages regulation order was that 'if a contract between a worker and employer to whom an order applies provides for the payment of less remuneration than the statutory minimum, it shall have effect as if it provides for the payment of the statutory minimum'.[138] Provided there was a contract therefore, of any type, whether of employment or for labour, the worker would be entitled to be paid the 'reasonable' remuneration established by the councils. In contrast to the Agricultural and Coal Mines (Minimum) Wage Acts, there was no requirement for the worker to be employed *under* a contract of service, or employment. Instead, the Act envisaged that the courts would imply an executory contract (in the ongoing relational sense) so

[135] Catering Wages Act 1943, 6 & 7 Geo VI c 24; Wages Councils Act 1945, 8 & 9 George VI c 17. See: HC Deb 16 January 1945, vol 407, cols 69–116, 110 (Mr Corquodale).

[136] Section 3.

[137] Section 13 (emphasis added).

[138] Section 11(1).

that workers would enjoy a contractual right to minimum remuneration, holidays with pay, and certain standard terms and conditions; benefits conditional upon employment rather than time working.

The policy behind the Act was consistent with that underpinning the National Insurance Act 1946, in that it envisaged a unitary model of employment premised upon ongoing mutual obligations of faithful service and social protection, a functional equivalent to the pre-industrial ideas of mutuality that the concept of tenure has been used in this book to express. This provided room for the courts to draw upon contractual techniques to transform the precariousness of the right to the wage into something resembling the stability of the salary. This it did by invoking the concept of remuneration, a contractual right to be paid that could be implied whenever labour was provided, thereby providing an additional dimension to the worker's right to be paid.

The rights envisaged by the Wages Councils Act, like other social welfare legislation enacted at this time, could only operate if the contract between the parties could be seen as ongoing and continuous in nature. It required more, therefore, than a series of contracts for work and wages and/or de facto control over labour on an ongoing basis. The contractual model envisaged by the legislation thus worked in tandem with the courts to reconstitute the labour relationship in a form in which it could be regulated, to imply a relational contract envisaging ongoing obligations of continued performance, and with it, certain mutual rights and obligations capable of securing workers a form of social wage, and employers faithful and obedient service.

By using the term 'remuneration', the Wages Council Act had been able to build upon the worker's absolute right to be paid wages for labour: by providing an additional contractual right to remuneration as an incident of the relationship which the market transaction expressed. Workers could still bring an action in debt, or under the Truck Act, for unpaid wages therefore, but they could also bring a contractual claim to recover remuneration in the event that the employer failed to pay.[139] In this way, the legal system made it possible to enforce a free bargain between legal equals in the market, an exchange of labour for a wage, while guaranteeing at the same time the subsistence wage and faithful service that this presupposed.

The gradual assimilation of the positions of the salaried employee hired to serve, with that of the subordinate and dependent wage worker had the effect of subjecting higher-status employees to the norms of subordination and obedience that wage labour had long implied, while at the same time extending to wage workers the legal obligation to provide faithful service that had been a condition for the

[139] The Act made express provision for this by virtue of s 13(4) of the Act: 'Nothing in this section shall be construed as authorising the making of any deduction, or the giving of remuneration in any manner, which is illegal by virtue of the Truck Acts, 1831 to 1940, or of any other enactment'.

latter's contractual right to remuneration. By these means, the proprietary relationship between a master and his servant had been re-established, given a new foundation, in the express or implied contract of employment—thereby integrating principles of property law with the modern law of contract.

6.6 The Legally Constituted Wage and Decasualization

Prior to the Second World War, legal intervention in the contractual relationship between higher-status employees and their employers had been minimal. Contractual remuneration for employment was not, in contrast to the wage, something that was deemed to be set by the market, nor was it something that was vulnerable to distortions that it was assumed to be the legal system's role to correct. In the mid-twentieth century, therefore, the question for the courts was how the use of the term 'wage' in legislation enacted prior to the war ought to be conceived in an age when it was assumed that the content of the right to be paid for employment could be legitimately influenced by considerations 'external' to the market. Rather than reading the concept of the wage as referring to the market wage that was payable for labour, the court instead assumed that the wage, particularly where paid for service, ought to be treated as equivalent to the concept of remuneration. This reflected, it seemed, an emerging idea that legal regulation of pay rates was concerned with more than guaranteeing that the employer paid the market wage, particularly where what was being purchased was personal service rather than (only) abstract labour time. In a sense, the legal system was beginning to redefine its relationship with society and the market, embracing a role in actively shaping the way in which the market, and the wage itself, was conceived.

These ideas are evident from the court's approach to statutory construction in *Re Walker's Decision*. Like *Roberts v Hopwood*, *Re Walker* was decided under s 62 of the Metropolis Management Act 1855, but after the Wages Councils Act had been enacted. Pursuant to its power to set the wages of its 'servants', the Council had set those of its male workers, providing for an additional sum to be paid by way of a children's allowance. The question for the court was whether in doing so the Council had exceeded its statutory power to set wages. The Court argued that it had not:

> [While] children's allowances could have no relation to the value of the employee's services [and] payment of them ... could not be regarded as a pecuniary return for services rendered ... [nonetheless] any sums paid by the corporation to their servants are wages.[140]

[140] *Re Walker* [1944] KB 644, 648.

Rejecting the view expressed in *Roberts*, the court argued that non-market considerations could be considered in setting wages, as the market rate could only ever be a guide. Sums such as that in question would still be classed as wages provided that they did not 'manifestly exceed the sums which would have been arrived at on economic principles'.[141] In particular, considerations as to the costs of living would be essential in calculating the proper price of labour, just as the price agreed between the two sides of industry would.[142] It was only if the rate was set by wholly 'philanthropic considerations' that they would be described as 'gratuities' and so fall outwith the definition of the wage.[143]

The clear divide between wages set by the market and remuneration as something that could be influenced by the law, could not, it seems, be practically maintained. However clear the distinction had become when viewed in the abstract, it was clear that the market wage could not be determined entirely independently from considerations about the costs of subsistence. Even payments for labour might deviate from the 'market rate' in the sense of the sum agreed between 'free and equal' subjects, particularly where Parliament had expressly provided for a wage that was to be set by third parties. The effect of these changes was thus to build into the *market wage* ideas about the subsistence function of the wage that the concept of remuneration had long implied.

This shift in thinking was also evident in the way that responses to the dock labour problem came to be conceived in the period following the Second World War. The failure of industry to put in place a system of maintenance pay (a guaranteed minimum *remuneration*) was now widely seen as unacceptable and potentially detrimental to the efficiency of the ports.[144] In 1937, decasualization had become a major issue again, primarily because the unions resumed their campaign for wage increases, arguing that underemployment must be compensated by higher wages. A modest wage increase was agreed, but more significantly, serious bargaining on the matter of decasualization took place from 1937 to 1939, although problems relating to implementation prevented any serious progress being made.

Things were to change, however, with the coming of the War, and the appointment, by Winston Churchill, of Ernest Bevin as Minister of Labour. For the first time, *compulsory* registration was to be brought in. In 1940, concerned by the shortage of dock labour at the major ports, the Dock Labour (Compulsory Registration) Order 1941 was passed, establishing a port registration committee to

[141] ibid 652.
[142] ibid 651.
[143] ibid 656.
[144] HC Deb 12 November 1945, vol 415, cols 1753–822, 1756 (Mr Isaacs): 'The dock worker, like any other worker, when he gives his life to that industry should have some sort of stability and some guarantee that when he turns out in the morning to go to work he will find a job. If he is not going to find a job there, and is not wanted at all, he should have some remuneration for the time he has given, and for the fact that he has to hold himself available to come back the next day once again, if wanted. We want this Bill to provide for regularity of employment.'

maintain a compulsory register of employers and dockers, preventing work from being undertaken except by registered employers and dockers. The scheme was deliberately designed to ensure a regularity in the supply of labour in exchange for greater stability of pay and employment, extending to all major ports in the country.[145]

In 1947, concerned to avoid a return to the pre-war position, a new statutory scheme was adopted, modelled on the wartime scheme, but administered by a specially created body, the National Dock Labour Corporation. The Board was made up of a chairman, two other appointed members, and three members from each side of industry, appointed by the National Joint Council. It appointed local boards to administer the scheme in each port, consisting of worker and employer representatives.[146] The Corporation was responsible for much more than allocating jobs and distributing guarantee payments. Individual dockers might have multiple employers per week, and this necessitated a body to pay him his total weekly wages, to calculate PAYE, stamp his card, and deduct insurance contributions, etc. The Corporation was also responsible for reviewing ports' demand for labour, and thus for ensuring that a sufficient amount of labour was available from port to port—paying travel and subsistence expenses as necessary. The scheme also charged the board with making 'satisfactory provision for the training and welfare of dock workers, including port medical services', contributing to the efficiency and productivity of the workers.[147] Dockers were to receive not only a reasonable income from employment, then, they were also to receive protection against many of the risks arising from employment—similar rights to those enjoyed by 'non-casual' workers engaged in other industries.

The aim of the scheme was to ensure that the board did what employers in ordinary industries were now being required to do for their own employees, but which was practically difficult in the docks given the plurality of employers and the irregular nature of the work. Here, then, the board assumed the role of centralized 'employer', and, while foremen continued to supervise the work on the ground, it alone had (non-delegable) powers of discipline and dismissal. The result was to confer on dock workers a form of 'office' of which they could not be deprived other than by due process, and with it an implicit right to be provided with regular work or pay.[148]

[145] In practice, two schemes were in effect during the war, in different ports. Each provided for certain guaranteed payments, a percentage levy made on each employer on the basis of the wages earned by dock workers. While those in the ministry of war transport scheme were in the employment of the ministry, guaranteed a payment for eleven turns of four hours each at a set rate, in the other scheme, men were guaranteed 'attendance money' at a set rate for every turn he attended but did not get work. This thus fell short of a guaranteed 'social wage' even if it marked significant progress in this direction. For details, see: Jensen (n 98) 136–37.

[146] ibid.

[147] ibid.

[148] *Barnard v National Dock Labour Board* [1953] 2 QB 18; [1953] 2 WLR 995.

The board's revenue was raised by a levy based on wages fixed by the board, but subject to a 25 per cent cap over which the Minister of Labour would have to be consulted. Negotiations over wages and terms and conditions continued to be left to both sides of industry in the National Joint Council. One of the provisions that the scheme guaranteed was a guaranteed wage per 'turn', 'attendance' money at *a lower* rate for turns when the docker made himself available but there was no work, and a set minimum below which total income could not fall. That is, *a guaranteed sum* which would be paid as a form of 'fall back' if employment in a given week proved insufficient. Falling short of a guaranteed social wage (payable regardless of the amount of work performed), the government emphasizing that pay for work ought to be more than pay for 'attendance', these advances nonetheless recognized that workers should be paid for time when they are available to work, and not just time 'actually working'. [149]

Problems of casual labour in the docks did not disappear entirely until 1967; it was only then that a true, 'social wage' was achieved. Following further waves of strikes (protesting against the dismissal of dock workers, and the 'loss' of freedom involved in the scheme), the Devlin Inquiry was set up to enquire into the 'problem'. The outcome of the Inquiry was a proposal for a reduction in the number of employers, and an elevation of the 'fall back' payment so as to guarantee all dockers a reasonable weekly minimum income—plus bonuses where work was performed. This time, then, the guaranteed minimum was to reflect the minimum sum that a regular worker was deemed to be entitled for a full week's work, and any pay for 'actual' work was to act as a form of 'bonus' designed to incentivize greater efficiency. The goal was to achieve 'the complete abolition of casual employment and the introduction of a system of permanent employment under which all dock workers would be allocated permanently to a particular employer and would be regularly employed by him'. —in other words, *total decasualization*.[150]

The Devlin reforms were primarily motivated by economic concerns; Britain was falling behind foreign ports in terms of mechanization and innovation, and the persistence of casualism could not be disassociated from this. But strong opposition continued vis-à-vis the degrading nature of casual work *in general*, and the need to 'humanize' hiring practices in the dock industry continued to be influential:

> permanency is vital . . . the dignity of the workers is important. I ask hon. Members to imagine themselves lined up in a pen . . . The boss examines the workers, decides that one is not a bad sort of fellow and that he will have him, but not another who is too old or almost dying, and so passes to the next man. What a humiliating experience for any human being . . . [151]

[149] HC Deb 12 November 1945, vol 415, cols 1753–822, 1756.
[150] HL Deb 11 July 1966, vol 246, cols 19–68, 21 (Lord Winterbottom).
[151] HC Deb 29 November 1967, vol 755 cols 554–99, 584 (Mr Heffer, MP for Liverpool).

By the middle of the twentieth century, then, there was considerable consensus on the importance of guaranteeing regular work and/or pay to all workers, regardless of the characteristics of the industry in which they were employed and regardless of whether they earned a 'salary' or a 'wage'. Distinctions between manual and 'professional' workers, and between trades and occupations, were thus no longer deemed to be relevant to questions of payment: all those who provided their labour (power) to others were deemed to be entitled to a guaranteed social wage—the costs of which was to be born, primarily, by employers, and where necessary, subsidized by the state. If the industry was, by its nature, casual, therefore, the goal was a system in which employers could take advantage of a reserve pool of casual labour *only if* they found ways to guarantee those workers a 'reasonable' and 'regular' income. The payment of a social wage was becoming to be seen as one of the conditions that ought to be imposed by law on employers' ability to purchase labour in the market.

6.7 Conclusion

Throughout the twentieth century, the legal system had begun to see a role for itself not just in facilitating the operation of the pricing mechanism, passively responding to prices freely agreed and remedying instances of distortion, but in actively shaping it, influencing the way in which value-based assessments were made. From this perspective, the market wage was itself something that was constituted by law as, at least in those contexts in which Parliament had sought to intervene, it could no longer be maintained that the wages set were dictated entirely from within the market process. Even the market wage would only be classed as such if it truly reflected a *social* perception of what labour was worth, and thus if it bore some relation to the costs of living informed by considerations of fairness. It was the legal system, therefore, which determined whether the pricing mechanism was operating effectively; wage rates could not be justified merely because they were left to the 'natural' forces of supply and demand. The legal system's role in providing the conditions for the labour market to function thus went beyond providing the conditions for its autonomy, for free competition, for by shaping the decision-making practices of the parties, making space for the parties' to express their own beliefs about what amounted to a 'fair' wage, the legal system played an active role in establishing the boundaries of the 'free agreement'.

In this context, two different types of regulation worked in harmony: the Wages Council Act, regulating the rate at which workers were remunerated on the one hand, and the Truck Acts and common law protection of wages on the other. The significance of the latter two was that they 'jealously guarded' the right to wages, preventing inequality of bargaining power from depriving workers of their right to be paid *at least* the market value of their labour. The Wages Council Act, by contrast, operated to ensure that in addition to this market wage, the social costs of labour would also be borne by the employer. These twin functions of the wage, its coordinating and social reproduction functions, were realized through the distinction that had now emerged between the legal concepts of the wage and remuneration; and work, and employment, as the different benefits in respect of which workers were paid.

It can be concluded from this that during the mid-twentieth century, the market wage that emerged through the 'free' play of market processes was the product of a set of institutional processes, central among which was a legally guaranteed right to subsistence—a social wage. To be recognized as capable of freely disposing of a commodity, workers had to act through an institutional framework that guaranteed their subsistence, making employee status and the social rights to which it gave rise, a precondition for the emergence of a market wage capable of coordinating decision making in the market. For this reason, the concept of the wage had itself gradually begun to connote ideas of fairness and subsistence, and, as we shall see, this was to gradually obscure the significance of the distinction between the legal concept of the wage and remuneration. If the amount that workers were paid could not be separated from social and political considerations, it made little sense to speak of the wage as if it were set by some abstract, or natural market. However implicitly, it seems that a naturalistic ontology had been decisively rejected.

7
The (Return of the) 'Market Wage'

7.1 Introduction

The period beginning the 1970s reflects a profound shift in the way that the law–market relationship was being conceived. This was parallelled by a change in the legal conception of the wage. No longer did the wage express the worker's right to subsistence, conveyed through a right to minimum remuneration; it was instead the price that the market required that employers pay for labour or 'work'.[1] Wage regulation could only be justified, therefore, if the wage rate did not exceed the natural market rate.[2] Labour law was increasingly being seen at this time as an exogenous 'interference' in an otherwise efficient system, and freedom of contract an innate and inviolable right with which the state could not, and should not, interfere. The result was that 'contract' came to be seen as the most appropriate mechanism through which to deal with problems such as low wages.[3]

The conceptual distinction between the wage as a price for labour and the concept of contractual remuneration was becoming blurred: the right to be paid was being reduced to a purely contractual right to be paid for time working. While this perhaps reflected the fact that workers' wage packets were becoming more complex, consisting of many fringe benefits not expressed in the wage, this conceptual disintegration has had significant effects on the scope of protection. It is in the Wages Act 1986 and the common law developments relating to it that this new perspective is most evident. To illustrate this, the first section of this chapter will explore the background to the Act before explaining how the Act has altered the legal regime concerning the worker's right to be paid. This includes changes to the wages councils system and changes to the law on deductions from wages. Section 2 will then explore the evolution of the concept of the wage through an in-depth analysis of the wage–work bargain and statutory protection against unauthorized deductions from wages.

[1] Wages Act 1986, c 48.

[2] See, for example, HL Deb 6 June 1986, vol 475, cols 1203–43, 1222 (Lord Teviot): 'In some industries they are regrettably necessary but if they are not careful they can set minimum wages which are out of line with market rates. If they do they will destroy jobs and not create them as we have all been seeking to do since the Government have come into power'.

[3] This was forcefully objected to by Lord Wedderburn in the debates over the Wages Bill 1986: '... The idea is too preposterous and I hope we shall hear nothing more about the justification by contract for sweeping away an elementary and basic right of workers not to have unreasonable deductions made by fines and the like'. HL Deb 06 June 1986, vol 475, cols 1203–43, 1233.

Labour and the Wage. Zoe Adams, Oxford University Press (2020). © Zoe Adams.
DOI: 10.1093/oso/9780198858898.001.0001

7.2 The Background to the Wages Act

The 1960s was a period of recurring economic crisis in Britain, a 'balance of payments deficit', resulting from a combination of post-war inflation and lagging growth rates.[4] At the same time, Britain was suffering at the international level with the loss of its colonial empire, calling into question its capacity to compete with major economic powers, such as the United States, on the global stage.

It is in this context that Britain's industrial relations system faced increasing criticism, and this was only to increase throughout the 1960s as the economic problems facing Britain became more pressing. Collective bargaining and the 'restrictions' it imposed on industry's capacity to adapt to changing conditions came to bear much of the blame for the situation in which Britain found herself, both domestically and abroad. As a result, the 1960s Conservative government made the industrial relations system a major focus of reform, and this included the wages councils; both of which were discussed at length by the Donovan Commission (the Royal Commission on Trade Unions and Employers' Associations) in 1968.

One of the conclusions of the Commission was that wages councils hindered the development of voluntary organization, and so were self-defeating. The wages councils had only ever been intended to be temporary, to no longer be necessary once voluntary bargaining mechanisms had developed. The problem was that the collective bargaining focus of the councils was somewhat ill-suited to the industrial environment to which the problem of low pay was proving endemic. Voluntary bargaining rarely developed in the newly emerging service industries in which the wages councils were most needed, and this, the Committee concluded, was due not to the structure of the industry or trades concerned, but to the wages councils themselves. The result was that by the end of the 1970s, it was widely believed that the councils had been unsuccessful, having failed both in their aim of facilitating joint regulation and (largely due to enforcement issues) to eradicate low pay.[5]

Despite this narrative, prior to 1979, there was still considerable consensus among employers and workers that the councils were important. In the government's consultation paper of 1975, the overwhelming argument was for reform rather than abolition.[6] Employers supported the system because it was

[4] Robert F Banks, 'The Reform of British Industrial Relations : The Donovan Report and the Labour Government's Policy Proposals' (1969) 24 Relations industrielles 333.

[5] 'Wages Councils Criticized over Low-Paid Workers' *The Times* (London, 18 August 1977) 2. *The Times Digital Archive*. Web. 12 March 2019. The low pay unit argued that the government was turning a blind eye to employer evasion and so was effectively encouraging employers to pay below the minimum rates, cutting the number of inspectors drastically in the early 1980s: Barrie Clement, Labour Reporter. 'Tories "Turn Blind Eye to Low Wages" ' *The Times* (London, 25 May 1983) 2. *The Times Digital Archive*. Web. 12 March 2019.

[6] Rosemary Lucas, 'The Wages Act 1986: Some Reflections with Particular Reference to the Licensed Residential Establishment and Licensed Restaurant Wages Council' (1990) 10 The Service Industries Journal 320, 322.

expedient and helped them to avoid complex local level wage bargaining. They also believed that it provided them with important protection against unfair competition, the presumption being that any competition was unfair if it had the effect of driving down workers' wages.[7] Even the trade unions, hostile at first to the threat the councils posed to voluntary bargaining had, by the 1970s, started to support the system, arguing for its extension alongside a new statutory minimum wage.[8] More than a decade of 'stagflation' had convinced both sides of industry that wage-fixing mechanisms were important for securing cooperation, helping both sides to adjust to challenging conditions.

The 1979 Conservative government had different ideas. Indeed, as early as 1968, Margaret Thatcher had stated categorically that it was:

> totally unacceptable that government should decide the increases of wages and salaries. Conservatives should arrange to reduce the range of government decision making and restore individual choice ... What we need now is a far greater degree of personal responsibility and decision, far more independence from government, and a comparable reduction in the role of government.[9]

In policy-making circles, decades of 'stagflation', industrial unrest, and rising unemployment had fostered opposition to collective bargaining, fuelling the belief that market forces were the most efficient mechanism for allocating resources.[10] Both the regulation of terms and conditions of employment and collective bargaining had distortive, and inflationary, effects therefore, and the wages council system embodied both. During the late 1970s and early 1980s, the councils were thus being criticized not only for failing to promote voluntary organization, but also because collective organization itself was deemed to be too great an intrusion on individual freedom of action in the market.[11] Imposing on the parties terms to which they had not expressly agreed, the councils necessarily, the argument went, set wages above what was seen as a 'natural' market rate.[12] They were inflationary, a

[7] Official Report, 19 March 1985, vol 75, col 817.

[8] House of Commons Employment Committee, *Wages Councils: Together with the Proceedings of the Committee* (HMSO 1985). On the strong defence of the Council by unions, see: 'Pledge to defend Truck Acts and Wage Councils' *The Times* (London, 7 September 1983) 4. *The Times Digital Archive*. Web. 12 March 2019. On employer support, see: Chris Pond and Emma McLean. 'Divided Views on Wages Councils' *The Times* (London, 20 March 1984) 13. *The Times Digital Archive*. Web. 12 March 2019. For a different view, however, see: RH Price, 'Future of Wage Councils' *The Times* (London, 31 October 1984) 13. *The Times Digital Archive*. Web. 12 March 2019.

[9] Quoted in Dennis Kavanagh, Thatcherism and British Politics: The End of Consensus? (OUP 1990) 10-11.

[10] Lucas (n 6) 322.

[11] Sandra Fredman, 'Deregulating Pay: The Wages Act 1986' [1986] Public Law 551.

[12] Government opposition was characterized as opposition to councils as they acted as 'a restraint' on the labour market' in David Felton (Labour Correspondent), 'Wages Councils' *The Times* (London, 20 March 1985) 8. *The Times Digital Archive*. Web. 12 March 2019.

threat to job creation, and partly to blame for rising unemployment.[13] Mr Richard Alexander argued, for example, that

> In addition to all this inflation which wages councils engender, in addition to their remoteness and their atmosphere of 'jobs for the boys', there is the expense ... They are not only expensive for the State but are costly and often ruinous to the employer, who is bound to comply with their awards.[14]

The government was explicit that it was better to have a job that paid below a 'living wage', than to have a system that guaranteed living wages, that 'pushed' employers out of the market or caused unemployment. The (mechanistic) relationship between minimum wages (set above the market rate) and unemployment was thus not questioned—despite convincing evidence that the wages councils did not threaten job opportunities, nor price young people out of the market.[15]

In 1986, in response to its consultation on the wages councils, the government enacted the Wages Act. This was to replace entirely the existing framework for the regulation of wages, curtailing the powers of the wages councils with a view to their eventual demise, while replacing the Truck Acts with a new statutory right for all workers not to be subject to unauthorized deductions from 'wages'. The premises underpinning the Act were explained when the bill was introduced into the House of Commons:

> The Bill is based on the central economic objective to which the Government have held since 1979 — to achieve an efficient and modern economy where economic growth is accompanied by low inflation, enabling us to compete in international markets and produce real, sustainable, productive jobs. To achieve that we need an efficient and productive private sector, not hampered by unnecessary Government-imposed regulations and restrictions. Secondly, we need an efficient labour market, where there is the minimum of constraints on the rights of employers and employees to agree to offer and accept jobs on contractual terms that suit them both.[16]

The Wages Councils Act had been modelled on a belief that the legal system played an important role in constituting and regulating the market. Individuals were not assumed to be naturally free and capable of bargaining as equals in the market. Rather, freedom was seen to be legally constituted, and thus dependent on

[13] Rosemary Lucas, The Wages Act; Department of Employment, 'Department of Employment, Wages Councils Consultation Document' 1988.

[14] HC Deb 11 March 1981, vol 1000, cols 980–84, 980.

[15] Barrie Clement (Labour reporter), 'Tories Split on Wage Council Abolition' *The Times* (London, 1 June 1985) 2. *The Times Digital Archive*. Web. 12 March 2019.

[16] HC Deb 11 February 1986, vol 91, cols 796–881, 796 (second reading) (Mr Clarke).

mechanisms like minimum wages and collective bargaining. The concept of the 'market wage' only made sense as an emergent property of an institutional framework in which these conditions were met, and so was not something which could be conceptualized independently from the legal framework in which the market was embedded. It only existed, therefore, *as a result* of wage regulation, and so was not seen as something that ought to be 'respected' (or 'replicated') by the legally mandated minimum wage rate.

In contrast to this, the conservative policy was premised on a much more passive, reactive conception of the law, one that saw the market and the bindingness of agreements as empirical facts that could be conceptualized independently from law and institutions. The presumption here was that the legal system simply responds to what is already there, a preformed fully functioning market system. The 'powers of the wages councils [therefore] undoubtedly impose complex and unnecessary burdens on business'.[17] The legal system can thus interfere with, or correct, that market, but it neither constitutes nor shapes it. Legal protection against deductions from wages is not part of the process by which the market wage is constituted therefore, but amounts to an interference in an inherently free bargain, and for this reason has an inevitably inflationary and distortive effect.[18] In the words of Ken Clarke:

> I do not regard labour as just another commodity, and I do not think that one can apply the rules of the market to the employment of people. However, if a system is introduced the aim of which is to put the cost of labour above that which it would otherwise be if freely entered into by an employer and an employee, by making labour more expensive people will be even less willing to take on labour and will look for labour-saving alternatives.[19]

As well as its attack on the wages councils system, the Conservative government was particularly concerned to 'recasualize' the docks: to dismantle the Dock Labour Scheme and shift the balance of power decisively in favour of the employers.

One of the effects of the 1967 reforms explored in Chapter 6 had been that the Dock Labour Board ceased to be the employer of the dockers, employing only the 'reserve pool' directly. This meant that dockers were to be contractually employed by the employers to whom they were allocated. One of the consequences of this was that, when opposition to the scheme grew, it was to prove much easier for employers to resist calls for joint negotiations.[20]

[17] HC Deb 17 July 1985, vol 83, cols 326–39, 327 (Mr King).
[18] See particularly: HC Deb 11 February 1986, vol 91, cols 796–881 (Mr Clarke).
[19] ibid 805.
[20] Peter Turnbull and Victoria Wass, 'The Greatest Game No More - Redundant Dockers and the Demise of 'Dock Work'' (1994) 8 Work, Employment and Society 487, 487.

In 1972, alarmed at the loss of jobs on the waterfront—as a result, mostly, of containerization—dockers picketed warehouses outside the dock areas where the containers were filled. They fell foul, however, of the newly enacted Trade Union legislation, and, in July 1972, five dockers were jailed for refusing to obey a court order to stop picketing. This led to a wave of protest strikes across Britain, in response to which the Trades Union Congress (TUC) eventually called a general strike; the government caved and the dockers were released.

The outcome of the unrest was the Jones-Adlington agreement, which, at the time, represented a major win for the dockers: the agreement abolished the temporary unattached pool entirely; the government would pay the employers a subsidy to compensate them for hiring surplus labour, and would also offer large pay-offs for dockers leaving their jobs. The agreement was, however, only to fuel subsequent opposition by employers and government to the state's role in the industry.[21]

In the years following the Jones-Adlington agreement, mechanization proceeded and the number of dockers declined year on year. In 1989, against the backdrop of new restrictive union legislation, and following a sustained campaign by port employers,[22] the Dock Labour Scheme was repealed—in the name of 'free' markets.

Urging for the repeal of the Scheme, Michael Fallon, Conservative MP for Darlington had argued that:

> the scheme was monopolistic, out of date, discriminatory and *anti-business*. It prevented ports from deploying their manpower in the most economical and efficient way and it prevented them diversifying … It was not simply destroying jobs, it was also preventing new jobs being created. *Abolition would establish much fairer competition between ports.*[23]

The opposition argument that 'we believe in job security. We believe in the dignity at work which the scheme has given dock workers … important benefits which

[21] ibid.

[22] Alan Hamilton Labour Staff. 'CBI and Hauliers Attack Dock Scheme "Monopoly"' *The Times* (London, 3 May 1975) 17. *The Times Digital Archive*. Web. 16 March 2019; Paul Routledge (Labour editor), 'Port Employers Condemn Proposal to Extend Dock Labour Scheme' *The Times* (London, 21 May 1975) 20. *The Times Digital Archive*. Web. 16 March 2019; George Clark (political correspondent), 'Government Facing Crucial Challenge on Dock Work Bill' *The* Times (London, 6 February 1976) 7. *The Times Digital Archive*. Web. 16 March 2019; Robin Oakley (political editor), 'MPs Urge End to Dock "Jobs For Life"' *The* Times (London, 21 January 1988) 2. *The Times Digital Archive*. Web. 16 March 2019.

[23] 'Conservative Call for Docks Change' *The Times* (London, 11 March 1988) 4 (emphasis added). *The Times Digital Archive*. Web. 16 March 2019. See similarly the comments by Mr Norman Fowler in 'Abolition for Dock Labour Scheme' *The* Times (London, 7 April 1989) 10. *The Times Digital Archive*. Web. 16 March 2019.

should not be thrown away'; was thus given little weight, given the 'overwhelming' case for reform.[24]

The mass redundancy of ex-registered dockers, particularly trade union activists, and the abolition of the Dock Labour Scheme, effectively put an end to what had become known as genuine 'quality' employment in the docks.[25] The so-called benefits of deregulation[26]—creating new jobs, much-needed investment, lower prices for port users and consumers, and improved international competitiveness—did not materialize. The government had failed to appreciate the non-competitiveness of the industry and the effects that the Scheme had had on the economic performance of the ports in the preceding decades. Deregulation thus served to exacerbate, rather than resolve, underlying structural weaknesses in the industry and effectively ushered in a new era of casual employment. This was, however, merely a reflection of a much broader trend, and was entirely consistent with the government's policy towards the wages councils system, and its more general attempt to deregulate the labour market.

7.3 The Changing Legal Landscape of the 'Wage'

7.3.1 Changes to the Wages Councils System

The first legal attack on the wages councils had come with the Wages Council Act of 1979 which consolidated a number of existing councils and cut back on the number of inspectors. According to the International Labour Organisation (ILO), this move meant that the typical establishment would now be visited only every twelve to fourteen years.[27] Then, in 1986, Part II of the Wages Act introduced a number of further, potentially more far-reaching, changes to the system:

Firstly, the Act significantly curtailed the powers of the boards, confining them to setting a single basic rate of pay, single overtime rate, and a maximum accommodation charge, removing the power to set holidays and to set minimum terms and conditions of employment.[28] Secondly, it introduced a single basic minimum rate and prevented councils from setting different rates in accordance with skill and job function, requiring that they have express regard, when setting the rate,

[24] Nicholas Wood and Roland Rudd. 'Docks Strike Threatened as Jobs Guarantee Goes'. *The* Times (London, 7 April 1989) 1. *The Times Digital Archive*. Web. 16 March 2019.

[25] Peter Turnbull and Victoria Wass, 'The Great Dock and Dole Swindle' (1995) 73 Public Administration, 513–34.

[26] On which see: 'Abolition for Dock Labour Scheme' *The Times* (London, 7 April 1989) 10. *The Times Digital Archive*. Web. 16 March 2019; 'Government Deceived Public on Dock Labour Scheme, says Foot' *The Times* (London, 9 May 1989) 12. *The Times Digital Archive*. Web. 16 March 2019.

[27] ILO Role of Consultive Organizations in Selected areas of Labor Administration, United Kingdom (Geneva ILO 1994), Chapter 3.

[28] Section 14.

to its potential effect on the level of employment.[29] Thirdly, the Act removed the minister's power to create new councils, while making the Secretary of State solely responsible for decisions as to abolition. Even though the decision to establish a council had previously been based on whether the prevailing rate of remuneration was, or was likely to be, adequate, there was no obligation to consider this when making decisions as to abolition.[30] Instead, the only requirement was that the minister 'have regard to current levels of remuneration'.[31]

Like the early trade boards, the wages councils were now to act as residuary mechanisms to check clear instances of low pay, confined to demonstrative instances of so-called market failure. Even here, however, it was believed that the wages councils would, in time, no longer have any role to play:

> I have to make it clear that I do not see a great role for statutory minimum wage fixing, or wage fixing at all, in today's society. It was only after consultation that we decided to retain them in those industries where both the employers and the trade unions did not feel ready to embark on the kind of world that we are used to in other industries, where these things are freely negotiated and entered into by both parties.[32]

Having previously operated at the level of an ongoing labour relationship, the wages councils were now to play a basic and minor role in regulating a market transaction, merely 'setting a minimum rate below which adults should not be employed'.[33] Even this rate was, however, subject to 'agreement': there was no longer any provision preventing the worker from agreeing in writing to a deduction that would take the rate below the minimum set by the wages order.[34] The entire purpose of the wages councils had been reconceptualized, recasting the minimum rates of remuneration previously implied as a matter of law as 'a form of retail price maintenance—you fix a price below which one may not lawfully buy labour—in the hope that it will save dangerous and damaging undercutting, unnecessary rivalry and all the other things that can arise in market competition'.[35] Beyond this narrow market-correcting role, wages councils had no role to play:

29 Section 14(6)(1).

30 (1945) 8 & 9 Geo VI, s 3.

31 Section 13(2)(a).

32 HC Deb 11 February 1986, vol 91, cols 796–881, 803 (Mr Clarke).

33 ibid 801.

34 See s 17(1) and (2). Compare this with the provision in the Catering Wages Act 1943, s 10(3) which provides: 'Where any benefits or advantages are provided, in connection with any employment, by the employer or by some other person under arrangements with the employer, then, whether or not the benefits or advantages are authorised to be reckoned as payment of wages in lieu of payment in cash, any sum paid by the worker in respect of those benefits or advantages shall be deemed for the purposes of this Act to have been deducted by the employer from his remuneration'. See *People's Refreshment House v Jones* [1954] 1 WLR 339; [1954] 1 All ER 317.

35 HL Deb 06 June 1986, vol 475, cols 1203–43, 1229 (Lord Houghton).

> Wages councils interfere with the freedom of employers to offer and job seekers to accept jobs at wages that would otherwise be acceptable.[36]

Despite the Act having redefined the councils' powers to set a mandatory level of reasonable remuneration as one requiring them to set a minimum basic wage rate, the Act did not replace the term remuneration with wages when referring to the minimum rate. This inconsistent, and, it could be said, careless use of juridical language further highlights the point that the wage was no longer being seen as a right which was 'above' or beyond the reach of contract; it was simply the sum that the employer agreed to pay under a contract of employment. The distinction between wages and remuneration thus had not only become blurred, it was implicitly dismissed as unimportant. This confusion between the once absolute right to wages and the contractual right to remuneration was, however, to create considerable confusion for the courts where these concepts had, until this point, been seen as distinct.

7.3.2 Changes to the Legal Regulation of Deductions from Wages

The origins of s 1(1) of the Wages Act, what is now s 13(1) of the Employment Rights Act 1996 (ERA), was the Truck Act 1831. This, it will be remembered, established a right for all those within the scope of the Act to be paid in full, and in coin, all wages earned by, or payable, in exchange for any 'labour done' and rendered void any agreement providing otherwise.[37] By definition, the Act provided workers with protection against deductions being made from wages, whether or not they were consented to in writing.[38] The 1896 Act made it explicit that all fines and deductions, other than those which were fair and reasonable, that had been imposed to compensate the employer for loss, and had been consented to in writing, were unlawful.[39] This requirement for fair and reasonableness was, however, now seen as something that could only be determined by the market:

> it is a matter of judgment as to what constitutes a reasonable deduction. The Government's approach is to leave this decision to the parties by saying that what they agree to as deductions is lawful. It puts deductions on a basis similar to that applying to other terms and conditions of employment.[40]

[36] Department of Employment Consultative Paper 1985, cited in: Sandra Fredman, 'Women at Work: The Broken Promise of Flexicurity' (2004) 33 Industrial Law Journal 299, 559.

[37] (1831) 1 & 2 Wil 4 c 27, s 3.

[38] Truck Act 1831, s 4.

[39] Truck Act 1896, 59 & 60 Vict c 44. Controversial cases concerning the scope of the 1831 Act include: *Chawner v Cummings* (1846) 8 QB 311, 115 ER 893 and *Archer v James* (1859) 2 B & S 61, 121 ER 996.

[40] HL Deb 06 June 1986, vol 475, cols 1203–43, 1242 (Lord Trefgarne).

The Truck Acts' protection only extended to manual workers but attached to the 'doing of labour' within a trade rather than to a particular form of contract. Thus, while the wage was defined as anything '*contracted* to be paid, delivered, or given as a recompense, reward, or remuneration for any Labour done or to be done', the Act provided that:

> any Agreement, Understanding, Device, Contrivance, Collusion, or Arrangement whatsoever on the Subject of Wages, whether written or oral, whether direct or indirect, to which the Employer and Artificer are Parties or are assenting, or by which they are mutually bound to each other, or whereby either of them shall have endeavoured to impose an Obligation on the other of them, shall be and be deemed a 'contract'.[41]

The Wages Act repealed this regime and replaced it with a single statutory right not to be subject to unauthorized deductions from wages.[42] This is now embodied in the ERA, s 13(1) which provides a right not to be subject to deductions (that have not met the Act's pre-notification requirements) from wages 'properly payable' at the date of the claim, where the wage is defined as 'any payment by an employer to his worker in connection with employment' (a definition that seems to correspond with the definition of 'remuneration').[43] This protection is conferred upon all those who are employed under a contract either of employment or to personally do work. The effect of this provision was that, provided that the pre-notification requirements in the Act are met, deductions from wages would be lawful, irrespective of quantum. The only exception to this was a 10 per cent limit on deductions from the wages of retail workers made in respect of stock shortages.[44] For all other workers, the statute no longer prevented contracting out from the right to be paid all wages in full and even exempted from the pre-notification requirements any deductions made in respect of strike action. In this way, it also weakened the mechanism of the strike as an alternative route through which to resist pressures to lower wages.[45]

The framework established under the Wages Act is based on a very different set of premises from those underpinning the Truck Acts. It extends to all workers, rather than just manual ones, but the emphasis has shifted from the provision of labour to the form of the contract under which it is provided. This has had knock-on effects for the scope of protection. The Wages Act did not replace the Truck Act's

[41] Truck Act 1831, s 25 (emphasis added).

[42] For a defence of the Truck Acts and a criticism of the then proposed changes to the law, see: Tamara Goriely, 'Arbitrary Deductions from Pay and the Proposed Repeal of the Truck Acts' (1983) 12 Industrial Law Journal 236.

[43] Wages Act 1986, c 48, s 7(1).

[44] Section 2(1).

[45] John Mcmullen, 'The Wages Act 1986' (1986) 15 Industrial Law Journal 266.

absolute right to be paid wages 'earned' in full. It simply provided a right to be paid in accordance with the terms of the agreement; the wages that are left once agreed sums have been withheld. It also changed the regime as it relates to fines, for there is no longer any requirement that fines be fair and reasonable; all that matters is whether or not the employer has obtained the worker's written consent.

Rather than providing protection for a workers' wages by treating the right as absolute, that is, preventing the parties from waiving that right by agreement, and coupling this with a contractual right to be paid a minimum remuneration for employment, the Wages Act simply stipulated a right to be paid wages for labour provided under a particular form of contract. For all but a very few (those engaged in retail), this right was to be left entirely to the parties' 'natural' freedom of contract, 'leaving this, [and all] ... decisions to the parties by saying that what they agree to as deductions is lawful'.[46]

Consistently with this, the Act included within its definition of the wage a number of payments referable to the contract, or employment relationship, rather than just to the provision of labour. It was, effectively, a definition of contractual remuneration. The government had argued that this broad definition of wages was necessary to assimilate the positions of blue- and white-collared employees. Status distinctions, it was said, had 'absolutely no place in modern industrialised society'. For this reason, this reform formed an integral part of the 'important new and modern set of rights for workers in respect of deductions from pay', because, by including envisaging ongoing contractual obligations within the definition of wages payments, the definition better recognized that many white-collared workers enjoyed a number of 'fringe benefits that are not offered to manual workers'.[47] The problem, however, is that the Act abolished the power of the wages councils to make provision for such fringe benefits for workers unable to negotiate them for themselves. In effect, therefore, it protected workers from having such benefits withheld without their prior consent, but did not actually help them to secure those benefits in the first place. Elevating the 'wage' to a level that might better secure workers' subsistence was, it seems, to be left to the 'higgling' of the market.

7.3.3 The Common Law and the Right to be Paid

In principle, it is only those sums that fall outside the statutory definition of 'wages' that are excluded from the scope of the industrial tribunal's jurisdiction in claims for unlawful deductions from wages—a definition which encompasses all those payments to which a worker is entitled to receive from his employer in connection

[46] HL Deb 6 June 1986, vol 475, col 1242.
[47] HC Deb 11 February 1986, vol 91, cols 796–881, 798 (Mr Clarke).

with his employment.[48] However, the effect of what is now s 14 of the ERA is that any deduction made in response to the events therein listed will also be excluded, and so must be assessed in the ordinary way in the common law courts. Particularly controversial here has been s 14(5) which refers to deductions made in response to industrial action. In principle, this section does not establish an independent right for the employer to withhold pay in response to a strike. Its only effect is to exempt such deductions from the procedural requirements in s 13. In a given case, the overall legality of a deduction will thus depend on the contractual or other common law propriety of making it. If the contract does not expressly provide for such a deduction therefore, the employee should be able to sue for it in the ordinary way.

In English law, a non-breaching party cannot unilaterally suspend his contractual obligations in response to the other party's breach. In bilateral contracts, therefore, it is no defence to argue that non-performance was a response to the other party's breach. If the non-breaching party affirms the contract, he cannot refuse to perform without placing himself in breach of contract. In the context of the contract of employment, basic principles of contract law would suggest therefore, that an employer who affirms the contract in response to his employee's refusal to work cannot unilaterally suspend his obligation to pay. If he refuses to pay, he will himself be in breach of contract. The Supreme Court has recently confirmed in *Hartley*, however, following the earlier decision in *Miles v Wakefield*, that an employer will not be in breach of contract if he unilaterally withholds pay from an employee in response to a refusal to work. This is so, it seems, not only for employees paid wages, or a 'salary' in the sense of a regular payment for *pre-defined* hours of work, but also for salaried professionals paid a periodical sum for a relatively open-ended and indeterminate obligation to serve.

The confusion underpinning these cases arise, it seems, from the courts' failure to distinguish, first, between the concepts of the wage, the salary, and remuneration and the different principles applicable to each, and second, between the contract by which labour was *historically* sold for wages, and the legal form of the relational contract of employment.

The previous chapter showed that it was only in the early twentieth century that the courts began extending this relational model to industrial workers' paid wages.[49] Prior to this period, wage workers would be hired by way of a contract that did not necessarily envisage any ongoing obligations between them and their employers beyond the immediate obligations of work and payment. That is not to say that each exchange did not translate in practice into implied obligations to perform

[48] The rest of this chapter draws on aspects of: Zoe Adams, '"Wage", "Salary" and "Remuneration": A Genealogical Exploration of Juridical Terms and Their Significance for the Employer's Power to Make Deductions from Wages' (2019) 48 Industrial Law Journal 34.

[49] Simon Deakin and Frank Wilkinson, *The Law of the Labour Market Industrialization, Employment, and Legal Evolution* (OUP 2005).

work and to employ. The point, however, is that such obligations were deemed to be limited to single units, an hour or day, of labour and payment.[50] For this reason, the worker's implied obligation to faithfully serve was not implied into an *ongoing* contractual relationship, an implied obligation to continue to offer labour service over time, but arose as an incident of servant status, a by-product of the annual hiring rule and the penal provisions of the master and servant legislation. From the contractual perspective, therefore, beyond the immediate wage–work exchange, there was no ongoing obligation on the employer to pay his worker, no 'mutuality of obligation' beyond the obligation to pay wages for labour. In Mark Freedland's terms, there was no 'relational' contract, no arrangement giving rise to a contractually protected interest in ongoing employment and payment.[51]

From the medieval period, the principal action for enforcing informal agreements such as the labour contract was the action in debt. Debt differed from covenant in that rather than being based on an underlying promise, the obligation to pay was said to derive from the underlying transaction, from the fact that some benefit had been provided pursuant to some form of reciprocal exchange.[52] To claim wages, therefore, a worker would have to prove that he had provided the full year's service for which the wage was paid. If the employer could show he had not enjoyed exclusive control over his servant for the entire period, such as if the servant had departed from service or been wilfully disobedient, he was under no obligation to pay.[53] He was not, in other words, in breach of any contractual obligation if he unilaterally withheld 'unearned' wages.[54]

The essence of the labour agreement was not mutual promises therefore, but actual *exchange*: in the context of an annual hiring, a full year's service for a full year's wages, and in eighteenth and nineteenth-century industry, a day or hour's work, or a finished good, in exchange for a time or piece wage. If a manual worker could not prove he had produced the good or performed the hour or day's work, therefore, he was not entitled to be paid. It was this premise that came to be embodied in the Truck Act 1831 and the absolute right to be paid *wages* for labour 'done or to be done' that it envisaged.

According to this logic, it is not difficult to see why the House of Lords in *Miles* might have assumed that an employer is entitled to withhold wages from a worker who refuses to work in breach of contract. In this approach, the employer's right to withhold is not the result of an implied condition in a bilateral contract of employment, however, but a right inherent in the legal form of the pre-twentieth century

[50] Mark Freedland, 'The Legal Structure of the Contract of Employment' in Freedland and others (ed), *The Contract of Employment* (OUP 2016) 46.
[51] ibid 91.
[52] David Ibbetson, *A Historical Introduction to the Law of Obligations* (new edn, OUP 2001) 21.
[53] ibid.
[54] *Spain v Arnott* (1817) 2 Stark 256, 171 ER 638; *Turner v Robinson* (1833) 5 B & Ad 789, 110 ER 982; *Ridgway v Hungerford Market Co* (1835) 3 Ad & El 171, 111 ER 378; *Saunders v Whittle* (1876) 33 LT 81.

labour contract as a simple exchange of commodities. Employers are not liable in damages for refusing to pay a worker who has not worked because their *only* obligation under the contract is to pay for labour rendered. But the distinctive feature of the relational contract of employment is that there are mutual obligations of ongoing performance. These early 'wage work' bargain cases should not be relied upon therefore, as authority for the cases arising today where the contract in question is a bilateral or relational contract of employment.

The courts' extension of the contractual model to industrial wage workers in the early twentieth century was particularly significant therefore, for helping to elevate the market wage into something more closely resembling a right to subsistence. Not only did it provide the basis for the new forms of minimum remuneration legislation explored in Chapter 6, but it also provided a mechanism for shifting onto the employer some of the social costs not reflected in the wage. This it did, first, by decoupling the right to be paid from the obligation to work, implying an obligation to pay remuneration for time in contractual employment, and second, by implying into that obligation the costs of the various labour rights and protections to which the contract of employment gave rise.

The result of these changes was that by the mid-twentieth century, the gap between the rights of wage workers and those of salaried employees had been narrowed. The courts no longer assumed from the fact that a wage was paid for work that there were no additional ongoing obligations between the parties, no obligation on the employer to retain and employ. In effect, they implied from the existence of a labour agreement a right to be paid that was independent of the right to be paid wages for work. Even if the contract stipulated for the payment of wages therefore, employers could not unilaterally withhold payment without placing themselves in breach of contract:

> Assuming that there has been a breach on the part of the servant entitling the master to dismiss him, he may if he pleases terminate the contract, but he is not bound to do it, and if he chooses not to exercise that right but to treat the contract as a continuing contract notwithstanding the misconduct or breach of duty of the servant, then the contract is for all purposes a continuing contract subject to the master's right, in that case, to claim damages against the servant for his breach of contract.[55]

The significance of the concept of remuneration, therefore, was that it helped extend to wage workers the relational model of the contract of employment that had previously been the preserve of the salaried employee. The rules applicable to the contract of employment, at least insofar as the questions of breach and payment

[55] *Hanley v Pease & Partners* [1915] 1 KB 698, 705.

were concerned, were no different from the rules applicable to bilateral contracts generally. However, the significance of the unitary model of the contract of employment that emerged in the mid-twentieth century was that it brought the labour contract within the mainstream development of contract law from which it had long been excluded. Through the legal concept of remuneration, moreover, the contractual wage could be elevated into something more closely resembling a right to subsistence. It provided a platform, in other words, through which to shift onto the employer some of the social costs of employment.

There remained an important distinction between the salary and the wage, however, when it came to the principles applicable in the context of the common law debt claim. Claims in debt for unpaid wages will fail in relation to time when the worker was not working. Claims in debt for unpaid salary, by contrast, will succeed provided that the employee can show that the contract continued during the payment period in question. One particular benefit of the contractual right to remuneration, therefore, is that it is only if the contract has been terminated in light of the employee's prior breach that the debt claim will have to be brought; otherwise, the burden is on the employer to bring a claim in damages to recover any loss caused.

If instead of affirming the contract the employer terminates it in response to the employee's prior breach, however, the only common law remedy available to the employee will be a claim in debt for any unpaid sums. In this context, wage workers will only be prevented from claiming any unpaid wages that correspond with time not working, whereas the situation for salaried employees is more complex because the salary is an indivisible payment for an entire obligation. Thus, at common law, as the period between pay dates is treated as an entire contract, if the employee is dismissed between payments they will be unable to claim anything in respect of the period in question unless they can prove that they have substantially performed.[56]

By the end of the nineteenth century, it was widely felt that this rule, the entire contract rule, operated unfairly vis-à-vis employees, particularly where the interval between payments was particularly long.[57] To mitigate the effects of this, therefore, the courts sought to extend the Apportionment Act 1870 to salaries payable under a contract of employment.[58]

The purpose of the Apportionment Act was to render apportionable periodical payments such as rents and annuities so that they could be apportioned between successors in title.[59] The problem that the Act responded to arose where an office-holder or landlord died midway through a payment period and it was necessary to

[56] *Taylor v Laird* (1856) 1 Hurl & N 266, 156 ER 1203; *Saunders v Whittle; Boston Deep Sea Fishing Co v Ansell* (1888) 39 Ch D 339

[57] See the discussion in *Hartley* v *King Edward VI College* [2015] EWCA Civ 455; [2015] ICR 143 (CA).

[58] Paul Matthews, '"Salaries" in the Apportionment Act 1870' (1982) 2 Legal Studies 302.

[59] ibid.

apportion payments between the deceased's estate and his successor.[60] To this end, and in order to include payments made to public-office holders, the Act included within the definition of annuities 'salaries and any other periodical payments' made in respect of tenure of the office.[61] The Act presupposed that the payee had a proprietary interest in the payment, that the payment would continue to be payable irrespective of who had the right to claim it. For this reason, it did not extend to salaries payable between an employer and employee under a contract of employment; it extended only to 'offices of a public nature' and the rents or payments issuing or being derived in respect of them.[62] Given that the premise behind the Apportionment Act was to render apportionable payments payable to successors in title, moreover, it only came into operation on death or if the payee otherwise ceased to be entitled.[63] It therefore only applied to payments '... as will still be made to someone, though the payment to a particular individual has ceased'[64] and so had no application if the individual's right to be paid continued.[65]

The extension of the Act to private employment was not uncontroversial: for despite the courts' growing use of the term 'salary' to denote the periodical payments made to contractual employees, in the late nineteenth century Parliament continued to interpret the salary much more narrowly, confining it to the payment due to holders of a public office.[66] Nonetheless, the problem that the Act addressed, the question of how to apportion payments between two parties, was structurally similar to that which faced a salaried employee following termination of the contract. Here too there was a dispute as to how much the employee, who had continued to serve but for less than the stipulated period, could claim, and how much the employer who had benefitted from the employee's services, but to a lesser extent than envisaged, could retain.[67] These issues only arose, however, if the contract had been terminated. Otherwise, the payment would still be payable on the same basis as before the breach. For this reason, despite its extension to private employment, it remained the case that it only applied if the contract had been terminated:[68]

[60] ibid.

[61] Section 5.

[62] *Lowndes v Stamford* (1852) 18 QB 425, 118 ER 160, 164–65; (in respect of the 1834 Act). See similarly *Treacy v Corcoran* (1874) IR 8 CL 40.

[63] Matthews (n 58).

[64] *Lowndes v Stamford* (n 62) 164–65.

[65] See the detailed discussion in *Sim v Rotherham* [1987] Ch 216.

[66] For example, in the Income Tax Act 1842, Schedule D referred to all private professions (the self-employed) and referred to 'Profits, Gains, and Emoluments of such Professions, Employments or Vocations' while in Schedule E, applicable to the public sector, it referred to 'Salaries, Fees, Wages, Perquisites, or Profits' and 'Annuities, Pensions or Stipends' (Schedule D, case 2, rule 2; Schedule E, rule 1)

[67] *Moriarty v Regent's Garage Co, Ltd* [1921] 1 KB 423, 429 (Lush J).

[68] *Moriarty v Regent's Garadge; Item Software (UK) Ltd v Fassihi* [2004] EWCA Civ 124; [2004] BCC 994; *Re Central de Kaap Goldmines* (1899) LJ Ch 18; *Re London & Northern Bank* [1901] 1 Ch 728; *McConnell's Claim* [1901] Ch 728; and *Healey v SA Francais Rubastic* [1917] 1 KB 947.

> The effect of s.2 of the apportionment Act 1870 is that, unless the parties otherwise stipulated, the salary of an employee *whose employment terminates during a pay period* shall be apportioned and paid in respect of the period actually worked.[69]

Prior to the enactment of the Wages Act 1986, therefore, the nature and scope of workers' right to be paid were relatively clear. The wage was seen as a divisible payment for divisible obligations for work, such that for the purposes of a debt claim, a worker would have to prove that he had provided work to be entitled to be paid. The salary, by contrast, was seen as an indivisible periodic payment for an entire obligation, one that accrued per month of employment, irrespective of whether, and how much, the employee worked. If the contract was terminated, the right to be paid would depend on questions of substantial performance and the position under the Apportionment Act. For those hired under a contract of employment, however, irrespective of whether the contract provided for a wage or a salary, the employer could not unilaterally withhold even 'unearned sums' without placing himself in breach of contract.

To engage with the decision in *Hartley*, where the Supreme Court reached the opposite conclusion, we need to revisit the House of Lords' decision in *Miles*.

Miles was an officer of the Crown, appointed under the Registration of Services Act 1953 and assigned to serve as a registrar of deaths, births, and marriages for Wakefield Council thirty-seven hours a week in exchange for a salary fixed by the statutory scheme. Miles refused, as part of a union-backed plan to place pressure on employers to improve registrars' financial status, to carry out marriage ceremonies on Saturday mornings in accordance with the scheme, although he continued to provide thirty-seven hours work per week as required. In response, the Council withheld 3/37th of his salary, after having told Miles he would not be paid for the Saturday mornings in question. Miles initially argued that he was entitled under the scheme to organize his own working time, but went on to argue that his salary was an unconditional payment for his occupation of the office, and so could not be unilaterally withheld even if he was found to be in breach.

Miles was an office-holder, and so because he had no contract with the council, he fell outside the scope of the Wages Act and the provisions on deductions from wages. Thus, while the House suggested that Miles could be treated as an employee for the purposes of the claim, to successfully defend Miles' claim for unpaid salary, the council had to find a common law basis for unilaterally withholding 3/37th of his pay.

The first issue that the House had to address concerned the distinction between salaries and wages and the implications of each for the scope of an employee's right to be paid. In this respect, the central question was whether a 'salary' payable to an

[69] *Item Software v Fassihi* (n 68) [117] (emphasis added).

'employee' was, as Counsel for Miles suggested, a contractual payment for contractual service, presupposing only the continuation of the contract, or whether the salary was payable only in respect of work or services actually rendered. The second issue turned on the relationship between salaries and wages on the one hand and remuneration on the other, and as such the claim in debt for unpaid wages and the employer's contractual obligation to pay.

7.3.3.1 Confusing the Wage and the Salary

It was clear from the terms of the statutory scheme that Miles was to be paid a *weekly* salary for a pre-defined period of work (thirty-seven hours per week). The House of Lords concluded from this that his position was no different from that of a 'wage' worker hired at a weekly wage. The obligations to work and to pay were, it argued, interdependent, for 'the employer pays for work and the worker works for his "wages"'. This is so, it seems, irrespective of whether the 'wage' is expressed as a weekly 'salary' or weekly wage for pre-defined hours of work.[70]

It seems from this that the House of Lords saw no meaningful distinction between a salary and a wage, at least when it comes to the conditions that must be satisfied for the purposes of the debt claim. It is arguable, however, that this was due to the specific nature of Miles' salary, the fact that their Lordships interpreted the scheme as creating a right to be paid for a pre-defined period of work. Lord Templeman expressly recognized, for example, that there is a difference between salaried office-holders whose obligations might require that they provide service on Sundays or Christmas as and when required and those with pre-defined hours of work like Miles, a distinction that would equally apply to private employees. He did not explain whether different principles might apply to each when it comes to the question of what earns the right to be paid.[71]

In *Miles*, the House of Lords had argued that a salary, or at least a salary that envisages pre-determined hours of work, is *not* an unconditional payment payable for (contractual) service over time. Instead, it is a payment for work done, where the obligation to pay is only triggered when that work has been duly performed. This meant providing work in accordance with the express and implied terms of the contract of employment, including the implied obligation to faithfully and obediently serve.[72] It thus implied that employees could not, by definition, be said to be working during a period of industrial action because 'an employee who works with an intention to harm his employer is no different from a worker who refuses to work at all'.[73]

[70] *Miles v Wakefield Borough Council* [1987] AC 539, 557.
[71] ibid 556.
[72] ibid 559 (Lord Templeman).
[73] ibid 561 (Lord Templeman). See also Lord Bridge, 551.

This interpretation was confirmed in *Wiluszynski* where the Court of Appeal argued that an employee is not entitled to remuneration under the contract of employment if he is not ready and willing to perform *that contract*.[74] Here, the employee's refusal to perform a small part of his contractual duties per day amounted to a failure to 'work' that permitted the employer to reject the work and withhold each day's payment without placing itself in breach of contract.[75]

The High Court adopted a similar approach in *Cooper*.[76] This case concerned a full day's strike among support staff at a sixth form college to which the employer responded by withholding not only a full day's 'salary' but also the holiday pay referable to the strike day in question. The court confirmed that an employer has *two* choices (short of dismissal) when it comes to responding to a strike: to deduct unearned sums (the '*Miles*' basis of deduction) or to claim damages by way of breach of contract (the '*Sim*' basis). For policy reasons, however, if the employer elected for the former, he was limited to deducting that which the employees could not sue for in a claim in debt. This meant the employer could not circumvent the Working Time Regulations by withholding an apportioned part of holiday pay.[77] This was not 'wages' in the sense of the value of labour to the employer, but part of the 'total consideration under the contract'.[78] Only the former, the court argued, could unilaterally be withheld.

The employees in *Cooper*, *Wiluszynski*, and *Miles* were all hired to provide a set amount of work per week.[79] In each case, therefore, although their contracts provided for a 'salary', the term does not seem to have been used in the technical legal sense to refer to a fixed periodic payment for contractual service over time. Instead, it is used in the generic sense to refer to the annualized total of that which is paid in exchange for a set amount of work throughout the year. The position in both *Sim v Rotherham*, decided while *Miles* was on appeal, and *Hartley v King Edward VI College* was different. Both these cases concerned industrial action by teachers who were paid a salary in the sense of a periodical payment for professional service over time. Rather than prescribing set working hours, therefore, the contracts envisaged that the employees 'provide a particular service to proper professional standards' such that their right to be paid could not be confined to any pre-determined working hours or time spent at the workplace.[80]

[74] *Wiluszynski v Tower Hamlets LBC* [1989] ICR 493; [1989] IRLR 259.

[75] For a discussion, see: Hazel McLean, 'Contract of Employment. Negative Covenants and No Work, No Pay' (1990) 49 Cambridge Law Journal 28.

[76] *Cooper v Isle of White College* [2007] EWHC 2831; [2008] IRLR 124.

[77] ibid [32].

[78] ibid [8].

[79] The case report does not give details of Wiluszynski's contract, but this can be inferred from the trial judge's discussion of the hypothetical possibility of reducing the salary 'by 2–3 hours' for the five-week period in question.

[80] *Sim v Rotherham* (n 65) 255.

For Scott J in *Sim*, the salary was something that vested in the teacher per month of employment. For this reason, even a breach of contract committed with an intention to harm the employer could not be equated with an absence from, or failure to, work.[81] Industrial action was not, in other words, to be equated with a total failure of consideration capable of excusing the employer's failure to pay, whether this took the form of a work-to-rule, as was the case in *Sim*, or a full day's strike. In *Sim*, therefore, where the teachers had refused to perform cover work in breach of an implied term of their contracts, the they had a good claim *i* for their salaries and, if the employer refused to pay them, for breach of contract. This was so even in respect of the salary due for the month during which the industrial action took place; since the contract was continuing, the employer continued to be bound by its contractual obligation to pay them. Scott J put this as follows: 'each month a contractual right to a salary payment vest in the teacher ... if in the course of a month there has been a breach of contract ... if the breach of contract has not given rise to any recoverable loss ... there is no deduction that can be properly made'.[82]

By the time *Hartley* was decided, however, the status of this argument was unclear. In *Miles*, Lord Oliver had referred to *Sim*, but had argued that for the purposes of a claim in debt for unpaid salary, the employee would have to prove he *had been* ready and willing to perform his contract of employment during the period in question.[83] Neither he nor the courts in *Cooper* or *Wiluszynski* drew any express distinction between a salary in the generic sense of an annualized payment for 'work' and a salary in the technical sense of a fixed periodical payment for contractual service over time. It seemed, therefore, that the principle in *Miles* would apply irrespective of the nature of the employee's contractual pay.

The dispute in *Hartley* arose when, following a day's strike by teachers at a sixth form college, the college sought to withhold 1/260th of their annual pay. Both the Court of Appeal and the Supreme Court accepted with little discussion the argument that the *Miles* basis for deduction applied, that 'pay for a strike day is never earned and cannot be claimed'.[84] The only question remaining was thus whether the college was entitled to deduct 1/260th of the salary, reflecting the number of weekdays in the year, or were limited to 1/365th to reflect the number of calendar days in the year. The answer to this depended on whether the salary was conceived as a payment for contractual service over time, apportionable by reference to calendar days, or, as in *Miles*, a payment for core working hours, apportionable by reference to time spent teaching at the workplace.

[81] ibid 263.
[82] ibid 255.
[83] *Miles v Wakefield* (n 70) 567.
[84] *Hartley v King Edward* (n 57) (SC) [11].

The court assumed, therefore, that it was necessary to find some basis for apportioning the salary. This followed from the idea that a single day's strike might amount to a total failure of consideration justifying the employer's refusal to pay. The problem, however, was that as in *Sim*, the teachers' salary was defined as a 'sum payable per annum, to be paid in monthly instalments'. Their contractual duties included working a minimum number of working days per year, referred to as 'directed time', and 'such additional hours as may be needed to enable you to discharge your duties effectively including, in particular, the marking of students' work, the writing of reports on students and the preparation of lessons, teaching material and teaching programmes'. The nature of this 'undirected time' was elaborated in the collective agreement, comprising a number of 'professional duties' neither limited to teaching hours, nor confined to tasks performed at the workplace. In light of this, the court recognized that the teachers' obligations extended far beyond an obligation to provide a minimum amount of 'directed time' at the workplace. Their salaries could not, therefore, be seen as divisible payments for a divisible obligation to work. Instead, they were fixed periodic payments for ongoing service such that, prima facie, the entire contract rule applied.[85]

To reconcile this with the decision in *Miles*, therefore, the Supreme Court had little choice but to find a basis upon which to apportion both the entire obligation to serve and the indivisible obligation to pay. For this purpose, it invoked the Apportionment Act and its equal daily rate of accrual. In so doing, however, the Supreme Court not only applied the Act in a context to which it was ill-suited, where the contract and the entitlement to payment continued, but also fundamentally subverted the basic rationale upon which the Act had been applied to contracts of employment. Rather than being used to provide protection for the employee's accrued salary in the event of wrongful dismissal, the Act had been relied upon to deprive employees of an apportioned part of the salary that they should never have been refused in the first place.

7.3.3.2 Dissolving the Distinction between Wages and Salaries, and Remuneration

In principle, the question as to what the employee must prove to make out a claim in debt for unpaid salary/wages is irrelevant when it comes to determining whether the employer is under a contractual obligation to pay.[86] The benefit of the contractual right to remuneration, as noted above, is that it prevents the employer from unilaterally withholding payment and placing the burden on the worker to establish his right to be paid. In *Miles*, however, the House rejected the premise of this argument, and the basic contractual principles on which it is based.[87] If a

[85] [2015] ICR 143 King Edward (SC) [11] and [25].
[86] Brian Napier, 'Aspects of the Wage Work Bargain' (1984) 43 Cambridge Law Journal 337.
[87] *Miles v Wakefield* (n 70) 565 (Lord Templeman).

non-breaching party affirms the contract, he is entitled to refuse payment if the other party's breach is an implied condition for the obligation to perform.

Miles was not an employee; he did not actually have a contract of employment with the Council so there was nothing to ground an action by the council for damages, nor a claim by Miles in respect of the council's failure to pay. The case was quite different from an ordinary employment case, therefore, as the sole issue was whether Miles, treated as an employee for the purposes of a debt claim, could make out his entitlement to the sums claimed. Thus, while Lord Oliver saw 'much force in [the] argument that the only route available to an employer would be a claim in damages for any loss flowing from the breach' he concluded that these principles were irrelevant on the facts because this was 'an action in which the plaintiff claimed certain sums as due to him by way of salary and in which, therefore, he assumed the burden of pleading and proving each essential allegation necessary to establish his entitlement'.[88]

If this is so, it could be argued that the case provides no real authority for the contractual aspects of the claim, the question as to whether the refusal to pay would amount to a breach of contract. It is clear from the judgments, however, that their Lordships decided the case *as if* there was a contract of employment between the parties that continued following the breach.[89] The decision can only be explained, therefore, by reference to the particular view of the contract of employment that their Lordships adopted: a contract that binds an employee to provide faithful service over time, but does not give rise to any binding and *enforceable* obligations on the employer to provide work and/or pay on an ongoing basis. The form of the contract is thus exchange, but the obligation to work is conceived in a form redolent of the relation of master and servant.

The cases that their Lordships relied upon to defend this position do not actually support the arguments made. First, most of the cases relied on are Scottish cases where 'there [is] nothing particularly novel' in the idea that 'all the conditions of a mutual contract are dependent upon their counterparts'.[90] English law does not recognize the 'mutual contract' as a distinct contract type, however, nor does it endorse the premise that a non-breaching party can withhold performance in response to another party's breach. It is not entirely clear, therefore, why these principles are being relied upon to justify a decision in relation to the English law of the contract of employment. Second, of the two English cases relied on, one, *Henthorn*, arguably supports the contrary argument, while the other, *Creswell*, rests on a similar misconception as that which underpins the decision in *Miles*.

[88] ibid 567 (Lord Oliver).

[89] ibid 565 (Lord Templeman).

[90] *Laurie v British Steel Corporation*, 23 February 1978 (unreported); *Turnbull v McLean & Co* (1874) 1 R 730; *Alexander Graham & Co v United Turkey Red Co Ltd* [1922] SC 533.

Henthorn was a dispute over the burden of proof in a claim for unpaid wages in respect of a period of 'work to rule'. The sole question for the court was whether it was for the employers or the employees to prove that the workers had (or had not) satisfied the condition for claiming wages. Lawton J suggested that 'when a plaintiff claims he is entitled to be paid money under a contract which he alleges the defendant has broken, he must prove that he was ready and willing to perform that contract'. It does not seem that he was saying, however, that the consideration for wages is the performance of, or readiness and willingness to perform the contract.[91] Instead, he was reiterating the point that the plaintiff must be so willing at the time he *seeks to compel the defendant to perform*, that is, when he brings a claim for breach of the contractual obligation to pay. It is exactly this, the workers' *ongoing* readiness and willingness to perform, rather than their willingness at the time of the breach, that the employers were disputing in this case.[92] Lawton J's remarks do not contradict the idea that to claim in debt wages for a prior period, the workers need only show that they worked, or were ready and willing to work, throughout the period in question. In fact, the implication of *Henthorn* for *Miles* would have been that because Miles was, at the time of the claim, ready and willing to perform his duties (ie he was no longer in breach), he would have been entitled to bring an action for breach of contract in respect of the council's failure to pay.[93]

In *Cresswell v Board of Inland Revenue* the court asserted the principle 'no work (or, at any rate, readiness to perform whatever work it is the employee ought to be willing to perform if physically able to do so)—no pay'.[94] In *Creswell*, however, the court had conceded that 'direct authority [for this point] is slight'.[95] The only (English) authority identified was *SS for Employment v ASLEF (no.2)* but, as Sedley QC for *Miles* noted, this case was concerned only with whether a work to rule *was* a repudiatory breach, and so said little on the effects of affirming the contract on the employer's obligation to pay.[96] The other cases relied upon were, once again, Scottish cases where the principle, in contrast to English law, is well established.[97]

The House of Lord's interpretation of the cases has, however, been confirmed by the decisions in *Wiluszynski* and *Cooper*. Both these cases simply assumed that an employer who does not wish to dismiss his employee following industrial action

[91] For a similar interpretation, see: Napier (n 86).

[92] *Henthorn and Taylor v Central Electricity Generating Board* [1980] IRLR. 361, 362–63. See: *ANAC v Robinson* [1977] VR 87 where the employee was unsuccessful because they failed to establish that they had been ready and willing to perform. Here, however, the claim was for *damages for breach of contract*, not a claim in debt. A claim in debt succeeded in *Welbourn v Australian Postal Commission* [1984] VR 256.

[93] *Henthorn and Taylor* (n 93).

[94] [1984] 2 All ER 713; [1984] ICR 508, 522.

[95] ibid.

[96] [1972] 2 All ER 949. But see Lord Denning's remark at 967.

[97] [1984] 1 CR 508, 522.

can either claim in damages for breach of contract and/or deduct such sums by way of equitable set off, or unilaterally withhold a sum reflecting that which the employee could not sue for in a claim for unpaid wages—without placing itself in breach of contract.

Neither the teachers nor the court in *Hartley* questioned the premise that, after *Miles*, an employer is entitled to unilaterally withhold a portion of a worker's wages and/or salary in response to a strike. However, because the court had recognized that the salary was an indivisible payment for an entire obligation—something emphatically denied by the House of Lords in *Miles*—the effect of applying the '*Miles*' basis of deduction was to create a situation in which one side of an entire contract appeared to have been suspended. Thus, while the teachers remained bound to continue to perform their ongoing obligation to serve, the employer could unilaterally suspend his *ongoing* obligation to pay. The situation was not dissimilar, therefore, from that which obtains following the termination of the contract. This might explain why the Supreme Court determined the question of apportionment by invoking principles applicable to contracts that have been terminated. Its argument that at common law a salaried employee is not entitled to be paid for a payment period of a strike only holds where the contract has come to an end; otherwise, the obligation to pay continues as before. Similarly, the Apportionment Act need not even be considered where the contract is continuing, because it is *only* following termination that questions of substantial performance and apportionment arise. This confusion all follows from the now widespread failure of both Parliament and the courts to carefully distinguish between the wage and the salary, and to differentiate the principles applicable to these two payments from the principles applicable to the employer's obligation to pay remuneration.

On the one hand, this shows a complete lack of awareness of the important social and economic function that the contract of employment, and the concepts intrinsic to it, emerged to perform. On the other, however, it reflects a much more significant shift in the way that the courts conceive the law–market relationship and the function of the contract of employment. The maxim, 'no work, no pay' that the House of Lords endorsed in *Miles* reflects a belief that the employer's obligation to pay is simply an obligation to pay the value of a commodity, a commodity, moreover, to which he expects to be given 'exclusive' access. Failure by employees to cooperate with their employers thus deprives the latter of the value of the 'good' for which the wage is said to be paid. Considerations about the socio-economic function of the wage, its function in securing social reproduction, are entirely excluded: the courts are seen to have the power only to police the boundaries of a simple exchange. The 'contract of employment' merely describes the legal mechanism through which that exchange is executed, therefore, and so is not being conceived as a regulatory device through which employment relationships are shaped and constituted in a form in which they can be both socially, and economically, sustainable.

7.4 Conclusion

Neither Parliament nor the courts recognize a distinction today between the sum that an employer agrees to pay for work and the legally constituted obligation to pay for ongoing service that the contract of employment had long implied. The function of the contract of employment is not, therefore, to provide stability to both parties' expectations, providing the employer with ongoing service and the worker with remuneration and social protection. It is simply the mechanism through which the employer guarantees that he will be able to make use of, and benefit from, the labour purchased by the wage.

Behind these premises lies a particular view of the role of the legal system and its relationship with the market. The legal obligation to pay is not a multifaceted one consisting of obligations to pay for work or labour, and obligations to pay for service implied from the worker's subordination and dependence. Instead, it is a single obligation to pay for labour rendered under a contract of employment. It is this that is expressed today by what have become synonymous terms: wages, salaries, and remuneration. The courts' role today is not to construe the employer's obligation to pay in light of labour law's broader function therefore, but simply to guarantee that the employer actually pays what he agreed to pay, and even then, only if he has actually received the full benefit of the work for which he agreed to pay it. The unique character of the labour commodity and its place within the broader social fabric is being ignored, as is the broader role that the contract of employment has historically performed in reconciling the coordination and subsistence functions of the wage.

The same ontology is implicit in the statutory framework. Rather than protecting workers from employers' abuse of power, from being pressured to consent to deductions from wages, statutory protection against deductions guarantees only a right to be paid what is left of the wage once agreed sums have been withheld. Legal protection for wages is not seen as a precondition for freedom of contract, therefore part of the institutional framework that *constitutes* the labour market and one of the conditions for the emergence of the labour commodity, rather it is something that exists entirely independently from that market and, restricting the parties' freedom, is to be narrowly construed.

The problem, however, is that both the common law and the statutory regime is built upon a legal framework that was based on a very different set of ontological premises. It is the courts' failure to engage with these premises that explains the confusion we see in the case law. Having lost sight of the distinctiveness of payments such as salaries and remuneration, *and* their protective connotations, this gives rise to a deceptive picture of the limits of what labour law can do when it comes to providing protection for workers' right to be paid. Decision in cases like *Miles* and *Hartley* are thus presented as natural and inevitable, when, in fact, they are a product of a particular set of assumptions about the nature of law and the wage which previous chapters have shown to be problematic.

8
The Statutory Minimum Wage

8.1 Introduction

This book has argued that, to be sustainable, labour markets presuppose that employers pay their workers a sum that covers not just the private, but also the social costs involved in their use of labour power. While workers' living costs could, conceivably, be secured through a system of state-provided wage supplements (or even, minimum income guarantee), by shifting the social cost problem onto the state and the community, such an approach would interfere with the wage's important signalling or coordination function at the cost of the long-run stability and sustainability of the system. Thus, if both the social reproduction and coordination functions of the wage are to be performed, it is extremely important that employers bear not only the private, but also the social costs of employment—guaranteeing workers not merely a minimum market wage for time working, but a guaranteed minimum income from employment. This would imply that wage supplements and tax credits ought to have only a very minimal role to play. Indeed, depressing wages below subsistence level are not effective from the perspective of capital accumulation/surplus value production for, regardless of its effects on the profits of *individual firms*, the overall surplus value produced in a given production cycle can only be known when the *full costs* of production are taken into account: and this necessarily includes the costs to *society*, of reproducing the labour power of all those whose labour power services, in one way or another, the 'needs' or 'demands' of capital.

This premise, that employers should bear primary responsibility for securing workers' living costs, was intrinsic to the medieval and early modern conception of the service relation and the system of wage regulation in which it was embedded. By the end of the eighteenth century, however, this idea was falling out of favour, as was the idea that the legal system had any role to play in the regulation of wages. For the first time, the market was being seen as the only appropriate mechanism through which to determine wage rates. As a result, it was not long before a gap began to open up between the wage and workers' costs of subsistence. It is in this context that we find early experimentations with wage supplementation.

The first experiment with wage supplementation came with the introduction of wage allowances along the lines adopted in the Berkshire district of Speenhamland in 1795. The Speenhamland 'system' arose out of a meeting at the Pelican Inn in the parish of Speen. The purpose of the meeting was to adapt current wage rates

Labour and the Wage. Zoe Adams, Oxford University Press (2020). © Zoe Adams.
DOI: 10.1093/oso/9780198858898.001.0001

in line with prices. For reasons which remain unknown, the magistrates decided instead to replace the system of wage regulation with an allowance policy, a wage supplement designed to top up the market clearing wage to subsistence level.[1] The magistrates thus committed themselves to making 'allowances for the relief of the poor for their own support and maintenance' by tying the wage supplement to the cost of a loaf of bread.[2] If a labourer was in private employment, the parish would be responsible for ensuring he received the recognized minimum, making up the difference between this and the wage his employer chose to pay him.

The Speenhamland system reflects an early attempt to externalize the social costs of labour from the market. By failing to set a mandatory pay rate, however, and resorting instead to the payment of allowances, the magistrates' decision undermined incentives for both workers and employers. Guaranteed a minimum income irrespective of whether they worked, and how much, workers had little incentive to find work or to work more efficiently. In turn, because employers could count on the parish to top up the wage to subsistence level, they had little incentive to pay much at all by way of wages.

In the roundsman system, an applicant for relief took a ticket to a farmer who could employ him for as long as he liked for whatever he wished to pay; the farmer paid the ticket, which was taken back to the overseer who made up the wage out of parish funds. The result of the system was that farmers employed surplus labour at less than the market rate. Strategies such as this simply further demoralized workers, and, at the same time, removed the employer's impetus to develop new production methods by investing in labour-saving machinery. In time, this imposed an impossible burden on the parish. By the early nineteenth century, even these 'charitable' supplements had dipped below subsistence level. Speenhamland had 'confirmed' the emerging view that even state provided wage supplements 'distorted' the market, depressing wages below the 'natural' subsistence rate.[3]

Criticism of Speenhamland lay at the heart of the poor law report that led to the new poor law of 1834. By withdrawing relief in aid of wages, the commissioners argued, labourers would become 'more steady and diligent' so giving farmers a higher return on capital, enabling them to pay higher wages. The poor law commissioners thus firmly endorsed a conception of society 'based on an interdependent market economy resting on self-interest, competition, and contract',—a highly naturalistic conception of the law–market relationship.

The reaction to Speenhamland was so negative that, after the repeal of the old poor law in 1834, the idea of paying wage supplements was not revived until the

[1] John Lawrence Hammond and Barbara Bradby Hammond, *The Village Labourer, 1760-1832: A Study in the Government of England before the Reform Bill* (Longmans, Green 1913) Chapter 6.

[2] Reproduced in ibid 140.

[3] See the evidence in: House of Commons Select Committee on Labourers' Wages (Russell), Report, Parliamentary Papers (1824) (392) VI 401.

early 1970s.[4] During this period, what the employer agreed to pay for work was more or less synonymous with how much the worker received in connection with his employment (what we might now refer to as 'remuneration'). Individuals had to subsist on their wages, therefore, and wage rates had to be dictated by the market: wages were not something with which the law could, or should, interfere. The poverty and squalor that resulted from this attitude towards wages ultimately led to the Trade Boards Act. However, as we have seen, this Act did little to qualify the general attitude towards wage regulation. Linking the right to be paid to the provision of a given quantity of labour, the Act continued the assumption that wages were, and *should* be, workers' sole source of subsistence—and that that wage was dictated not by law, but by the market. The role for the minimum wage in this context was simply to provide for the 'competitive wage' that would have emerged 'but for' market failure—to ensure the payment by employers of the market price of the worker's commodity. The legal system's only role was to facilitate the identification and enforcement of the 'real' market rate.

It is in light of these observations that the wages councils can be seen as a significant staging post in the evolution of the minimum wage. The councils reflected a comprehensive attempt to shift the social costs of employment onto employers, signalling a willingness by Parliament to embrace a constitutive role for the legal system in the setting of wages. Rather than seeing social reproduction as a process that exists externally to the market, to be guaranteed *in addition* to the market wage, the labour market was seen to be integrated, or embedded, within a much broader process of social reproduction; a process in which law was deemed to be integral.

Working in conjunction with a relational model of the contract of employment, the Wages Councils Act had provided, in the industries to which it applied, for a guaranteed minimum weekly income irrespective of how much work was performed. If an employer sought to purchase labour with wages, therefore, it was implicit that he would have to pay a sum believed to reflect the social costs associated with its use.[5] This was achieved through the Act's use of the term remuneration which, attaching to the employment relationship rather than the provision of labour, performed a functionally similar role to the servant's implied right to be maintained. The concept of remuneration reflected the idea that, irrespective of how much was payable as wages, the person responsible for paying those wages ought to bear the costs of subsistence—to take responsibility for the wellbeing and subsistence of the worker. For this reason, the councils set the minimum rate of remuneration, not by reference to any pre-conceived notion of a natural

[4] See: Simon F Deakin and Frank Wilkinson, *Labour Law, Social Security and Economic Inequality* (Institute of Employment Rights 1989) A full narrative account of Speenhamland is outside the scope of the book. The reason for including it here is to set the scene for the analysis of the modern law on tax credits.

[5] HC Deb 16 January 1945, vol 407, cols 69–116, 74–75 (Mr Bevin).

market-clearing wage, but by reference to what both sides of industry regarded as fair or adequate, taking into account considerations about the costs of living.[6]

In terms of the structure of the Act, what was unique here was that the obligation to pay contractual remuneration and to bear the costs of the various employment rights arising from the contract of employment was independent from the obligation to pay wages for labour. Underpinning the Wages Councils Act, therefore, was a certain economic understanding of the need for employers to meet a greater part of the social costs of the reproduction of labour power, so that these costs did not fall entirely on the worker and/or the state.

> We have renamed the boards Wages Councils, and they will be given a general power to fix remuneration, and remuneration includes the fixing of a guaranteed weekly wage. I am sure that no one will now object to their having that power. The restriction hitherto placed upon them as to the number of holidays they can give will be removed; they will be able to deal with that question on its merits ... by the passing of this Bill we can turn our backs upon that bit of our industrial history.[7]

The role for the state was not to supplement the wage, but to provide for a comprehensive social insurance system where earnings-related contributions and benefits could ensure that a subsistence income could continue during sickness, unemployment, and retirement.[8] For William Beveridge, the aim was a 'national minimum', achieved not only through the wages councils, but through a combination of social insurance and public assistance (including universal education and children's allowances) based on the principle of 'guaranteeing to everyone, on condition of working and contributing while he can work, an income sufficient for his subsistence and that of his family' including those periods 'when for any reason, of sickness, accident, old age or unemployment, he cannot work'.[9] The task, he argued, was the creation of a labour market that was a seller's, and not a buyer's, market, where a 'national minimum' for all was the ultimate goal towards which markets and public policy were directed.[10]

The wages councils thus formed part of a broader, demand-oriented macroeconomic policy that saw a key role for the state in providing the framework through which market activity could take place. This included not only the central pillars of the welfare state, social insurance, education, and public assistance, but also centralized demand-management. Introduced with a view to targeting inflation, experimentation with incomes policies expressed a similar sentiment, a

[6] See the discussion in Chapter 7.
[7] HC Deb 16 January 1945, vol 407, cols 69–116, 75 (Mr Bevin).
[8] Deakin and Wilkinson (n 4).
[9] William Henry Beveridge, *Full Employment in a Free Society* (Allen & Unwin 1944).
[10] ibid.

commitment to maintaining an alignment between wages and prices. In such a context, wages, including tax and social insurance payments made in connection with employment, performed a social reproduction, or subsistence, function, and so were not seen as a product of some abstract laws of supply and demand:

> It is true that wages, for example, are settled by a balance between the amount demanded and the amount the employer is able and willing to pay. To this extent the general level of demand in the economy is important, because, as we have seen in the past, an excessive level of demand leads to labour shortages, large increases in money wage rates and wage drift on a large scale ... But in seeking agreement on an incomes policy we are not attempting to supersede supply and demand in this sense, but rather to moderate the forces which affect this balance.[11]

Supply and demand were seen during this period as forces that emerged from a particular institutional framework, in the construction of which law played an integral part. There were not, therefore, any fundamental economic laws to which the law responded: rather, those forces were seen to be institutional, and thus, to a great extent, a product of law. In such a context, law did not simply react to market decisions made by economic actors, but actively constituted these relations with a view to achieving a balance of risks and costs between workers, employers, and the state. To avail itself of rights in labour, an employer would have to bear the social costs involved in its use—irrespective of how much that employer agreed to pay by way of wages. This is the same attitude that we saw in relation to dock work. In the same way that the obligation to work implied an obligation to faithfully and obediently serve, therefore, the obligation to pay wages implied an obligation to bear the social costs of employment. There was little room in this framework for a system of tax credits and wage supplements designed to top up wages in order to 'make work pay'.

8.2 Tax Credits and the National Minimum Wage Act 1998

As discussed in Chapter 7, in the 1970s and 1980s, the wages councils were the subject of considerable critique by the Conservative government(s), part of their much broader criticism of the social and economic policies of the post-war period. Experiences during the 1960s and 1970s seemed to support the idea that trade unions caused inflation; incomes policies were ineffective; and wages councils were a barrier to employment. In such an environment, as we have seen, neoliberal ideas about individualism and free markets began to flourish.

[11] HC Deb 14 April 1964, vol 693, cols 264–65.

From the government's perspective, where social policy had gone wrong in the post-war years was in conceptualizing unemployment as a problem of aggregate demand, rather than a product of labour market rigidities—including labour law and collective bargaining. This 'revelation' or the 'real' causes of unemployment led to a widespread attack on unions, and, at a macro-economic level, a shift to supply-side policies. In practice, this meant using the tax-benefit system to incentivize employers to offer more jobs, and to encourage workers to accept them—at whatever wage was being offered.

Central to this new policy paradigm was the government's new wage supplement, the family credit, an extension of the family income supplement introduced as a temporary measure in 1971. The purpose of the credit was primarily to subsidize employers, to encourage them to hire workers at rates they could 'afford', particularly given that the wages councils were to be setting rates above the level 'required to fill jobs' ... 'prevent[ing] employers from developing pay systems wholly in accordance with the best interests of their businesses'.[12] Thus, as the opposition argued, it seemed that:

> The real policy underlying [the credit] is to try to force down wage levels by paying family credit through the employer, thereby encouraging employers, in addition to the other methods that the Government are using, to force down the wages of the low paid.[13]

The 1970s and 1980s thus reflected a return to the pre-1940s belief in the existence of an objective market-clearing wage which ought not be artificially raised to take into account considerations about the costs of living. The result was a tax credit system *but no minimum wage*. Even the scope for market failure, therefore, the premise that the labour market might not actually clear in practice, had been implicitly rejected.[14] Labour markets could operate competitively provided that the state did not 'intervene', and *any* attempt to do so by setting wage rates could not but lead to unemployment. As then Conservative MP Enoch Powell argued:

> [payment of relief to] persons in full-time employment ... is something which is bound profoundly to distort the wage system and to frustrate the ambition ... that a man should receive as near as may be the full value of his work in cash.[15]

The only exception to this principle was the limited system of wage supplementation targeting low wage-earners with dependent children, payable to mothers even

[12] Department of Employment, Consultation on Wages Councils 1988, 5; Social Security Act 1986, Part II, and SI 1987/1793.

[13] HC Deb 01 July 1986, vol 100, cols 813–15, 814 (Ms Short).

[14] HC Deb 03 June 1985, vol 80, cols 34–51, 35.

[15] HC Deb 10 November 1970, vol. 806, cols 262 and 264–5 (Mr Powell).

when the eligibility was in respect to the father's earnings. Even this was, however, seen as a continuation of the premise that employers cannot be required to pay above the market rate, for 'the essence of family allowances is that they are not related to the income of the recipient except via the tax system, which is a quite different matter'[16].

> ... employers cannot be expected to pay more than the market rate for labour to their employees, regardless of their employees' commitments. ... There will, thus inevitably be cases where the market rate is sufficient for single men and women to live in reasonable dignity, but is not sufficient for a married couple to do so even when they have only one child, let alone more. This situation is not new. It is one in which society has felt again and again compelled to intervene.[17]

Having significantly curtailed the powers of the wages councils under the Wages Act, wages councils were finally abolished in the Trade Union and Employment Reform Act of 1993. The press release accompanying the Act stated clearly that:

> Wages Councils were established in the early 1900s when there were no employment rights, no general health and safety legislation and little social security protection. They have no role to play in the 1990s.[18]

The abolition of the councils did not, however, have the effect that the Conservative government had forecast. While the result was that about one half of the jobs in the retail sector paid below the old minimum rates, there was also a net loss of about 18,000 jobs in retail and catering. Lower pay and fewer jobs was the result of 'free' bargaining over wages therefore, and not the other way round.[19]

By the mid-1990s, with no legally binding minimum wage and no comprehensive system of wage supplementation to top up wages to subsistence level, concerns about rising levels of in-work and child poverty increased.[20] While the Labour party had historically been committed to Keynsian demand management and full employment, progressive taxation and redistributive expenditures, under the leadership of Tony Blair, attitudes had begun to shift.

Blair jettisoned the economic policy of 'Old Labour', placing emphasis on the intrinsic efficiency and fairness of markets, advocating no new tax initiatives, restraints on public expenditures, and restrictions on unions' ability to call strikes. In relation to social policy, while the traditional push had been on extending benefit

16 ibid 262 and 279 (Mr Powell).

17 ibid 262 and 279 (Sir Brandon Rhys Williams).

18 Department of Employment press release, 5 November 1992.

19 Low Pay Network, *After the Safety Net* (Low Pay Network 1994).

20 HM Treasury, 'Tackling Poverty and Making Work Pay: Tax Credits for the 21st Century' (2000) 6 The Modernisation of Britain's Tax and Benefit System.

programmes, New Labour now spoke of social inclusion and the need for responsibilities to be connected with rights. The idea of the national minimum wage fitted neatly into this new policy paradigm: it required no increase in taxation, and only minimum public expenditure. But it also placed emphasis on work as a source of social inclusion, linking ideas of decent living standards with ideas of effort, hard work, and personal responsibility—ideas central to the neoliberal world-view perpetuated under Thatcher.[21]

These ideas formed the background to Labour's 'Welfare Contract', also known as 'the New Deal', a series of reforms intended to 'make work pay'. This was to be achieved through a reformed tax credit system designed to increase incentives to work backed up by a statutory minimum wage. Concerned to keep business on their side, however, labour's minimum wage was packaged as part of a 'flexibility-plus' paradigm that would ensure protection for 'ethical' employers, while remaining sensitive to the 'economic circumstances of the time'.[22] The case for the minimum wage was built on an economic rationale that stressed its efficiency-enhancing effects, its capacity to reduce taxpayer subsidies to companies that were paying below-market wages—with very little emphasis placed on the needs of the low-wage workers themselves.

Labour's minimum wage was never intended to be a living (or social) wage. The main purpose of the National Minimum Wage Act (NMWA) was to prevent employers responding to the tax credit regime by decreasing wages, reducing incentives to work, where the overriding policy focus was labour market flexibility, personal responsibility, and a duty to work.[23] Making work pay was not to be confused with 'making *employers* pay'. This was not the function of the minimum wage:

> By setting a floor for wages, [the national minimum wage is] essential to ensure that low-income workers enjoy the full benefit of the tax credit.[24]

The minimum wage was seen as integral to a policy aimed at 'correcting' the market, restoring competitiveness. As Mrs Beckett, introducing the bill into the House of Commons argued:

> Despite the previous Government's assertions, having no floor at all for wages has in itself created considerable problems in the labour market. It has increased

[21] Jerold Waltman, *Minimum Wage Policy in Great Britain and the United States* (Algora Publishing 2008) Chapter 3.

[22] ibid 82.

[23] HM Treasury, 'Tackling Poverty and Making Work Pay: tax credits for the 21st Century' (2000) HMSO.

[24] ibid 17. For the current tax credit regime see: Welfare Reform Act 2012, Part I, Universal Credit Regulations 2013, SI 2013/376, and Universal Credit (Work Allowance) Amendment Regulations 2015, SI 2015/1649. For a commentary, see: Keith Puttick, '"21st Century Welfare" and Universal Credit: Reconstructing the Wage-Work-Welfare Bargain' (2012) 41 Industrial Law Journal 236.

> costs and pressures on the public purse and it has undermined many efficient and worthwhile companies which are at risk of losing market share as they are undercut by cowboy operators.[25]

Statutory minimum wages were very much a continuation of the supply-side policies of the Conservative government, a system based around incentives to work. Different wage rates were established for different age groups—with no variation depending on industry, location, or costs of living. Workers aged 18 and below were expressly excluded from the scope of the Act, and those aged 21 and under paid at a lower minimum rate. The premise that employers could hardly be expected to pay the same rate to 'inexperienced workers' further highlights that the minimum rate was conceived in terms of the market value of the labour provided, rather than the needs of the individual providing it.

Consistently with this, Labour's attention when it came to combatting poverty and social exclusion lay elsewhere. This was not the function of wage regulation, but of tax credits and social security. The tax credit system was thus expanded in 2002 with the introduction of the working tax credit and the child tax credit. In addition to providing a supplementary source of income to persons 'engaged in qualifying remunerative work' this regime also made it possible for tax credits and other forms of income support (such as statutory sick pay) to continue during periods of illness, incapacity, maternity, or adoption leave. These are periods when the contract is continuing, but contractual pay (wages or sick pay) is no longer being paid.[26] In effect, rather than requiring employers to pay workers a social wage as a quid pro quo for the benefit of having them employed under a contract of employment *when work was not being provided*, the state assumed these costs, confining employers' pay-related obligations to the payment of the private costs of a commodity. In this way, a distinction was emerging between the wage, now understood as the market wage adjusted for imperfections, and the deemed subsistence income—the difference between the two being covered by the state.

Labour had implicitly accepted the premise that there is a direct link between 'above market' wages, and unemployment. For this reason, the minimum wage rate had to be set 'sensibly' in the sense of being subject to employer ability to pay. While for Beveridge, the labour market had to be a seller's market because while 'a person who has difficulty in buying labour that he wants suffers inconvenience or a reduction in profits . . . A person who cannot sell his labour is in effect told that he is of no use. The first difficulty causes annoyance or loss. The other is a personal catastrophe';[27] for the 1997 Labour government, as for the Conservatives, the labour

[25] HC Deb 16 December 1997, vol 303, cols 162–239, 163.

[26] Tax Credits Act 2002 and Working Tax Credit (Entitlement and Maximum Rate) Regulations 2002, SI 2002/05. It also assisted 'seasonal' workers and employees affected by suspension from work while complaints or allegations were being investigated, as well as providing (limited) protection to strikers.

[27] Beveridge (n 9).

market was a buyers' market where the demands flowing from the process of capital accumulation placed limits on how far the law could go towards guaranteeing workers a social wage.

8.2.1 Universal Credit and the National 'Living' Wage

In 2012, the Coalition Government replaced the working tax credit, and the five other existing means-tested benefits, with universal credit, to be phased in gradually.[28] The tag-line for this policy was, once again, 'to make work pay', but the emphasis had shifted away from seeing tax credits as a mechanism for bridging the gap between wages and workers' subsistence needs, towards a much tighter dovetailing between tax credits and minimum wages to reduce dependency on all forms of state assistance. In this way, it intended to 'remove barriers to employment, smooth transitions back to work and remove distortions in the current system that prevent people from doing extra hours when available'.[29] It does this, however, by opening up low-paid, insecure, and part-time workers to a series of behavioural conditions that had previously been applicable only to the unemployed. To be entitled to state support, those in work as well as those out of work must meet a minimum (and progressive) earnings threshold, and must secure themselves additional hours and/or higher paid work/second jobs as a condition for claiming the credit.[30] The focus of the 'claimant's commitment', the 'contract' that claimants must sign before being given access to the scheme, is thus on requiring claimants to meet certain work-search, work-preparation, work-training and work-preparation requirements, to make it more likely that they will 'obtain paid work (or more paid work or better-paid work)' so as to avoid having their income reduced.

Intrinsic to this policy was the introduction, from 2016, of the national living wage (NLW).[31] On its face, this would seem to be aimed at providing to all workers (over 25) a statutorily guaranteed social wage capable of meeting at least the basic costs of living.[32] In practice, however, it falls short of doing so in many respects. Designed to work alongside universal credit's conditionality requirements, the

[28] Universal Credit Regulations 2013, 2013/376; The Welfare Reform Act 2012 abolished the following benefits: income based jobseekers' allowance under the Jobseekers Act 1995; income related employment and support allowance under Part 1 of the Welfare Reform Act of 2007; income support under s 124 of the Social Security Contributions and Benefits Act 1992; housing benefit under s 130 of that Act; council tax benefit under s 131 of that Act; child tax credit and working tax credit under the Tax Credits Act 2002. See: Welfare Reform Act 2012, s 33.

[29] Matthew Pennycook, 'What Price a Living Wage' [2012] Resolution Foundation 4.

[30] Welfare Reform Act 2012 s 4(1), and ss 13, 14, 17, and 18 in particular. See parallel provisions in Universal Credit Regulations 2013.

[31] National Minimum Wage (Amendment) Regulations 2016, SI 2016/68.

[32] Interview with George Osborne, 'Chancellor George Osborne's Summer Budget 2015 Speech—GOV.UK' <https://www.gov.uk/government/speeches/chancellor-george-osbornes-summer-budget-2015-speech> accessed 7 August 2017.

NMW's principal purpose is to reduce benefit dependency by requiring workers to take on more hours and second jobs at the 'NLW' level—without any express concern to tie that level to the costs of living. Instead, the wage is set to rise to a minimum rate of 60 per cent of hourly median wages by 2020—making no direct link between the wage and workers' needs.[33] The NLW is not a 'living wage' in the sense implied by the Living Wage Foundation, therefore, an organization that encourages employers to pay a voluntary living wage that is linked with the public's perception of what amounts to an adequate minimum standard of living.[34] Whereas the 'real' living wage attempts to make work pay by making *employers* pay a sum that reflects the social costs of labour, the NLW simply alters the distribution of those costs between employers and the state.

The National Minimum Wage Act 1998[35] already contained a power to pass regulations to provide for different rates of pay for those under 26 years of age. In fact, the 2015 regulations[36] set out four minimum wage rates, corresponding with different age bands. Thus, when it came to implementing the proposals for the 'national living wage' all that was required was a new 'tier' to the age bands already provided in the 2015 regulations, renamed, however, as the 'national living wage'. This is exactly what was achieved by the National Minimum Wage (Amendment) Regulations 2016, reg 3 of which simply added reg 4A to the 2015 regulations providing a wage supplement to workers aged 25 and over.[37] In practice, the introduction of the national living wage constituted a statement to the effect that workers below 25 years of age were not entitled to be paid a living wage, while those above that age, were entitled to be paid something that was, in practice, a market wage plus a wage premium that still fell far below the level that would be required to cover the costs of living. That different age groups are currently paid a different rate—but still incur broadly similar living costs—further shows that this 'living wage' is not seen to perform a subsistence function in the same way as had the minimum rates of remuneration envisaged by the Wages Councils Act where, through collective bargaining, rates were expected to vary between trades, classes of workers, and geographical locations—to reflect, in other words, workers' *needs*.

[33] For a discussion, see: Gavin Kelly and Conor D'Arcy, 'Analysing the National Living Wage: Impact and Implications for Britain's Low Pay Challenge' (Resolution Foundation) <http://www.resolutionfoundation.org/publications/analysing-the-national-living-wage-and-its-impact-on-britains-low-pay-challange/> accessed 26 July 2015. The 60 per cent target is the international standard required by bodies such as the European Social Committee, referred to as the 'decency threshold'. It is also linked with the poverty line, defined at 60 per cent of household income. The Bain review that led to the NLW came up with the 60 per cent figure having analysed how this would place the UK vis-à-vis its international competitors.

[34] Conor D'Arcy and Gavin Kelly, 'Analysing the National Living Wage', 'What Is the Real Living Wage? Living Wage Foundation' (Living Wage Foundation 2016) <https://www.livingwage.org.uk/what-is-the-living-wage> accessed 2 July 2017.

[35] Section 3.

[36] SI 2015/621.

[37] SI 2016/68.

The express motivation for the post-2012 reforms was the government's desire to 'reduce the welfare bill'.[38] It was not, in other words, an attempt to introduce a minimum wage framework that saw the wage as something that ought to reflect the costs of living. The primary purpose served by a higher minimum wage rate was to help reduce unemployment and the costs of the tax credit system to the taxpayer. It did not, therefore, reflect a shift in the way that the law–market relationship was conceived: wages set above the market rate were still seen to 'cause' (inevitably) unemployment:

> It is extremely worrying that those on the Opposition Benches would rather see young people out of work and without opportunities than in work, learning and getting the skills for their future. All the evidence shows that if we set the rate too high we see youth unemployment, which is exactly what happened under the previous Labour Government.[39]

All the NLW does, therefore, is change the arithmetical relationship between the minimum wage and the tax credit system—without touching the former's conceptual foundations. No accompanying change was made to the structure of the NMWA and NMWR, nor the link between work and payment which they reflect. Framed as a new wage supplement to be paid to more experienced workers aged 25 and over, with the 'real' minimum wage remaining in place, the policy is much more about encouraging workers to work as hard, and as much, as would be required at prevailing wage rates, than it is about seeing the satisfaction of the subsistence needs of the working classes as a conditioning factor on the rate of wages, and thus on the rate of profit.[40]

8.3 The Conceptual Structure of the National Minimum Wage Act (NMWA) and National Minimum Wage Regulations (NMWR)

The NMWR distinguishes between employment, coterminous with the existence of the contract that establishes the worker's rights under the NMWA, and work: the period for which the wage can be claimed.[41] In practice, this means that the right

[38] Department for work and pensions, 'Universal Credit Impact Assessment' <https://www.gov.uk/government/uploads/system/uploads/attachment_data/file/220177/universal-credit-wr2011-ia.pdf> accessed 29 August 2017.

[39] HC Deb 17 April 2018, vol 639, cols 173–74, 173 (Elizabeth Truss).

[40] Department of Business Innovation and Skills, 'Low Pay Commission Remit 2016' <https://www.gov.uk/government/uploads/system/uploads/attachment_data/file/443328/BIS-15-409-NMW-Low-Pay-Commission-Remit-2016.pdf> accessed 7 August 2017.

[41] National Minimum Wage Regulations 2015, SI 2015/621, regs 57–58, and National Minimum Wage Act 1998, s 54.

to be paid the minimum wage extends to all those employed under a contract of employment or to personally provide work.[42] Nonetheless, the right to be paid a minimum wage is a right to be paid wages for 'work', rather than a right to be remunerated for time employed; personal service over time.[43] This makes the meaning of work central when it comes to determining the scope of the worker's right to be paid, and, because neither the NMWA nor the NMWR define the concept of 'work', the scope of protection is very much left in the hands of the courts.

There is nothing in the NMWA or the NMWR that would prevent the courts from taking a functional approach to statutory interpretation. This would mean treating the meaning of work as something that depends on the time and/or duties for which the court believes the employer should pay, in light of the benefit it derives from this and the burden it places on the worker. For the most part, however, this is not the approach that the courts have taken. The courts instead tend to defer to the individual contract, identifying what the parties agreed the employer would pay for, seeing the meaning of work itself as something determined by 'agreement'. By taking this passive, reactive view of the law's role in this context, much is left to the parties' relative bargaining power when it comes to determining the scope of the employer's minimum wage obligations.

8.3.1 The Concept of 'Work' and the National Minimum Wage

For the purposes of determining whether an employer has complied with his minimum wage obligations, the NMWR distinguishes between time work, broadly corresponding with 'wage work' payable for hours actually worked, 'salaried hours work', applicable to those paid for a set basic number of hours a year, 'output work', such as commission and piece rates, and 'unmeasured work', a residual category designed to catch all those whose working arrangements which fall outside the other three categories.

By virtue of special deeming provisions contained in regs 27 and 32, salaried hours workers and time workers also have a right to be paid the minimum wage for time that is not work, but which is deemed to be for the purposes of the Act. This covers periods of 'down time' when the worker is effectively on call—available at or near the place of work for the purposes of working—but not actually working within the context of the Act. It excludes, however, time spent waiting for work at home (neither 'at or near' the workplace), time when the worker is 'not awake for the purposes of working', periods of leave that are expressly unpaid, and periods of industrial action. There is no right to be paid the minimum rate for travel time,

[42] Lydia Hayes, 'Care and Control: Are the National Minimum Wage Entitlements of Homecare Workers at Risk under the Care Act 2014?' (2015) 44 Industrial Law Journal 492.

[43] ibid.

therefore, for overnight lay-overs, for sleeping shifts, unless they fall within the contractual definition of 'work', nor for periods of industrial action short of a strike when some work has been provided.[44]

This narrow definition of what counts as work can be particularly problematic for workers reliant on tax credits for topping up their wage to subsistence level. Take, for example, care workers. Care workers' contracts customarily provide that only direct 'contact' time will be paid. To claim working tax credit, however, workers must show that they are engaged in 'qualifying remunerative work' for at least thirty hours a week.[45] Because this corresponds with time for which the claimant is, or expects to be, paid, it will only cover this 'contact time' and not the substantial periods devoted to driving to and from work and between clients' homes. A care worker may thus be 'working' in the broad sense for more than thirty hours, but will be excluded from claiming the tax credit because of the narrowness of the contractual definition of 'work' for which she is entitled to be paid. True, he/she will receive the minimum wage, but that will be *all* he/she will receive, and this is so in a context in which the minimum wage is deliberately *not* designed to be sufficient to cover workers' living costs, because the tax credit system, from which such workers struggle to benefit, are intended to make up for any shortfall.

It is also clear from the Act that 'salaried work' is not to be confused with the historical concept of the term introduced in Chapters 5 and 6.[46] It applies to those whose contracts lay down a set number of basic hours for which they have, in theory, a right to be paid 'regardless of the number of hours actually worked in a particular week or month'.[47] It is not confined, therefore, to those who are employed in a particular capacity to provide their professional services over time. In practice, moreover, because the courts defer to the individual contract to determine which of the worker's contractual obligations count as work beyond the right to sickness and holiday pay, even those engaged in statutory salaried hours work will only be paid for time when work is, or is deemed to have been, provided.[48] For those whose contracts do in fact envisage ongoing service, therefore, the employer's minimum wage obligation will only extend to a fraction of the time that their contracts require them to devote to their employer's business (see below).

[44] Regulation 34 expressly excludes time travelling between home and the workplace. This has harsh implications in certain industries, as can be seen in: *Aslam v Uber BV* [2018] EWCA Civ 2748; [2019] IRLR 257. See also: *Thera East v Mr J* [2017] IRLR 878 where the court left it to the contract to decide whether travel time was 'work' that warranted a right to be paid. On overnight lay-overs, see: *Baxter v Titan Aviation Ltd* (unreported) 30 August 2011 (EAT).

[45] Working tax credits are gradually being replaced by universal credit, but the transition is still ongoing. See Working Tax Credit (Entitlement and Maximum Rate) Regulations 2002, SI 2002/2005, reg 4.

[46] Regulation 21(5).

[47] ibid.

[48] For particularly restrictive readings of this see: *South Manchester Abbeyfield Society Ltd v Hopkins* [2011] ICR 254; [2011] IRLR 300 (EAT); *Hughes v Jones (t/a Graylyns Residential Home)* [2008] UKEAT/0159/08MAA.

The category of 'unmeasured work' reflects an alternative to salaried employment for employers wanting to benefit from having a worker on hand to work and to do as much work, as and when required, without having to pay for the benefit of doing so. This category applies to workers whose hours of work are not specified, and who are required to work when needed or when work is available. Rather than being paid a fixed salary for time in employment, however, with the employer committing in advance to providing a minimum income or minimum hours of work, these workers are paid to complete a particular job or task, regardless of how long it takes them to do so and regardless of how (ir)regularly they are called upon to work. For minimum wage purposes, they must be paid for those hours spent performing what is classed by their contracts as work.[49]

In *South Holland v Stamp*, care wardens at a sheltered housing scheme were bound by their contracts to be on site continuously for 103 hours per week. The Employment Appeals Tribunal (EAT) rejected the argument that all these hours could be classed as 'work'. Instead, it was necessary to refer to a list of her contractual duties so that her eligibility for working time could be more tightly circumscribed:

> ... time spent by the respondents when they are not carrying out the contractual duties required of them under their contract cannot be counted [...] thus when a warden is at home on call but sleeping, washing, entertaining or carrying out domestic chores [the time does not qualify for national minimum wage payments].[50]

Regulation 44 on unmeasured work operates in conjunction with reg 49 which makes provision for the parties to approve a 'daily average agreement' to determine 'the daily average number of hours the worker is likely to spend in carrying out the duties required'. In *Stamp*, reg 49 had not applied because no such agreement was in place. The effect of such an agreement would be to provide a degree of certainty by specifying the minimum number of hours a worker could expect to be paid. Nonetheless, if the worker agreed that she would normally be engaged in performing her duties for twelve hours a week, but the tasks prove so demanding (for reasons outside the worker's control) that she in fact performs closer to twenty, she has effectively waived her entitlement to claim the minimum rate for the additional eight hours.[51] The premise behind the provision is that the NMWA ought not increase the costs of hiring labour on a casualized basis, nor decrease the attractiveness of 'flexible' forms of work. The inclusion of this provision is important, the courts suggest, to avoid a situation where the NMWA leads to the 'probable ending of [socially useful] employment ... [by] pricing it out of the market'.[52]

[49] Regulations 44–50.
[50] *South Holland v Stamp* [2003] EAT/1097/02 RN [37].
[51] For a discussion of this, see: Lisa Rodgers, 'The Notion of Working Time' (2009) 38 Industrial Law Journal 80.
[52] *Walton v The Independent Living Organisation Ltd* [2002] ICR 1406 (EAT) 1412 (Holland J).

This argument was invoked in *Walton v Independent living organisation*. Walton was a home care worker who worked three days on and four days off to provide a continuous service in the home of a severe epileptic. Walton claimed that she was paid by the day ('time work') and engaged in time work throughout a daily period of fourteen hours when she was awake and providing care and supervision. The Court of Appeal rejected the argument that all aspects of her activities during the day could be classed as work, classifying her work as unmeasured work for the purposes of calculating the minimum wage. The daily average agreement stated that Walton's caring tasks only consumed six hours and fifty minutes in any twenty-four-hour period. In fact, however, she was required to be on the premises at all times in case the patient required assistance.[53] Nonetheless, the court treated this as discretionary labour which did not attract the minimum wage, falling outside the tasks specified as work in the contract and extending beyond the hours agreed in the daily average agreement.

Both *Walton* and *Stamp* involved employees engaged in care work for what the courts classed as unmeasured work. Similar problems arise, however, for those engaged in time or salaried work whose contracts require that they remain responsive to clients'/employers' needs on an ongoing basis.

In this context, the courts have drawn a distinction between those hired to make themselves available to wait for work such as security guards or telephone operators, and those whose 'core work' duties can (arguably) be distinguished from contractual duties that require that they also be on call outside core working hours.[54] The EAT in *Focus Care Agency* noted that the courts have also tended to draw a 'clear dichotomy' between those cases where a worker is working merely by being present at the employer's premises, whether or not they have been provided with sleeping accommodation, and those where the worker is provided with sleeping accommodation and is simply on call (or available).[55] In the former case, the worker will be treated as working throughout the full duration of the shift. In the latter, however, the deeming provisions in regs 27 (salaried hours work) and 32 (time work) will apply. This means that only the time when the worker is available to work 'at or near' the workplace, and is 'awake for the purposes of working' will be time to which the right to the minimum wage will attach.

If the contract clearly defines the work for which the employer is willing to pay, therefore, and requires in addition to that work that the worker perform a number of duties during 'non-work' hours, the worker will have to rely upon the deeming

53 ibid [3].

54 Compare: *British Nursing Association v Inland Revenue* [2003] ICR 19 (CA) (telephone service), *Scottbridge Construction Ltd v Wright* [2003] IRLR 21, and *Burrow Down Support Services Ltd v Rossiter* (EAT) [2008] UKEAT 0592/07/2506 (night watchman) with *Wray v J W Lees & Co (Brewers) Ltd* [2012] ICR 43 (EAT) and *South Manchester Abbeyfield Society* (n 48) (duty housekeeper with sheltered accommodation).

55 *Focus Care Agency Ltd v Roberts* [2017] UKEAT 0143_16_2104, 31. See also: *Whittlestone v BJP Home Support Ltd* [2014] ICR 275; [2014] IRLR 176.

provisions to claim a right to the minimum wage in respect of those additional hours. By careful drafting, therefore, the employer can narrowly circumscribe how much of the time from which it in fact benefits is time to which the obligation to pay the minimum rate will apply. This can be illustrated by the decision in *Edinburgh Council v Lauder*.[56]

In *Lauder*, the employee was engaged as a support worker in a sheltered housing facility. Her contract provided for tied accommodation, and required that she work thirty-six hours a week, and an additional emergency response for four nights a week. The question for the court was whether providing the emergency response could be classed as work for the purposes of the Act. Lady Smith found that *Lauder* had specific core day-time hours, that the emergency response cover was something required in addition to work, and so would only attract the minimum wage to the extent that regs 16(1) and (1A) applied.[57] This meant that she could not claim the minimum wage for time spent waiting for work beyond the workplace, or time when she was not 'awake for the purposes of working', notwithstanding that the contract required that she make herself available to be called on during the entire night. She was not paid for employment, in other words, for the benefit of providing her services over time, but for 'work' as defined by the contract.

The approach in *Lauder* was doubted by Langstaff J in *Whittlestone*, later endorsed by the EAT in *Focus Care Agency* (above). Langstaff J argued that concepts such as 'on call' or 'core hours' are liable to mislead. He was happy with the distinction between people who are working by being present, and people who are not, but saw 'substantial difficulty' in accepting a distinction between 'core hours' and other hours in the contract. In Langstaff J's view, if a contract provides that hours are to be worked then they are working hours regardless of their classification as 'core' or 'non-core'.[58]

Building on this, the EAT in *Focus Care Agency* argued that the courts should apply a 'multifactorial approach' to determining whether the worker is to be treated as working merely by being 'available'.[59] This requires a close examination of the parties' contract, with particular emphasis on: (i) the employer's particular purpose in engaging the worker; (ii) the extent to which the worker's activities are restricted by the requirement to be present and at the disposal of the employer; (iii) the degree of responsibility undertaken by the worker; and (iv) the immediacy of the requirement to provide services if something untoward occurs or an emergency arises.

This is closer to the functional approach advanced above, but it still rejects any active constituting role for the court. This is because these factors are only relevant,

56 [2012] UKEAT/0048/11/BI. See similarly *Hughes v Jones* (n 48) and *South Manchester Abbeyfield Society* (n 48).
57 This corresponds with what is today reg 32(1).
58 *Whittlestone* v BJP (n 55) [53].
59 *Focus Care Agency* (n 55) [44].

it seems, if the contract does not itself clearly define what counts as work for the purposes of the right to be paid. It has thus been confirmed that the *Focus Agency* test requires that the courts 'start with the contract'.[60] This is why, rather than deriving any general principles, the EAT was content to leave each case to turn on the terms of the individual contract, including how the contract provides for pay to be calculated. If the worker is *in fact* paid per shift, therefore, there will be a presumption that she is to be paid the minimum wage for the entire duration of each shift. If she is *in fact* paid by reference to tasks performed or time spent awake at the workplace, this would not be the case.[61] The courts will not, therefore, impose an obligation to pay if it is not clear from the broader factual matrix that the time in question was something for which the employer was willing to pay. Indeed, the EAT in *Focus Agency* expressly endorsed the decision in *Walton*, which suggests that different principles are applicable to unmeasured work. In light of this, it may be that more employers, particularly in the care sector where on-call night shifts are common, will take advantage of this provision so as to further limit the scope of their minimum wage obligations.[62]

When *Focus Care* reached the Court of Appeal, the court overruled the EAT to the effect that sleep-in shifts will not be classed as work for the purposes of the regulations.[63] Rather, Underhill J argued that the deeming provisions were 'self-evidently' intended to apply to sleep-in shifts, such that care workers engaged on such shifts were 'available for work' and not 'actually working'. Thus, the only time for which carers would be entitled to be paid were those hours when they were actually awake for the purposes of 'working':

> the self-evident intention of the relevant provisions is to deal comprehensively with the position of sleep-in workers. The fact that their case is dealt with as part of the availability provisions necessarily means that the draftsman regarded them as being available for work rather than actually working. That is hardly surprising: it would not be a natural use of language, in a context which distinguishes between (actually) working and being available for work, to describe someone as 'working' when they are positively expected to be asleep throughout all or most of the relevant period.[64]

Before the decision was released, Martin Green, the Chief Executive of Care England, stated that 'if the existing decision of the Employment Appeal Tribunal is upheld it would be a watershed moment for the sector, with profound effects for the

[60] *Abbeyfield Wessex Society Ltd v Edwards* [2017] UKEAT/0256/16/BA.

[61] *Focus Care Agency* (n 55) [42].

[62] *Focus Care Agency* (n 55) [35]–[37].

[63] *Royal Mencap Society v Tomlinson-Blake and Shannon v Rampersad* [2018] EWCA Civ 1641; [2019] ICR 241.

[64] ibid [43]. Underhill J reiterated these sentiments in his dissenting opinion in *Aslam v Uber* (n 44).

viability of residential domiciliary and supported care'.[65] How far these concerns influenced the Court of Appeal is an open question. It is clear from the judgment, however, that the EAT's multifactorial approach was seen to go too far, to be an 'unnecessarily elaborate approach' which is not necessary given the clear intentions behind the deeming provisions contained in the Regulations.[66] The NMW (and, by implication, the NLW) was quite clearly not intended to provide for any form of 'living wage' *despite the name of those regulations*, to prevent employers from benefitting at the expense of workers without adequately remunerating them. It was simply concerned with how much was paid by way of 'wages' for 'work', where work corresponds with tangible productive activities, and not merely 'time' at the employer's disposal.

This prevailing conception of the 'wage' poses particular problems for individuals engaged in the so-called 'gig-economy'. This refers to individuals hired on a task-by-task basis, usually via a digital intermediary (or 'app'), (often) described in their contracts as independent contractors, but who have little or no control over the conditions in which their work (or the product in which it is incorporated) is sold.[67] Not only have these individuals struggled to establish worker status, so as to bring them within the scope of the NMWA (and other statutory labour laws), even when worker status has been established before a court or tribunal, there has been considerable opposition to the idea (much as is the case with care workers, above) that these individuals might be paid for time when they have the app on, but when they have not accepted a 'task' or 'trip'.[68]

The question of when gig-workers should be considered to be 'working' for the purposes of earning the minimum wage was addressed in *Aslam v Uber BV*. Having decided that Uber drivers fell within the statutory definition of the 'worker', the Court of Appeal went on to assess the scope of Uber's minimum wage obligations. It is clear from the judgment that the Court did not consider Uber drivers to be 'employed' on an ongoing basis. Rather, they made themselves available 'for hire' for the purposes of individual shifts. The only question, then, once worker status was established, was whether they should be paid when they were available to work, with the app switched on, or whether they should only be paid for trips actually accepted.[69]

[65] 'Royal Mencap Society v. Tomlinson-Blake' <https://www.dentons.com/en/insights/newsletters/2018/july/31/uk-employment-law-roundup/uk-employment-law-round-up-july-2018/royal-mencap-society-v-tomlinson-blake> accessed 3 November 2018.

[66] *Royal Mencap* (n 63) [57].

[67] The term 'gig-work' is often used in a more colloquial sense to refer to a variety of forms of contingent or temporary work. For a discussion of the term, see: Emily Hong, 'Making It Work: A Closer Look at the Gig Economy' (New America 2015) <https://www.newamerica.org/weekly/94/making-it-work-a-closer-look-at-the-gig-economy/> accessed 23 March 2019.

[68] Notable cases include: *Addison Lee Ltd v Lange* [2019] ICR 637; *Leyland v Hermes Parcelnet* [2017] 1800575/2017; *Pimlico Plumbers v Smith* [2018] UKSC 29; [2018] ICR 1511; *Aslam v Uber BV* (n 44); *Independent Workers' Union of Great Britain (IWGB) v RooFoods Ltd (t/a Deliveroo)* [2018] IRLR 84; *Dewhurst v CitySprint UK* (2017) (unreported).

[69] *Aslam v Uber BV* (n 44).

The opinion expressed in the Taylor review, published following the Employment Tribunal decision in *Aslam*, was that: 'no individual should be expecting to be paid for all the time that he or she has the app open (regardless of whether or not they are seeking work)'. The 'correct' approach, it argued, would be to adapt the 'legislation on piece-rates' so as to provide for payment based on 'number of tasks performed'.[70] The reason for this was that 'if an individual knowingly chooses to work through a platform at times of low demand, then he or she should take some responsibility for this decision'.

The Employment Tribunal, by contrast, had argued that because having a large number of drivers on its books is central to Uber's business model, drivers should be treated as working whenever they have the app switched on and they are available for work—regardless of whether any trips are actually performed.[71] While the Court of Appeal did not address this issue in depth, it argued that it was at least debatable that this should be the case. This view was, however, vociferously opposed by Underhill J in the minority, and so, is likely to be revisited on appeal:

> In my view, if drivers provide services to, and under a contract with, [Uber]at all it is only during the period when they have accepted a trip. It is common ground that drivers are not obliged to accept any particular trip when offered. The only basis on which the ET held that they are nevertheless under a contractual obligation to Uber while the App is switched on is that they are liable to be disconnected for a specified period if they reject trips, or cancel them, too often. But . . . I do not believe that that implies a positive contractual obligation on the part of drivers to accept (and not cancel thereafter) a minimum number of trips offered. I would add that if there were such an obligation it would be necessary to specify what the minimum obligation was.[72]

One of the challenges, directly confronted by the court in Uber, was that, as for many gig-economy workers, their contracts permit them, in theory, to accept work from other 'similar' platforms when they have not accepted a trip from Uber. If they are 'working' for Uber, then, during 'availability' time, they are not doing so *exclusively*. According to Underhill J, this created an intractable problem: an individual could not be working for two employers simultaneously. And, if indeed he was, how could a court decide which of the two employers should be responsible for guaranteeing payment for the time in question? In other words, how is it possible for more than one employer to have rights in the same portion of labour power simultaneously? Indeed, this 'problem' would exist not only in relation

[70] Matthew Taylor, 'Good Work; The Taylor Review of Modern Working Practices' (Gov.uk 2017) 36–37 <https://www.gov.uk/government/uploads/system/uploads/attachment_data/file/627671/good-work-taylor-review-modern-working-practices-rg.pdf>.

[71] [2017] IRLR 4 [100]

[72] *Aslam v Uber* (n 44) 161.

to minimum wage legislation, but to employment law more generally. And, if this argument succeeds on appeal, it would effectively allow practical difficulties concerning *the implementation* of substantive labour law rights to influence courts' decisions concerning (analytical) questions of scope.

As we saw in Chapters 5 to 7, however, when Parliament confronted a similar practical issue in the context of dock work, not only did this not alter the prevailing conception of the employment status of dock workers (as 'workmen'), it did not lead Parliament to conclude that the appropriate solution was to exclude dock workers from the employment rights that other 'workmen' enjoyed either. Having first suggested that, for the purposes of unemployment insurance, the solution was that the first employer, of the week (or day) would be responsible for that week/day's contributions, Parliament later instituted a system of centralized wage and contribution payments so as to ensure a guaranteed minimum income to all (registered) dock workers; administered initially through the Board of Trade, and later, through the National Dock Labour Board. Requiring all dock employers to be registered as a condition for hiring 'casual' dock labour, and preventing unregistered workers from being employed, this system made it possible, in the docks, to combine a degree of 'flexibility' and 'casualism' with a form of social wage without requiring dock employers to hire particular dock workers on a permanent basis, and without requiring dock workers to take 'responsibility' for the casual nature of their work.

8.4 Exclusions

The prevailing conception of the wage, as a payment for economically valuable work (judged from the standpoint of the employer), has created a situation where an individual's entitlement to the minimum wage depends, to a great extent, on the employer's willingness to recognize the individual's activity as a valuable one, and to do so by agreeing to a pay a (monetary) wage.[73] This has, as we have seen, reduced the scope of many workers' minimum wage entitlements. It also, however, circumscribes which individuals come to be recognized as workers who are entitled to the minimum wage in the first place.

First, in the absence of a contractual right to payment, there is a risk that the courts will characterize the relationship as a voluntary one. As such, as there will be no 'mutuality of obligation', worker status will not be established.[74] Second, various categories of worker have been expressly excluded from the scope of the NMWA,

[73] Exclusions not considered in this section, for reasons of space, include the exclusion of share fisherman, serving members of the armed forces, persons living in a religious communities, and the under 16s. The lower youth rate is discussed in passing in the analysis of interns and apprentices. Company directors are also not included, unless they are also hired under a contract of employment or workers' contract. See also certain specific categories excluded by the National Minimum Wage Regulations 2015.

[74] See the discussion of *Quashie v Stringfellows Restaurants* [2012] EWCA Civ 1735; [2013] IRLR 99 in Chapter 9.

due to the seemingly low economic value of their work. As we will see, in relation to these groups, the 'non-economic' context in which they work, the reasons for which they do so, and/or the 'quality' of their labour has been deemed to be such that they do not merit payment of the minimum rate. This is so, for example, for voluntary workers, apprentices and interns, prisoners, detainees, and domestic workers providing work in a 'familial' context.

8.4.1 Volunteers and Voluntary Workers

A central element of the Conservative Party Manifesto of 2010, and the then Coalition's Programme for Government, was the concept of the 'Big Society', the idea that public service contracts should be opened up to voluntary organizations, and that individuals should be encouraged to participate in voluntary or 'community' work, allowing charities and social enterprises to compete with private firms to offer public services. One of the consequences of this policy has been an increasing involvement of charities and voluntary organizations in public services, providing services which were traditionally delivered by paid state employees or local authorities.[75] This includes, for example, ambulance services, mental health services, legal services, transport, probation, etc: services that can be provided by voluntary organizations at more competitive prices because they are under no legal obligation to pay the individuals who work for them the minimum wage.

'Genuine' volunteers, persons under no legal (contractual) obligation to work, fall outside the scope of the NMWA entirely, while individuals who would otherwise satisfy the statutory definition of 'worker', will be excluded from the scope of the Act if they fall within the definition of 'voluntary workers' in s 44. This section includes 'workers' who work for charities, voluntary organizations, associated fund-raising bodies, and statutory bodies, and who receive no remuneration or benefit in kind (other than reasonable subsistence or accommodation) except for expenses incurred in the performance of their duties. People who are not *in fact* paid for their work, provided they work for a voluntary organization, will not, therefore, enjoy a legal *right* to payment.

Behind s 44 is an assumption that, if an individual does not, in fact, get paid for the work they perform, that work must be provided voluntarily *for non-financial reasons*, and that the individual therefore does not need/expect, (or even merit), payment.[76] To require payment in such circumstances is assumed to

[75] Colin Rochester, Angela Ellis Paine, and Steven Howlett, *Volunteering and Society in the 21st Century* (Basingstoke 2010) 3, 222–26.

[76] 'People volunteering for charities, voluntary organisations and other relevant organisations contribute a huge value to society, *and they do so without an expectation of being paid* the National Minimum Wage'. Minimum Wage: Voluntary Work, 26 February 2019, WQ 222589 (Kelly Tolhurst).

be undesirable: not only does it contravene the parties' clear intentions, but also, if matters were otherwise, 'important' services provided by voluntary organizations would cease to be economically viable, (raising the cost to the government of securing the delivery of public services that it is determined to out-source to non-governmental organizations).

Motivations to work are complex. Individuals may choose to undertake work for a variety of reasons not linked to the possibility of financial reward. In practice, however, the possibility of engaging in unpaid work is a privilege that few can afford: there exists considerable scope for abuse. While volunteers may be motivated by various 'altruistic' reasons, there are often also complex structural factors influencing decisions to engage in unpaid work. For example, labour market conditions are often such that unpaid work is the only entry route available to the individual when it comes to obtaining (future) paid employment. This is so for marginalized groups unable to hold down a regular job for example, as well as for individuals seeking employment in industries in which, given an over-supply of labour, firms make work 'experience' a condition for obtaining a (future) paid position. Rather than tackling discriminatory hiring practices, therefore providing positive support to marginalized groups to facilitate their access to employment, many such groups are instead being pushed into the voluntary sector where they act as a source of 'cheap' (or free) labour. And this is something that the NMWA and NMWR positively encourage. And, by encouraging voluntary organizations to compete for contracts for the delivery of public services, there is a real risk that paid employees will be replaced by unpaid alternatives.

8.4.2 Interns

One group particularly affected by the exclusion of volunteers is young persons seeking work experience and/or training. The first group to consider in this context is apprentices. Apprenticeships include both the traditional common law apprenticeship and the 'modern' apprenticeship introduced in 1995 (now regulated by Apprenticeships, Skills, Children and Learning Act 2009 ('ASCLA') and the Apprenticeships (Form of Apprenticeship Agreement) Regulations 2012/844). The most significant difference between these forms of apprenticeship is that, while traditional apprenticeships were of fixed (long-term) duration, and imposed strict duties on the master to instruct and maintain his apprentice, the modern apprenticeship does neither. Qualification is to be awarded as soon as the apprentice has demonstrated the necessary competence in every element of a defined framework, and the only payment-related obligation on the employer is to pay the reduced minimum wage to those apprentices to which the NMWA applies (see below). In turn, as of 2012, modern apprenticeships are contracts of service and not common law contracts of apprenticeship.[77] They will not, for this reason, be subject to the strict common law rules concerning dismissal (as it such rules apply only to traditional 'apprentices').[78]

The reduced minimum wage, or 'apprenticeship rate', found in reg 4A of the National Minimum Wage Regulations 2015, SI 2015/621 (£3.90 at the time of writing), applies to anyone employed under a common law apprenticeship or a 'modern' apprenticeship (in the above sense), who is under the age of 19 and/or within the first twelve months of their apprenticeship. Apprentices over 19 and in the second or third year (etc) of the apprenticeship are entirely exempted from the NMWA. Many internships and work experience placements will also very often fall outside the scope of the Act. While it is possible that individuals hired under such schemes will satisfy the statutory definition of 'worker', most such individuals will fail to prove an obligation to provide personal services (or, relatedly, a right to wages), sufficient to bring themselves within the scope of the Act. This is particularly so, as will be explained below, where the arrangement is described as work 'experience' or 'shadowing' such that the employer can show that the provision by the individual of 'economically valuable' work was never envisaged.

From the sixteenth century, masters would be allowed to accept an apprentice only if it could be shown they had sufficient means by which to support and maintain him. Failure to do so was, as with the servant, good justification for departure/termination. Given that apprentices today no longer live in the household or workshop of their master, however, no such 'maintenance' obligation exists. But nor, it seems, is there any obligation on employers to pay a social wage—to cover the apprentices living costs—by way of replacement. Instead, the courts have emphasized that the lower (below market rate) 'remuneration' that apprentices tend to receive is justified on the basis that 'the difference should have been made up to him by the benefits of apprenticeship, such as the benefit of training, instruction and experience in the various departments of the works'.[79]

While, historically, the lower wage rate commonly paid to apprentices was largely off set by the master's legal obligation to provide for, and support, the apprentice throughout the duration of the training, today, apprentices have to rely on alternative sources of income to fund them throughout. This makes apprentice schemes a privilege that not everyone can afford. As is clear from *Edmonds v Lawson*,[80] the courts do not see this as an avoidable outcome, a political choice,

[77] With effect from 6 April 2012, the combination of the Apprenticeships, Skills, Children and Learning Act 2009 (ASCLA) and the Apprenticeships (Form of Apprenticeship Agreement) Regulations 2012, SI 2012/844 introduced a new statutory regime in relation to apprentices employed on or after that date. The ASCLA has been amended a number of times, including by the Deregulation Act 2015, the Enterprise Act 2016 and the Technical and Further Education Act 2017.

[78] If the agreement fails to comply with the prescribed requirements of the ASCLA, however, the contract may well be found to be a common law apprenticeship: *Flett v Matheson* [2006] EWCA Civ 53; [2006] ICR 673.

[79] *Dunk v George Waller & Son* [1970] 2 QB 163; [1970] 2 WLR 1241, 167 (Lord Denning).

[80] *Edmonds v Lawson* [2000] QB 501.

and thus an outcome the law might prevent. Rather, it is seen to follow inevitably from the lower value of the work that 'untrained' apprentices perform and the 'non-economic' nature of the arrangement between the apprentice and his/her master—an arrangement whose 'principle purpose' is to provide education and training. From this perspective, in other words, it is an outcome that is 'dictated' by the market.

In *Edmonds*, the Court of Appeal held that a pupil barrister was not entitled to be paid the national minimum wage because she had no obligation to provide 'valuable services' for any member of the chambers. Moreover, even if she did undertake such services, the relevant Code of Conduct provided that she would be paid for those services. This meant that the recipient would become the client of the barrister, purchasing her services directly, rather than her employer—the claimant would therefore fall outside the scope of the NMWA because she had not undertaken to perform work or service for a party who was not a client (per s 54(3)(b))[81].

The Court of Appeal assumed that the claimant pupil was not performing economically valuable work, because, as an as yet unqualified barrister, any work she performed would have to be checked by a qualified barrister before it could be used for the purposes of a case. There was not, the court argued, any valuable consideration given to the pupil master because everything the pupil did in the course of the pupillage was oriented towards her own professional development, rather than the benefit of that member of the chambers.[82] Because the primary motivation was not immediate financial reward, the pupil was held to have not intended to provide valuable consideration.

The court took a broader view of the relationship between the pupil and the chambers, recognizing the benefit, to the chambers, of the pupillage system as a means through which to attract potential talent.[83] It thus concluded that, on this basis, a contract of sorts could be said to exist between the pupil and the chambers. That was not to say, however, that it was a contract within the scope of the NMWA (which applies to contracts of employment, apprenticeship, and personal work). Because each of these contracts presuppose an obligation to serve and the pupil did not undertake to do anything that was not conducive to her own professional development, no such contract could be said to exist. The value of her work to the chambers was purely incidental, the main purpose of the arrangement being one of education and training.

[81] Had she been under 26, she would have fallen within the scope of reg 12 of the NMWR 1998, which prescribes the lower, apprentice, rate.

[82] *Edmonds v Lawson* (n 81) [24]

[83] See similarly: *Gabe v United Reformed Church*, 24 November 2017 (ET) (unreported) at [44] where the ET held that the services the respondent provided were not consideration for the payments and allowances paid to the pupil; 'that was not the reason why the apprentice master or chambers/pupil supervisor or solicitor's firm or carpenter pays the apprentice. The benefits for the chambers or the firm or the carpenter are more generalised and more long-term'.

In coming to this conclusion, the Court of Appeal emphasized that 'the object of the National Minimum Wage Act 1998 was not, as we understand, to enlarge the categories of those entitled to be paid wages but to ensure that those entitled to be paid wages are not paid at anything less than a specified minimum level'.[84] Indeed,

> the fact that the generality of barrister pupils have been unpaid, not just in the distant past but also in modern times, is in our view of significance in determining whether a relationship of or equivalent to apprenticeship exists. For although trade apprentices have always received reduced wages, reflecting both *the value of the practical training they receive and their reduced productivity*, they have always in modern times received some wages and in earlier times received board and lodging.... While solicitors' articled clerks may once have been in very much the same position as pupil barristers, they have in more recent times been entitled to payment. The fact that pupil barristers have up to the present been unpaid in our view reflects *the lack of expectation that they will render services of value*; hence the requirement in the Code of Conduct that, *if they do produce work of value*, they shall be paid.[85]

The Court of Appeal in *Edmonds* thus left it to the employer to decide whether the 'work' undertaken was economically valuable, and thus worthy of being remunerated in 'wages'. The NMWA was, it assumed, concerned only with ensuring that those employers *who had already agreed to pay wages*, would, in fact, pay at least the minimum rate as specified in the regulations and only for those activities for which that employer was willing to pay.[86] Rather than shaping employment practices through law, a well-established practice of non-payment in a particular industry or sector was instead taken by the courts to justify a finding that there is no entitlement to be paid in the context of a specific case.

While apprenticeships generally guarantee the individual a recognized qualification and very often future employment, internships generally provide no recognized qualification nor any guarantee of future employment. Even so, many firms make some form of work experience a condition for obtaining employment in the industry, and so offer various 'unpaid' internships to 'attract' potential talent. Interns that undertake 'work' personally will, most likely, be classed as a 'worker' for the purposes of the NMWA. Nonetheless, if the firm makes no provision for payment, and the arrangement is characterized as shadowing or work experience, the apparent absence of economically valuable work will, as in *Edwards*, likely be taken as strong evidence that there was is no entitlement to payment. Thus,

[84] *Edmonds v Lawson* (n 81) 509.
[85] *Edmonds v Lawson* (n 81) [34] (emphasis added).
[86] This is entirely consistent with the discussion of education and training of 16 and 17 year olds in the Low Pay Commission's report of 1998: Low Pay Commission. 'First Report of the Low Pay Commission' (1998) 68 and 71.

provided the employer can show that the objective of the arrangement was not the provision of economically valuable work in exchange for payment, the individual will not be able to claim the minimum wage.[87]

In light of this analysis, it is concerning, if not surprising, that in 2010 the TUC estimated that one in three interns were unpaid (less expenses)—a number that has increased dramatically in recent years.[88] The prevailing approach to the NMWA is such that, for businesses, unpaid internships prove particularly cost-effective recruitment processes, which, simultaneously, provide a convenient source of cheap labour. Because they presuppose that the individual can support him/herself throughout the duration of the scheme, moreover, they remain a privilege of the most wealthy—and so too, by implication, do the full-time paid jobs to which they provide access.

8.4.3 Prisoners

It is not only work provided for 'free', or for non-financial reasons, that will fall outside the scope of the NMWA. Other paid work will also not attract a right to the minimum wage if it is deemed by the legislature to be of little economic value (or otherwise not deserving of payment). This is the case, for example, with the work of prisoners and detainees.

Prisoners providing work for prison authorities, or for private sector firms pursuant to work-placement schemes, have long been distinguished, at common law, from employees. This is because: 'There [is] no contractual relationship, no intention to create legal relations and no mutuality of obligation … The [putative employer] could not choose whether a prisoner would be provided with work; the defendant was obliged by statute to provide it: rule 31(1) of the Prison Rules.' Prison work is not, in other words, a 'voluntary, mutual relationship for the mutual advantage of employer and employee' and so cannot be said to be provided pursuant to a contract of employment.[89]

The courts have held prison authorities, and/or the private sector firms for which a prisoner directly works, vicariously liable for torts committed in the course of the prisoner's 'employment': for these purposes, the relationship is said

[87] *Regulations implementing the National Minimum Wage: A Report by the Secretary of State for Trade and Industry* laid before Parliament on 16 February 1999 as required by s 5(4) of the National Minimum Wage Act 1996, para 23.

[88] Richard Wachman, 'One in Three Interns Works for Nothing, Says TUC' *The Guardian* (London, 26 March 2010) <https://www.theguardian.com/business/2010/mar/26/interns-unpaid-work-tuc> accessed 24 June 2019. In 2018, the Sutton Trust estimated that of the 100,000 interns working in Britain each year, around 58,000 are unpaid: Sally Weal, 'Graduates Trapped in Unpaid Internships, Study Finds' *The Guardian* (23 November 2018) <https://www.theguardian.com/money/2018/nov/23/graduates-trapped-in-unpaid-internships-study-finds> accessed 14 December 2019.

[89] *Cox v Ministry of Justice* [2016] UKSC 10 [39].

to be sufficiently 'akin' to employment.[90] The situation is different, however, when it comes to claims in relation to labour law, where it is the person performing the work, rather than a third party, seeking to assert rights. In *M & P Steelcraft Ltd v Ellis (HM Prison Service v Ellis)*,[91] for example, the EAT refused to recognize a contract of service between a serving prisoner and a firm at which he had undertaken a work placement (pursuant to the Prison Service's resettlement programme). While it acknowledged that the individual worked on terms comparable to those of 'ordinary' employees, and that the contract *appeared* no different from a contract of service, the purpose of the contract had to be considered before a conclusion could be made on this point. The provision of the prisoner's personal services was, the court argued, a secondary purpose: the purpose of the arrangement being to assist in the prisoner's rehabilitation. The effect, in this case, was that a term in the contract that stated that there was no intention to create legal obligations was not void under s 203 of the Employment Rights Act 1996 (ERA) (which prevents the parties from contracting out of labour legislation), and so was legally effective.

The EAT noted in this case that 'there is no doubt that . . . had there simply been a contract on the same terms as contained in the written particulars, the claimant would be an employee. Indeed, that is the status which everyone accepts the claimant had had from the time he left prison; and it was the status of similarly placed workers.'[92] Even so 'the crucial question, . . . is whether the agreement takes on a different character when seen in the context of the tripartite arrangement and the resettlement scheme. We agree with the respondents that it does.'[93]

The deciding factor in *M & P* was the objective or purpose of the arrangement. That is, because the arrangement was not motivated exclusively by economic considerations, because there was a degree of legal compulsion involved and the purpose of the scheme was rehabilitation, the relationship was not a voluntary 'market' relationship in the same sense as is 'free' employment. The objective of the prison authorities, who had control over the prisoner, was to facilitate the latter's rehabilitation, and this was a purpose with which the firm for which the claimant worked was willing to participate. The absence of any say on this matter by the prisoner, and the clear economic benefit to the firm, was, implicitly, irrelevant.

The defendant prison service had argued in this case that a positive finding on the employment status question would make firms increasingly reluctant to participate in work placement schemes, given the higher costs involved, to the detriment of the prisoner's potential rehabilitation. Noting this argument, the EAT

90 ibid.
91 *M & P Steelcraft Ltd v Ellis* [2008] ICR 578; [2008] IRLR 355.
92 ibid [58].
93 ibid [77].

stated that 'whilst policy does not dictate the result, we do draw some comfort from the fact that our conclusions will not exacerbate the risk that the operation of the resettlement scheme will be undermined'.[94]

The reasoning in *M & P* and the 'policy' concerns voiced by the EAT, are given statutory expression in s 45 of the NMWA, which exempts prisoners from the scope of the national minimum wage. This exclusion was said by the government to be necessary because, without the exclusion, prisoners would often satisfy the criteria for worker status in the context of the Act—an outcome that, it was assumed, should be avoided. If prisons, or firms, were required to guarantee the receipt of a minimum wage by prisoners for the purposes of work undertaken pursuant to prison rules, private sector firms might be less willing to provide work opportunities to prisoners: the higher (perceived) risk involved in hiring a prisoner would no longer be off set by the advantages of cheap labour.

Excluding prisoners from the scope of the national minimum wage, and employment law more generally, is presented as necessary and unavoidable. It is due to the lower value of prisoners' labour to firms, and the overriding importance of providing work opportunities to prisoners which would be 'impossible' if firms were required to pay above the 'market rate' for prison labour. By separating prisoners from the rest of the labour force, however, this policy actively encourages the exploitation of forms of labour power outside the formal labour market, and thus, and by implication, outside of the regulatory framework in which it exists. It allows firms to gain a competitive advantage therefore, by removing any obligation on them to assume the costs of (prisoners') subsistence, and, relatedly, of their subsequent social reintegration—notwithstanding the benefit to the firm of prisoners' work.

While the government presents this policy towards prisoners' wages as an inevitable consequence of the lower value of prisoners' work, essential for prisoners' rehabilitation, it also actively promotes prison workers to firms as sources of cheap labour. For example, the government argues that prison labour can help 'resolve' skills shortages and, at the same time, 'reduce ... overheads, saving organisations substantial sums'.[95] It is little surprise, then, that many private sector firms are doing business in prisons, reducing the size of their standard workforce and increasing the size of their prison contract.[96] Prisoners are paid often less than £2 an hour (pursuant to prison rules), and are very often required to work in excess of sixty hours a week.[97] From the government's perspective, however, given that it

[94] ibid 597.

[95] 'Employing Prisoners and Ex-Offenders' (GOV.UK, 23 May 2018) <https://www.gov.uk/government/publications/unlock-opportunity-employer-information-pack-and-case-studies/employing-prisoners-and-ex-offenders> accessed 22 March 2019.

[96] Arianna Silvestri, 'Prison Conditions in the United Kingdom' (2013) European Prison Observatory, 32.

[97] ibid.

actively promotes such practices, this is not an example of exploitation, but something that is inevitable due to the 'low' value (and thus, cost) of the work provided.

8.4.4 Detainees

It is not only prisoners that are excluded from the scope of the NMWA during detention, individuals detained in immigration centres are also excluded because 'detainees are in an equivalent position to prisoners remanded before trial, in that they are prima face offenders against the immigration rules'.[98] Hence, detainees must not be paid more than the prescribed maximum cap of (at the time of writing) £1, or £1.25 an hour.[99]

Paid activities were introduced into UK immigration centres by the Blair government in 2003, (apparently) to prevent boredom and frustration amongst detainees. Concerned that detainees would be regarded as workers for the purposes of the NMWA, the government introduced an express provision excluding detained persons from the Act on the grounds that granting detainees the national minimum wage 'would not be viable financially, nor reflect the *true* economic value of the work likely to be carried out'.[100]

The government has stressed that 'this money is not a wage as the ordinary working population would see it'. Rather, the purpose of the work is to alleviate boredom and occupy detainees whose 'position regarding pay rights is not the same as for those who are not in detention'.[101] When the wage rate was challenged in judicial review proceedings, the High Court endorsed this view, arguing (inter alia) that:

> it is not ... inhumane to set a fixed rate for paid activity that a detained person is not compelled to do. Paid activity is only one of a range of activities contemplated [by the rules] to meet the 'recreational and intellectual needs' of detained persons and for 'relief of boredom'... 'It is not part of the legislative purpose ... to ensure that detained persons have the opportunity to earn money to meet their basic or other needs'.[102]

The legislative scheme has thus been constructed so as to create status distinctions between ordinary workers and 'lesser' persons (persons in purported

[98] HC Deb 04 July 2017, vol 401, cols 783–90, 789 (Baroness Williams). Detainees are exempt from the provisions of the minimum wage by way of section 59 of the Immigration, Asylum and Nationality Act 2006.

[99] Home Office, UK Border Agency, Detention Services Order 01/2013, s 6.

[100] HC Deb 16 November 2005, vol 439 col 1016 (Tony McNulty) (emphasis added).

[101] HC Deb 04 July 2017, vol 401, cols 783–90, 789 (Baroness Williams).

[102] R (*Morita & ors*) *v SSHD* [2019] EWHC 758 (Admin) [73]–[65].

violation of certain rules) whose labour is assumed to be less economically viable and/or not economically motivated. This is a similar strategy to that employed elsewhere in the NMWA to justify the payment to young persons of a lower minimum rate, and the exclusion of certain persons (as with volunteers) from the scope of the right entirely. When asked whether the measures in relation to detainees would enable private firms to profit at detainees' and paid employees' expense (as, it could be argued, is the case with prisoners), the government argued that this was not the purpose of the measure: the 'beneficiaries' of the £1/£1.25 maximum wage per hour were said to be the detainees themselves.[103]

One of the premises behind the exclusion of detainees from the scope of the NMWA seems to be that, requiring firms to pay detainees the market/minimum rate for ordinary workers, as embodied in the NMWR, would prevent firms hiring them at all, and this would necessarily be harmful to the detainees who depend on paid work to 'alleviate boredom'.[104] Because they will, however, be assuming the position of employees (or, at the very least, workers), it is nonetheless deemed necessary to expressly exclude them from the scope of the NMWA, and to legislate a maximum wage cap to prevent a court finding that they are entitled to the minimum wage. This is the only way, apparently, to ensure the economic viability of their employment. Because the majority of immigration removal centres in the United Kingdom are outsourced to private corporations, however, as Kate Bales has argued, the regime 'makes immigration detention a highly profitable sector of the incarceration industry'.[105] This, it seems, is the real rationale underpinning the policy.

It is difficult to see how either policy, towards prisoners or detainees, can be justified. True, neither prisoners nor detainees have to contribute to accommodation and food costs during periods of detention. They do, however, very often have families to think about, and, moreover, need to make provision for their release. In addition to this, however, by excluding certain groups from the scope of the minimum wage, the policy actively encourages employers to make use of the labour of individuals whose position is already extremely precarious, and to do so at the expense of other paid employees and other firms.

The policy towards detainees and prisoners emphasizes well how the minimum wage is currently being conceived: it is seen as an expression of the market rate for labour, and it is only because the minimum wage is set so low (for 'ordinary' workers) that it can be justified at all. For those individuals whose labour is deemed to be less valuable than the ordinary low paid worker therefore (interns, prisoners, detainees), the minimum rate cannot be justified: hence, these groups must be

[103] HC Deb 04 July 2017, vol 401, cols 783–90, 790.
[104] ibid.
[105] Katie Bales and Lucy Mayblin, 'Unfree Labour in Immigration Detention: Exploitation and Coercion of a Captive Immigrant Workforce' (2018) 47 Economy and Society 191.

expressly excluded from the scope of the Act. The legal framework is thus actively promoting, and facilitating, the use by firms of cheap labour, shifting the social cost onto society, workers, and the state. This is, therefore, not merely an example of the market promoting forms of unfair competition: the legal system has established a legal framework that facilitates forms of labour expropriation that would not be possible had that framework not been established.

8.4.5 Domestic Workers

One further category excluded from the minimum wage is domestic workers providing work as part of an employer's family. In enacting this exception, the government had in mind, most specifically, au pairs and nannies, particularly 'foreign nationals in the UK under the au pair scheme who undertake light household duties or child care and are treated as members of the host family'.[106] These individuals 'deserve different treatment', it was argued, 'because of their integration within the family context'[107] and the importance of preserving employment opportunities that were predicted to disappear if employers were to be required to pay the minimum wage.

To fall within the exemption, the worker must be treated as a member of the employer's family, particularly vis-à-vis the provision of accommodation and meals, and the sharing of tasks and leisure activities. The implicit assumption is that work done in circumstances broadly comparable to the 'unpaid' work performed by 'family members' in the home is properly regarded as outside the economic or market sphere, and so, is beyond the purview of the formal labour market—and, by implication, the proper scope of legal regulation of wages.

The domestic home worker exception effectively reinforces social norms about the type of work that family members, particularly women, are expected to do for free, to the detriment of domestic workers seeking paid employment.[108] As is the case with the other categories considered above, the effect is to downgrade the work these individuals perform, and to reinforce assumptions about the low economic value of domestic work more generally—justifying exploitative practices. By framing the work as 'familial', and thus as being motivated by non-economic reasons (love, devotion, community), the government justifies non-intervention in this purely private sphere, while obscuring the precarious financial and legal position of many domestic workers and the complex factors influencing the acceptance by them of low paid positions.

[106] HC Deb 25 February 1999, vol 990, cols 633–35.

[107] *Regulations implementing the National Minimum Wage* (n 87) para. 21.

[108] Judy Fudge and Sandra Fredman., 'The Contract of Employment and Gendered Work' in Freedland and others (ed), *The Contract of Employment* (OUP 2016) 231–52.

The various exclusions contained in the NMWA are not inevitable; a result of something intrinsic to the work that these groups perform, nor to the conditions in which they do so. Rather, they reflect political choices that themselves actively shape and constitute the boundaries of the market and the economic. In so doing, the legal system plays an active part in influencing how resources are used and distributed throughout the economy—even if it denies that it is playing such a role in practice. At the same time, this strategy reinforces social norms concerning the value of different forms of activity, and the fairness of different types of working arrangements, legitimizing and promoting forms of surplus value extraction beyond the wage.

8.5 The Boundaries between Wages, Tips, and Remuneration

Once the scope of the individual's minimum wage entitlements has been ascertained, it becomes necessary to determine which of the payments received by the individual can be counted as part of the 'wage' when it comes to assessing whether their employer has complied with its minimum wage obligations. Particularly controversial in this respect have been payments made in connection with employment, but which are either not part of the contractual sum that the employer is obliged to pay, paid instead by third parties, or are not paid in respect of, or by reference to, the amount of labour provided. This is particularly so with regard to tips and gratuities which, prior to 2009, were expressly included within the payments that count towards the minimum wage.

Long recognized by the courts as part of a worker's contractual remuneration, tips would seem to fall outside the definition of the wage as a payment by an employer for labour. Consistently with this, tips were excluded from the definition of wages in the Truck Acts, and could not be considered as part of the minimum rates set by the trade boards because they were not deemed to be part of the price that an employer paid, or was required to pay, for 'personal labour'.[109] In contrast, tips had long been considered part of workers' taxable earnings for the purposes of income tax legislation, the damages payable for breach of contract, and, during the twentieth century, the 'earnings' to be considered when calculating compensation under the Workman's Compensation Acts.[110] Tips were thus something to which the worker was entitled, either by contract or custom, but not part of the exchange value of labour: the wage.[111]

[109] Truck Act 1831, s 25. See: HL Deb 03 June 1943, vol 127, cols 814–56, 823 and *Cofone v Spaghetti House Ltd* [1980] ICR 155.

[110] See: *Manubens v Leons* [1919] 1 KB 208 (claim for wrongful dismissal); *Blakistan v Cooper* [1907] 2 KB 688 (Easter offerings payable under an office taxable under Sched E Income Tax Act).

[111] See: Einat Albin, 'A Worker–Employer–Customer Triangle: The Case of Tips' (2011) 40 Industrial Law Journal 181, 193; HL Deb 03 June 1943, vol 127, cols 814–56, 842.

Prior to the nineteenth century, tipping had largely fallen outside the scope of wage and labour legislation,[112] both as regards the 'vails' given by visitors to wealthy households to their host's servants by way of appreciation for extra services, and tips paid to waiters in tea and coffee houses as an incentive for better service.[113] This was still the case throughout the nineteenth century, at which time it had been common for proprietors of commercial establishments to charge members of the waiting profession for the privilege of working in their establishment.[114]

By the end of the century, as the industry expanded, employers became increasingly concerned about their profitability and reputation and sought to exercise greater control over their waiters through their pay, thereby replacing these customary arrangements with contracts for wages. Because they paid so little, however, the waiters continued to be highly dependent upon tips for their earnings.[115] In many establishments, moreover, waiters continued to 'pay the employers for their jobs',[116] with employers imposing a number of fines and charges to reduce the sums that could be claimed.[117]

Because waiters had long been seen as independent professionals engaged in the provision of a service, they fell outside the scope of the labour protection that was developing during this period to provide protection for (manual, and in some contexts, clerical) workers' rights to be paid. In particular, they fell outside the scope of the Truck Acts, where such practices would have been forbidden as stoppages from wages. The first attempt to regulate tip payments came in the Catering Wages Act 1943. This legislation was enacted with a view to remedying low pay in industries where tip payments were common and, because workers tended to be hired under customary/casual arrangements, it would prove difficult to do so through the frame of the (relational) contract of service or employment.[118] While those hired on a casual basis were excluded from the scope of the Wages Councils Act, the Catering Wages Act expressly included 'casual workers' within its scope, extending protection to occupations where tip-based pay was common, such as those of waiters, barmen, and extra waiting hands. To achieve this, the legislation applied to workers employed in a catering undertaking, or

112 Albin (n 111) 190.

113 On vails, see: Ofer H Azar, 'The History of Tipping—from Sixteenth-Century England to United States in the 1910s' (2004) 33 Journal of Socio-Economics 745; on tipping in tea and coffee houses, see:Marc S Mentzer, 'The Payment of Gratuities by Customers in the United States: An Historical Analysis' (2013) 30 International Journal of Management 108, 109.

114 Catering Wages Commission, *Catering Wages Act, 1943. Report of the Catering Wages Commission on Their Recommendation for the Establishment of a Wages Board for Licensed Non-Residential Establishments*, (HMSO 1945) 34.

115 Albin (n 111) 191.

116 Catering Wages Commission (n 114) [16285]–[16288].

117 ibid.

118 ibid.

when their work was performed due to an arrangement, express or implied, by way of trade.[119]

The Catering Wages Act was intended to guarantee that employers would pay decent wages, rather than relying on customers or guests to cover the costs of labour.[120] In contrast with the Wages Councils Act, therefore, its primary concern was *who paid*, rather than what the worker received. In this particular industry, this question was deemed to lie at the heart of the problem of low pay:[121]

> ... a large number of those employed in hotels and restaurants receive no wages. Waiters, chambermaids, cloakroom men and porters sometimes receive a nominal 5s. a week, and sometimes nothing at all, and in some cases, they even pay for their position. Therefore, when we go to a hotel or restaurant and give a tip we are not handing something to the servants for special services which they have rendered to us but we are, in fact, contributing to wages which in other trades and industries would be paid by the employers.[122]

Parliament deliberately invoked the term 'wages' to circumscribe the scope of the board's rate-setting powers, in order that the setting of minimum wages did not influence workers' tips. By (implicitly) excluding tips from the scope of the minimum rates, employers themselves had to pay their workers a minimum sum, regardless of how much they received in tips from customers. The Act's purpose was thus to ensure that employers bore the full cost of labour, and so it left open scope for workers to receive tips as *additional* remuneration to complement their new legally guaranteed wages. For this reason, Parliament expressly distinguished wages and remuneration, confining the tips to the latter:

> This is a Bill for the regulation of the payments to be made by an employer to his employee. A tip is not a payment made by an employer to his employee. It is a payment made by a third person to somebody else's employee.[123]

In *Wrottesley v Regent Street Restaurant*, the court confirmed this interpretation of the Act.[124] This was so notwithstanding that the term 'remuneration' appeared regularly throughout the legislation.[125] This term was only invoked because 'there

[119] See also: Wages Regulation (Licensed Residential Establishment and Licensed Restaurant) Order 1948 which expressly included casual workers who were, however, excluded from the scope of other wage-fixing legislation.
[120] HL Deb 03 June 1943, vol 127, cols 814–56, 842 (Viscount Simon).
[121] See the discussion in: HL Deb 20 May 1943, vol 127, cols 567–617.
[122] HC Deb 05 February 1937, vol 319, cols 2011–22, 2012 (Mr Holmes).
[123] HL Deb 20 May 1943, vol 127, cols 567–617, 598–99 (Lord Nathan).
[124] [1951] 2 KB 277, 283.
[125] Sections 8, 9, and 10. But sections 8(1) and 10(2) make it clear that the term corresponds with the more precise concept of the wage as the price of labour.

are certain deductions from wages which are authorised by s. 10 so that remuneration is an apt word to indicate the net payment'.[126] Here, the court argued that tips have long been deemed part of a worker's 'earnings' for the purposes of income tax legislation, and part of the contractual remuneration considered to be comprised in the compensation payable under the workman's compensation legislation. They are thus sums to which, whether expressly or impliedly, the workers are entitled. Moreover, as they were most often paid directly in cash by a customer to a worker, they were the worker's property, and so could not be used by the employer to discharge his minimum wage obligations as they could not be said to be paid *by* him to his worker.[127]

By the time *Nerva* was decided in 1990, however, the custom of paying tips in cash was in decline.[128] Rather than providing workers with a right to retain cash tips, employers sought to recoup those tips themselves by imposing service charges that were due as part of the bill. This situation was exacerbated because cheques and credit card payments were becoming more common, so workers would rarely receive cash tips in hand.[129] Despite the court's assumption in *Wrottesley* that workers would go on receiving tips as a supplement to their guaranteed wage, therefore, there was no longer much scope for workers to be able to claim tips *in addition* to the minimum wage.

In *Nerva*, consistent with the principle, albeit not the spirit, behind the decision in *Wrottesley*, the court argued that if tips paid directly to workers are workers' property, the same (or, rather, the inverse) must be true of tips paid directly to the employer. If he used such sums to pay his worker, therefore, they were a payment by him to his worker and so would go towards discharging his minimum wage obligations.

In *Nerva*, between 1983 and 1986, the employer fell within the jurisdiction of the Wages Councils Act 1979 and between 1986 and 1989, the Wages Act 1986, rather than the Catering Wages Act as in *Wrottesley*. The court, engaging with the conflicting statutory language—the use in the Wages Councils Act of the term 'remuneration', and in the Wages Act of the term 'wage'—argued that there was no longer any meaningful distinction to be drawn between them: each referred to a compulsory payment made by an employer to his worker. Notwithstanding the use of the term 'remuneration', therefore, both the Wages Councils Act and the Wages Act were said to be concerned with what the employer paid his worker, rather than what the worker received by way of remuneration for employment.[130]

Like the court in *Wrottesley*, Straughton LJ pointed out that although the Catering Wages Act used the term 'remuneration', it was clear that it was concerned

[126] *Wrottesley v Regents Street* (n 124) 283.
[127] *Wrottesley v Regent Street* (n 124).
[128] *Nerva v RL&G Ltd* [1997] ICR 11; [1996] IRLR 461.
[129] ibid [22]–[23].
[130] ibid 14.

with payment by an employer to a worker—which, in the context of the Wages Act at least, was exactly what was meant by the term 'wage'. The wage was no longer simply the price of labour, it seemed, but the price payable under a contract between a worker and his employer—hence the blurring of the lines between remuneration and wages. Therefore, the difference was no longer to be drawn by reference to the subject matter of the contract, by reference to that for which the payment was made, but instead by reference to *who paid*. This made it possible to assimilate the legal protections provided in what had been very different models of minimum 'wage' protection.

As explained in Chapter 7, the term 'remuneration' had been deliberately invoked in the Wages Councils Act as something that is payable for employment, as opposed to something that reflects the price of labour. Parliament argued in favour of the term because it ensured workers not just a right to be paid for work, but a guaranteed minimum weekly income that attached to stable employment.[131] By reframing the distinction between the concepts in terms of *who pays*, however, the court in *Nerva* assimilated the purposes of the Catering Wages Act and the Wages Council Act to ensure that the employer rather than the public bore the direct, or private, costs of labour. The distinction between that which is payable for work and that which is paid for ongoing service had thus been lost, and with it, the distinction between wages and remuneration.

The effect of this interpretation in *Nerva* was to leave employers free to provide workers with a right to tips if they wished, but to leave them equally free to claim tips for themselves and to use these sums to discharge their minimum wage obligations. It is this that came to be reflected in the NMWA: tips other than those paid in cash directly to the worker can be considered part of the remuneration payable as part of the minimum wage.

In 2009, the NMWR was amended to exclude from the definition of wages tip-payments made via a tronc system.[132] The purpose of this was to better protect customer expectations, to 'empower customers through clear information on what happens to the service charge, tip or gratuity when they leave'.[133] It was a response to employers' attempts to use tronc systems to avoid PAYE obligations, leaving it unclear to customers how their tip payments would be used.[134] The amendment did not change the basic position where the employer recoups tips in the form of a service charge, or when tips are paid directly via cheque or credit card. These would

[131] HC Deb 16 January 1945, vol 407, cols 69–116, particularly 73–76 (Mr Bevin).

[132] This did not affect the position in Part I of the Employment Rights Act (corresponding with Part I of the Wages Act 1986), however, where tips continue to be part of the 'wages' to which the provisions on itemized pay statements and deductions apply.

[133] Department of Business Innovation and Skills, 'The National Minimum Wage: A Code of Brest Practice on Service Charges, Tips, Gratuities and Cover Charges' (2009) 4.

[134] It was partly a response to: *Revenue and Customs Commission v Annabel's (Berkeley Square)* [2009] ICR 1123.

still be deemed part of the employer's property and thus the fund from which he was entitled to pay wages.[135]

The 2009 amendment is entirely consistent with the policy behind the NMWR and the Wages Act more generally: to guarantee that employers, rather than the public, bear the full private costs of labour. In form, the position is the same as that which obtained under the Catering Wages Act. In practice, however, the effect is quite different. The Catering Wages Act had been enacted in a context in which the practice of paying workers cash tips was so widespread that it could be assumed that workers would continue to receive tips in addition to their wages. By the 1990s, however, this was no longer the case.[136]

The harsh implications of this policy became clear in 2018 when the *Bristol Post* published an article exposing the practices of a local chain of restaurants that exploited the definition of wages in such a way as to 'recover' any tips received above the level of the minimum wage:

> A few months ago, a local newspaper in Bristol, the Bristol Post, exposed a tipping practice at a local chain of restaurants called Aqua Italia that involved managers levying a 3% charge on all table orders regardless of tips received. In practice, that meant that waiters and waitresses could, on occasion, be asked to go to the cashpoint after their shift to withdraw their own money to pay the levy to their employers, even if they did not have any tips themselves. Those funds were then recycled to help pay the wage bill—in essence, charging workers to work...
>
> ... Amazingly, I am told that that is apparently legal—that is, if, in a reference period, such as a weekly pay period, the average hourly wage after deductions does not fall below the national minimum wage, it is legal, but if it does fall below the national minimum wage, it is not. That is because there are no useful laws on the regulation of tips in the hospitality sector or, as in the case of Aqua Italia, on charging workers to work.[137]

The government responded to calls to address this problem by referring to the need to promote 'competitiveness':

> ... employers who play fair are disadvantaged compared with unscrupulous employers. It is a competitive market. We have heard the figures for how much unscrupulous restauranteurs and people in the industry can make as a result of that kind of scheme, which provides them with an unfair advantage in the marketplace

[135] Jamie Elliott, 'Tip off: Waiters Still Paid Minimum Wage out of Your Service Charge' *The Guardian* (London, 7 June 2009) <https://www.theguardian.com/money/2009/jun/07/waiters-tips-restaurants-minimum-wage> accessed 6 February 2017.

[136] HC Deb 16 December 1997, vol 303, cols 162–239, 165 (Mrs Beckett).

[137] HC Deb 07 March 2018, vol 636, cols 188–205, 202 (Darren Jones).

> among their competitors who are doing the right thing. I am very mindful of that, so we will remedy the situation *if the industry does not act on the abuses that are sometimes reported* ... It is important to get it right so any action is targeted and benefits the workers, while burdens on legitimate, well-meaning businesses are minimised. Employers should not be out of pocket, and I entirely accept that they may need to retain a small proportion of tips to cover the administrative cost of processing them, as I said earlier.[138]

The government is not opposed in principle, it seems, to allowing employers to claim a portion of workers' tips as 'compensation' for some of the costs involved in employing them. The overriding concern is with preserving customer expectations, and preventing unfair competition. The role of tips in compensating for some of the precarity and insecurity endemic in certain forms of employment, such as casual work in the hospitality sector, has been completely overlooked. The problem (of employers claiming tips to lower labour costs) is conceptualized as a market distortion that the law might have to 'correct', if, and only if, the market does not itself 'self-adjust'.

In the *Bristol Post* example, the workers in question were paid a wage, but because they were being charged for the opportunity to earn tips, the effect was to reduce their overall remuneration. For other individuals, the fact that their remuneration is not classified as a wage, but as tips or shares, will have the effect of excluding the individual from the scope of the NMWA entirely. This is the case, for example, for 'share fishermen',[139] and certain individuals engaged in personal service industries, such as sex-work or lap-dancing, where it is customary for the individuals to pay a club or organization for the 'opportunity' to earn tips or fees by performing for its clients—an issue that will be explored in more detail in Chapter 9.[140]

8.6 Conclusion

The legal framework governing deductions from wages, tax credits, and the NMWA and NMWR all rest on the same basic ontological premises: the law has no role to play in shaping employment practices, in imposing an obligation to pay that alters the parties' incentives, encouraging employers to offer more stable, regular employment if they are to avoid being driven out of the market.

Since the 1980s, the policy underpinning minimum wage regulation in English law has been played out through the changing relationship between statutory

[138] ibid (Andrew Griffiths) (emphasis added).

[139] Section 43 of the National Minimum Wage Act 1998.

[140] This is implied by the Court of Appeal decision in *Quashie v Stringfellows Restaurants* [2012] EWCA Civ 1735 discussed in Chapter 9.

minimum wages and tax credits. Prior to 1998, in the absence of a statutory minimum wage, subsistence costs were to be born not by employers, but by the state through a system of wage supplements and tax credits. The introduction of the statutory minimum in 1998 did little to change this: the minimum wage was aimed more at correcting market distortions than it was at shifting social costs onto employers. For this reason, the tax credit system continued to bear most of the weight when it came to topping up wages to subsistence level.

This chapter has shown that these ideas are reflected in the NMWA's conceptual structure, and the distinction it draws between 'employment', as a condition for claiming the minimum rate, and 'work' as that for which workers are entitled to be paid, and the deference it affords to employers when it comes to their choice of payment system. Little attempt has thus been made to prevent employers from using the contract and its definition of work to shift economic risk on to workers. Moreover, because the wage continues to be conceptualized as an expression of the value of a commodity, the legislature was reluctant to extend the scope of the NMWA to individuals whose work is deemed to be of such low 'economic value' that a minimum market wage is inappropriate. Rather than discouraging exploitative employment practices and therefore facilitating the involvement of disadvantaged groups in the labour market, the government has instead actively encouraged the exploitation of these groups (or rather, the *expropriation* of their labour), by excluding them from access to the regulated, or formal, labour market entirely.[141]

The shift in policy from 1998 to today should not be underestimated. While during both periods, the conception of the wage at the heart of the NMWA was a market wage that corresponded with the price of a commodity, prior to the more recent reforms, there was at least a tax credit system in place that was expressly designed to top up that wage to subsistence level. It is true, as has been argued, that this itself is not conducive to long-term stability and efficiency, but it did at least take seriously the need to provide for the subsistence needs of working households. The premises on which universal credit is built, however, are quite different. Rather than acting as a bridge between wages and workers' subsistence needs, the tax credit system is more explicitly tailored with a view to providing incentives to work—however irregular, short term, or precarious that work may be. The overriding premise is that *a job* is better than *no job*, and that low wages and a deregulated labour market is the means through which jobs will be 'created'. While the

[141] 'Expropriation' refers to the use of resources, by capital, for less than its costs of reproduction. It goes beyond, therefore, 'exploitation' in the historically specific sense that is intrinsic to capitalist wage labour (the appropriation of *surplus* labour) because it involves attempts by capital to pay not even for *socially necessary* labour. It is a form of accumulation whereby capital appropriates, for its own benefit, social or natural 'use values' produced outside its circuit, such as the reproductive labour involved in reproducing the labour power for which some employers refuse to fully pay (by paying below subsistence wages). On this distinction between forms of 'accumulation', see: Nancy Fraser, 'Expropriation and Exploitation in Racialized Capitalism: A Reply to Michael Dawson' (2016) 3 Critical Historical Studies 163.

NLW does suggest that ideas about the subsistence wage are resurfacing, the aim that the NLW embodies is unlikely to be achieved in practice. This is due to the wider changes being made to universal credit, further casualizing work, the absence of any weekly or monthly minima, and, as has been shown in this chapter, the fact that the NLW is being given effect through the same conceptual structure as the (original) NMW. If the broader institutional environment remains hostile to stable employment, promoting casualization, increases in the minimum rate alone will do little to help many of the lowest paid.

9
Mutuality of Obligation and the Social Wage*

9.1 Introduction

In the United Kingdom, there are three main legal categories under which individuals can perform work: employee (employed under a contract of employment or service), independent contractor (carrying on a profession of business undertaking on one's own account and contracting with clients or customers), and 'worker'—colloquially known as the 'limb (b)' worker. While there is some academic debate as to whether workers should be seen as a sub-class of the employed (as opposed to the self-employed), the legal position today is relatively clear: workers are, at common law at least, a sub-class of the self-employed: individuals who carry out their work as part of someone else's business.[1]

While employees enjoy the full scope of employment law protections, and independent contractors enjoy very few, workers enjoy an intermediate range of protections—including trade union rights, minimum wages, holidays and working time, and protection from discrimination. They are excluded from the right to sick pay, statutory maternity/paternity pay, redundancy pay, the right to claim unfair dismissal, and the right to notice for termination: such rights are only available to employees (and, for the most part, employees with a minimum period of continuous service).

While the tax and employment law systems are not completely aligned, the tests applied in each area are similar. The key difference, however, is that, for tax purposes, there are just two categories: employed and self-employed. As, theoretically, a sub-class of the self-employed, workers will (usually) be treated as self-employed for tax and social security purposes, even though they are entitled to certain basic employment rights as workers. At present, this means that there are considerable advantages to an employer hiring an individual as a worker (rather than an employee)—most particularly, because the employer will not pay national insurance contributions on that worker's behalf. Workers also benefit because they will be

* Aspects of this chapter have been published as: Zoe Adams, 'Labour Law and the Labour Market: Employment Status Reconsidered' Law Quarterly Review <https://doi.org/10.17863/CAM.35039> (forthcoming).

[1] *Clyde & Co LLP v Bates van Winkelhof* [2014] UKSC 32.

Labour and the Wage. Zoe Adams, Oxford University Press (2020). © Zoe Adams.
DOI: 10.1093/oso/9780198858898.001.0001

subject to the more favourable income tax rules applicable to self-employed persons. This state of affairs encourages firms to make creative use of boiler-plate terms with a view to avoiding a finding of employment status, while, simultaneously, discouraging individuals from self- identifying as employees (and thus from attempting to claim employee status in a court of law).[2] In recent litigation concerning the employment status of workers in the gig-economy, for example, the 'workers'' representatives, the Independent Workers of Great Britain, have been particularly explicit that they are not seeking employee status for their members. What they want is a legal finding that their members are workers, and action by the government to extend the labour rights, which are currently only available to employees, to workers (in their capacity as 'self-employed' persons able to benefit from the tax position that this implies.

This underlying incentive structure is not irrelevant, then, when it comes to exploring why the courts have, in recent years in particular, tended to classify 'casual' workers as either independent contractors or workers—without considering whether they might (or *ought*), in fact, be employees. In fact, the existence of statutory worker status has removed the impetus for the courts to adapt traditional tests for employment to take into account the reality of modern working practices, by allowing them to fall back on the worker concept whenever they are faced with a labour relationship that does not fit with conventional assumptions about the nature of employment. In combination, this means that, for the most part, casual workers will fall outside the scope of many of the most important labour protections, including the right not to be unfairly dismissed.

The statutory framework does not, however, *dictate* that casual work arrangements be classed as contracts for personal services ('worker' contracts), rather than contracts of employment. Rather, this is a product of a particular judicial attitude, and a particular conception, held by the courts, of their role in the context of the capitalist system. As previous chapters have shown, there is an important difference between a court that sees its role as enforcing the agreement the parties have made, and a court that recognizes that the law plays an important role in shaping that agreement, and as such, the labour relationship itself. The first perspective leads the court to take a passive role, taking formal contracts at face value, prioritizing the express terms of the agreement over terms implied by law or conduct. The second perspective sees the court as having a more constitutive role in defining contract types, implying contracts from conduct, and reading implied terms into the contract as necessary incidents of employment status in order to further labour law's socio-economic function.

Thus, while the passive ontology tends to narrow the scope of protective legislation allowing the 'market' to dictate the terms on which labour power is sold,

[2] Abi Adams, Judith Freedman, and Jeremias Prassl, 'Rethinking Legal Taxonomies for the Gig Economy' (2018) 34 Oxford Review of Economic Policy 475.

the constitutive ontology facilitates a functional approach to questions of employment status that allows considerations of public policy about the importance of labour to the individual and the community to override freedom of contract. This latter approach increases the scope for labour law to secure a social wage because it matches labour rights, not to a specific contractual form, but to relationships that arise when one party has no choice but to provide their labour to another, attributing labour law rights and obligations based on considerations about how labour *should* be sold, and used, in (a sustainable) capitalist society. Importantly, and until Parliament intervenes to improve the protections available to workers, this latter approach would allow the courts to more readily *imply* contracts of employment, so to better provide even casual workers, with greater stability and protection. To allow, in other words, considerations of public policy to override any prior commitment to 'freedom' of contract.

This approach is not, however, one that is presently favoured by the courts. This can be seen, as we shall see, from the way that the concept, or test, of mutuality of obligation is currently being conceived. The confusion that exists in the case law concerning the meaning, and function, of this concept reflects deep controversies about the role of the relationship between law and social practices, a controversy that has significant implications when it comes to how the courts approach questions of employment status, and thus to the overall effectiveness of labour law when it comes to coordinating the provision of a social wage.

9.2 Mutuality of Obligation Today

The term 'mutuality of obligation' is used in two different senses in case law today. The first sense refers to the requirement for consideration: there must be a contract of some type between the parties before the question of employment status even arises, an 'irreducible minimum of obligation' on both sides. Mutuality of obligation in the second sense, by contrast, refers to the idea that there is something distinctive about employment relationships that distinguishes them from a basic exchange of work for wages.

The idea of mutuality as consideration is reflected in McKenna J's judgment in *Ready-Mixed Concrete*: 'There must be a wage or other remuneration. Otherwise, there will be no consideration, and without consideration, no contract of any kind.'[3] Nonetheless, there is considerable disagreement concerning the nature of this irreducible minimum of obligations, as 'sometimes the employer's duty is said to be to offer work, sometimes to provide pay'. Nonetheless, it seems that:

[3] *Ready Mixed Concrete (South East) Ltd v Minister of Pensions and National Insurance* [1968] 2 QB 497, 515.

> The critical feature ... is that the nature of the duty must involve some obligation to work such as to locate the contract in the employment field. If there are no mutual obligations of any kind then there is simply no contract at all, as *Carmichael v National Power plc*[4] makes clear; if there are mutual obligations, and they relate in some way to the provision of, or payment for, work which must be personally provided by the worker, there will be a contract in the employment field.[5]

The next section will show that mutuality in the consideration sense has long been a condition for establishing employment status, in the sense of being a condition to the entitlement to wage and labour protection. It is reflected, for example, in the requirement for 'quid pro quo' in claims for wages in the fourteenth and fifteenth centuries, and for a 'lawful hiring' in the context of the poor law (see below). Historically, this has required proof that labour (power), rather than a contracted for result or task, has been provided pursuant to some form of reciprocal exchange transaction. The focus of the tests employed by the courts was thus on the nature of the rights enjoyed by the employer, and the socio-economic position of the worker. The added requirement for 'mutuality' simply referred to the fact that purely gratuitous transactions would not fall within the purview of the law. In the presence of a written contract, this would be readily implied, but even in the case of informal (oral) contracts, evidence that labour had in fact been provided in expectation of some benefit would have been sufficient to establish the existence of a legally binding arrangement. This would then have provided sufficient 'mutuality' to ground a right to statutory, or reasonable, wages.

In recent years, however, particularly in the higher courts, the causal flow has been reversed. Rather than the *obligation* to pay wages being implied from evidence of the provision of labour, this obligation will only exist if the parties provide for it in their contract. The Employment Appeals Tribunal (EAT) in *Stack v A-Jar-Tec Ltd* concluded, for example, that the fact that there was no express provision for remuneration meant there was no consideration, and as such, no contract of employment into which a right to remuneration could be implied.[6] This was so notwithstanding the finding that the individual had agreed to provide his personal services to the company and had in fact done so for a considerable period of time.

Stack v A-Jar-Tec involved a company director. The decision of the EAT on this point was overturned on appeal. The Court of Appeal argued that 'the EAT had overlooked that the process of contract formulation might be partly express and partly by implication. It was not fatal to the existence of a concluded contract that the directors had not expressly agreed [to] a term concerning remuneration'.[7]

[4] *Carmichael v National Power plc* [1999] 1 WLR 2042; [1999] 4 All ER 897.
[5] *James v Greenwich LBC* [2007] ICR 577, 581–82; [2007] IRLR 168, 170 (emphasis added).
[6] *Stack v Ajar-Tec Ltd* [2013] UKEAT/0293/13/DA.
[7] ibid [30].

The courts have taken a less favourable position, however, towards low-paid casual workers engaged in personal service industries in which, rather than being paid a regular wage, they instead receive an 'opportunity' to earn tips or fees from third parties. The problem here is that because the express consideration under the contract does not take the form of a right to wages, the courts refuse to imply an obligation to pay wages that would contradict the obligations to which the employer has freely agreed. If the employer does not offer to pay a regular wage, therefore, the contract will lack the 'irreducible minimum of mutuality' to establish the existence, not of a contract per se, but a contract *relevant to the employment field.* By implication, the fact that there is no express promise to pay wages will prevent the worker from claiming any *right* to wages as a result of having provided, for example, the benefit of their personal service pursuant to some form of reciprocal exchange. This is the approach we see in cases such as *Hong Kong Golf Club* and *Quashie* (see below).

This approach shifts the focus of the enquiry away from the question of whether labour has been provided, as opposed to a job or task, towards the form of the contract. The question is not whether labour has been provided in expectation of some reciprocal benefit, therefore, but whether the contract imposes on workers an obligation to provide services personally, and on employers an obligation to pay monetary remuneration. This goes against the trend of the early twentieth century cases, as epitomized in Lord Shaw's warning in 1916 that:

> It would be a strange answer to this absolute obligation to pay a minimum wage to his servant that the employer should say 'This statute cannot apply to me because I have done better than give him less than the minimum wage: I have bargained to give him no wages at all.'[8]

This is, however, the effect of the majority decision in the *Golf Club* case, for example, and the Court of Appeal decision in *Quashie.*[9] In the latter, the Court of Appeal argued that a contract that required a dancer to perform a minimum number of evenings per week in the 'employer's' club in exchange for an opportunity to earn fees from its clients lacked the type of mutuality of obligation that is characteristic of employment (as compared with self-employment). The 'most important finding' in this respect was that there was no *express* contractual obligation to pay,[10] and there was 'nothing inherently implausible in the finding … that the club was obliged to pay nothing … it is what the terms of the agreement say, and the judge found that it was [the dancer's] understanding … Since … there is

[8] *Churm v Dalton Main Collieries Ltd* [1916] 1 AC 612, 634. See also Lord Parker at 643.

[9] *Cheng Un Yuen v Royal Hong Kong Golf Club* [1998] ICR 131; *Quashie v Stringfellow Restaurants* [2012] EWCA Civ 1735; [2013] IRLR 99 (CA). See also *Pimlico Plumbers v Smith Appeal* [2014] UKEAT/0495/12/DM [40].

[10] *Quashie v Stringfellow* (n 9) [46].

no mutuality of obligation, which is an essential element of the contract of employment . . . the Claimant was not an employee of the Respondent on a continuing basis or by *separate contracts* but was self-employed'.[11]

Establishing mutuality in this basic consideration sense is only the first hurdle. This is clearly a requirement for both worker and employee status for it goes to the question of the existence of the contract by which labour is provided. The essence of any relationship in the employment field, whether worker or employee, is said to be the existence of a contract to do work personally (subject to the proviso that the individual's status by virtue of that contract is not that of a client or customer etc) and this presupposes a legally binding obligation to provide labour as opposed to a completed job or task. Nonetheless, to prove that that contract to do work personally is a contract of employment, mutuality in what this chapter will refer to as the 'relational' or 'continuity' sense, must also be proven. That is, the relationship must be one that envisages ongoing obligations of future performance, an obligation *on the worker* to provide his labour on an ongoing basis. Today, this is encapsulated in the idea that the employer must promise to provide work, and the worker to accept it, on an ongoing basis.

This 'relational' conception of mutuality is broadly consistent with Mark Freedland's 'secondary tier' of mutuality of obligation, in the sense of mutual promises of future employment. In Freedland's work, however, mutuality in this secondary or 'relational' sense is not a *test* for establishing employment status, but something that is *ascribed* to employment relationships so-established:

> where there is such an exchange or a series of exchanges of work and remuneration taking place in the context of a personal work relationship, the employer or employing enterprise and the worker *should* be regarded and treated as being committed to reciprocal co-operation in the conduct of that contractual relationship ('the reciprocity principle').[12]

From this perspective, an approach that characterizes much of the pre-1970s case law, mutuality of obligation is not so much a test for establishing employment status, as a general idea about the way in which the labour relationship should, and has historically been, constituted in law. Mutuality of obligation is not an empirically observable reality, or particular contractual form, that the courts can identify, but a juridical idea, namely, the idea that the parties' mutual expectations as to the worker's ongoing service *should* be expressed in law in a particular form: today, as a contract of employment in which certain standard mutual rights and obligations are implied.

[11] ibid [48].

[12] Mark Freedland, 'The Legal Structure of the Contract of Employment' in Freedland and others (ed), *The Contract of Employment* (OUP 2016) 16 (emphasis added).

In *Airfix Footwear*, for example, the EAT suggested that 'where work is done consistently over a substantial period a tribunal would be entitled to reach the conclusion that a contract of employment had been created between the parties'.[13] Similarly, in *Nethermere*, Slynn J stated 'I cannot see why well-founded expectations of continuing homework should not be hardened or refined into enforceable contracts by regular giving and taking of work over periods of a year or more' with the result that 'outworkers … might become … employees under contracts of service'.[14]

In contrast to this approach, the more recent tendency has been for the courts to adopt one of two positions. In the first, they invoke the term mutuality of obligations expressly in order to refer to the idea of continuity, or ongoing performance, as an essential feature of, or condition for, a contract of employment. From this perspective, even evidence of a wage-work exchange and the presence of control will not be sufficient to establish a contract of employment during periods of work, if there are no express obligations to provide and accept work on an ongoing basis.

For example, the Court of Appeal in *O'Kelly* suggested that 'mutual obligations are a crucial prerequisite of a contract of service [because] a contract of service is a continuing relationship between employer and employee;' intermittent performance of work is 'inconsistent with [there being] *continuing obligations*'.[15] In *Stevedoring & Haulage*, therefore, it was argued that where the contract 'expressly negatives mutuality', or expressly states that the work is to be casual, or denies any obligation to provide or accept a minimum amount of work, there will be no contract of employment.[16] This means that even a 'lengthy course of dealing' will not '… somehow convert itself into a contractually binding obligation … to continue to enter into individual contracts' sufficient to establish a contract of employment if there are no express contractual obligations to provide and accept work on an ongoing basis.[17]

These decisions have been followed in a number of cases involving claims by agency and/or casual workers to statutory employment rights.[18] They have thus

[13] *Airfix Footwear Ltd v Cope* [1978] ICR 1210; [1978] IRLR 396, quoted in *Nethermere (St Neots) Ltd v Gardiner* [1984] ICR 612, 619 and 630; [1984] IRLR 240, 243 and 248 (Kerr J).

[14] *Nethermere* (n 13) 628. See also: *Greig and Others v Insole and Others* [1978] 1 WLR 302, 326; [1978] 3 All ER 449, 472: 'where a contract of employment by its terms imposes on an employee a binding obligation to work, without expressly imposing on the employer a corresponding obligation to provide work, the court will in an appropriate case readily imply such an obligation on the part of the employer, if it is satisfied that such implication is the proper way of giving to the transaction the business efficacy which both parties must have intended it should have'. For a more recent example, see: *Drake v Ipso Mori UK Ltd* [2012] IRLR 973.

[15] Described in *Nethermere* (n 13) (emphasis added). The EAT in *O'Kelly* (unreported) rejected the argument that the workers were individual contractors on the grounds of a lack of 'mutuality of obligation', but this position was reversed on appeal.

[16] *Stevedoring & Haulage Services Ltd v Fuller* [2001] EWCA Civ 651; [2001] IRLR 627 [10].

[17] *Nethermere* (n 13) (Kerr J dissenting) 630.

[18] *Carmichael v National Power* (n 4); *James v Greenwich* (n 5).

posed considerable hurdles to those hired under zero-hours contracts, through employment agencies, and/or to perform gigs or shifts when it comes to claiming basic employment protections. In these cases, it is assumed that 'even where the work-wage relationship is established and there is substantial control, there may be other features of the relationship which will entitle a tribunal to conclude that there is no contract of employment in place even during an individual engagement'.[19]

In the second approach, reflected in another line of cases, although the term mutuality of obligation is expressly invoked as an essential element of a contract of employment, its primary function has been to determine whether the contract is a short-term one envisaging a single shift, or an 'umbrella' contract envisaging ongoing performance.[20] This is important because many employment rights can only be claimed by employees who have a specified period of continuous service. In this context, a lack of mutuality will not *necessarily* prevent a finding that there is a contract of employment when work is being provided.[21] However, if the contract does not establish an obligation to maintain that relationship in being between shifts, the courts will not imply an ongoing or 'umbrella' contract in order to provide workers with more stable and continuous employment.[22] Even if an individual is an employee while working, therefore, their contracts are effectively treated as being lawfully terminated (without notice) at the end of each shift, preventing them from establishing the necessary continuity of service required to claim those very employment rights designed to provide the stability and security they are de facto denied.

From the perspective of the worker's right to be paid, this latter interpretation of mutuality would provide access to statutory protection for the right to be paid wages for labour actually provided, but would not go as far as to transform this right into a contractual right to be remunerated for time in employment. There being no binding executory obligations underpinning the relationship between engagements, the conditions for claiming rights to sickness and maternity pay, for example, or a statutory right to notice capable of providing more stable employment, would not be established.

It is only in very few cases that the courts have recognized that where there is a contract of employment

> for individual assignments—a casual employee may have worked so regularly and for such a period as to acquire continuity under these provisions. Such an

[19] *Quashie v Stringfellow* (n 9) [14].
[20] *Carmichael v National Power* (n 4); *Clark v Oxfordshire Health Authority* [1997] EWCA Civ 3035; [1998] IRLR 125.
[21] For example, *McMeechan v Secretary of State for Employment* [1997] ICR 549; [1997] IRLR 353; *Cornwall County Council v Prater* [2006] EWCA Civ 102; [2006] 2 All ER 1013.
[22] *Hellyer Brothers Ltd v McLeod* [1987] ICR 526; [1987] 1 WLR 728.

> employee will, to the eyes of anyone other than an employment lawyer, scarcely appear casual anymore; and it is not inherently surprising that such an employee should acquire employment rights.[23]

The willingness of the courts to disregard 'no mutuality' clauses (an '*Autoclenz-style*' sham) will, moreover, depend on how far the written terms can be said to reflect the *real agreement* between the parties.[24] Thus, if the employer has no intention of providing regular work and the worker has no choice but to accept casual employment, the courts will not imply such an obligation to protect a reasonable expectation on the worker's part to be provided with a stable, and secure, income.[25]

This short discussion of the mutuality concept and the various guises in which it appears today highlights that there is considerable tension in the way in which that concept is currently conceived. This is due in part to the co-existence of competing ontological positions within and between the courts. The difference between the decisions in *Nethermere, Airfix, Stack*, and the EAT in *Quashie*, and cases such as *O'Kelly, Stevedoring & Haulage*, the EAT in *Stack* and the Court of Appeal in *Quashie*, is two different ontological positions, two different views as to the relationship between law and the social reality of employment. From one perspective, 'mutuality of obligation' is an idea that is implicit in the way in which the labour relationship is conceived in law. This is the approach we see in cases such as *Nethermere* and *Airfix*. Rather than referring to a prior reality, the express terms of the parties' agreement, it is something that arises as a consequence of the contract of employment that the courts imply in order to shape the relationship that the wage–work exchange establishes. From the alternative perspective, by contrast, the contract of employment is itself constitutive of the labour relationship, a prior reality to which the courts must respond. Mutuality of obligation is thus something that describes the particular contractual obligations that parties to such a contract agree, and which, as a result, renders them subject to labour rights and obligations. This is what we see in cases such as *O'Kelly, Stevedoring & Haulage*, and *Quashie* (CA): if ongoing obligations are not established by the agreement, there are no rights or obligations for the legal system to enforce, and thus nothing to which labour law can apply.

The rest of the chapter will trace the evolution of the two different conceptions of mutuality, in the 'consideration' sense and in the 'relational' or continuity sense, and their relationship to the concepts of employee and worker.

[23] *Drake v Ipso* (n 14) [27].

[24] *Autoclenz v Belcher* [2011] UKSC 41; [2011] 4 All ER 745.

[25] This can be contrasted with the earlier decision in *Devonald v Rosser & Sons* [1906] 2 KB 728, discussed in Chapter 6.

9.3 Historical Antecedents to Mutuality of Obligation

9.3.1 Prior to the Nineteenth Century

From the fourteenth century, as we saw in Chapter 5, service was compulsory for all those without alternative means of subsistence. The contract by which dependent persons provided their service was something that was imputed from that person's dependence, with the obligation to serve, and the right to wages it established, something that was implied through that contract as a result of the statutory regime. If a person undertook work on a casual day-to-day basis, therefore, it was implicit that they were not dependent in the same sense as servants were; had they been, they too would have been compelled to serve.[26]

During this period, the corollary to the legal obligation to serve was the right to be maintained by one's master. For this reason, only those with sufficient land to support their servants were entitled to compel a servant into service.[27] Employers' rights to service, like Lords' to the service of their villeins, thus came to imply an ongoing right to subsistence, associating with the concept of service certain relational ideas of mutuality of obligation.

In the sixteenth and seventeenth centuries, and even up to the middle of the nineteenth century, the courts had to elaborate upon the meaning of service given the central role that it played within the framework of the poor law. During this period, service was not only something that was mandated for those with insufficient means, imposing on employers an obligation to maintain and protect, but something that imposed on the parish similar obligations in times of unemployment.[28]

The Poor Relief Act 1691 provided that 'if any unmarried person shall be lawfully hired into any Parish or town for a year, such service shall be deemed and adjudged a good settlement therein'.[29] This meant that both a lawful hiring envisaging a year's service, and a year's actual service, would have to be proven to establish a settlement.

In relation to the need to prove service, Chapter 5 has shown how this requirement was associated with proprietary ideas linked with leasehold; exclusive control over the servant for the duration of the hiring. Implicit in this was the servant's complete subordination to the employer's command, and thus his inability to refuse to work as and when required. These obligations were 'mutual'

[26] (1364) YB Trin 38 Edw 3, fo 12b, pl 1. 'He did not have sufficient land to have a servant, but was a serving man himself': (1426) YB Pasch 4 Hen 6, fo 19b, pl 5.

[27] (1364) YB Trin 38 Edw 3, fo 12b, pl 1.

[28] Prior to 1691, while outdoor relief was a Parish function, service was not given as an express statutory basis for claiming a settlement. See earlier legislation: (1530) 22 Hen VIII c 12; (1535) 27 Hen VIII c 25; (1597) 39 Eliz 1 c 4; (1601) 43 Eliz 1 c 2; (1662) 14 Cha II c 12 (Settlement Act).

[29] (1692) 3 & 4 W & M c 11, s 7.

to his right to be maintained, however, in the sense that the employer's failure to provide adequate food and board would provide a good defence to an action for departure.[30]

In relation to the statute's requirement for a lawful hiring, the courts interpreted this as requiring that service had been provided pursuant to a reciprocal and enforceable contract.[31] Even so, the courts readily implied such a contract from evidence of service (as executed consideration). The issue was only problematic, therefore, where the contract was made by a minor and/or a servant already bound into the service of another.[32] For questions of status, the courts thus placed greater emphasis on the parties' conduct and the scope of the employer's control, than they did on the terms of any express agreement.

The courts took a similar approach when it came to claims for wages. Informal contracts only being actionable in debt, it had long been the case that the basis for the claim to wages was the entitlement, rather than the promise to pay.[33] It was thus proof of service, the exchange transaction, rather than the contract itself, that provided the basis for the claim.[34] Even in the sixteenth century, as assumpsit gradually came to replace debt as the main mechanism for the enforcement of informal agreements, the courts would imply a promise to pay from the fact of service, for it was the exchange itself, the transfer of value, that provided the basis for the obligation to pay wages.[35]

Prior to the nineteenth century, therefore, we can identify two distinct *ideas* associated with the concept of mutuality. The first refers to the basic idea that the courts are only concerned with transactions of a legal nature. In a context in which written contracts were rare, this required evidence that labour had been provided pursuant to some form of reciprocal exchange. Given that for most labour was compulsory, however, and wages provided by statute, such would be readily inferred from evidence of service. This depended upon the nature of the relationship between the parties, and the degree of the servant's dependence.

The second idea of mutuality reflects ideas about the nature of the labour relationship, a particular form of property relationship that envisages ongoing rights

[30] In 1354, the court confirmed that a failure to provide livery constituted a good defence in an action for departure: (1354) YB Mich 28 Edw 3, fo 21B, pl 18. In turn, a person without sufficient land of their own was not permitted to retain a servant under the statute: (1364) YB Trin 38 Edw 3, fo 12b, pl 1.

[31] See, for example, *R v The Inhabitants of Beaulieu* (1814) 3 M & S 229, 235–36, 105 ER 595.

[32] *The Parish of Anmy Crusis v Barnsly* (1721) 11 Mod 365, 88 ER 1092 (already apprenticed to another); *R v The Inhabitants of Chesterfield* (1702) 12 Mod 132, 88 ER 1215 (no valid contract as no mutual consent).

[33] George Hall, *The Treatise on the Laws and Customs of the Realm of England Commonly Called Glanvill* (Clarendon Press 1993) X, 3–5; David Ibbetson, *A Historical Introduction to the Law of Obligations* (new edn, OUP 2001) 19; Cecil Fifoot, *History and Sources of the Common Law: Tort and Contract* (Greenwood Pub Group 1949) 249; *Alice's Case* (1458) YB 37 Mich Hen 6, fo 8, pl 18.

[34] On what had to be proven in debt, see: (1472) Pasch 12 Edw 4, fo 8, pl 22. See: Ibbetson (n 33) 39.

[35] David Ibbetson 'Assumpsit and Debt in the Early Sixteenth Century: The Origins of the Indebitatus Count' (1982) 41 CLJ 142, 153; David Ibbetson and John Barton, 'Consideration and the Theory of Contract in Sixteenth-Century Common Law' [1990] Towards a General Law of Contract 67.

to personal service. In this context, the concept expresses the premise that an employer's right to service *ought to be* made conditional upon his securing the servant a right to subsistence. Rather than require the employer to keep his worker employed, providing him with regular work, the courts instead imposed an obligation on the employer to maintain and protect him for the entire period of the hiring, irrespective of how much work was performed. Mutuality of obligation was not something that the courts sought to identify, therefore, nor a test used to determine the scope of social legislation, but a distinctive idea about the nature of the labour relationship and the way it should be constituted in law when it came to questions of enforcement. It was, in other words, the product of, rather than the condition for, labour law rights and obligations.

9.3.2 The Nineteenth Century

In the nineteenth century, these distinct ideas of mutuality continued to play a role in determining the scope of labour legislation. In the context of the Truck Acts, mutuality in the primary 'consideration' sense continued to require as a condition for wages proof of actual performance; that labour had actually been provided pursuant to some form of reciprocal exchange. Evidence of reciprocity still being readily inferred where some form of benefit had been provided pursuant to an 'Agreement, Understanding, Device, Contrivance, Collusion, or Arrangement whatsoever on the Subject of Wages',[36] the emphasis was less on the form of the contract or the relationship between the parties than it was on whether what had been provided was in fact labour, rather than some concrete task or job.

The Act defined the 'wage' as 'any Money or other Thing had or contracted to be paid, delivered, or given as a Recompence, Reward, or Remuneration for *any Labour done or to be done*...' and applied to all Artificers, 'all Workmen, Labourers, and other Persons in any Manner engaged in the Performance of any Work, Employment, or Operation, of what Nature so ever, in or about the several Trades and Occupations aforesaid'.[37] This meant that questions of scope turned primarily upon whether the payment could be classed as a wage that was payable for labour 'done or to be done' rather than a price to be paid for a contract:

> [The Act] applies only to those persons who are to receive wages as the price of their labour, and that the term 'wages' is to be understood in its popular sense, and does not include wages which are the price of a contract.[38]

[36] Section 25.
[37] Section 25.
[38] *Riley v Warden* (1848) 2 Ex 59, 154 ER 405 (Rolfe B).

The focus of the case law was thus upon whether the parties intended that the worker provide his services personally, and thus that he provided labour, rather than promising to secure the completion of a specific job or task. This meant that it was only if 'the nature of the contract is such that it is not a contract for labour but the result of labour [that] the case is not within the Act'.[39] Despite a much more restrictive reading towards the end of the nineteenth century, quickly reversed by the legislature,[40] the courts' approach, for the most part, was to look at 'the nature of the work, the contract and position of the parties' and derive from this the terms of the contract.[41] This was because the courts assumed that 'the legislature intended to protect a particular class' such that all these factors would have to be considered to 'say whether [an individual] was of that class'.[42] Thus, while it was necessary that there be a contract to personally do work, the terms of that contract were *implied* from the nature of the work and the socio-economic status of the parties.[43] Mutuality in this context merely reflected the idea that where labour was provided it would readily be presumed that it was provided pursuant to a reciprocal exchange transaction, thereby triggering the legal right to be paid.

Mutuality played a different role, however, in the context of the Master and Servant Acts. The Acts presupposed 'service' such that while it applied to servants in husbandry and 'artificers, handicraftsmen, miners, colliers, keelmen, pitmen, glassmen, potters and other labourers employed for any certain time, or in any other manner',[44] it provided masters with a remedy in the event of a departure from service and imposed criminal penalties for desertion of work. It thus envisaged not only an exchange of commodified labour for wages but ongoing service, an obligation to provide labour to one master exclusively on an ongoing basis.[45]

To avail himself of the 'protection' under the Acts, the *employer* had to prove that there had been more than an exchange of labour for wages, that he had promised to provide work in exchange for the service which he sought to compel.[46] If no such promise existed, the claim would fail for 'want of mutuality'.[47] By the mid-nineteenth century, however, the courts would imply such a promise from evidence of regular work, constituting the wage–work exchange itself as a contract

[39] *Sleeman v Barrett* (1864) 2 Hurl & C 934, 159 ER 386.
[40] Truck Act 1887, s 10.
[41] *Bowers v Lovekin*; (1856) 6 El & Bl 584, 591, 119 ER 982 (Erle J). Contrast with *Squire v Midland Lace* [1905] 2 KB 448.
[42] *Bower v Lovekins* (n 41) 591. See also Erle J in *Ingram v Barnes* (1857) 119 ER 1190; 7 El & Bl 115; and Maule J in *Sharman v Sanders* (1853) 13 CB 166, 138 ER 1161.
[43] Similarly, in *Riley* it was the nature of the task and the status of the parties from which the terms of the contract were derived.
[44] (1757) 31 Geo II c 11, s 3.
[45] *Lancaster v Greaves* (1829) 9 B & C 628, 631–32, 109 ER 233, confirmed in *Ex Parte Gordon* (1856) 25 LJMC 12, 14.
[46] See Chapter 4, and *R v Welch* (1853) 2 El & Bl 357, 118 ER 800 (Lord Campbell CJ) 362; *Pilkington v Scott* (1862) 153 ER 1014.
[47] *Lees v Whitcomb* (1828) 130 ER 972; *Sykes v Dixon* (1839) 9 Ad & El 693, 112 ER 1374; *Aspdin v Austin* (1844) 5 QB 671, 114 ER 1402; *Dunn v Sayles* (1844) 5 QB 685, 114 ER 1408.

of service so as to provide employers with a right to his worker's ongoing service. In theory, this went hand in hand with a right for servants to be provided with regular work from which to earn a (market) wage.[48] In fact, however, for much of the nineteenth century, the courts proved reluctant to enforce the implied obligation to provide work in favour of workers, particularly when it came to claims for wages in respect of periods of lay off.[49] However embedded were ideas of mutuality within labour law discourse, that is, the idea that service went hand in hand with some form of right to subsistence, the courts had not yet given expression to these ideas through a relational conception of the contract of service.

It is clear, however, that employment status for the purposes of the Master and Servant Acts was highly dependent upon the courts embracing an active constituting role, implying a contract of service where, in light of its implications in the context of the statutory framework, this was something to which it was assumed the parties were entitled. During this period, therefore, we can still see two distinct ideas of mutuality; one going towards establishing the basic right to wages to which all workers were entitled, the other towards establishing the specific protections associated with ideas of service. Thus, mutuality in the primary consideration sense referred to the requirement that labour have been provided pursuant to a reciprocal exchange, a condition for statutory protection for wages, while mutuality in the relational sense expressed the premise that the courts ought to provide employers with a right to ongoing service and to provide in exchange some form of proxy for the industrial servant's right to be maintained.

9.3.3 The Late Nineteenth and Early Twentieth Century

The Employers and Workmen Act 1875 replaced the penal provisions of the Master and Servant Act with a special power for the magistrates to impose fines for breaches of work discipline and to require specific performance of the contract of service.[50] Thus, although long-term hirings were becoming less common, and criminal penalties for breach of contract removed, the Act continued to provide employers with a mechanism to compel ongoing service from the contract by which labour was sold for wages.[51]

[48] *Re Bailey* (1854) 3 El & Bl 60, 118 ER 1269; *R v Welch* (n 46); *Saunders v Whittle* (1862) 2 B & S 49. Contrast with those paid a fixed salary for service. Here the salary provided sufficient 'mutuality' such that the courts refused to imply an additional obligation to provide work: *Collier v Sunday Referee Publishing Company Ltd* [1940] 2 KB 647; [1940] 4 All ER 234 [50]; *Lagerwall v Wilkinson, Henderson & Clarke* (1899) 80 LT 55; and *Turner v Sawden* [1901] 2 KB 653; *Midland Counties District Bank, Ltd v Attwood* [1905] 1 Ch 357, 362.

[49] *Williamson v Taylor* (1843) 5 QB 175, 114 ER 1214.

[50] Section 3.

[51] On changes in work organization during this period, see: Simon Deakin and Frank Wilkinson, *The Law of the Labour Market Industrialization, Employment, and Legal Evolution* (OUP 2005) 77–78.

The Act applied to 'workmen', defined as 'any person (except domestic servants) who, being a labourer, servant in husbandry, journeyman, artificer, handicraftsman, miner, or otherwise engaged in *manual* labour … has entered into or works under *a contract* with an employer … express or implied, oral or in writing … a contract of service or a contract personally to execute any work or labour'[52] This definition was later adopted in the Employers' Liability Act of 1880, and the Workmen's Compensation Act of 1897, although the latter dropped the requirement for manual labour.[53]

In 1940, the term 'artificer' in the Truck Act was replaced with the term 'worker', defined by reference to the definition of 'workman' in the 1895 Act, and from this point onwards, the term 'worker' became the primary term to be used to denote dependent employment in protective labour legislation.[54] Higher-status salaried employees were, by contrast, at least until the term 'employee' began to be used (eg in the Contracts of Employment Act 1963), deemed to be beyond the scope of protective labour law.[55] For the purposes of the Employer and Workman Act this was because the term 'labourer' invoked in the definition of 'workman' was said to exclude those engaged in 'a higher class of labour' such as 'developing ideas … in furtherance of the business of the firm'.[56] Elsewhere, this was achieved both through the courts' interpretation of the term 'worker', as 'presupposing a position of dependence' and certain express statutory exceptions excluding those earning above a certain threshold from the scope of protection.[57]

By the middle of the twentieth century, the worker definition became the standard approach to defining the scope of protective labour legislation, modified, or qualified by various express exclusions depending upon the nature of the rights in the Act in question. For example, under the Wages Councils Act, although there was no requirement for a contract of service, the Act nonetheless excluded 'any person who is employed casually' as well as those employed 'otherwise for the purposes of the employer's business'.[58] Because the Act provided an ongoing right to be paid that was independent of time spent working, it presupposed a relationship whereby a single employer enjoyed the benefit of the worker's ongoing service, and it was this that these statutory exceptions had intended to achieve. For this reason,

[52] Section 10.

[53] Section 7.

[54] Section 29(3). The only Acts that retained the reference to manual labour were the Truck Act 1940 and the Employer and Workmen Act 1875.

[55] This parallelled the differential tax treatment of higher-status employees and wage workers. See: Mark Harvey and Norman Geras, *Inequality and Democratic Egalitarianism: Marx's Economy and Beyond and Other Essays* (OUP 2018).

[56] *Jackson v Hill & Co* (1884) 13 QBD 618, 622.

[57] *Simpson v Ebbw Vale Steel, Iron & Coal Co* [1905] 1 KB 453, 458 and *Gordon v Jennings* (1882) 9 QBD 45. The National Insurance Act 1911 excluded those whose remuneration exceeded £160. The Workmen's Compensation Act 1906, s 13 adopts the same definition of worker but excludes those whose remuneration exceeds £200 and whose employment is of a 'casual nature'.

[58] Section 23(1). See similarly: Workmen's Compensation Act 1925, s 3(2)(b).

the courts were open to the possibility that 'an outworker working on his own account and without a team and working exclusively for a particular [employer] might well be an employee [sic] although an outworker as well'. This ultimately depended on where the balance lay between 'service and servitude' and 'independence and freedom' when all the circumstances were considered.[59]

In industries such as catering where casual labour was particularly common, Parliament tied the scope of the right to minimum wages to the performance of a particular type of work, rather than to the existence of an ongoing relationship involving the provision of labour. Thus, it applied to workers 'employed' in an undertaking involved in 'the supply of food or drink for immediate consumption, the provision of living accommodation for guests or lodgers' and expressly provided that 'for the purposes of this Act, any worker who, for the purposes of any undertaking or part of an undertaking, performs any work in pursuance of an arrangement express or implied made by the worker by way of trade with the persons carrying on that undertaking shall be deemed to be employed by them in that undertaking or part'.[60] In *Pauley v Kenaldo*, this meant that a cloakroom assistant who was not 'employed' under a contract of employment but was nonetheless engaged in the work to which the minimum rate was applicable, fell within the scope of the Act, the casual nature of the arrangement notwithstanding.[61] This approach broadly followed the approach taken in the Trade Board Acts where the courts allowed workers to claim the minimum rate whenever the type of work typical of the trade had been provided. This meant that casual workers, and even outworkers who employed a number of other outworkers, were entitled to the minimum rate, notwithstanding the lack of an ongoing employment relationship.[62]

For much of the nineteenth century, beyond the Factory Acts whose scope was determined by reference to enterprise type, and the Truck Acts which applied to (most) manual workers, labour legislation had been concerned primarily with reenforcing employers' control over workers in production, providing them with a mechanism for compelling into service those who merely sold their labour power for wages. By the mid- twentieth century, however, this function was increasingly being performed by a relational contract of service.[63] The result was to exclude from the scope of labour protection persons hired on a casual basis, those unable to bargain for a relational contract and who, as a result, were deprived of the stable and continuous employment that the contract of service now provided. It was in

[59] *Westall Richardson v Roulson* [1954] 1 WLR 905, 909 (obiter).

[60] Catering Wages Act 1943, s 1(2) and 1(4).

[61] *Pauley v Kenaldo* [1953] 1 WLR 187; [1953] 1 All ER 226

[62] *Street v Williams* [1914] 3 KB 157; *Skinner v Jack Breach* [1927] 2 KB 220. This also meant that if the worker was paid piece wages and was not given sufficient work to enable him to earn the minimum basic piece rate, the court would imply an obligation to pay a higher rate per piece: *Nathan v Gulkoff and Levy* [1933] Ch 809.

[63] See, for example, the courts' interpretation of the contract in: *Parkin v South Hetton Coal Co* (1907) 98 LT 162, 164; *George v Davies* [1911] 2 KB 445; and *Hanley v Pease & Partners* [1915] 1 KB 698.

order to address this problem that Parliament introduced the new statutory concept of the employee.[64] The effect of this was to extend to all the employed, those providing work personally, the relational model of the contract that had once been the preserve of the higher-status salaried employee, parallelling developments taking place in tax and social security legislation.

The first statute to use the term 'employee' to circumscribe the scope of labour legislation was the Contracts of Employment Act 1963. This introduced the right to notice and to a written statement of particulars that is now embodied in s 86 and s 1 of the Employment Rights Act (ERA).[65] The Act reproduced the definition of the 'worker' used in previous statutes, and now referred to these persons as 'employees'.[66] These were persons who, providing their labour pursuant to a contract in the generic sense, were now to be deemed in law to be hired under a relational contract of employment. If there was evidence that labour had in fact been provided continuously over a particular period of time, or that labour was being provided in a context in which ongoing service was mutually expected, workers would be able to claim this new employee status and, after accumulating the requisite continuity of service, the statutory rights to which that contract gave rise.

> [The Bill] offers the worker a legal contract of employment, something he has never had before. Of course, many employers give their employees a contract and some measure of security. All employers, however, are not good employers. And, in any case, it is a new thing that they are now legally entitled to a contract which sets out not merely the period of notice but conditions relating to holidays, sick pay, pension rights and many other things. (HL Deb 21 June 1963, vol 250, cc1494–528, 1516 (Lord Robertson))
>
> We want to *bring about a situation* in which hardly anyone working in this country can be dismissed at a few hours' notice.[67]

The Act explicitly envisaged a constituting role for the courts, implying from an exchange of work for wages a relational contract envisaging ongoing performance.[68] It was only if the parties' mutual expectations were inconsistent with this that the claim to employee status would fail, the burden being on the employer to prove that an implied right to notice was inconsistent with the parties' expectations.[69]

The statutory requirement for a minimum period of continuous service was separate from the question of whether a contract of employment could be implied.

[64] The source for this appears later in this section, in the Hansard references to the debates behind the Contracts of Employment Act 1963.
[65] Sections 1 and 4.
[66] Section 8(1).
[67] HC Deb 01 May 1963, vol 676, cols 1092–115, 1096 (Mr Prentice) (emphasis added).
[68] HL Deb 21 June 1963, vol 250, cols 1494–528, 1516 (Lord Robertson).
[69] HC Deb 01 May 1963, vol 676, cols 1092–115, 1103 (Mr Diamond).

It was introduced to preserve the important role that probationary periods were deemed to perform for both workers and their employers, enabling both parties to end the relationship at will where the job, or the worker, proved unsuitable. It was stressed, therefore, that the question of continuity was not concerned with the separate issue of status, but was 'an argument about when a man has passed his period of probation and ... an employee having passed his period of probation, it is only a question whether the employer can look ahead for one week'.[70]

The Industrial Relations Act 1971 reduced the twenty-six-week qualifying period established in the Contracts of Employment Act to thirteen weeks and introduced a new statutory right for all 'employees' not to be unfairly dismissed after 104 weeks' continuous service.[71] The right not to be unfairly dismissed was to be treated separately from the collective labour rights provided for elsewhere in the Act, rights which applied to all 'workers'. The Act thus drew an implicit distinction between those in regular and stable employment, able to claim rights under the Wages Councils Act (individuals providing work who were not employed on a casual basis in industries to which Wages Orders applied), the Contracts of Employment Act (employees), and unfair dismissal, and those who provided work and wages on a one-off or intermittent basis to whom a much more limited set of rights applied, rights concerned most directly with working conditions and the terms upon which labour was provided in the market.

In the debates surrounding the passing of the Act, the government argued that although the worker concept had Victorian connotations, 'we have to include employees in the literal sense, *and* those that come under a contract of service'.[72] This was because there was no justification for limiting collective labour rights, nor the restrictions on their exercise, to employees. Instead, such rights were to be extended to all those *employed*, those who normally work, or seek to work 'under a contract of employment ... or any other contract (whether express or implied, and, if express, whether oral or in writing) whereby he undertakes to perform personally any work or services for another party to the contract who is not a professional client of his'.[73]

In this way, the 'employee' concept was coming to include both the 'servant' under a contract of service and the 'intuitive' employee, the higher-status managerial or professional salaried person. However, once this shift had taken place, this new unitary concept of the employee had to be distinguished from the somewhat larger group of workers who included many of those we now call limb (b) workers. The latter needed collective rights but could not easily be made to fit into the employee concept once dismissal rights were strengthened. The result was

70 ibid.
71 Section 19(1) and 28.
72 HC Deb 14 December 1970, vol 808, cols 961–1076, 964 (Mr Carr).
73 Section 167(1).

that a link was being established between ideas about the subsistence wage and a *stable and continuous model of employment*—one to which the broader institutional framework has been becoming increasingly hostile over time.

In 1986 when the Wages Act was being debated, the definition of 'worker' caused considerable concern. The Industrial Relations Act's definition of the worker, as re-enacted in the Trade Union and Labour Relations Act 1974, was substantially the same as the formulation adopted in previous Acts, but had added the proviso 'is not a client or customer of any profession'. In 1986, the government sought to add the further phrase '*or business undertaking* carried on by the individual'. This substantially mirrored the requirement in the Wages Council Act that the individual should not be providing work 'other than for the purposes of the employer's business'. The idea, according to Lord Trefgarne, was to ensure that 'anyone who is employed by someone else would be protected ... but if the person doing the work is doing so as part of a business he is running he should not be covered by the protections of the Bill'.[74] The government believed that with this qualification the definition would be adequate to incorporate all but the genuinely self-employed.[75] This is the definition we now find in the ERA (the limb (b) worker), the National Minimum Wage Act 1998, and the Working Time Regulations 1998–99.[76] This is the legal framework that forms the background to the discussion of the two types of mutuality of obligation explored in the previous section.

Both ideas of mutuality, in the sense of reciprocity or consideration, and in the relational sense associated with the right to subsistence, can be found during the period from the 1960s to the 1980s, although the statutory requirement for continuity somewhat blurred the distinction between them. Following the introduction of the new employee status in 1963, it was relatively clear that the statutory concept of worker continued to be synonymous with the dependent employed. These were persons who could prove mutuality in the primary sense, that they provided their labour in exchange for wages. Many of these workers would also be able to claim that they were employees hired under a contract of employment if they could prove that they had provided, or were expected to provide, that labour on an ongoing basis.

By the end of the 1970s, therefore, mutuality as a condition for access to labour law implied simply that labour, rather than some contracted for result, had been provided pursuant to a contract in the generic sense of some form of reciprocal exchange. The form of the contract was largely irrelevant, therefore, provided that labour power had been provided in exchange for some form of remuneration.

Beyond this idea of mutuality as consideration, mutuality of obligation was not a term that was used by the courts when it came to questions of status. Instead, the

[74] HL Deb 24 June 1986, vol 477, cols 228–74, 263.
[75] HL Deb 24 June 1986, vol 477, cols 228–74, 264 (Lord Wedderburn).
[76] Working Time Regulations 1998, SI 1998/1833; SI 1999/3372.

idea of mutuality of obligation was embedded in the broader function that protective labour legislation had emerged to perform, with the contract of employment the juridical technique through which it did so. In exchange for the ongoing service that at one time coercive labour legislation, and later the relational contract, had provided, labour and social welfare legislation had secured certain protective rights that were 'mutual' to the employer's rights in service, rights which together went towards providing workers with a form of subsistence wage.

Prior to the 1980s, the contract of service was not itself seen to be *by its nature* continuous, in that the statutory criteria for continuity continued to be treated independently from the question of status. Thus, although judges accepted 'that the relationship of master and servant is normally conceived of as a continuous relationship, and that the fact that there is a series of contracts is more consistent with those contracts being contracts for services than contracts of service' they would nonetheless typically 'doubt whether this factor can usefully be considered in isolation'.[77]

It is not clear from this how far the introduction of the limb (b) worker explains the more restrictive interpretation of the employee concept that the courts adopted from the 1980s. Nonetheless, prior to the decision in *O'Kelly* at least, the distinction between an exchange of work for wages, and an exchange of ongoing service for remuneration and social protection, seemed to reflect a distinction between the *empirical reality* of employment for many manual workers, and the *normative consequences* of the rights and protections that the legal system (albeit selectively) conferred upon them by way of compensation. In this sense, the ongoing or relational aspect of employment was a function of the contract of employment that was implied in order to provide workers with a more stable income and regular employment. It was not, therefore, a condition for labour protections, a test for establishing employment status in the first place.

9.4 Conclusion

Prior to the 1980s, mutuality in the relational sense, today associated with the employee concept, was neither an express legal doctrine invoked by the courts, nor a condition for claiming labour rights. It reflected a distinct legal idea, an assumption embedded in the legal conception of service, that the working relationships *ought* to be structured in such a way as to give rise to particular mutual rights and obligations. The premise behind the concept was that employers ought not to be able to benefit from a worker's ongoing service unless they provided in exchange some form of social wage—that bundle of rights and entitlements provided, at

[77] *Market Investigations Ltd v Minister of Social Security* [1969] 2 QB 173, 187 (Cooke J).

various times, through the legal form of contract of service (or employment) and associated with 'labour' (and/or social security) law. In the medieval period this had been guaranteed through the servant's legal right to be maintained, a right that was mutual to the employer's right to exclusive service; in the nineteenth century it had been provided (imperfectly) through the employer's obligation to provide work in exchange for his rights to compel service under the master and servant legislation, and in the mid-twentieth century, through the worker's right to contractual remuneration and to the labour and social protections arising from the relational contract of employment.

The distinction between workers and employees cannot be fully understood today, therefore, without engaging with the historical idea of mutuality that has shaped how dependent labour and the contract of service has been conceived. Workers should be seen as a broad category that includes all those who provide labour power in exchange for some benefit, and who, as a matter of law, have a right to be paid a market wage. This is today (imperfectly) provided through a combination of in-work benefits, minimum wage entitlements, and statutory protections against deductions. The term 'employee', by contrast, refers to those workers whose working arrangements lend themselves to being structured, in law, through the legal form of the concept of employment—the legal mechanism through which a form of social wage has, historically, been guaranteed. In this sense, the concept of the 'employee' should be seen as a legal status that would, in many circumstances, be conferred on those who provide their labour for wages (including, then, those persons currently classified as 'workers') were an active constituting role for law to be embraced—even if the work arrangement in question was casual in nature.

It is in light of this observation that we can recognize the limits of the 'purposive' approach to employment status that has gained considerable support in recent years following the Supreme Court's decision in *Autoclenz*. In this case, the Supreme Court argued

> ... the relative bargaining power of the parties must be taken into account in deciding whether the terms of any written agreement in truth represent what was agreed and the true agreement will often have to be gleaned from all the circumstances of the case, of which the written agreement is only a part. This may be described as a purposive approach to the problem.[78]

On its face, this purposive approach would seem to mark a radical departure from contractual orthodoxy. In practice, however, it remains rooted in the same naturalistic ontology that has underpinned the case law since the 1980s. It proceeds,

[78] *Autoclenz v Belcher* (n 24) [35]. *Firthglow Ltd v Szilagyi* [2009] EWCA Civ 98; [2009] ICR 835 (Smith J); *Consistent Group v Kalwak* [2007] IRLR 560 (EAT) [57] (Elias J).

therefore, 'from first principles of contract law'[79] and involves, simply, an analysis of what the 'actual legal obligations are' by having regard to what the parties agreed.

The purposive approach stops far short, then, of recognizing an active constituting role for law, recognizing that there are certain inderogable mutual rights and obligations that are implied into labour relationships in light of labour law's broader function. It does not imply that public policy concerns might justify the courts in imposing working arrangements that differ from that which the parties seem to have 'intended' therefore, or indeed, from what are presumed to be their legal obligations 'in fact'.

The purposive approach will not help claimants such as *Quashie*, therefore, when arguing that they have a right to be paid wages (minimum or otherwise) (so as to establish a work contract) if the contract envisages a system of entirely tip-based pay when this is entirely consistent with what happens in practice. Nor will it assist claimants who seek to claim labour law rights when both parties agreed to a work arrangement in which there was no obligation on either party to offer and accept work if this is the basis on which the relationship proceeded. In effect, if the parties agree to a work arrangement that does not provide for a form of social wage, if such an arrangement is structured so as to fall outside the prevailing legal concept of a contract of work or employment, the legal system will not intervene so as to render that work arrangement socially and economically sustainable: public policy has no role to play.

The purposive approach rejects, then, a constitutive role for the law—a role for the legal system in shaping employment relations, and thus how capitalism develops. It does not attempt to narrow the gap between the social reality of work for those employed on a casual basis, and the normative ideal of stable and continuous employment, therefore; it simply attempts to align the terms of the written contract with how the parties conduct themselves in practice. Legal obligations are still assumed to flow from the parties' agreement, therefore, such that an inter-personal agreement between individual contracting parties remains the touchstone for determining questions of employment status. In effect, such an approach 'depoliticizes' the employment status question, leaving questions of status to 'the market'.

The courts' discussion of this purposive approach reveals a lot about prevailing understandings of the role of labour law in a capitalist economy, and, relatedly, of the relationship between legal concepts and 'social practices'. In this frame, labour law is not seen as a mechanism through which to structure working practices, to determine the conditions on which employers are permitted to have access to labour power; rather, it is seen as a means for supporting 'economic activities' that exist, to a great extent, 'independently' from law.

[79] *Autoclenz v Belcher* [2009] EWCA Civ 1046 (Aikens J) [87].

Rather than seeing the contract of employment as a description of a social reality that may or may not be agreed by the parties, what is required today is that we take seriously law's role in constituting socio-economic relations, taking the contract of employment as a prescriptive device that the legal system imputes to dependent labour relationships with a view to shaping them. And, where such an approach is precluded—by the nature of the work, or industry concerned—policy-makers can, and arguably must intervene. In this way, it might once again be possible to embrace the role that labour law can, and arguably must, play in ensuring that the labour market operates in a fair and sustainable way, guaranteeing all workers the sort of social wage that is implicit in the historical concept of mutuality of obligation.

10
Labour Law: Limits and Potential

10.1 Introduction

This book began with the observation that low pay and under-inclusive employment status are widely recognized as being some of the most pressing problems facing workers today. It noted, however, that labour law is generally assumed to have failed to adequately address these problems. Prevailing explanations for why this might be so were, however, shown to be inadequate; they attributed such problems to non-legal 'exogenous' factors, and/or simply assumed that labour law had the capacity to 'address' them.

The Marxian inspired ontology advanced in this book provides an alternative approach that sheds new light on these questions. By emphasizing the importance of engaging with questions of ontology and form, this new approach forces us to engage with the way in which the form of law, and its relationship with capitalism, influences the purposes to which law can (successfully) be put; the 'values' and 'purposes' that tend to be attributed to it (and thus the 'philosophical theories' invoked to 'ground' it); as well as legal theory and practice. At the same time, it helps us better understand the constitutive role of law, the functions it performs in capitalism, and the complex ways in which it contributes to, and constitutes, many of the 'problems' it is often called upon to address. In this way, it facilitates a fresh perspective on labour law's 'crisis', the 'problems' of low pay and unclear employment status, as well as on the broader question of labour law's emancipatory potential.

One of the benefits of this new approach is that, by exploring the distinctive properties of law, and labour law, and situating them in a broader theory of the nature (and historical specificity) of the capitalist system, it allows us to explore the *structural* factors explaining contemporary social problems, and labour law's apparent 'failure' to deal with them, while, at the same time, helping to distinguish the various contingent, or historical factors influencing the nature and prevalence of such problems today. This makes it possible to reveal the limits and potential of law when it comes to bringing about changes in society, while suggesting certain mechanisms through which it might be possible to do so.

Of course, like this book, critical labour law scholarship in the United Kingdom has long emphasized the importance of situating labour law in the context of capitalism. However, it has done so largely at the expense of privileging questions of content (the substance of labour market policies) over those of form. As a result, it has tended to focus almost exclusively on the various conflicts and power struggles

Labour and the Wage. Zoe Adams, Oxford University Press (2020). © Zoe Adams.
DOI: 10.1093/oso/9780198858898.001.0001

that shape labour market policy, directing its critique (primarily) towards the 'illegitimate domination, inequality, and democratic deficits in social life', rather than the structures and contradictions that frame and condition them.[1] In this book, by contrast, rather than developing a critique of 'the substance of laws and legal systems which placed workers in a situation of vulnerability and subordination relative to their employers',[2] taking as its starting point certain shared (and thus contestable) values (some theory of social justice), the focus has been on understanding the contradictions inherent in the dynamics of capitalism's development, and the normative expectations and ideals, that it and law presupposes. This did not mean ignoring questions of content, nor the real, lived, social struggles that shape (and have historically shaped) campaigns for reform; but it did mean situating these struggles within a broader theory of the objective contradictions that underpin them—recognizing that it is only by understanding these contradictions and crisis tendencies that we can discover the seeds, or potential for change.[3]

In taking such an approach, the book contributes to a wider strand of Marxist legal scholarship that has attempted, particularly although not exclusively in the context of international law, to refocus legal critique on questions of legal form, without losing sight of questions of content, so as to shed light on the limits and potential of law as a mode of regulation[4] This book is unique, however, in applying these insights to labour law, and to the social category of the wage in particular, and in the emphasis it places on the significance of the legal system's internal ontology to the effects of law on the ground. That is, the book explored how the ontological assumptions implicit in legal discourse, a product, in part of the (socially conditioned) beliefs of legislators and judges, influences legal practice. It also explored how those assumptions come to be embedded in particular legal concepts so as to influence capitalism's development, and how those assumptions are themselves framed or influenced by particular socio-economic conditions. One of the book's key insights, then, was that, how the legal system conceptualizes the employment relationship and its central features, and how it understands its own role in relation to society, are important factors that cannot be excluded when it comes to

[1] Karl Klare, 'On Ruth Dukes, *The Labour Constitution: The Enduring Idea of Labour Law*' [2018] Jurisprudence 1, 5.

[2] Ruth Dukes, 'Critical Labour Law: Then and Now' in Emilios Christodoulidis, Ruth Dukes, and Marco Goldoni (eds), *Research Handbook on Critical Legal Theory* (Edward Elgar 2019) 2.

[3] Nancy Fraser and Rahel Jaeggi, *Capitalism: A Conversation in Critical Theory* (John Wiley & Sons 2018).

[4] China Miéville, 'The Commodity-Form Theory of International Law' in Susan Marks (ed), *International Law on the Left* (CUP 2008); China Miéville, *Between Equal Rights a Marxist Theory of International Law* (Aakar Books 2016); Susan Marks, 'International Judicial Activism and the Commodity-Form Theory of International Law' (2007) 18 European Journal of International Law 199; Robert Knox, 'Marxism, International Law, and Political Strategy' (2009) 22 Leiden Journal of International Law 413; Paul O'Connell, 'Law, Marxism and Method' [2018] Forthcoming in triple C: Communication, Capitalism and Critique (2018); Grietje Baars, *The Corporation, Law and Capitalism: A Radical Perspective on the Role of Law in the Global Political Economy* (Brill 2019).

explaining labour law's 'crisis'—its failure to 'address' the problems of low pay and under-inclusive employment status—today.

10.2 Law, Labour Law, and the Contradictory Functions of the Wage

The importance of the legal system's 'internal ontology' was demonstrated in Part II through the genealogy of the category of the wage. During the medieval and early modern periods, the courts developed their ideas of wage labour by reference to a particular form of property relationship characterized by what has been referred to in this book as 'tenure'. The defining characteristic of such relationships was that one party sought to exercise exclusive control over a valuable social resource in which the owner and the community retained an interest. By imputing to such relationships a contract of service, the courts made it possible to constitute those relationships in a form in which certain obligations of fair use and protection could be guaranteed. The result was that, by the end of the seventeenth century, it was largely taken for granted that the servant's right to subsistence, implied in, but payable independently from, the wage, was an implied condition for the employer's (exclusive) rights in labour.

This analysis revealed how feudal ideas of property rights and service obligations shaped the way that the labour relationship came to be conceived in the particular context of the United Kingdom. Even so, the prevalence of these ideas in legal discourse and judicial reasoning has shifted as capitalism has developed. During the eighteenth and nineteenth centuries, therefore, the idea of tenure as the foundation of a social wage was eroded. In its place, there emerged the idea of a wage as a payment made to a worker for an alienable commodity. In this context, what the worker needed to subsist (ie the 'socially necessary wage') came to be equated with the wage that the market itself set, and it was this premise that came to be embedded in early minimum wage legislation.

Even so, throughout the course of the twentieth century, the courts rediscovered, albeit implicitly, the constitutive role that law had played prior to the emergence of the modern labour market, and these ideas began to shape how minimum wage legislation developed during, and following, the Second World War. This shift can be seen, for example, in the concept of remuneration and the role it played in minimum 'wage' legislation: the premise that in exchange for ongoing service, the employer ought to pay a sum capable of adequately maintaining his worker, and in the ideal of mutuality of obligation as something to which the contract of employment should aspire. These ideas can even be seen in 'casual' industries such as dock work, where they implicitly underpinned programmes for 'decasualization' and a 'guaranteed' weekly income.

Since the 1980s, this framework and the legal system's conception of its relationship with social practices, has begun to break down. This is evident from the passive or reactive role that the courts take both to questions of status, and when determining the nature and scope of the worker's right to be paid. Its practical effects can be seen in the erosion of the distinction between 'wages', 'salaries', and 'remuneration'; the confusion that exists in relation to the scope of the worker's right to be paid; the structure of the National Minimum Wage Act and Regulations; prevailing attitudes towards the benefits (and inevitability) of 'casual work;' and the confusion that has arisen in relation to the role that mutuality of obligation plays in relation to questions of employment status.

Despite this process of 'disintegration,' many of the ideas embedded in these concepts, such as the notion of the social wage, remain deeply entrenched in the structures of the contract of employment; even if they are rarely acknowledged today. One of the benefits of the genealogical approach, therefore, was that it helped to reveal the potential of legal concepts such as 'remuneration,' and 'mutuality of obligation', shedding light on how they might be reconstructed and re-used today in a way that might better realize the ideals they express.

10.3 Law's Constitutive Role

Engaging with capitalism's contradictions and the (contradictory) role of law, and labour law, in mediating them, allowed for a detailed analysis of law's 'constitutive' role—that is, law's contribution to the emergence and reproduction of capitalist social relations. By exploring the mechanisms through which law 'constitutes' capitalist social relations, the analysis went far beyond abstract and vague claims that law is constitutive of social relations and relatively autonomous 'from' society, to explain in clear and precise terms what a constitutive account of law entails—and the significance of this observation for legal theory and practice.[5]

First, to say that law is constitutive of capitalism is to make an argument about the historical specificity of 'law' as a particular form of social regulation that is specific to societies based on private ownership of the means of production; capital accumulation; wage labour, and generalized commodity exchange. Law, on this view, is a historical category or form that is unique to capitalism. Its features must thus be grasped as emerging from, and being integrally related to, the practices and relations specific to capitalist societies.

[5] It thus avoids the trap identified by Christopher Tomlins, namely, a tendency to speak about law's autonomy *in* relation to society, without engaging with the ways law can be said to be *part of* or constitutive of it: Christopher Tomlins, 'How Autonomous Is Law?' (2007) 3 Annual Review of Law and Social Science 45.

Second, to refer to law as *constitutive* is to make a broader point about the relationship 'between' the law and 'the market'. Capitalistic markets, are, like law, conceived as historically specific and so are not to be confused with mere exchange. Markets are spheres of interaction in which spontaneously (through the mechanism of competition) generated 'prices' serve to coordinate decision making, and in which transactions are mediated by money as a 'universal' equivalent. They are, moreover, mechanisms through which both society's surplus and its productive inputs, *including labour power*, are allocated. The relevance of law's 'constitutive' role is that it emphasizes that the relationship between law and markets is one of mutual implication—they imply each other, in that they are *mutually constitutive*, historically specific, elements of the capitalist system conceived as a whole.

The law does not 'respond' to the existence of markets therefore, 'intervening' to ensure their efficient functioning. Rather, law is both presupposed by, and a precondition for, the practices through which capitalistic markets emerge and are reproduced. This includes not only particular institutions (such as property and contract) but also a particular discourse, and certain fundamental (legal) concepts, in which certain historically specific assumptions, intrinsic to market practices, are embedded, and systematically reproduced.

To refer to law as constitutive is also, then, to make a more general point: to suggest that law does more than merely 'regulate' or 'facilitate' behaviour, influencing outcomes by altering individuals' incentives. Law makes an irreducible difference to the course of events, shaping socio-economic outcomes in ways that cannot be reduced to the conscious decisions of individual agents. Law is implicit in the very practices it regulates, and, as such, is also implicit in the attempts by social and legal actors to influence or change it. Because individuals are always acting from a particular position and in a particular context, no outcome can be seen as the product of 'individual' choice alone—so-called structures, and agency, will always be playing a role—and, by definition, so too will the norms, values, and assumptions implicit in the legal framework through which features of the world are conceived, in the legal concepts through which they find legal expression.

These dimensions of law's 'constitutive role' help us to better understand how an analysis of capitalism's contradictions contributes to our understanding of law. Capitalism, it has been shown, presupposes the performance of certain functions, and these functions can only be performed by law and legal discourse. Because capitalist social relations are grounded in deep-seated contradictions, however, and because these contradictions manifest in the form of law itself, these functions can never be performed 'perfectly' or 'completely'.

There are things that the law *must* do in a capitalist society, and which it will nonetheless constantly struggle to achieve in practice. Hence, capitalism is inherently prone to crisis—not only of accumulation and/or social reproduction, but also, potentially, of legitimacy—and the same is true of labour law. These crisis tendencies express the limits inherent in what can be achieved in a capitalist society, and thus in what law, and labour law, can achieve within the existing structures—the 'purposes' to which it can be put. This observation has to be taken seriously when it comes to thinking about paths to reform.

Once the constitutive role of law is recognized and understood, and thus its need to shape social relations, it becomes clear that there can be no single 'natural' approach to questions of employment status or to contract construction; that the parties 'agreement' need not be seen as the touchstone when it comes to determining their legal rights and obligations. But what the genealogical analysis has shown is that this proposition is not only true in the analytical or ontological sense—in terms of what capitalism 'presupposes' about law and labour law—but also in the *historical* sense—when it comes to how questions of employment status have been approached in the past, and thus the legal 'resources' available to us today. Contrary to the assumptions implicit in the purposive approach,[6] labour law was never something that 'intervened' or 'qualified' a natural freedom of contract; rather, it was a body of rules and principles developed from feudal ideas of tenure and mutuality that set the boundaries in which freedom of contract would be allowed to operate with respect to a valuable, communal, resource.

When viewed in this light, it is not 'illegitimate' (in terms of the criteria for legitimacy historically developed in the United Kingdom) for the courts to determine the conditions on which an employer will be allowed access to labour; rather, it is essential to its historic role as protector of public, and private, property. True, English law may not have a concept of public order to parallel that which exists in civil legal systems, and labour law may take effect today to a great extent *through* the contract of employment, but property law principles have evolved in order to perform a similar function. They can, therefore, be invoked today as a perfectly 'legitimate' (in the historically specific sense) way of furthering labour law's socio-economic function. To see contract as an emblem of freedom and property of oppression, as legal scholars and courts tend to do, is ahistorical, and, arguably, misplaced; the two can, and have, worked in tandem so as to make protection of dependent workers compatible with a cognitive framework in which 'freedom of contract' is, and arguably must be, assumed to be guaranteed.

By helping us to view labour through an alternative lens, through the lens of property law principles and feudal ideas of tenure, the historical analysis actually makes it easier to justify, in terms more amenable to policy-makers and judges, and *without* recourse to abstract moral theory, why courts *should* do more than merely 'uphold' and 'respect' the parties' agreement. By emphasizing the qualified nature of the property acquired by the wage, the concurrence of the employer's,

[6] See also the argument that: 'The normative justification for labour law must therefore reach beyond the justifications for private law rules, and discover more compelling arguments and justifications for partly overriding those private law rules with different, often mandatory, regulations': Harry Arthurs, 'Introduction: Does Labour Law Need Philosophical Foundations?' in Hugh Collins, Gillian Lester, and Virginia Mantouvalou (eds), *Philosophical Foundations of Labour Law* (OUP 2018).

the worker's, and the community's interests in labour, these ideas provide an alternative justification for conditioning the employer's rights to use a worker's labour on his obligation to provide for his maintenance and protection—*even if* the effect of doing so is to squeeze (what are ultimately inefficient) firms out of the market. Principles of contract law, based on individualistic considerations about the interests of particular contracting parties rather than broader systemic considerations, are insufficient to adequately protect the complex, and conflicting, interests at stake. But the property law ideas, already buried within the structure of the contract of employment, are much more suited to this purpose—and can, potentially, be revived today in a way that is better suited to a changing socio-economic environment. In this way, a more 'active' or 'protective' stance might be adopted by the courts in a way that is entirely consistent with the historic role played by the common law in relation to property and contract—one which can, therefore, help redefine how questions of legitimacy are conceived—and in a way that draws on values, and assumptions, already embedded in the law.

10.4 Practical Implications: Low Pay, Labour Market Casualization, and Employment Status

Engaging with the constitutive role of law and the contradictory nature of capitalist social relations can help us question approaches to labour law that seem natural and inevitable, and thus think more creatively when it comes to questions of reform. In this respect, the historical analysis reveals (at least) three potential avenues down which labour law policy might proceed:

10.4.1 Minimum *Remuneration* Legislation

The historical analysis has shown that there are a number of possible models of wage regulation; that there are more options available to us than simply tinkering with the rate at which the wage is paid when it comes to addressing the problem of low, and irregular, pay. The analysis of the Wages Councils Act and the National Minimum Wage Act showed, for example, that the conceptual structure of a piece of labour legislation is extremely important for setting the limits of what a given body of legislation can achieve. The premise that the wage should be paid for 'work', and that this expresses the limits of the worker's rights to be paid, is not, this book has shown, as self-evident as is often supposed. Rather, there exists a practical alternative to today's framework, based as it is on a link between work and wages, which would be better capable of providing protection against low and precarious pay, a model based on the principle of a minimum *remuneration* for employment—and thus the possibility for a legally guaranteed right to be paid that might be tied to employment, rather than to a given quantum of labour—a guaranteed daily, weekly, or monthly 'wage'.

10.4.2 Decasualization

Contemporary discussions concerning the minimum wage entitlements of 'gig-workers' takes it as given that an individual's 'free' acceptance of a casual work arrangement means that they ought to take 'some responsibility' for this decision—not expecting to be paid for time spent on-call.[7] For the courts, the practical difficulties of guaranteeing a minimum wage for on-call time is a further justification for restricting these rights—not only might it discourage socially desirable forms of work arrangement, but it would also create considerable hardship for employers of workers who could, conceivably, be 'working' for more than one employer during the same period.[8]

The example of the dock industry shows, however, that these 'obstacles' are not insurmountable. Rather, during the mid-twentieth century, a policy of decasualization was deliberately adopted, notwithstanding that prevailing labour law techniques had proven insufficient for this purpose. Thus, through a combination of registration, centralized wage payment, and a levy on employers' wages bills, the payment by employers (collectively) of a social wage was made a condition for their access to a pool of casuals. In effect, therefore, the legal system determined the conditions on which casual work practices could be adopted; the market did not *dictate* which work arrangements *had* to be permitted, nor the terms on which they were to be conducted.

This could not have been possible, however, had policy-makers not had a particular view of the nature of capitalism, and the role of law and the state within it. Policy-makers rejected the premise that what was 'good' or 'preferable' for individual firms and/or workers, was what was best for society at large. For this reason, how working relationships were to be structured could not be based on 'decisions' and 'preferences' revealed in the market; rather, this was seen to be a fundamentally political question, to which questions of sustainability, stability, and fairness were intrinsic.

Policy-makers and courts did not, during this period, conflate the analytical question of which individuals were in fact wage dependent, and thus in need of the protections that were beginning to be provided through labour law, with the practical question of how those protections were to be guaranteed in practice. Thus,

[7] Matthew Taylor, 'Good Work; The Taylor Review of Modern Working Practices' (Gov.uk 2017) <https://www.gov.uk/government/uploads/system/uploads/attachment_data/file/627671/good-work-taylor-review-modern-working-practices-rg.pdf> accessed 31 August 2017.

[8] *Aslam v Uber BV* [2018] EWCA Civ 2748; [2019] IRLR 257 [162].

once the *need* for a guaranteed weekly income was recognized, the task was simply to explore how this might best be achieved in different industries (eg catering) and/or in relation to different types of work arrangements (eg casual or seasonal employment).

At this time, wages were not seen as the mere price of labour either, as something determined, ultimately, by the market. Rather, they were seen to be something to which workers were absolutely entitled; a precondition for employers being allowed access to labour power, and thus to compete. This 'wage' was not, moreover, something that the market could, or should be allowed to set; rather, it was something that had to be based on considerations of need. Collective bargaining, and living costs, were thus deemed to be essential when it came to establishing the appropriate rate—a rate that was to be payable, moreover, regardless of how much work was, in fact, performed.

Central to the decasualziation programmes of the mid-twentieth century was a particular *ideal* of employment embodied in the concepts of 'mutuality of obligation' and 'remuneration'. Of course, these concepts were not expressly invoked in discussions about dock decasualization, but the ideas they expressed, ideas embedded in other aspects of the legal framework, played a significant role in guiding the approaches of policy-makers and, in other contexts, the courts. The premise that employment in capitalism ought to involve certain mutual rights and obligations—that in exchange for their labour, workers ought to be paid a guaranteed weekly income—was, in other words, an assumption deeply embedded in the law.

10.4.3 Employment Status

One of the challenges facing labour law today is how to prevent workers *in need* of a socially necessary wage (workers *in fact)* from being excluded from the scope of labour law *in practice*, as a result of the nature of the industry in which they are engaged, and/or the form of their contract. While the purposive approach prevents formal contractual wording from defeating a claim to employment status, it does not, at present, prevent a firm from structuring a work arrangement in such a way that it falls outside prevailing legal criteria for employment. In the words of Underhill J, *Autoclenz* [and the purposive approach it adopted]

> gives no warrant for disregarding the terms of the Agreement. Autoclenz is an important tool in tribunals' armoury because it enables them to look to the reality of a relationship rather than a false characterisation imposed by the employer. But the premise is that the characterisation is indeed false. As I have said, *Autoclenz does not permit the re-writing of agreements only because they are*

disadvantageous. Protecting against abuses of inequality of bargaining power is the role of legislation[9]

While the courts assume that it is for Parliament to intervene to bring excluded groups within the scope of labour law, the Taylor review indicates a decisive reluctance on behalf of the government to adopt such an approach. Instead, it is simply assumed that, provided the legal criteria are known by the parties, those parties should be free to 'decide' how to structure their arrangement, and thus whether or not to 'opt in' to labour law's scope.

This problem, the tendency for certain groups of workers to fall outside labour law's personal scope as a result the nature of their work, and/or the industry in which they work, is not new. However, in the past, Parliament proved much more willing to legislate so as to protect specific groups or industries, and/or to develop industry-specific regimes to achieve outcomes that, in other contexts, would be realized through labour law and the contract of employment. In this respect, two examples from the previous chapters are particularly instructive: first, the taxi industry, and second, catering.

In the early twentieth century, because taxi-drivers failed to satisfy the common law criteria for a contract of service, Parliament expressly intervened so as to ensure that persons who were deemed to be 'workers' (or 'workmen') by reason of their socio-economic status, who worked long hours for little pay, and in a regulatory environment that constrained their capacity to bear economic risk, would enjoy the labour law protections that such a status was deemed to imply—notwithstanding that the 'employers' had little control over how and when they worked.

Similarly, in the 1940s, casual workers in the catering industry, deemed to be in need of legally guaranteed minimum wages, were expressly catered for through the creation of a distinct, industry-specific wage-regulation regime, tailored to the particular challenges associated with the industry in question—namely, the casual nature of the work and the prevalent practice of tipping.

In neither context, then, was failure to satisfy the common law criteria for a contract of employment/service the final word in assessing whether certain groups should be within the scope of labour law. Nor was there deemed to be one single 'solution' when it came to guaranteeing different workers the substance of the protections provided, for most, through labour law and the contract of employment.

The scope for such an approach to be adopted today, while precluded by prevailing conceptions of labour law's role in capitalist society, is already explicitly provided for in legislation. Section 23(2) of the Employment Relations Act 1999 makes express provision for the Secretary of State to extend the scope of existing labour legislation to any individuals not currently within its personal scope. At

9 ibid [147].

the time of writing, however, such a provision is yet to be used. That is not to say that this power would be a panacea. A statutory presumption in favour of employment status would be a further important move—and even this would be meaningful only if accompanied (among other things) by the above mentioned reforms to the minimum wage framework, and, potentially, more active support for collective bargaining. Even so, invoking such a power would, however, represent an important step, one that is far from being unprecedented, and which has, in fact, been used in some of the very industries in which much litigation concerning employment status is taking place today.[10]

10.5 Conclusion: Labour Law and Social Change

What, then, is the implication of the analysis in preceding chapters for the limits and potential for labour law to bring about social change, and, relatedly, for the role of legal and social actors when it comes to realizing that potential today?

In order to answer these questions, it is necessary to distinguish between two levels of analysis. First, at a structural or systemic level, the analysis in this book implies that there are objective limits on how far labour law can challenge, directly, the inequality and exploitation inherent in capitalist social relations, and thus capitalism's deep structures. This is because this particular form of inequality and exploitation is presupposed by, and systematically reinforced by, the legal concepts through which labour laws must be expressed if they are to be perceived as legitimate (in the context of capitalism). Even so, in order to uphold its, and the legal system's, legitimacy, labour law must operate through those concepts with a view to placing limits on how far that inequality and exploitation can extend. This contradiction, labour law's tendency to presuppose and reproduce, but simultaneously limit inequality and exploitation, is such that there actually exists considerable scope for variation in the precise content of labour market policies, and thus what outcomes capitalism actually produces in practice.

At the second level, then, it is ultimately a *historical* question as to how these structural contradictions manifest in practice, and thus the conditions in which individuals actually live and work at a particular time. This historical question is framed, or influenced, moreover, by the concrete political struggles and conflicts through which capitalism's contradictions are substantively played out and through which the *content* of labour market policies must, inevitably, be forged.

The precise balance between labour's exploitation and its limits is not, then, pre-given in the form or structure of capitalist society, nor by anything inherent in the form of law. The balance between use and exchange value, between the

[10] Andrew James, 'Extending Rights for Workers' (The Institute of Employment Rights 2015) <https://www.ier.org.uk/blog/extending-rights-workers> accessed 31 May 2019.

conflicting but inter-dependent 'demands' of capital accumulation and those of social reproduction, have been struck differently in different times and places—and it is through labour law and the social form of the contract of employment that this balance has, historically, been fought out. Expansions and contractions in labour law's personal scope, and the deregulation and reregulation of labour markets and working relations, in this sense reflect shifts in the balance of power in society—and the ever-changing scope that exists for social and legal actors to shape how that society develops. While there are limits to how far labour law can transcend the inequality and exploitation presupposed by capitalism, and this has to be taken seriously when it comes to thinking about paths to reform, that is not to say that the values embedded in the legal system's constitutive concepts cannot be exploited by human agents to shape how those relations develop. To ignore the ontological basis of those concepts and thus to apply concepts without an appreciation of how they relate to the structure of capitalist society, is, however, liable to produce unintended effects—hence the importance of engaging directly with questions of ontology.

Recognizing the constitutive role of law, and labour law, their role in reproducing capitalist social relations, does not mean, therefore, resigning ourselves to accept as pre-given, a particular institutional framework or set of socio-economic outcomes. Rather, it actually opens our eyes to the scope that exists for shaping capitalist social relations, for changing the way in which the capitalist system is lived, and experienced, in practice.

For this to be possible, however, legal and social actors must thus take seriously the causes of the ideologies driving labour market policies today, rather than simply dismissing them and offering alternatives. The market only appears as a natural order, and individuals as naturally equal and free, in particular socio-historical conditions, and the role of law and legal discourse in upholding this image must not be overlooked. Nor, however, should it be uncritically accepted. Defending labour law policies in the name of 'universal' values of human dignity, freedom, and equality, without exploring why these values appear so important to us, and in what conditions, overlooks the role these values themselves play in the reproduction of the relations through which substantive inequalities are systematically reproduced.

Rather than seeing legal concepts as social tools that can provide direct solutions to social demands, or empty shells which it is for policy-makers to fill with content, therefore, legal scholars, policy-makers, and the courts must thus engage with the nature of the legal system's internal evolutionary dynamics and its relationship with the structural features of the capitalist system. This means taking seriously the values embedded in its higher-level concepts, recognizing the scope that exists not only for path dependence and lock-in to constrain the path of the law, but also the inherent potential of such concepts when it comes to thinking about how to bring about social change.

Taking seriously the role of labour law in the reproduction of capitalist social relations, and relatedly, in making those relations socially and economically viable, as the ontological approach allows us to do, can thus open our eyes to the different sorts of outcomes to which we *can* aspire, and which are possible within capitalism—notwithstanding the limitations and tendencies inherent in the legal form. And, because labour law really does have the capacity to bring about meaningful changes in the material conditions of life and work, to alter the balance of power between capital and labour, it may well be that it can act as a catalyst for more far-reaching structural change. For this to be possible, however, labour lawyers must take seriously, and engage reflexively, with the contradictory role of labour law in a capitalist society, and thus the assumptions embedded in the concepts through which labour law policies take effect.

Bibliography

Adams Z, 'Understanding the Minimum Wage: Political Economy and Legal Form' (2019) 78(1) Cambridge Law Journal 42–69

—— '"Wage", "Salary" and "Remuneration": A Genealogical Exploration of Juridical Terms and Their Significance for the Employer's Power to Make Deductions from Wages' (2019) 48 Industrial Law Journal 34–65 <https://doi: 10.1093/indlaw/dwy003> accessed 22 September 2018

Albin E, 'Labour Law in a Service World' (2010) 73(6) Modern Law Review 959–84

—— 'A Worker–Employer–Customer Triangle: The Case of Tips' (2011) 40(2) Industrial Law Journal 181–206

Archer MS, *Realist Social Theory: The Morphogenetic Approach* (CUP 1995)

—— *Culture and Agency: The Place of Culture in Social Theory* (CUP 1996)

—— *Structure, Agency and the Internal Conversation* (CUP 2003)

Arthur CJ, 'Value, Labour and Negativity' (2001) 25 Capital & Class 15

—— 'On Robert Albritton's Dialectics and Deconstruction in Political Economy' (2002) 10 Historical Materialism 251

—— *The New Dialectic and Marx's Capital*. Historical Materialism Book Series 1 (Brill 2004)

Arthurs H, 'Can Davidov's Legal Slingshot Slay the Goliath of Political Economy? On Guy Davidov's A Purposive Approach to Labour Law' (2017) 16(1) Jerusalem Review of Legal Studies 1–14

Azar OH, 'The History of Tipping—from Sixteenth-Century England to United States in the 1910s' (2004) 33(6) Journal of Socio-Economics 745–64

Baars G, *The Corporation, Law and Capitalism: A Radical Perspective on the Role of Law in the Global Political Economy* (Brill 2019) <http://brill.com/view/title/31854> accessed 24 August 2019

Bailey D, *The Truck System: A Book for Masters and Workmen* (Bath: Pitman 1859)

Bales K and Mayblin L, 'Unfree Labour in Immigration Detention: Exploitation and Coercion of a Captive Immigrant Workforce' (2018) 47 Economy and Society 191

Bales K, Bogg A, and Novitz T, '"Voice" and "Choice" in Modern Working Practices: Problems With the Taylor Review' (2018) 47(1) Industrial Law Journal 46–75

Berg M, *Markets and Manufacture in Early Industrial Europe (Routledge Revivals)* (Routledge 2014)

Beveridge WH, *Full Employment in a Free Society* (Allen & Unwin 1944)

Bhaskar R, *Reclaiming Reality* (Verso 1989)

—— *Dialectic: The Pulse of Freedom* (Routledge 2008)

—— *Scientific Realism and Human Emancipation* (Routledge 2009)

—— *A Realist Theory of Science* (Routledge 2013)

—— *The Possibility of Naturalism: A Philosophical Critique of the Contemporary Human Sciences* (Routledge 2014)

Biernacki R, *The Fabrication of Labor: Germany and Britain, 1640-1914* (rev edn, University of California Press 1997)

Blackburn S, 'The Problem of Riches: From Trade Boards to a National Minimum Wage' (1988) 19(2) Industrial Relations Journal 124–38

—— *A Fair Day's Wage for a Fair Day's Work?: Sweated Labour and the Origins of Minimum Wage Legislation in Britain* (Ashgate Publishing Ltd 2007)
Bogg A, 'Labour, Love and Futility: Philosophical Perspectives on Labour Law' (2017) 33 International Journal of Comparative Labour Law and Industrial Relations 7
von Böhm-Bawerk E, *Karl Marx and the Close of His System* (Ludwig von Mises Institute 1949)
Booth C, *Labour and Life of the People*, vol 1 (Williams and Norgate 1891)
Brenner R, 'The Agrarian Roots of European Capitalism' (1982) 97 Past & Present, 16–113
Brown A, 'Reorienting Critical Realism: A System-wide Perspective on the Capitalist Economy' (2007) 14(4) Journal of Economic Methodology 499–519
Brown A, Slater G, and Spencer DA, 'Driven to Abstraction? Critical Realism and the Search for the "Inner Connection" of Social Phenomena' (2002) 26(6) Cambridge Journal of Economics 773–88
Brown KD, *English Labour Movement, 1700-1951* (Gill and Macmillan 1982)
Burn R, *W. Strahan & W. Woodfall* (15th edn, W. Strahan & W. Woodfall 1785)
Bythell D, *The Sweated Trades: Outwork in Nineteenth-Century Britain* (St Martin's Press 1978)
Campbell BMS, 'Factor Markets in England before the Black Death' (2009) 24(1) Continuity and Change 79
Christodoulidis E, 'Labour Constitutionalism in a Genealogical Key' (2018) 9 Jurisprudence 1–5
Christodoulidis E and Dukes R, 'Dialogue & Debate: Labour, Constitution and a Sense of Measure: A Debate with Alain Supiot' (2010) Social & Legal Studies 19(2) 217–52
Clark A, *The Working Life of Women in the Seventeenth Century* (Routledge 2013)
Clark E, 'Medieval Labor Law and English Local Courts' (1983) 27(4) American Journal of Legal History 330–53
Clark JM, *Studies in the Economics of Overhead Costs* (University of Chicago Press 1947)
Collins H, *Marxism and Law* (OUP 1982)
Collins H, Lester G, and Mantouvalou V (eds), *Philosophical Foundations of Labour Law*. Philosophical Foundations of Law (OUP 2018)
Dalton M, *The Country Justice: Containing the Practice of the Justices of the Peace Out of Their Sessions, Gathered for the Better Help of Such Justices of Peace as Have Not Been Much Conversant in the Study of the Laws of This Realm* (W. Rawlins and S. Roycroft 1655)
Daunton M, *Progress and Poverty: An Economic and Social History of Britain 1700-1850* (1st edn, OUP 1995)
—— *Wealth and Welfare: An Economic and Social History of Britain 1851-1951* (OUP 2007)
Davidov G, 'A Purposive Interpretation of the National Minimum Wage Act' (2009) 72(4) Modern Law Review 581–606
—— *A Purposive Approach to Labour Law* (OUP 2016)
—— 'Putting the Purpose of Labor Law to Work: A Response to Comments' (2017) 16(1) Jerusalem Review of Legal Studies 68–82
—— 'The Status of Uber Drivers: A Purposive Approach' (2017) 6(1–2) Spanish Labour Law and Employment Relations Journal 6
Davis J, *Medieval Market Morality: Life, Law and Ethics in the English Marketplace, 1200–1500* (CUP 2011)
Deakin S, 'Evolution for Our Time: A Theory of Legal Memetics' (2002) 55(1) Current Legal Problems 1
—— 'The Contribution of Labour Law to Economic and Human Development' in Langille B and Davidov G (eds), *The Idea of Labour Law* (OUP 2011) 156–75

—— 'Conceptions of the Market in Labour Law' in Numhauser-Henning A and Rönnmar M (eds), *Normative Patterns and Legal Developments in the Social Dimension of the EU* (Bloomsbury Publishing 2014)
—— 'Juridical Ontology: The Evolution of Legal Form' (2015) Historical Social Research/Historische Sozialforschung 170–84
—— 'Labor Law: The Pragmatist's Guide—Comments on A Purposive Approach to Labour Law' (2017) 16(1) Jerusalem Review of Legal Studies 28–39
—— 'Tony Lawson's Theory of the Corporation: Towards a Social Ontology of Law' (2017) 41(5) Cambridge Journal of Economics 1505–23
Deakin S, Gindis, D, Hodgson GM, Huang K, and Pistor K, 'Legal Institutionalism: Capitalism and the Constitutive Role of Law' (2017) 45(1) Journal of Comparative Economics, Institutions and Economic Change 188–200
Deakin S and Green F, 'One Hundred Years of British Minimum Wage Legislation' (2009) 47(2) British Journal of Industrial Relations 205–13
Deakin S and Wilkinson F, *Labour Law and Economic Theory: A Reappraisal* (ESRC Centre for Business Research 1998)
Denning AT, 'Wages During Sickness' (1939) 54 Law Quarterly Review 353
Dobb M, *Wages* (Nisbet & Co Ltd 1933)
—— *Theories of Value and Distribution since Adam Smith: Ideology and Economic Theory* (CUP 1975)
Drake B, 'The Waiter', in S Webb and AJ Freeman, *Seasonal Trades* (Constable & Company Limited 1912)
Edelman LB, 'Rivers of Law and Contested Terrain: A Law and Society Approach to Economic Rationality' (2004) 38(2) Society Review 181–98
Edelman LB and Stryker R, '23. A Sociological Approach to Law and the Economy' in Smelser NJ and Swedberg R (eds), *The Handbook of Economic Sociology, Second Edition* (Princeton University Press 2010)
Ehrbar H and Glick M, 'The Labor Theory of Value and Its Critics' [1986] Science & Society 464
Elder-Vass, D, *The Causal Powers of Social Structures* (CUP 2010)
—— *The Reality of Social Construction* (CUP 2012)
—— 'Towards a Realist Social Constructionism' (2012) 70 Sociologia, Problemas e Práticas 5–24
Elias, P, 'Changes and Challenges to the Contract of Employment' (2018) 38 Oxford Journal of Legal Studies 869
Elliott J, 'Tip off: Waiters Still Paid Minimum Wage out of Your Service Charge' *The Guardian* (7 June 2009) <https://www.theguardian.com/money/2009/jun/07/waiters-tips-restaurants-minimum-wage> accessed 6 February 2017
Fifoot CHS, *History and Sources of the Common Law: Tort and Contract* (Greenwood Pub Group 1949)
Finkin MW, '"The Kindness of Strangers": The Tip and the Minimum Wage in France, Germany, and the United States' (2016) 32(1) International Journal of Comparative Labour Law and Industrial Relations 3–31
Fletcher R, 'Legal Forms and Reproductive Norms' (2003) Social & Legal Studies 12(2) 217–41
Foley DK, 'Rethinking Financial Capitalism and the "Information" Economy' (2013) 45 Review of Radical Political Economics 257
Fredman S, 'Deregulating Pay: The Wages Act 1986' [1986] Public Law 551–61
Freedland MR, *The Contract of Employment* (Clarendon Press 1976)

—— *The Personal Employment Contract*. Oxford: OUP, 2005

Fudge J, 'Fragmenting Work and Fragmenting Organizations: The Contract of Employment and the Scope of Labour Regulation' (2006) 44 Osgoode Hall Law Journal 609

—— 'The Future of the Standard Employment Relationship: Labour Law, New Institutional Economics and Old Power Resource Theory' (2017) 59 (3) Journal of Industrial Relations 374–92

—— 'Modern Slavery, Unfree Labour and the Labour Market: The Social Dynamics of Legal Characterization' (2018) Social & Legal Studies <https://doi.org.10.1177/0964663917746736> accessed 13 November 2019

Geras N, 'Essence and Appearance: Aspects of Fetishism in Marx's Capital' (1971) 65 New Left Review 69

Gintis H and Bowles S, 'Structure and Practice in the Labor Theory of Value' (1981) 12 Review of Radical Political Economics 1

Goldway D, 'Appearance and Reality in Marx's "Capital" ' (1967) 31 Science & Society 428–47

Goodrich P, *Reading the Law: Critical Introduction to Legal Method and Techniques* (Wiley-Blackwell 1986)

Gunn R, 'Marxism and Philosophy: A Critique of Critical Realism' (1989) 13 (1) Capital & Class 87–116

—— 'Practical Reflexivity in Marx' (1987) 1 Common Sense 39–51

Hammond JL and Barbara BH, *The Village Labourer, 1760-1832: A Study in the Government of England before the Reform Bill* (Longmans, Green 1913)

Harvey D, *A Companion to Marx's Capital*, vol 1 (Verso Books 2010)

Harvey M and Geras N, *Inequality and Democratic Egalitarianism: Marx's Economy and Beyond and Other Essays* (OUP 2018)

Hay D and Craven P, *Masters, Servants, and Magistrates in Britain and the Empire, 1562-1955* (University of North Carolina Press 2005)

Hicks JF, 'The Contractual Nature of Real Property Leases' (1972) 24 Baylor Law Review 443

Hilton GW, *The Truck System: Including a History of the British Truck Acts, 1465-1960.* (W. Heffer 1960)

Hilton RH, 'Freedom and Villeinage in England' (1965) 31 Past & Present 3–19

HM Treasury, e-Comms Team. The Chancellor's 1998 Budget Speech, 17 March 1998

Hobsbawm Prof E, and Rude G, *Captain Swing* (new edn, Phoenix 2001)

Holdsworth WS, *A History of English Law*, vol 1 (Methuen 1922)

Horwitz MJ, 'The Historical Foundations of Modern Contract Law' (1974) 87(5) Harvard Law Review 917

Hutchins BL and Harrison A, *A History of Factory Legislation* (PS King & Son 1911) 10

Huws U, *Labor in the Global Digital Economy: The Cybertariat Comes of Age* (Monthly Review Press 2014)

Hyde A, 'What Is Labor Law?' in Davidov G and Langille B (eds), *Boundaries and Frontiers of Labour Laws: Goals and Means in the Regulation of Work* (Hart Publishing 2006)

Ibbetson D, 'Assumpsit and Debt in the Early Sixteenth Century: The Origins of the Indebitatus Count' (1982) 41(1) Cambridge Law Journal 142–61

—— *A Historical Introduction to the Law of Obligations* (new edn, OUP 2001)

Ibbetson DJ and Barton JL, 'Consideration and the Theory of Contract in Sixteenth Century Common Law' (1990) Towards a General Law of Contract 67–124

Ilyenkov EV, *The Dialectics of the Abstract and the Concrete in Marx's Capital* (Aakar Books 2008)

Jaeggi R, *On the Critique of Forms of Life* (Ciaran Cronin tr, Belknap Press 2018)

Jensen VH, *Hiring of Dock Workers and Employment Practices in the Ports of New York, Liverpool, London, Rotterdam, and Marseilles* (Harvard University Press 1964)

Kahn-Freund O, 'The Wages Councils Bill' (1945) 8(1–2) Modern Law Review 68–72

—— 'Minimum Wage Legislation in Great Britain' (1949) 97(6) University of Pennsylvania Law Review 778–810

Kaidesoja T, 'The Concept of Social Structure in Roy Bhaskar's Critical Realism' [2009] JyväskyläStudies in Education, Psychology and Social Research 376

Kaufman BE, 'How a Minimum Wage Can Improve Efficiency Even in Competitive Labor Markets: The Webbs and the Social Cost of Labor' (2008) Andrew Young School of Policy Studies Research Papers Series

—— 'Labor Law and Employment Regulation: Institutional and Neoclassical Perspectives'in Dau-Schmidt K, Harris S, and Lobel O (eds), *Labor and Employment Law and Economics* (Edward Elgar 2009) 3–14

—— 'Sidney and Beatrice Webb's Institutional Theory of Labor Markets and Wage Determination' (2013) 52(3) Industrial Relations: A Journal of Economy and Society 765–91

Keynes JM, *General Theory of Employment, Interest and Money* (Atlantic Publishers & Dist 2016)

Klare K, 'On Ruth Dukes, *The Labour Constitution: The Enduring Idea of Labour Law*' (2018) 9 Jurisprudence 1–6

Knox R, 'Marxism, International Law, and Political Strategy' (2009) 22 Leiden Journal of International Law 413

Lang ATF, 'The Legal Construction of Economic Rationalities?' (2013) 40(1) Journal of Law and Society 155–71

—— 'Market Anti-Naturalisms' in Desautels-Stein J and Tomlins C (eds), *Searching for Contemporary Legal Thought* (1st edn, CUP 2017) 312–29

Langille B, 'Labour Law's Theory of Justice' in Davidov G and Langille, B (eds), *The Idea of Labour Law* (OUP 2011) 101–19

Laski HJ, 'Judicial Review of Social Policy in England: A Study of Roberts v. Hopwood et Al.' (1926) 39(7) Harvard Law Review 832–48

Lawson T, 'A Realist Theory for Economics' (1994) New Directions in Economic Methodology 257–85

—— *Economics and Reality* (Psychology Press 1997)

—— 'Comparing Conceptions of Social Ontology: Emergent Social Entities and/or Institutional Facts?' (2016) 46(4) Journal for the Theory of Social Behaviour 359–99

—— *Reorienting Economics*, vol 20 (Psychology Press 2003)

Lewis PA, 'Tempered Steele? On the Merits of Critical Realism and the "Ontological Turn" in Economics' (2011) 23 Critical Review 207

Littler CR, *The Development of the Labour Process in Capitalist Societies: A Comparative Study of the Transformation of Work Organization in Britain, Japan, and the USA* (Heinemann Educational Publishers 1982)

Low Pay Commission, 'First Report of the Low Pay Commission' (1998)

Lucas R, 'The Wages Act 1986: Some Reflections with Particular Reference to the Licensed Residential Establishment and Licensed Restaurant Wages Council' (1990) 10(2) Service Industries Journal 320–35

Lucas R and Radiven N, 'After Wages Councils: Minimum Pay and Practice' (1998) 8(4) Human Resource Management Journal 5–19

Luhmann N, *Law as a Social System* (Ziegert KA and Kastner F trs, OUP 2004)

—— *Social Systems* (Stanford University Press 1995)

Malthus TR, and Pullen J, *TR Malthus: Principles of Political Economy*, vol 2 (CUP 1989)

Manning A, *Monopsony in Motion: Imperfect Competition in Labor Markets* (Princeton University Press 2003)

Marks S, 'International Judicial Activism and the Commodity-Form Theory of International Law' (2007) 18 European Journal of International Law 199

Marshall A, *Principles of Economics: Unabridged Eighth Edition* (8th edn, Cosimo, Inc 2009)

Marx K, 'Instructions for the Delegates of the Provisional General Council' (1866) 20 CW 190

—— *Capital, Volume I.* (Penguin/New Left Review 1867)

—— *Grundisse: Foundation of the Critique of Political Economy (Rough Draft)* (Penguin Books 1973)

—— *Selected Writings*, vol 77 (McLellan D ed, OUP 1977)

——and Engels F, *Selected Works: In Three Volumes*, vol 3 (Progress Publishers 1977)

——and Engels F*Collected Works of Karl Marx and Frederick Engels. Volume 3 Marx and Engels, 1843-1844: Marx, Engels, 1843-44 v. 3.* (Lawrence & Wishart Ltd 1987)

——and Engels F *Wage-Labour and Capital* (International Publishers 1969)

—— Engels F, and Lapides K, *Marx and Engels on Trade Unions* (International Publishers Co 1990)

Matthews P, '"Salaries" in the Apportionment Act 1870' (1982) 2(3) Legal Studies 302–07

Mayhew H, *The Morning Chronicle Survey of Labour and the Poor: The Metropolitan Districts*, vol 2 (Routledge 2016)

McClelland J, 'A Purposive Approach to Employment Protection or a Missed Opportunity?' (2012) 75(3) Modern Law Review 427–36

McGaughey E, 'Uber, the Taylor Review, Mutuality and the Duty Not to Misrepresent Employment Status' (2019) 48 Industrial Law Journal 180

Megarry R, Harpum C, Wade W, Bridge, and Dixon MJ, *The Law of Real Property* (Sweet & Maxwell 2012)

Miéville, C, *Between Equal Rights a Marxist Theory of International Law* (Aakar Books 2016)

Millward R, 'The Emergence of Wage Labor in Early Modern England' (1981) 18(1) Explorations in Economic History 21–39

Milsom, SFC, *Historical Foundations of the Common Law* (Butterworth-Heinemann 1969)

Moseley F, *Money and Totality: A Macro-Monetary Interpretation of Marx's Logic in Capital and the End of the 'transformation Problem'* (Brill 2015)

Mummé C, 'From Control through Command to the Control of Discretion: Labour Time, Labour Property and the Tools of Managerial Control in Early Twentieth Century Ontario' (2016) 45(2) Industrial Law Journal 176–206

Murray M, *The Law of the Father?: Patriarchy in the Transition from Feudalism to Capitalism* (Routledge 2005)

Murray P, *The Mismeasure of Wealth: Essays on Marx and Social Form* (Brill 2016)

Napier BW, 'Contract of Service: The Concept and Its Application' (Doctoral thesis, University of Cambridge 1976) <https://www.repository.cam.ac.uk/handle/1810/250705> accessed 13 November 2019

—— 'Aspects of the Wage Work Bargain' (1984) 43 Cambridge Law Journal 337–48

O'Connell P, 'Law, Marxism and Method' [2018] Forthcoming in triple C: Communication, Capitalism and Critique (2018)

Ojha S, 'Regulating Work: Decasualisation of Dock Labour in Colonial India' (2014) 42 (3/4) Social Scientist 77–89

Ollman B, *Dance of the Dialectic: Steps in Marx's Method* (University of Illinois Press 2003)

Orth JV, *Combination and Conspiracy: A Legal History of Trade Unionism, 1721-1906* (OUP 1991)

Palermo G, 'The Ontology of Economic Power in Capitalism: Mainstream Economics and Marx' (2006) 31(4) Cambridge Journal of Economics 539–61

—— 'Power, Competition and the Free Trader Vulgaris' (2016) 40(1) Cambridge Journal of Economics 259–81

—— 'Competition: A Marxist View' (2017) 41(6) Cambridge Journal of Economics 1559–85

Palmer RC, *English Law in the Age of the Black Death, 1348-1381: A Transformation of Governance and Law* (University of North Carolina Press 2000)

Pashukanis E, *Law and Marxism: A General Theory* (new edn, Pluto Press 1987)

Picchio A, *Social Reproduction: The Political Economy of the Labour Market* (CUP 1992)

Pilling G, *Marx's 'Capital': Philosophy and Political Economy* (Routledge 1980)

Plucknett TFT, *A Concise History of the Common Law* (The Lawbook Exchange Ltd 2001)

Polanyi K, *The Great Transformation: The Political and Economic Origins of Our Time* (2nd edn, Beacon Press 2002)

Pollock Sir F and Winfield Sir PH, *Principles of Contract* (13th edn, Stevens 1950)

Porpora DV, 'Cultural Rules and Material Relations' (1993) Sociological Theory 212–29

—— *Reconstructing Sociology: The Critical Realist Approach* (CUP 2015)

Postone M, *Time, Labor, and Social Domination: A Reinterpretation of Marx's Critical Theory* (CUP 1995)

Prassl J, *The Concept of the Employer* (OUP 2015)

—— *Humans as a Service: The Promise and Perils of Work in the Gig Economy.* (OUP 2018)

Raghunath TR, 'Marx's Theory of Ideology' (PhD Thesis, McMaster University 1988)

Ricardo D, *On the Principles of Political Economy, and Taxation* (John Murray 1821)

Rittich, Kerry. 'Making Natural Markets: Flexibility as Labour Market Truth Special Issue: Continuing towards an Economic Sociology of Law' (2014) 65 Northern Ireland Legal Quarterly 323–44

Rodgers L, 'The Notion of Working Time' (2009) Industrial Law Journal 38(1) 80–88

Rogers JET, *Six Centuries of Work and Wages: The History of English Labour*, vol 2 (GP Putnam's sons 1884)

Rule J, *The Labouring Classes in Early Industrial England, 1750-1850* (Routledge 2014)

Samuels WJ, 'Markets and Their Social Construction' (2004) Social Research 71(2) 357–70

Sayer A, *Realism and Social Science* (Sage 2000)

—— *Method in Social Science* (revised 2nd edn, Routledge 2010)

Schmiechen JA, 'Sweated Industries and Sweated Labor: A Study of Industrial Disorganization and Worker Attitudes in the London Clothing Trades, 1867–1909' (1976) 36(1) Journal of Economic History 283–86

Schmiechen JA, *Sweated Industries and Sweated Labor: The London Clothing Trades, 1860-1914* (University of Illinois Press 1984)

Segrave K, *Tipping: An American Social History of Gratuities* (McFarland 1998)

Sekine T, 'The Dialectic of Capital: An Unoist Interpretation' in Ollman B and Smith T (eds), *Dialectics for the New Century* (Palgrave Macmillan 2008) 200–10

Simpson AWB, *A History of the Land Law* (Clarendon Press 1986)

—— *A History of the Common Law of Contract: The Rise of the Action of Assumpsit* (OUP 1987)

Simpson B 'A Milestone in the Legal Regulation of Pay: The National Minimum Wage Act 1998' (1999) 28(1) Industrial Law Journal 1–32

—— 'Implementing the National Minimum Wage—the 1999 Regulations' (1999) 28(2) Industrial Law Journal 171–82

Smith A, *An Inquiry into the Nature and Causes of the Wealth of Nations* (W. Strahan and T. Cadell 1776)

Snell KDM, *Annals of the Labouring Poor: Social Change and Agrarian England, 1660–1900* (CUP 1985)

Steedman C, 'The Servant's Labour: The Business of Life, England, 1760-1820' (2004) 29(1) Social History 1–29

——*Master and Servant: Love and Labour in the English Industrial Age*, vol 10 (CUP 2007)

Steinfeld RJ, *The Invention of Free Labor: The Employment Relation in English and American Law and Culture, 1350-1870* (UNC Press Books 1991)

——*Coercion, Contract, and Free Labor in the Nineteenth Century* (CUP 2001)

Steuart J, *An Inquiry into the Principles of Political Oeconomy: Being an Essay on the Science of Domestic Policy in Free Nations*, vol 2 (Millar & Cadell 1767)

Stirati A, *The Theory of Wages in Classical Economics: A Study of Adam Smith, David Ricardo, and Their Contemporaries* (Edward Elgar Publishing 1994)

Stryker R, 'Mind the Gap: Law, Institutional Analysis and Socioeconomics' (2003) 1(3) Socio-Economic Review 335–67

Supiot A, *Homo Juridicus: On the Anthropological Function of the Law* (Verso Books 2007)

Swedberg R, 'The Case for an Economic Sociology of Law' (2003) 32(1) Theory and Society 1–37

Tawney RH, *The Agrarian Problem in the Sixteenth Century*, vol 1 (Longmans, Green 1912)

Taylor AJ, 'The Sub-Contract System in the British Coal Industry' in Pressnell P (ed), *Studies in the Industrial Revolution* (Athlone Press 1960) 215

Taylor M, 'Good Work: The Taylor Review of Modern Working Practices'(gov.uk 2017) <https://www.gov.uk/government/uploads/system/uploads/attachment_data/file/627671/good-work-taylor-review-modern-working-practices-rg.pdf> accessed 25 May 2018

Teubner G, *Dilemmas of Law in the Welfare State*, vol 3 (Walter de Gruyter 1986)

——*Autopoietic Law—A New Approach to Law and Society* (Walter de Gruyter 1987)

Theobald W, *A Practical Treatise on the Poor Laws, as Altered by the Poor Law Amendment Act... and an Appendix of the Statutes, Etc.* (S. Sweet; Stevens & Sons 1836)

Toner JP, 'Regulation in the Taxi Industry' (1992) Working Paper 381, 17 <http://www.its.leeds.ac.uk/> accessed 25 October 2016

Tucker E, 'Renorming Labour Law: Can We Escape Labour Law's Recurring Regulatory Dilemmas?' (2010) 39(2) Industrial Law Journal 99–138

Turgot ARJ, *Reflections on the Formation and Distribution of Wealth*. History of Economic Thought Books (E Spragg 1795)

—— *Turgot on Progress, Sociology and Economics: A Philosophical Review of the Successive Advances of the Human Mind, on Universal History Reflections and on the Formation and the Distribution of Wealth* (CUP 1973)

Van den Eeckhout P, 'The History of Labour and Labour Relations in Hotels and Restaurants in Western Europe and the United States in the Nineteenth and Twentieth Centuries: an Introduction' (2013) 11(2) Food and History 199–221

—— 'Waiters, Waitresses, and Their Tips in Western Europe before World War I. (2015) 60(3) International Review of Social History 349–78

Vinogradoff Sir P, *Villainage in England: Essays in English Mediaeval History* (Clarendon Press 1892)

Waltman JL, *Minimum Wage Policy in Great Britain and the United States* (Algora Publishing 2008)

Webb S and Freeman AJ, *Seasonal Trades* (Constable 1912)

Webb S and Webb B, *Industrial Democracy*, vol 2 (Longmans, Green 1897)

——*Problems of Modern Industry* (Longmans, Green 1902)

——*The History of Trade Unionism* (Longmans, Green 1920)

—— *English Local Government: English Poor Law History* (Longmans, Green 1929)Weinrib EJ, 'Legal Formalism: On the Immanent Rationality of Law' (1988) 97(6) Yale Law Journal 949–1016

Whyte WH, *Decasualization of Dock Labour, with Special Reference to the Port of Bristol.* University of Bristol Studies, No. 2. Bristol (published for the University of Bristol by J.W. Arrowsmith Ltd 1934)

Williams S, *Poverty, Gender and Life-Cycle Under the English Poor Law, 1760-1834* (Boydell & Brewer Ltd 2013)

Wonnacott M, *The History of the Law of Landlord and Tenant in England and Wales* (The Lawbook Exchange Ltd 2012)

Wood D, *Medieval Economic Thought*. Cambridge Medieval Textbooks (CUP 2002)

Wood EM, *The Origin of Capitalism: A Longer View* (Verso 2002)

Žmolek MA, *Rethinking the Industrial Revolution: Five Centuries of Transition from Agrarian to Industrial Capitalism in England* (Haymarket Books 2013)

Official Publications

(1819) House of Commons Select C Committee on the Poor Laws (Bourne), Report, Parliamentary Papers (1819) (529) II 249

(1824) House of Commons Select Committee on Labourers' Wages (Russell), Report, Parliamentary Papers (1824) (392) VI 401

(1828) House of Commons Select Committee on the Poor Laws (Slaney), Report, Parliamentary Papers (1828) (494) IV 137

(1834) Commission for Inquiring into the Administration and Practical Operation of the Poor Laws, Report, Parliamentary Papers (1834) (44) XXVII 1

(1866) House of Commons Select Committee on Master and Servant (Elcho), Report, Parliamentary Papers (1866) XIII 1

(1875) Royal Commission on Labour Laws (Cockburn), Second and Final Report, Parliamentary Papers (1875) XXX 1

(1890) House of Lords Select Committee on the Sweating System (Derby), Fifth Report, Parliamentary Papers (1890) (169) XVII 257

(1894) Royal Commission on Labour (Devonshire), Fifth and Final Report, Parliamentary Papers (1894) XXXV 9

(1908) Charity Organisation Society (London, England). Special Committee on Unskilled Labour: Report and Minutes of Evidence, June, 1908

(1908) House of Commons Select Committee on Home Work (Whittaker), Report, Parliamentary Papers (1908) (246) VIII 1

(1918) Reconstruction Committee, Sub-committee on Relations between Employers and Employed (Whitley), Interim, Report on Joint Industrial Councils (Cd 8606) Parliamentary Papers (1917–18) XVIII 415

(1920) Transport Workers Court of Inquiry, Report and Minutes of Evidence of the Inquiry (London 1920) (2 vols Cmnd 936 and 937) ('The Shaw Report')

(1922) Great Britain, Ministry of Labor, Minutes of evidence taken before the committee of inquiry into the working and effects of the trade board acts (London, HMSO 1922, Cmnd 1645) ('Cave Report')

(1929) Committee on Industry and Trade (Balfour), Final Report (Cmd 3282) Parliamentary Papers (1928–29) VII 413

(1931) Committee on Port Labour: Port Labour Inquiry Report (London, HMSO 1931) 61–70 (Chaired by Donald Maclean)

(1938) Report of the Committee on Holidays with Pay (Amulree Committee) (Cmd 5724)

(1943) Catering Wages Commission, Catering Wages Act, 1943. Report of the Catering Wages Commission on Their Recommendation for the Establishment of a Wages Board for Licensed Non-Residential Establishments (London, HMSO 1945)

(1956) Committee of Inquiry into the Working of the Dock Labour Scheme (Devlin Committee) Report. (London, HMSO 1956)

(1965) Committee of Inquiry into Certain Matters concerning the Port Transport industry: 'Final Report of the Committee of Inquiry under the Rt Hon. Lord Devlin' (Cmnd 2734) (London, HMSO 1965)

(1985) Employment Committee, Wages Councils: Together with the Proceedings of the Committee (London, HMSO 1985)

(1988) Department of Employment, Wages Councils Consultation Document Employment for the 1990s (Cm 540)

(1998) Low Pay Commission, The National Minimum Wage. First Report of the Low Pay Commission

(1988) *Fairness at Work*, London, Department of Trade and Industry, May 1998 Cmnd3968,

(2000) HM Treasury, Tackling Poverty and Making Work Pay— Tax Credits for the 21st Century, The Modernisation of Britain's Tax and Benefit System no 6

(2002) HM Treasury, Budget Report

(2016) Great Britain, and Low Pay Commission, National Minimum Wage: Low Pay Commission Report Autumn 2016

Index

Note: *For the benefit of digital users, indexed terms that span two pages (e.g., 52–53) may, on occasion, appear on only one of those pages.*